Additional Praise for *Too Big to Save?*

"Americans need to understand the financial crisis shaking this country. Bob Pozen offers a great guide to inner workings gone wrong and a clear agenda for getting the system right again. Read this book and understand."

> —Tom Ashbrook, Host of NPR's *On Point*

"Bob Pozen is among the most knowledgeable and thoughtful commentators on America's financial system today. Based on decades of practical experience and years of penetrating analysis, his book *Too Big to Save?* presents new ideas that should be essential reading for laymen and experts alike, especially our top policy makers."

> —Jeffrey E. Garten, Juan Trippe Professor of International
> Finance and Trade, Yale School of Management;
> Former Undersecretary of Commerce, Clinton Administration

"America's financial system is sorely in need of fundamental reform, and the aftermath of the recent crisis represents a historic opportunity to do something about it. *Too Big To Save?* is full of the kind of knowledge-based common sense that only someone with Bob Pozen's rich background of experience in the securities industry is likely to bring to today's debate about what to do and who should do it. The country will stand a better chance of getting these reforms right if everyone pays attention to his thinking."

> —Benjamin M. Friedman, William Joseph Maier Professor
> of Political Economy, Harvard University;
> Author, *The Moral Consequences of Economic Growth*

"There will be many books written about the financial crisis of 2007–2009. But if you want to read just one, read this book. Bob Pozen's account of what went wrong and how to prevent future crises is a tour de force, clearly written for the nonexpert and powerfully argued."

> —Robert E. Litan, Vice President for Research
> and Policy, The Kauffman Foundation;
> Senior Fellow, The Brookings Institution

"Bob Pozen reviews some extremely complex concepts in a straightforward, easy-to-read manner for people to digest the sheer quantity of coverage about all the elements of the credit crisis. Using charts and summaries, he helps nonexperts understand what happened and gives them the tools needed to evaluate the most critical financial issues."

> —Peter Lynch, Former Portfolio Manager, Fidelity Magellan Fund

To my wife Liz, who has patiently endured months of obsessive writing, and from whom I have learned so much about life and love.

Too Big to Save?

How to Fix the U.S. Financial System

Robert Pozen

WILEY

John Wiley & Sons, Inc.

For general information on our other products and services or for technical support, please
contact our Customer Care Department within the United States at (800) 762-2974,
outside the United States at (317) 572-3993 or fax (317) 572-4002.

Wiley also publishes its books in a variety of electronic formats. Some content that appears
in print may not be available in electronic books. For more information about Wiley
products, visit our web site at www.wiley.com.

Library of Congress Cataloging-in-Publication Data:

Pozen, Robert C.
   Too big to save : how to fix the U.S. financial system / Robert Pozen.
     p. cm.
   Includes bibliographical references and index.
   ISBN 978-0-470-49905-4 (cloth)
     1. Finance—Government policy—United States. 2. Financial crises—Govern-
ment policy—United States. 3. Global Financial Crisis, 2008-2009. 4. United States—
Economic policy—2009- I. Title.
  HG181.P67 2010
  332.10973—dc22
                                                   2009032794

Printed in the United States of America
10 9 8 7 6 5 4 3 2 1

Contents

Foreword   vii

Acknowledgments   ix

The Financial Crisis: A Parable   xi

Part I: The U.S. Housing Slump and the Global Financial Crisis   1

Chapter 1   The Rise and Fall of U.S. Housing Prices   7

Chapter 2   Fannie and Freddie   27

Chapter 3   Mortgage Securitization in the Private Sector   47

Chapter 4   Credit Default Swaps and Mathematical Models   69

    Appendix to Chapter 4   95

Part II: Impact on Stock and Bond Markets   97

Chapter 5   Short Selling, Hedge Funds, and Leverage   101

Chapter 6   Capital Requirements at Brokers and Banks   129

Chapter 7   Impact on Short-Term Lending   153

Chapter 8   Insuring Deposits and Money Market Funds   179

**Part III: Evaluating the Bailout
Act of 2008**   **201**

Chapter 9   Why and How Treasury Recapitalized So
              Many Banks   205
Chapter 10   Increasing Lending Volumes and Removing
              Toxic Assets   235
Chapter 11   Limiting Executive Compensation and Improving
              Boards of Directors   263
Chapter 12   Were Accounting Rules an Important Factor
              Contributing to the Financial Crisis?   295

**Part IV: The Future of the American
Financial System**   **319**

Chapter 13   The International Implications of the Financial
              Crisis for the United States   321
              Appendix to Chapter 13   353
Chapter 14   The New Structure of U.S. Financial Regulation 355

Notes   393
Glossary   435
About the Author   445
Index   447

Foreword

Every time there is a major financial crisis, and there have been quite a number of them in history, we find that there are many who are ready to dwell on blaming people and institutions; and only very few who offer really serious and constructive new proposals for improvements in our financial system that can repair the damage and reduce the impact of future crises. It is much harder to do the latter, as it requires coming to an understanding of the real origins of the crisis. The causes of the crisis are typically multiple, and understanding them requires extensive knowledge of the real nature of financial arrangements as they appear at this point in history, of the laws and conventions that regulate them, and of the kinds of human failures that underlie their misapplication. Constructive solutions require also an analytical framework that allows us to use basic economic theory to evaluate government responses.

Too Big to Save? provides us with just such an understanding and analytical framework. The policy proposals offered here should be taken seriously.

The review of the crisis that is provided here is a pleasure to read. First, it brings together a strong list of relevant facts in connection with an illuminating interpretation. For example, Bob documents how very low interest rates created a demand for mortgage-backed securities with high yields—which could be met due to the weak regulation of mortgage lendings and the eagerness of the credit rating agencies to hand out AAA ratings. He provides a wealth of information that can enable the reader to assess his argument.

Second, Bob develops several principles for evaluating the government's bailout efforts. He criticizes the Treasury's peculiar reliance on preferred stock as an instance of one-way capitalism—where taxpayers bear almost all the downside losses of bank failures with little upside if a troubled bank is rehabilitated. Ironically, federal officials appear to have chosen to use preferred stock rather than common stock in part because they wanted to keep the appearance of capitalism (not nationalizing the banks) more than its substance. This is a book about the real substance of our capitalist economy.

He also articulates specific tests for justifying bailouts and then shows why many recent bailouts do not meet these tests. We need to view bailouts in terms of our economic theory as well as we can, for only then can we have any semblance of an economic justification for these last-minute measures—rule changes in the midst of the game.

Third, Bob presents an integrated view of how U.S. financial regulation should be structured in the future. He puts meat on the bones of systemic risks—with the Federal Reserve as the monitor of such risks and the functional regulators implementing remedial measures. Since government guarantees have become so broad, he argues for a different type of board of directors to help regulators monitor the financial condition of mega banks.

Of course, not everyone will agree with all his proposals since the book includes so many. This is not a book with a lengthy discussion of the past plus a few future-looking proposals outlined in the last few pages. It is a thoughtful account on nearly every page. It keeps its momentum going, bringing us to a position where we can really evaluate how we ought to proceed from here and how our financial economy should evolve over the coming years.

—ROBERT J. SHILLER

Acknowledgments

I t takes a village to write a 400-page book in five months. I was the
lucky beneficiary of so many people who researched and read
the manuscript.

Noha Abi-Hanna did an excellent job of researching Part I, as
did Laura Coyne and Jeff Schneble on Part II. In Part III, Matt Filosa
and Charles Beresford each took the lead in drafting a chapter, while
McCall Merchant provided significant support on the other two chapters. Mary Ellen Hammond did extensive work in putting together the
drafts of Part IV, which benefited greatly from close readings by Ben
Friedman, Steve Hadley, and Dan Price.

The book went through several drafts, with reviewers providing
very helpful comments at each stage. I am deeply appreciative of the
comments from the following reviewers: Dan Bergstresser, Ronnie
Janoff-Bulman, Maria Dwyer, Jeff Garten, Lena Goldberg, Richard
Hawkins, Rick Kampersal, Julia Kirby, Bob Litan, Rob Manning, Deb
Miller, Betsy Pohl, Mark Polebaum, Brian Reid, Jim Stone, Preston
Thompson, Eric Weisman, and Rich Weitzel.

I am particularly grateful for the hard work and dedication of my
editorial assistant, Benjamin Kultgen, who copyedited each draft and

designed most of the charts. Mark Citro and Dan Flaherty provided technical assistance on charts and sources, respectively. In addition, Josh Marston and Jim Swanson were helpful consultants.

My special thanks goes to Courtney Mahoney, my wonderful assistant, who typed and revised draft after draft. She was helped whenever needed by Kathy Neylon and Lee Ann Carey.

In addition, I was encouraged to write this book by Shirley Jackson, and encouraged to reach out to the nonexperts by Jerry Kagan who also read several drafts. At John Wiley, I enjoyed strong support from David Pugh and Kelly O'Connor.

But I take full personal responsibility for any errors or other deficiencies in the book. It represents my own views, and not the views of MFS Investment Management or its parent Sun Life of Canada.

The Financial Crisis: A Parable

J ohn and Amy Barton had always envied the larger white house with the pool down the street from their home in Phoenix.[1] But they never thought they could swing the difference between their $400,000 current home and the $505,000 price tag on the white house. That is, until January 2005 when they met a local mortgage broker named Marjorie Spencer who offered them "a deal they couldn't refuse."

Spencer told them that they could sell their old house and buy the new house with a down payment of only $5,000. If they financed their new home with a 30-year fixed mortgage at 7 percent, their monthly payments would increase by only about $665, from $2,660 to $3,325. And they'd have no problem qualifying for the larger loan. Spencer said she would draw up a no-income-verification loan, and all the Bartons had to do was list the old home as a rental property, with a monthly rental income of $1,000.

Amy, though, had an uneasy feeling about Spencer, a loud, fast-talking woman who always wore a business suit. In fact, Amy wanted to sell their old home as soon as possible, and was not even sure that it could be rented. "We can say that your home has been rented in the past," said Spencer. "Trust me, nobody will notice." Amy ultimately gave in to the excitement of upgrading to a new home, so she and John signed all the papers that Spencer slid in front of them to make the deal official.

A few days later, the Bartons' new mortgage was sold to a large mortgage servicer, which collects monthly payments and sends them to the current holders of the mortgages. As soon as the mortgage servicer accumulated a large enough number of mortgages, it retained the servicing agreement but sold the mortgages again—this time to Wall Street Dealer. Finally, Wall Street Dealer put the mortgages into a shell company, went through the process of creating securities backed by these mortgages, and sold these securities to investors around the world. (See Figure 1.)

This process of securitization, illustrated in Figure 1, was creative. The principal and interest payments of the mortgages could be carved into separate securities, called tranches, each with different claims on the payments from the underlying mortgages. To take a very simple example, a risky tranche with a high potential yield might take the first loss on the mortgages in the event of a borrowers default, and a conservative tranche with a low interest rate might take the last loss on the mortgages.

The job of creating tranches with different risks and yields was done at Wall Street Dealer by a brilliant group of young college graduates. One such whiz kid was Peter Antonov, a 25-year-old MIT graduate who had impressed everyone with his amazing acumen for numbers. Antonov's job was essentially an exercise in profit maximization. Understand the risk appetite of your investors, analyze the expected cash flows from the mortgages, and ultimately create packages of mortgage-backed securities to fit the different needs of investors.

Once the security tranches were created, the next step was to get them rated by two of the three top rating agencies: Moody's, Standard & Poor's, and FinCredit. Like Antonov, the experts at the rating agencies had their models, which incorporated factors such as expected cash flow on the mortgages, diversification across geographic regions, and the chance that housing prices would fall—a very low likelihood according to their models.

Still, the rating process was a game, with the two winning agencies taking home $400,000 each for a complex deal like this one, and Antonov knew the rules of engagement. He and his colleagues called on these three credit-rating agencies to see what proportion of the securities backed by this particular group of low-quality mortgages

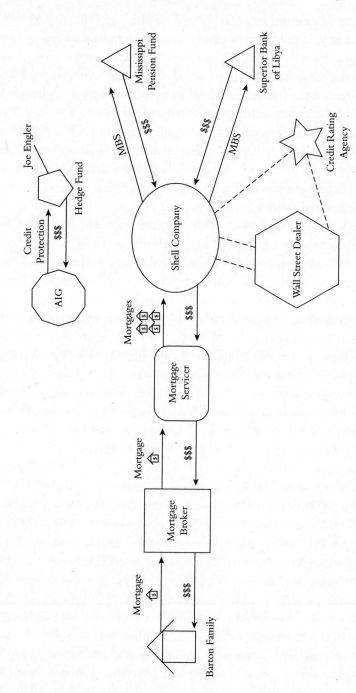

Figure 1 The Securitization of the Bartons' Mortgage

(called subprime) would be rated triple-A, the highest rating possible. A triple-A rating in the bond business was like the Good Housekeeping seal of approval.

Fin Credit came in at 50 percent, Moody's at 55 percent and S&P at 60 percent. Then Antonov had an idea: "Call Fin back," he told a colleague, "and tell them they were so far off we won't be using them for this deal." Two hours later, Antonov got a call from a Fin vice president who said, "We're willing to make some adjustments to get into this deal. Will 60 percent be enough?" With their triple-A ratings for 60 percent of the mortgage-backed securities, these were now ready for sale to investors around the globe.

Mortgage-backed securities were in great demand in early 2005 because they paid higher rates than the 4 percent available on 5-year U.S. Treasuries, and their triple-A rating indicated a very conservative investment. Only a handful of public companies had triple-A ratings in 2005.

The employees of Wall Street Dealer pitched the offering to Tom Paige, the investment director of Mississippi's state pension fund, covering 30,000 state employees. Paige took a call one afternoon from one of his plan consultants, who had been poring over the offering statement. "These securities are backed by a stable flow of income, they're generating good relative returns, and best of all they've got a triple-A rating," the consultant told him. Soon thereafter, Mississippi's state employees owned approximately $100 million of these securities.

Similar stories played out overseas. At the Superior Bank of Libya, chief investment officer Saddiq al-Massir had been keeping a close eye on the low level of U.S Treasury yields. Libya was one of the oil-rich countries in the Persian Gulf region whose dollar reserves grew rapidly in tandem with the rise in the price of oil (which is denominated in U.S. dollars). The bank's board of directors had given al-Massir a succinct directive regarding his investment goals. "Diversify the portfolio, and find higher relative returns." The mortgage securities of Wall Street Dealer fit the bill on both counts; al-Massir was particularly impressed by the AAA rating on the securities. He decided to place an order for $200 million.

Meanwhile, Joe Engler, a Los Angeles-based hedge fund manager, was impressed by Wall Street Dealer's offering but from the opposite perspective. He told his partners: "Housing prices can't keep soaring like this. Pretty soon, the fault lines will surface in the weakest subsector, subprime mortgages." To bet against the popular wisdom, Engler's fund sold $10 million of the triple-A portion of Wall Street Dealer's offering, but bought $10 million of protection against the default of this same portion. AIG was pleased to sell him protection for this portion at a premium of $25,000 per year for five years.

The first signs of real trouble began to crop up in 2006. Borrowers began to default more often on their mortgage payments, and Wall Street firms started to see more of their transactions fall apart. These were early warning signs that something was seriously wrong in the U.S. mortgage market. By the end of 2007, close to 16 percent of all subprime mortgages were in default.

Meanwhile, in Phoenix, housing prices were falling rapidly and the Bartons still couldn't find someone to rent their old house, much less buy it. So in the fall of 2007 they forfeited their $5,000 down payment on the new house and walked away from their new $500,000 mortgage. Under Arizona law, the Bartons were not personally liable for any shortfall if the proceeds from selling the new house did not cover the remaining mortgage on the house.

The employees of Wall Street Dealer began telling the bad news to investors; they would not be receiving the expected yields on their mortgage securities. But Antonov was no longer there. After pocketing a $2 million bonus in 2006, he had quickly found a better paying job at Lehman Brothers.

Tom Paige got ready to explain the pension fund's losses to the Labor Committee of the Mississippi State Senate, and Saddiq al-Massir was anxious as he was called before the bank's board of directors to defend his purchase of the Wall Street Dealer's mortgage-backed securities.

But Joe Engler was a happy camper. He received a large payment from AIG to cover losses on the mortgage-backed securities of Wall Street Dealers. As Joe uncorked a bottle of champagne for his partners, he kept repeating, "The trend is not your friend."

What This Book Will Tell You

Although the people and transactions depicted above are fictitious, they are typical of the situations that occurred between 2003 and 2006 in the United States. These situations were repeated so often not because of individual mistakes but because of powerful economic forces—such as low interest rates, excessive debt, and weak regulation—that led to a severe financial crisis in 2008 and 2009. This book will answer three key questions about this financial crisis:

1. How exactly did a steep drop in U.S. housing prices result in a severe financial crisis throughout the world?
2. In responding to this financial crisis, what did the U.S. government do right and what did it do wrong?
3. What actions should be taken in the future to resolve this financial crisis and help prevent others from happening?

In order to answer the first question, we must understand the unique role of nonbank financial institutions in the United States. In most countries, banks are the dominant financial institution. In the United States, by contrast, the majority of financial assets are held by nonbanks, such as mutual funds, credit-card issuers, and pension plans. In 2007, banks supplied only 22 percent of all credit in the United States.[2] Individual borrowers obtained loans through nonbank lenders like car finance companies; corporate borrowers sold bonds to institutional investors like life insurers. Over the last decade, nonbank lenders sold an increasing volume of mortgages and other loans to Wall Street firms, which repackaged and resold them as asset-backed securities based on the cash flows from these loans.

This book will show that the global financial crisis resulted from the burst of the U.S. housing bubble, which was financed through excessive debt spread around the world by mortgage securitization. As illustrated by the parable, unscrupulous brokers persuaded overextended buyers to take out mortgages with minimal down payments. These mortgages were then sold to a Wall Street firm, which pooled them together in a shell company. With top credit ratings based on dubious models, that company sold mortgage-backed securities across the world to investors looking for higher yields than U.S. Treasuries.

Like most financial innovations, mortgage securitization provided significant benefits as well as substantial hazards. Before mortgage securitization, lenders held their mortgages until they were paid off. By selling mortgages for securitization, lenders could obtain cash to make more loans. Loan securitization also provided investors with an easy way to diversify into securities based on payments from mortgages. American and foreign investors could choose among various types of mortgage-backed securities with conservative to risky credit ratings.

However, when the mortgages underlying these securities began to default, losses were incurred by investors throughout the world. As the default rates reached record highs, investors in the mortgage-backed securities with even the most conservative ratings suffered heavy losses. Because of widespread investor discontent, the volume of securitization of all loans plummeted from $100 billion per month in 2006 to almost zero in late 2008.[3] This debacle in the market for securitized loans was the catalyst for the failure of several financial institutions, the freezing up of short-term lending and the steep decline in the stock markets.

But this book does more than explain the origin of the financial crisis. It also answers the second question: In responding to the financial crisis, what did the U.S. government do right and wrong? The high level of government intervention in the financial markets was generally justified by the severity of the financial crisis, but some of the *methods* of intervention were inconsistent with several principles of sound regulation.

In supporting financial institutions, the federal government should avoid whenever possible the creation of moral hazard, an economic term for the situation created by broad loss guarantees that remove all incentive of private investors to perform due diligence on their investments. For example, the FDIC has guaranteed for up to three years 100 percent of over $300 billion in debt of banks, thrifts, and their holding companies.[4] As a result of these 100 percent guarantees, sophisticated investors in bank debt have no incentive to look at the financial condition of these banks. The financial system would be better served by 90 percent guarantees from the FDIC, so it would have the aid of sophisticated bond investors in keeping these institutions away from excessively risky activities.

In 2008, the federal government bailed out many large banks as well as large securities dealers and insurance companies that were deemed too big to fail. These bailouts not only created moral hazard, but also increased concentration in the financial sector and decreased competition for financial services. Therefore, the federal regulators should *not* save a large financial institution unless its failure would cause the insolvency of significant players in the financial system. For example, why was American Express bailed out although most of its liabilities are widely dispersed among merchants and customers?

From October, 2008 through January, 2009, the U.S. Treasury invested almost $200 billion of capital in over 300 banks.[5] In making such investments, the federal government often engaged in one-way capitalism, in which the government absorbs most of the losses when financial institutions fail, but receives only a small portion of the profits if these institutions are rehabilitated. This was unfair to American taxpayers. For example, after investing $45 billion of capital in Bank of America, the Treasury owns mainly the Bank's preferred stock and only 6 percent of its voting common shares. To gain the upside as well as the downside, the Treasury should own the majority (but not 100 percent) of the voting common shares of a troubled mega bank bailed out because it was deemed too big to fail.

In answering the third question, about which actions we should take to help prevent future financial crises, we should try to find the least burdensome regulatory strategy with the best chance of resolving the most critical issues. Because financial crises tend to spread across the world, in theory the international community should develop a global solution to a global problem. In practice, no country is prepared to cede its sovereignty to global regulators. Some countries will form coalitions of the willing, like colleges of supervisors, to coordinate supervision of global financial institutions; other countries will provide more financing to the International Monetary Fund (IMF). At most, the largest countries can exert collective pressure to prevent the erection of new protectionist barriers to global trade and capital flows.

In the United States, the Treasury should concentrate less on recapitalizing banks and more on reforming the loan securitization process. Recapitalized banks have not increased their loan volume.[6] Because higher loan volume is critical to reviving the economy, and the securitization of loans drives the volume of loans, the United States must fundamentally reform the securitization process. Similarly, the federal government should concentrate less on buying toxic assets from banks, and more on helping underwater borrowers, whose mortgage balances exceed the current value of their homes. These are the borrowers mostly likely to default on the mortgages underlying these toxic assets, whose value ultimately depends on this default rate.

In reforming the U.S. regulatory structure, Congress should focus on keeping up with financial innovation and coping with systemic risks. It should close the gaps in the federal regulatory system, which covers new products like credit default swaps and regulates growing players like hedge funds. It should also ask the Federal Reserve to monitor the systemic risks of significant financial firms, where the adverse effects of one firm's failure could bring down the whole financial system. But Congress should not create an omnibus agency to oversee all financial services; we need a nimble set of regulators to follow the rapid changes in each part of the financial sector.

In light of the fast pace of financial innovation and the growing complexity of transactions, regulatory officials will be hard pressed to monitor a mega bank's activities. Given the increase in moral hazard and the decline in competitive constraints, the regulators should seek help from the directors of a mega bank in holding its top executives accountable for generating consistent earnings without taking excessive risks. This challenging role requires a new type of board—a small group of super-directors with the financial expertise, the time commitment, and the financial incentive to be effective watchdogs. Only with such a board at every mega bank can we move from one-way capitalism to accountable capitalism.

How the Book Is Organized

The answers to the three questions addressed in this book synthesize a huge amount of public information on the financial crisis. This book generally does not attempt to create new sources of information; the information already available is overwhelming. Instead, this book organizes the publicly available information into useful categories, presented in a roughly chronological order. It then analyzes the relevant information and generates a large number of practical recommendations.

The book is not geared to financial experts, who might prefer an extensive discussion of each of the many issues identified here. Rather, this book is aimed at intelligent readers, who are not financial experts. For these readers, the back of the book has a glossary of financial terms.

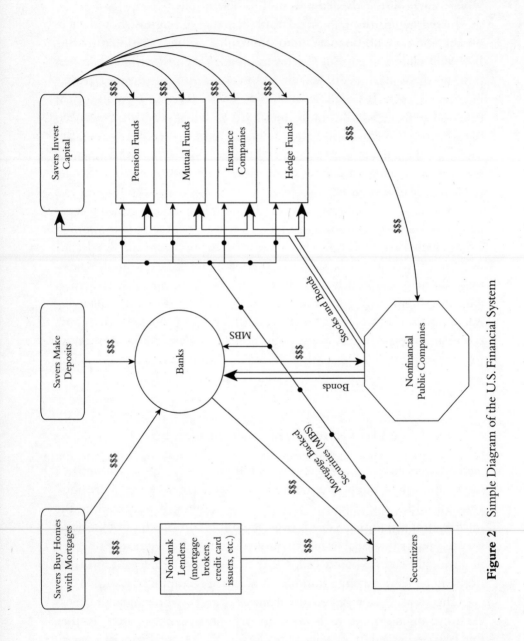

Figure 2 Simple Diagram of the U.S. Financial System

Also, Figure 2 presents a simplified diagram of the main private-sector players in the U.S. financial system. (Figure 14.1 in Chapter 14 outlines the current regulatory framework for U.S. financial institutions.)

As Figure 2 shows, savers are the initial source of capital for the financial system: they make deposits in banks and provide capital to other types of institutional investors, such as pension plans, mutual funds, insurance companies and hedge funds. Savers also use their capital to buy houses financed with mortgages from banks or nonbank lenders. At the next level, public companies outside of the financial sector as well as banks sell their stocks and bonds to institutional investors and sometimes directly to individual savers. Banks and nonbank lenders also sell mortgages to specialized entities, securitizers in the diagram, which turn these mortgages into mortgage-backed securities. These securities are bought by institutional investors and banks in the United States and abroad.

Each chapter of this book will analyze the impact of the financial crisis on a major part of the U.S. financial system. Each chapter will address all three of the questions posed earlier in this Introduction, explaining how the United States got into trouble in this financial area, evaluating the governmental responses in this area and suggesting practical reforms in this area. Most of these suggestions are my own, though some draw on the work of other commentators. In either case, the recommendations in this book are printed in bold to highlight them for readers.

In four chapters, Part I will analyze the globalization of the financial crisis through the sale of mortgage-backed securities around the world.

Part II, composed of Chapters 5 through 8, will assess the impact of the financial crisis on the stock markets, the capital of banks and the availability of short-term loans.

In four chapters, Part III will evaluate the federal bailout of financial institutions through buying their stock, refinancing their toxic assets and limiting their executive compensation.

Chapter 13 in Part IV will discuss the threat posed by this financial crisis for the free flow of international capital and trade. The final chapter in the book will discuss the implications of the current crisis for redesigning the American system of regulatory financial institutions.

In short, this book will give you a framework to analyze the daily barrage of information about the financial crisis. It will help you to avoid repeating the past mistakes of others, and to envision an effective plan for fixing the financial system in the future.

Part One

THE U.S. HOUSING SLUMP AND THE GLOBAL FINANCIAL CRISIS

The United States has experienced a few severe housing slumps since World War II—notably, the sharp decline in housing prices from 1989–1993. But as Figure I.1 shows, declining housing prices from that slump were not reflected in falling prices of U.S. stocks. In fact, the Standard & Poor's 500 Index (S&P 500) rose by over 15 percent for the years 1989 through 1993, while the home price index fell by over 13 percent.[1]

Other countries have experienced even more severe housing slumps than the United States—for example, the fall in Japanese housing prices during the 1990s. Although this Japanese housing slump was paralleled by a decline in the Japanese stock market during the 1990s, neither led to a global decline in stocks or bonds. Indeed, prior to 2008, no housing slump in any country has ever led to a global financial crisis.

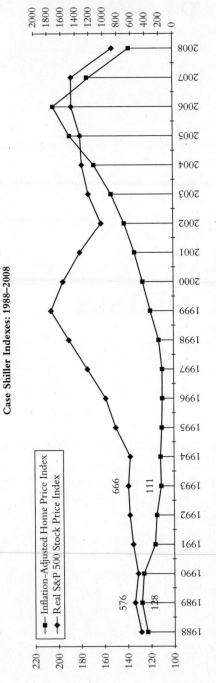

Figure I.1 Inflation-Adjusted Home Price Index vs. Real S&P 500 Stock Price Index

SOURCE: Robert Shiller irrationalexuberance.com.

So why did the U.S. housing slump in 2007 and 2008 trigger a global financial crisis? The answer lies in the excessive debt of American families and financial institutions, combined with the securitization process that spread mortgage–backed securities (MBS) across the world.

After being burned by stocks in the burst of the dot–com bubble, investors in 2001 were looking for other places to put their money. Most Americans felt that real estate was a safe bet because they believed that home prices always went up. With lots of mortgage financing available at low interest rates, many Americans bought housing and piled on the debt. By 2007, U.S. household debt reached a record high of over 130 percent of household income.

To increase their profits, many U.S. financial institutions also borrowed heavily to buy assets, supported by relatively small amounts of capital. In 2004, the Securities and Exchange Commission (SEC) allowed the five largest investment banks to double their ratio of assets to capital to over 30:1. The largest banks created separate shell companies to issue bonds, which could be found only in footnotes of their financial statements. Moreover, money poured into unregulated hedge funds, which often took out large loans to pursue aggressive trading strategies.

As long as the music was playing, everyone kept dancing. But when the music stopped in late 2006, all the dancers ran for the exits at the same time, crushing each other in the panic. As prices of housing and mortgage-backed securities plummeted, many investors tried to sell assets to raise cash and pay down their debts. These sales, in turn, drove asset prices lower, leading to more selling and more losses.

Huge losses were suffered not only by American investors but also by foreign financial institutions due to the global distribution of mortgage-backed securities. Traditionally, when lenders made home mortgages, they held on to them until they were paid off. But now lenders could sell most of their mortgages to specialized entities created by Wall Street banks or to either of two quasi-public corporations called the Federal National Mortgage Association (Fannie Mae) and the Federal Home Loan Mortgage Corporation (Freddie Mac). In turn, these entities and corporations sold MBS and bonds to investors across the world.

Figure I.2 provides a simple flow chart for the mortgage securitization process. A woman buying a house borrows money from a lender and signs a mortgage on the home, which secures her promise to repay

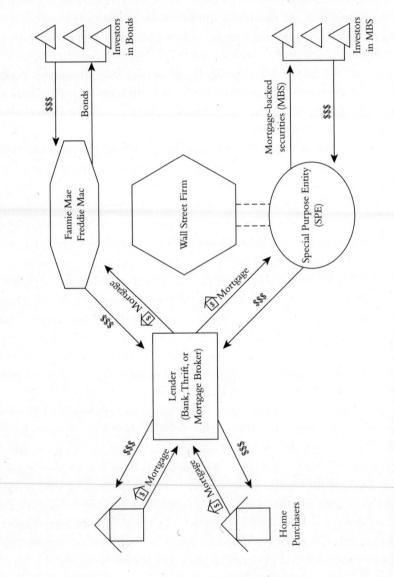

Figure I.2 Mortgage Securitization Process

the loan. She then makes monthly payments of principal and interest on the *mortgage* to the lender. This is the M in MBS. If she fails to repay her loan, the lender has the right to foreclose on the mortgage and take the house. The lender may sell the mortgage to Fannie Mae or Freddie Mac, which finances the purchase by selling bonds to investors. Alternatively, the lender may sell the mortgage to a special purpose entity (SPE), a shell corporation formed by a Wall Street firm to gather mortgages into a pool. An SPE raises money to buy these mortgages by selling to investors various types of bonds that are *backed* by (the B in MBS) the monthly payments from the mortgages in the pool. These bonds are *securities* (the S in MBS).

As the total residential mortgage debt in the United States more than doubled from 2000–2007, so did the total amount of MBS that were sold to investors throughout the world. The total residential mortgage debt in the United States skyrocketed—from approximately $5 trillion in 2000 to over $11 trillion in 2007—as U.S. home prices soared. In parallel, the total amount of MBS doubled from $3.6 trillion in 2000 to $7.3 trillion in 2007.[2]

Following the huge run-up in U.S. home prices from 2000–2006, these prices plummeted in 2007 through 2009 as the housing bubble burst and mortgage defaults rose to record high levels. In turn, these higher rates of mortgage defaults led to dramatic decreases in the prices of MBS based on these pools of troubled mortgages. Prices fell because the monthly mortgage payments backing the MBS were evaporating at an unforeseen rate. Because large amounts of MBS were held by financial institutions in the United States and abroad, this dramatic decline in MBS prices resulted in significant capital losses at institutions across the world. As a result, the securitization of loans has virtually halted since the end of 2008.

Although flawed, the securitization process still has significant benefits so it needs to be fundamentally reformed, rather than eliminated. Most importantly, securitization multiplies the volume of lending by increasing the liquidity of mortgages. Instead of holding mortgages to maturity, lenders can sell them to investors and use the proceeds to originate another round of loans. To take a simple example, compare two identical lenders—one that makes and holds one $400,000 mortgage that pays off after 15 years, while the second lender makes a $400,000 mortgage each year for 15 years and sells a $400,000 mortgage each year to investors.

Over 15 years, the second lender will use the same monies to lend $5.6 million more than the first lender. Thus, the securitization process provides more loans to Americans and, with more money available to fund mortgages, lowers interest rates on mortgages across the country.

At the same time, the securitization of mortgages offers the benefits of risk diversification to both banks and investors. Before mortgage securitization, banks located in a particular region of the country were vulnerable to declining housing prices in that region. Now regional banks can sell mortgages on local homes and buy a portfolio of MBS based on pools of mortgages from across the country. Investors can choose the specific package of risks they want because one pool of mortgages often issues several separate types of MBS (called tranches) with different risk characteristics. For instance, a low-risk tranche of an MBS with a relatively low yield might have the right to the first principal and interest payments from the pool. In contrast, a high-risk tranche of an MBS would have a much higher yield, but would incur the first loss if any mortgage in the pool defaults.

In short, the challenge is to retain the substantial benefits of the mortgage securitization without its negative aspects that led to investor losses around the world. Part I will rise to this challenge by analyzing the mortgage securitization process in four chapters. Each chapter will explain one important aspect of the securitization process, evaluate the reforms taken so far and offer further proposals to remedy the abuses in that aspect of the process.

- Chapter 1 will identify the driving forces behind the United States housing bubble and suggest what should be done to reduce the likelihood of another bubble.
- Chapter 2 will explain why Fannie Mae and Freddie Mac went bankrupt despite their government charters and assess what role, if any, they should play in the future.
- Chapter 3 will analyze why the private process of mortgage securitization came to an abrupt halt and delineate what reforms are needed to restart the process.
- Chapter 4 will propose a new regulatory framework for credit default swaps and, more generally, discuss the lessons learned from the misuse of mathematical models.

Chapter 1

The Rise and Fall of U.S. Housing Prices

C ontrary to popular perceptions, residential housing prices in the United States rose by only 10 percent above the rate of inflation from 1949–1997—going from an index of 100 to an index of 110, as demonstrated by Figure 1.1. Next, housing prices rose sharply by 21 percent above inflation between 1997 and 2001 (from an index of 110 to an index of 133), and then suddenly took off like a rocket between 2001 and 2006—rising 53 percent higher than the inflation rate (from an index of 133 to 203). But this meteoric rise was unsustainable; at the end of 2008, U.S. residential housing prices had plunged by 33 percent from their 2006 high (from an index of 203 to 137), and have declined further during 2009.[3]

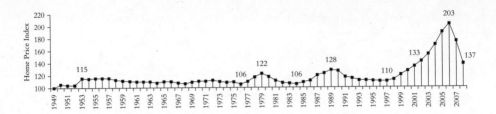

Figure 1.1   Inflation Adjusted Home Price Index: 1949–2008
Source: Robert Shiller irrationalexuberance.com.

Many factors contributed to this rise and fall of housing prices. In this chapter, we will focus on three key factors: abnormally low interest rates, unscrupulous sales practices of certain mortgage lenders, and incentives for certain house purchasers to avoid personal responsibility. (We will discuss additional important factors in other chapters, for instance, Chapter 5 on short selling by hedge funds and Chapter 6 on excessive leverage of financial institutions.)

The Fed Kept Interest Rates Too Low

Low interest rates in the United States were a key factor driving domestic housing prices sky high between 2001 and 2006. Because mortgages were so cheap, some purchasers were willing to pay more for homes that they were going to buy and other purchasers were able to afford homes for the first time. United States interest rates were pushed lower during this period by a combination of the savings glut in the emerging markets and the Federal Reserve's extended response to the 2001–2002 recession.

Between 2000 and 2007, the foreign exchange reserves of central banks in emerging markets ballooned from less than $800 billion to over $4 trillion.[4] In part, this sharp increase resulted from the rising prices of oil and gas in countries with natural resources, such as Saudi Arabia, Brazil, and Russia. In part, this sharp increase resulted from the rapid growth in trade surpluses of China and other Asian countries with the United States, where American consumers gobbled up imports.

In turn, the central banks in the commodity-producing countries and Asian exporters invested much of their rising foreign currency reserves in U.S. Treasuries. Such investments boosted the value of the

U.S. dollar, which supported the price of oil (denominated in U.S. dollars) and encouraged Americans to buy relatively cheap imports from Asia. Between 2000 and 2007, U.S. Treasuries owned by foreign investors rose from $1 trillion to $2.4 trillion. China alone increased its holdings of U.S. Treasuries from $60 billion in 2000 to $478 billion in 2007.[5]

In other words, there was an implicit agreement on a global recycling process. By consuming massive amounts of imported goods and oil, the U.S. ran huge trade deficits, which resulted in large trade surpluses with oil producers and Asian exporters. These two groups of countries then recycled most of these surpluses back to the United States by investing in U.S. Treasury securities. This global recycling process kept the rates on long-term Treasury bonds approximately 1 percent lower than they otherwise would have been.[6]

The role of the Federal Reserve in elevating U.S. housing prices is more complex. In response to the 2001 recession resulting from the burst of the dot-com bubble and the September 11, 2001 terrorist attacks on the World Trade Center, the Fed aggressively lowered the interest rate on short-term U.S. Treasuries (e.g., one week to three months), which declined to almost 1 percent at the end of 2002. The Fed then held the short-term rate close to 1 percent until the middle of 2004. Concerned about the fragility of the economic recovery, the Fed held interest rates too low for too long. Only toward the very end of 2006 did the Fed bring the short-term interest rate back to normal levels.[7] To see how far the Federal Reserve suppressed interest rates during this period, consider Figure 1.2.[8] The chart compares the actual low level of interest rates set by the Federal Reserve to the level determined by the Taylor rule—a well-recognized method of setting central bank rates developed by Stanford University professor and former Treasury official John Taylor. As the chart shows, actual rates were dramatically below those suggested by the Taylor rule from 2001 through 2005.

Low Interest Rates Stimulated Appetite for High-Yield Mortgages

The decline in interest rates on U.S. Treasury bonds stimulated the appetite among foreign investors for higher yields from other types of debt securities. Between 2001 and 2006, foreign ownership of MBS increased from 6 percent to over 18 percent.[9] Similarly, U.S. investors

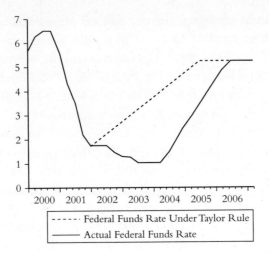

Figure 1.2 Taylor Rule
SOURCE: John Taylor for Federal Reserve Bank of Kansas City (September 2007).

had been burned by the crash in Internet stocks and were not receiving satisfactory yields on their bond portfolios. The mantra of U.S. investors became, "Give me yield, give me leverage, give me return."[10]

In order to offer higher yields, sponsors of MBS shifted toward pools with larger portions of subprime mortgages, which paid higher interest rates than prime mortgages. A prime mortgage is a loan meeting normal credit standards with proper documentation. A subprime mortgage is a loan to a home buyer who cannot meet the credit standards normally required to obtain a prime mortgage.

Interest rates on fixed-rate mortgages are mainly influenced by the rate on long-term Treasuries, which did not drop along with short-term rates. However, the interest rate on adjustable rate mortgages (ARMs) generally moves together with the rate on short-term Treasuries. With ARMs, the interest rate on the mortgages resets periodically (e.g., every year) in line with movements in short-term rates. From the fall of 2002 to the fall of 2004, the volume of new ARMs exceeded the volume of new fixed-rate mortgages as the interest rate on one-year ARMs fell to 4 percent or lower. This increased volume of ARMs contributed to the general surge in U.S. housing prices up to 2006.

In particular, the very low rates set by the Fed on short-term Treasuries and consequently ARMs encouraged the growth of subprime mortgages. Figure 1.3 shows how the volume of subprime mortgages rose from $120 billion in 2001 (under 6 percent of all mortgages originated) to $600 billion in 2006 (over 20 percent of all mortgages originated).[11] As former Federal Reserve Governor Edward Gramlich explained, "This whole subprime experience has demonstrated that taking rates down could have some real costs, in terms of encouraging excessive subprime borrowing."[12] While recognizing that subprime loans had helped promote home ownership among minority groups, Gramlich was alarmed by the hidden fees and prepayment penalties in most subprime loans, as well as their very low teaser rates that ratcheted up later. "Why are the most risky loan products sold to the least sophisticated borrowers?" Gramlich asked. "The question answers itself—the least sophisticated borrowers are probably duped into taking these products."[13]

Because of Gramlich's concerns about subprime loans, he urged Fed Chairman Alan Greenspan, as early as 2000, to send federal examiners into the mortgage affiliates of banks. But he was rebuffed by Greenspan, who feared that federal examiners would not spot deceptive practices and would inadvertently give a government seal of approval to dubious loans. In 2004, Gramlich reiterated his concerns about abusive lending practices, which were echoed by housing activists to Greenspan.

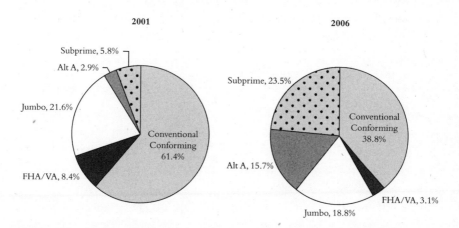

Figure 1.3 Mortgage Originations by Loan Type: 2001 and 2006
SOURCE: Inside Mortgage Finance Data in Major D. Coleman IV, Michael LaCour-Little, and Kerry D. Vandell, "Subprime Lending and the Housing Bubble: Tail Wags Dog?" (2008), http://papers.ssrn.com/sol3/papers.cfm?abstract_id=1262365.

But Greenspan again refused to utilize the Federal Reserve's authority to restrict mortgage lending practices.[14]

Lending Rules: Too Little, Too Late

Gramlich's concerns turned out to be well-founded. The default rate on subprime mortgages began to climb—from 10.8 percent in 2005 to 15.6 percent by 2007. In comparison, the default rate on prime mortgages went from 2.3 percent to 2.9 percent for the same period,[15] as shown by Figure 1.4. By the second half of 2007, investor concerns about this trend "led to a virtual collapse of the primary and secondary markets for subprime and nontraditional mortgages and contributed to disruptions in broader financial markets."[16] In 2006 and 2007, the federal banking agencies issued joint statements to depository institutions on how they should manage the risks associated with subprime lending and other nontraditional mortgage products. However, responding to comments from the mortgage industry, the final versions of the statements did not restrict or prohibit specific types of mortgage products or practices.

As the default rate on subprime mortgages continued to rise to 18.7 percent, the Fed in 2008 under its new Chairman, Ben Bernanke, finally adopted significant amendments (effective in 2009) to its rules on mortgage disclosures and unsafe lending practices for substandard mortgages. The new rules prohibit lenders from making a loan without

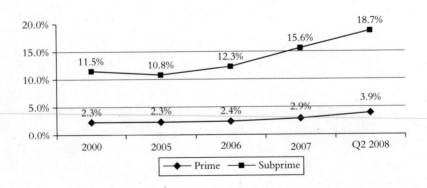

Figure 1.4 U.S. Mortgage Delinquency Rates (Total Past Due) 2000–2008
SOURCE: HUD Historical Data www.huduser.org/DATASETS/pdrdatas.html.

considering the ability of the borrower to repay out of income and assets other than the home's value. They require lenders to ensure that subprime borrowers establish escrow accounts or other arrangements to pay for property taxes and homeowners insurance on first-lien mortgage loans. The rules also ban any prepayment penalties if the terms of these penalties can change within the initial four years of the mortgage. Furthermore, they establish stricter advertising standards for mortgages and require certain mortgage disclosures to be provided to the borrower earlier in the transaction.[17]

Although these new rules go in the right direction, they are deficient in several major respects. Most critically, the Fed rejected a proposal that brokers disclose bonuses paid to them by lenders for steering customers to higher interest loans. These steering bonuses, often worth thousands of dollars, are typically paid to brokers for arranging more costly mortgages to borrowers with weak credit histories. For instance, Kimberly Marumoto of Hermosa Beach, California, said she used a broker to obtain a mortgage for her home and learned later, from her accountant, that she could have qualified for a lower interest rate. "It's almost like if you went to the store, and the store didn't tell you could actually get this item for 20 percent off," said Marumoto, who sells bedding and table linens. "This whole home loan business thing is very daunting to a first-time buyer."[18] As this example illustrates, steering bonuses can provide brokers with a significant incentive to originate mortgages with higher interest rates than those for which the borrower would have been eligible. **Therefore, steering bonuses should be banned or fully disclosed to the borrower.**[19]

Second, on disclosure generally, many subprime borrowers did not understand significant terms in their mortgages, for instance, the reset of the interest rate or the imposition of prepayment penalties. In part, this lack of understanding was caused by the dense pile of documents involved with mortgage applications. In response, Alex Pollock, former president of the Federal Home Loan Bank of Chicago, has made an excellent suggestion: **All applicants for home loans should be provided with a one-page summary form a few days prior to closing.**[20] **That form should outline the essential features of the mortgage, such as its monthly cost, principal amount, prepayment penalties and criteria for resetting interest rates if applicable.** This one-pager would drive home to borrowers the obligations they are assuming in signing the mortgage.

Third, the new rules fail to restrict the use of negative amortization loans. Such loans allow borrowers to pay back less than even the interest due on the loan each month. The shortfall is added each month to the loan's principal—the negative amortization—leading to larger monthly payments at the end of a specified period or at the maturity of the mortgage. Many home owners could not afford these larger monthly payments. **Negative amortization loans should be allowed only in special circumstances, such as restructuring a mortgage on the brink of foreclosure.**

Finally, and more broadly, most of the new rules apply only to subprime and Alt A mortgages. An Alt A mortgage is a loan to a home buyer who may be creditworthy, but does not meet the standards for a conforming mortgage—in many cases, the borrower cannot provide the normally required documentation. (Alt A stands for alternative documentation.) **But the new rules codify sound practices for advertising, underwriting, and servicing mortgages, so they should generally be extended to all first-lien mortgages on primary residences.**

In May, 2009, the House of Representatives approved the Mortgage Reform and Anti-Predatory Lending Act,[21] which imposes more restrictions than the Fed's new rules in several key areas. For example, it prohibits steering bonuses to encourage brokers to sell higher-priced home mortgages. It outlaws mandatory arbitration clauses in any residential mortgage and credit insurance with one advance premium. It bans mortgages with negative amortization (with certain exceptions), and outlaws prepayment penalties in ARMs. It also provides borrowers with a defense of rescinding the loan in a foreclosure proceeding. The House bill has not yet been voted on by the Senate as of September 1, 2009.

Many Mortgage Lenders Were Unregulated

The growth of subprime lending, especially mortgages with low teaser rates that later ratchet up, has been the main driver of mortgage losses. The growth of subprime lending was, in turn, driven by the willingness of mortgage sponsors to include subprime loans as part of mortgage pools underlying the issuance of MBS. As the demand for MBS increased, mortgage originators were able to sell all of their subprime loans quickly to the sponsors of the MBS. Therefore, mortgage originators had strong financial incentives to increase their volume of mortgages at the expense of loan quality and due diligence on borrowers.

Under substantial pressure to produce, mortgage lenders in many cases duped borrowers into taking out loans they could not afford to repay. In many Mexican-American communities of California, such a loan is called "la droga"—Spanish for drug and Mexican slang for a crippling debt. One of the highest concentrations of subprime loans in Orange County, California, was on Camile Street in Santa Ana. A 2007 story in the *Orange County Register* read, "On Camile Street every variety of la droga is on display: adjustable-rate loans with low teaser payments that quickly escalate; prepayment penalties so large that home owners cannot refinance; 'piggyback loans' so low-income buyers can own a house with no money down. All are described in long, complex documents that many Spanish-speaking buyers cannot read."[22]

Overzealous mortgage lenders used pressure tactics to close as many subprime loans as possible. For example, a mortgage broker named Troy Musick was so desperate to close a deal that he followed Ruth DeWitt into the waiting room of an Indiana hospital while Ms. DeWitt's husband was having quadruple heart bypass surgery. She recalls him saying: "It's now or never." The result was a $143,400 loan that the couple was not able to afford.[23] Similarly, New Century Mortgage provided Mr. Ramirez, a strawberry picker from Benito, California, who earned $15,000 per year, with a $720,000 loan to purchase a new home. The Ramirez family members say that they were told by their broker that they could refinance the monthly payments down to $3,000 per month. But this never happened and the actual $5,378 monthly payment was more than the Ramirez family could handle.[24]

The majority of the originators of subprime mortgages were independent mortgage lenders or brokers, called nonbank lenders. In 2005, for example, brokers represented around 60 percent of subprime originations, but only 25 percent of prime originations. As summarized in Figure 1.5, 14 of the top 25 originators of subprime and Alt-A loans in 2006 were nonbank lenders.[25]

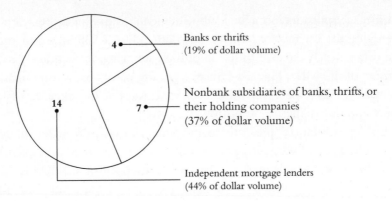

Figure 1.5   Top 25 Originators of Subprime and Alt-A Loans in 2006
SOURCE: Government Accountability Office: Westley Presentation using Inside Mortgage Finance and Federal Reserve Data.

The joint statements of the banking agencies on subprime loans and nontraditional mortgage practices, mentioned earlier, did *not* apply to nonbank lenders; these statements applied only to FDIC-insured banks, thrifts, and their affiliates. The 2008 amendments to the Fed's mortgage rules finally applied to all nonbank lenders. Similarly, until 2008, nonbank lenders were not required to be registered or regulated by any federal agency. Instead, licensing of nonbank lenders was left to the states, which often engaged in little or no supervision of nonbank lenders.[26] In other words, a majority of the mortgage lenders in the United States were essentially unregulated until quite recently.

Not SAFE Enough

In the summer of 2008, Congress finally passed the SAFE Mortgage Licensing Act (SAFE = Secure and Fair Enforcement). This Act establishes minimum standards for state licensing and registration of local mortgage lenders, and requires federal banking agencies to establish a joint registry of loan originators at federally regulated banks, thrifts, and their affiliates. The Act also requires the Department of Housing and Urban Development (HUD) to establish a backup licensing and registry system for loan originators in any state that fails to set up its own system within one or two years.[27]

The enforcement of the new Act is likely to be uneven. Some states will not only register nonbank lenders but also will institute other reforms. For example, California now prohibits lenders from initiating foreclosure proceedings until 30 days after contacting the borrower or making due diligence efforts to do so. This common sense requirement should apply in all states. Yet there is virtually nothing HUD can do if other states establish a registry and licensing system for nonbank lenders, and then do little to supervise them.

In addition, SAFE requires HUD to make recommendations to Congress on appropriate legislative reforms to the Real Estate Settlement and Procedures Act (RESPA) to promote transparency and comparative shopping on mortgage loans. In late 2008, HUD announced revisions of the RESPA requirements so that lenders would provide borrowers, in advance of a closing, with a "good faith estimate" of interest rates, other fees, and prepayment penalties as well as the possibility of later increases in monthly payments. These revisions were needed, according to HUD Secretary Steve Preston, because "many people made uninformed decisions" in taking out loans and these decisions contributed to a surge in mortgage defaults.[28] According to Preston, however, HUD does not have the authority or resources to enforce these RESPA revisions.

In the Stimulus Act of 2009, Congress authorized the Federal Trade Commission (FTC) to ban deceptive lending practices, which is a high priority for the FTC.[29] The FTC will be getting help from the Justice Department, which enforces federal criminal laws against fraud in connection with obtaining mortgages. These laws have long applied to prospective borrowers. In 2009, Congress extended these federal criminal laws to fraud by mortgage lenders.[30]

There are too many federal agencies involved in the regulation of mortgage lending, which also involves the 50 states under SAFE. **Therefore, Congress should create a new agency oriented toward consumer protection, such as the one proposed by the Obama Administration,[31] to police all the federal laws on mortgage lenders and provide that agency with additional enforcement resources in this area. To consolidate jurisdiction over this area, Congress should also transfer the authority to issue mortgage disclosure rules from the Federal Reserve Board to this new** agency. The Fed should be focused primarily on macro economics and systemic risk, not consumer protection.

Lenders Need Skin in the Game

As long as lenders can sell 100 percent of any mortgage they originate and retain no material risk of loss on that mortgage, lenders will have little incentive to do proper diligence on the borrower and structure the mortgage in a manner that it is highly likely to be repaid. Academic studies confirm the common sense intuition that mortgage lenders usually perform more rigorous due diligence when they are retaining the risk of a subprime mortgage's default, than when they are originating to distribute, that is, issuing subprime mortgages so they can be sold quickly to the secondary market.[32] In other words, lenders need to retain some skin in the game as an incentive to make and document sound loans.

On the other hand, many mortgage lenders do not have much capital. A high retention requirement would put them out of business and dramatically decrease competition in the mortgage lending sector. Balancing these considerations, the U.S. Congress is giving serious consideration to a bill requiring mortgage lenders to retain at least 5 percent of the face value of any mortgage they originate and sell.[33] The European Commission has proposed a directive requiring Member States to implement a similar 5 percent retention requirement for all new securitizations starting in 2011.[34]

Some House Purchasers Were Gaming the System

While some home purchasers were rushed or confused by mortgage lenders, others willingly participated in deceptive practices involving their mortgages. Consider the case of the Mottos, a family with four children, who, in 2005, agreed to pay $540,000 for a new three-bedroom house in Clarksburg, Maryland. The builder offered to supply them with a mortgage, but became concerned that the Mottos might not qualify for the loan. So the builder inflated the couple's income by incorrectly stating that they would be collecting rental income from

leasing their old house. Although the Mottos claim they were uncom-
fortable with misrepresenting their income, they nonetheless signed
the loan documents and bought the new house. Like the Bartons
in the parable at the start of this book, the Mottos could not sell or
lease their old home and were struggling to meet the mortgages on
both dwellings.[35]

An Oakland woman candidly told a similar story to the *San Francisco
Chronicle* about exaggerating her income in response to suggestions by
her mortgage broker: "He said, 'If you made $60,000, we could get you
into the lowest interest level of this loan; did you make that much?'
I said, 'Um, yes, about that much.' He went clickety clack on his com-
puter and said, 'Are you sure you don't remember any more income,
like alimony or consultancies, because if you made $80,000, we could
get you into a better loan with a lower interest rate and no prepayment
penalty.' It was such a big differential that I felt like I had to lie, I'm lying
already so what the heck, I said, 'Come to think of it, you're right, I did
have another job that I forgot about.'"[36]

Stories like that of the Mottos and the Oakland woman were
repeated many times. The top types of mortgage fraud include the
following:[37]

- Misrepresentation of income, assets or other debt
- Forged or fraudulent documents such as tax returns or rent
  verifications
- Misrepresentation of the borrower's intent to occupy the house as
  his or her primary residence
- Identity fraud through the unauthorized use of another person's
  Social Security number
- Straw buyers (someone who is not the actual buyer) used to help
  family or friends obtain a house

Of course, mortgage lenders and federal authorities should try to
prevent these practices by borrowers and take legal actions when these
practices are discovered. At the same time, the United States should
address three structural incentives that encourage home purchasers to
overextend themselves: mortgage loans with no down payments, state
exemptions from foreclosure liabilities, and unduly broad tax deductions for mortgage interest.

The FHA Allowed No Down Payment Loans

During the 1990s, the Federal Housing Administration (FHA) participated in several new programs offering no down payment loans to first-time home purchasers through gifts from nonprofit organizations. These programs were analyzed by FHA's Inspector General, who found that the default rate in 2001 was almost 20 percent on a large sample of such no-down-payment loans.[38] Nevertheless, the FHA continued until the middle of 2008 to allow the purchaser to meet its normal requirement for a 3 percent down payment by a gift from a nonprofit group, which, in practice, was often affiliated with the developer or builder of the home. In 2005 and 2006, for example, 40 percent of all first-time buyers took out mortgages with no down payments, according to the National Association of Realtors.[39]

Many no-down-payment loans were facilitated by allegedly charitable organizations that were "being used to funnel down payment assistance from sellers to buyers through self-serving, circular financing arrangements."[40] The program works like this: A seller makes a charitable donation to a nonprofit organization, which in turn gives a down payment gift to the house buyer. The source of the seller's donation is the sale proceeds of the house. Howard Glaser, a former HUD official, said, "It's a well-intentioned program that's turned into little more than a federally financed mortgage scam. The victim is often the borrower, who is lured into a home they can't afford by a federal program."[41] In 2006, the IRS began to investigate nonprofit groups funded by home builders and other sellers. **Although the IRS has revoked the nonprofit status of many front organizations for housing developers, a few continue to operate and should be closed down.**

As of October, 2008, the FHA required a purchaser to make a down payment of at least 3.5 percent of a home's purchase price to obtain a FHA mortgage. However, FHA materials stress that this down payment requirement can be fully satisfied by tax credits for first-time home purchasers, as described later. This use of tax credits is just another way for the FHA to make loans to home buyers with no skin in the game.

Moreover, home purchasers have already found that the U.S. Department of Agriculture will still help guarantee no-down-payment loans in rural areas, generously defined to include some outer suburbs of cities. In fact, the General Accounting Office (GAO) found 1,300 instances of areas qualifying as rural that were closely integrated with urban areas. For example, Belpre, Ohio was designated "rural" by GAO standards in 2005. That same year the Census Bureau reported that Belpre was "densely settled," with an average population density of 1,000 residents per square mile, and also that it was contiguous with the urban community of Parkersburg, West Virginia, which had a population of around 33,000 at the time.[42] **The Department of Agriculture should require at least a 3.5 percent down payment for all home mortgages in its programs and should more accurately define rural areas.**

Limit Tax Credits for First-Time Home Purchasers

In order to provide an additional incentive for home ownership, Congress enacted a tax credit in late 2008 for first-time home buyers with joint annual income of $150,000 or less. This credit applied to home purchases in 2008 and the first half of 2009, but must be repaid by the home purchaser in $500 annual installments over 15 years. The Stimulus Act of 2009 expanded this tax credit to $8,000, and included all buyers of principal residences who have not owned a home in the last three years and whose joint annual adjusted income does not exceed $170,000. The credit can be applied to any principal residence purchased through November 30, 2009, and it will *not* have to be repaid if the residence is held for at least 36 months.[43]

 If Congress wants to help first-time home purchasers below a certain income, it should offer them tax credits instead of mortgages with no down payments. But the tax credits should be designed to ensure that these home purchasers have skin in the game. Specifically, the amount of the tax credit should not cover more than half of the down payment for the house.

 With the rise of no-down-payment loans and the fall of housing prices, the national average of home owners whose mortgage debt exceeds the current value of their homes (underwater mortgages) was 18 percent as of September 30, 2008, rising to 22 percent by March 31, 2009.[44] Figure 1.6 shows the four states with the highest such percentage (other than Michigan with its auto problems).

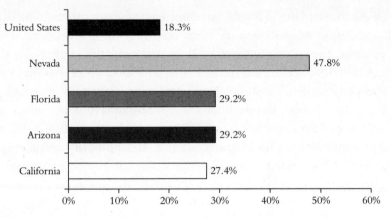

Figure 1.6   Percentage of Underwater Home Owners in Four States as of
Sept. 30, 2008
SOURCE: First American CoreLogic published in "State Has Highest Percentage of 'Under Water'
Households," *Wall Street Journal* (Oct. 31, 2008).

States Should Restrict Their Antideficiency Laws

California and Arizona both have laws that usually protect borrowers if
they default on their home mortgages and the proceeds from the home
sale are less than the amount of their mortgages. If a lender sells the
home underlying a mortgage, it generally may not collect any deficiency
from the borrower in these two states. **California and Arizona should
narrow or eliminate their antideficiency statutes, because they
encourage purchasers to buy as expensive a house as they can
and obtain close to 100 percent financing, with little concern
about personal liability if they default on their mortgage.**

In California and Arizona, the mortgage holder can elect one of
two remedies when a borrower defaults on a home mortgage. First, the
mortgage holder can sell the home subject to the mortgage in order
to recover as much as possible of the loan. In that case, the borrower
is not liable for any deficiency from the home sale, that is, the difference between the mortgage amount and the sale proceeds. Second,
the mortgage holder can sue the borrower personally for the amount
of the mortgage. In that case, the mortgage holder cannot attempt to
sell the home subject to the mortgage. This second alternative is unat-
tractive to most mortgage holders since the defaulting borrowers rarely
have personal assets worth more than their homes.

Both Nevada and Florida have homestead exemptions, which protect a person's primary home from creditors in many circumstances. In Nevada, the homestead exemption protects the owner of a primary residence from most creditors up to $550,000 of equity in their home.[45] In Florida, this homestead exemption essentially has no upper limit, leading people like O.J. Simpson with massive debts to purchase multimillion dollar homes there. However, both states allow lenders to foreclose and collect on a mortgage that is specifically secured by all the owners of a home.

Congress Should Narrow Tax Deductions for Mortgage Interest

Other incentives for home owners to overextend themselves are found in the U.S. tax code. Most Americans agree that mortgage interest on their primary residence should be tax deductible. However, the United States goes much further than other countries in tax deductions for mortgage interest. Interest deductions are available for mortgages on second homes, as well as for mortgages on any number of homes acquired by speculators hoping to sell or flip them quickly for a profit. House purchases by speculators were a significant factor behind the surge in housing prices and subsequent rise in mortgage defaults. In 2005, according to a real estate trade group, investors purchased almost one out of every three homes in the United States.[46]

Although the United States does not allow tax deductions for interest on credit cards or consumer purchases, interest on home equity loans is tax deductible. Yet the purpose of both types of loans is often the same. This tax policy on home equity loans is inconsistent and unwise. Home equity loan balances have ballooned from $1 billion to more than $1 trillion since the early 1980s.[47] During the surge in housing prices, many owners took out home equity loans not to improve their homes but to buy consumer goods. Similarly, cash-outs from refinancing home mortgages amounted to $327 billion dollars in 2006 alone.[48] From 2001 to 2007, $350 billion was shifted from credit card balances to home equity loans or refinanced mortgages.[49] As a result, U.S. household debt relative to personal disposable income rose from 77 percent in 1990, to just over 90 percent in 2000, to over 130 percent in 2007.[50]

Congress should give serious consideration to limiting the interest deduction to one mortgage for the primary residence of each family. In addition, Congress should seriously consider the elimination or restriction of the interest deduction for home equity loans and mortgage refinancings, unless the remaining equity in the home exceeds 20 to 25 percent of its current market value. This limit would allow home owners to realize some of the built-up equity in their home without jeopardizing the ability of the first mortgage holder to protect its interest.

Summary

The recent crash in U.S. housing prices was caused by multiple factors. A leading factor was the abnormally low rate of interest from late 2001 through mid-2005, which was driven by the global glut of savings and the Federal Reserve's policy decisions. This low interest rate made housing much cheaper for many Americans and created a huge demand among global investors for mortgage-backed securities (MBS) with higher yields and higher risks. The result: a huge increase in the volume of high-yield, subprime loans originated by mortgage lenders and sold to Wall Street firms, which packaged and sold them as MBS throughout the world. Unfortunately, these subprime loans were often made to borrowers who could not afford the monthly payments, and who soon began to default at an alarming rate. These high defaults contributed to a sharp decline in U.S. housing prices and an abrupt halt to the mortgage securitization process.

The origination of subprime loans was heavily concentrated in mortgage lenders, which were not required to be licensed until 2009. Although these mortgage lenders will now be licensed by each state, Congress should promote adequate and uniform supervision of the mortgage origination process by creating a federal mortgage agency. More fundamentally, to incent mortgage lenders to underwrite sound loans, they should be required to retain at least 5 percent of the default risk of the mortgages they sell in the secondary market.

Although the Federal Reserve has finally toughened the rules on mortgage disclosures and lending practices, it should go further by requiring disclosure of bonus payments to brokers for originating high-yield loans, and limiting the use of mortgages with negative amortization. Further restrictions on the practices of mortgage lenders may be adopted through legislation, or new Fed rules in response to possible legislation. In the future, the job of setting rules on mortgage practices, as well as the resources for enforcing these rules, should be transferred to a new federal mortgage agency with more of a focus on consumer protection than the Fed.

States like Arizona and California should limit their statutes that encourage home owners to avoid personal responsibility on their mortgages. If home owners default on their mortgages, the holders of those mortgages should have the ability to bring suit against these owners for at least some portion of the difference between the outstanding balance on the mortgages and the proceeds from the home sale. In 2008, the Federal Housing Administration (FHA) finally stopped insuring mortgages with no down payments. However, FHA should also stop allowing home owners to satisfy the agency's requirement for a 3.5 percent down payment entirely with tax credits. Similarly, the Department of Agriculture should eliminate or severely restrict the use of no-down-payment loans in its home ownership programs and narrowly define rural areas.

Tax credits are a sensible way to encourage first-time home buyers if the down payment on the home substantially exceeds the value of the tax credit given to the homebuyer. However, if the United States is to avoid another speculative bubble from overinvestment in housing, Congress should reconsider the scope of the tax subsidies for home ownership. Congress should continue to allow the deduction of interest on first mortgages securing the primary residence of the taxpayer. But Congress should consider repealing or limiting the interest deduction on home equity loans or mortgage refinancings, unless the remaining home equity exceeds 20 to 25 percent of the fair market value of the home. Similarly, Congress should consider repealing or limiting the interest deduction on mortgages used to buy vacation houses or other types of second homes.

Chapter 2

Fannie and Freddie

The critical link between the crash in U.S. housing prices and the global financial crisis lies in the process of mortgage securitization. This process was dominated by two quasi-public institutions, the Federal National Mortgage Association (Fannie Mae) and the Federal Home Loan Mortgage Corporation (Freddie Mac), both of which had public charters with housing missions but were owned entirely by private shareholders. These two institutions, together with a federal program for guaranteeing mortgages called the Government National Mortgage Association (Ginnie Mae), owned or guaranteed close to half of all U.S. mortgages by 2003. They also were large purchasers of subprime mortgages and mortgage-backed securities (MBS) backed by subprime loans.

Because of high default rates on these subprime loans, Fannie Mae and Freddie Mac reported huge losses in the fall of 2008 and were put into a federal conservatorship by the U.S. Treasury. In exchange for preferred stock, the U.S. Treasury pledged to provide as much as $100 billion of capital to each institution so they could both maintain a positive net worth in September of 2008. The Treasury later increased that amount to $200 billion per institution. In 2008, Fannie Mae's losses exceeded $57 billion and Freddie Mac's losses exceeded $50 billion.[1]

This chapter will outline the historic role of Fannie Mae and Freddie Mac, and explain how they contributed to the crash in U.S. housing prices as well as the global financial crisis. (Chapter 3 will address mortgage securitization in the private sector.) This chapter will show that the fundamental flaw embedded in both institutions was the conflict between their public mission to promote low-income housing and their private objective of obtaining good shareholder returns. This chapter will evaluate future options for both institutions in light of which functions should be performed by the federal government and which by the private sector.

A History of Mixed Messages

Fannie Mae was created as a federal agency in 1938 as part of the Congressional response to the Great Depression. Its mandate was to buy up mortgages from lenders so they could make more home loans. For its initial three decades of existence, Fannie Mae concentrated on buying mortgages insured by the Federal Housing Administration (FHA).

As part of a plan to limit on-budget spending in 1968, Congress created Ginnie Mae, which took over Fannie Mae's role of purchasing FHA-insured mortgages. At the same time, Congress transformed Fannie Mae from a federal agency to a corporation owned by private shareholders. Yet this shareholder-owned corporation retained an express public mission to buy up mortgages from low and moderate-income families, provide stability and liquidity in the trading market for mortgages, and promote access to mortgage credit throughout the country.

In 1970, Congress chartered Freddie Mac with a public mission similar to that of Fannie Mae. Congress created Freddie Mac partly to promote competition with Fannie Mae, and partly to have a federal entity that worked more closely with savings and loan associations than Fannie Mae, which was thought to cater mainly to the needs of mortgage bankers. In 1989, Freddie Mac was privatized as a corporation owned by shareholders, although it retained its public mission to support the U.S. mortgage market.

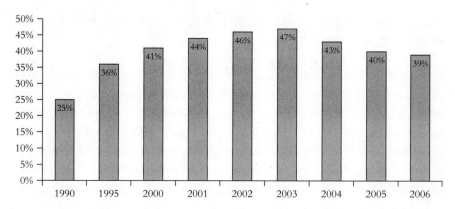

Figure 2.1   Fannie and Freddie Share of Residential Mortgage Debt
Outstanding
SOURCE: OFHEO 2008 Report to Congress.

Fannie Mae and Freddie Mac raised money by selling to investors
their own bonds, as well as MBS they had guaranteed. For years, they
used the proceeds from these sales mainly to purchase an increasing
share of mortgages in the U.S. market. As Figure 2.1 shows, the share
of the mortgage market controlled by these two institutions increased
from 25 percent in 1990 to a peak of 47 percent in 2003. By law, they
have been limited to purchasing nonjumbo mortgages, defined for 2008
as mortgages below $417,000 on single-family homes with exceptions
for high-cost areas.[2]

The Privileges of a Government Charter

To facilitate their purchase of mortgages for low and middle-income
families, Congress exempted from state and local income tax the interest payments on the debt securities issued by both Fannie Mae and
Freddie Mac. In addition, these institutions were granted a $2.25 billion
line of credit from the U.S. Treasury. Fannie Mae and Freddie Mac
were granted other special privileges as well. For example, they were
exempt from Securities and Exchange Commission (SEC) registration
of their securities, and banks insured by the Federal Deposit Insurance
Corporation (FDIC) were allowed to invest in the securities of these

two institutions without the limits normally applied to investments in shareholder-owned corporations.[3]

Due to these privileges normally associated with a federal agency, the bonds of both institutions were widely perceived by investors to constitute moral (not legal) obligations of the U.S. government. In other words, investors assumed that the federal government would come to the rescue of Fannie Mae and Freddie Mac if either became financially troubled. Due to this perceived implicit guarantee, the interest rates on the bonds of these two institutions were significantly lower than the rates on the bonds of other large and top-rated institutions competing to buy mortgages.

Setting Affordable Housing Goals

In exchange for these governmental privileges, the Secretary of HUD was empowered to set affordable housing goals for Fannie Mae and Freddie Mac. Specifically, HUD was authorized to determine the percentage of their business that should be devoted to promoting low and moderate income housing. That rate was increased successively from 42 percent in 1996 to 56 percent by 2008.[4]

As Fannie Mae and Freddie Mac devoted more of their resources to promoting low and moderate-income housing, the percentage of American home owners grew from 65 percent in 1995 to 69 percent in 2005. See Figure 2.2. This incremental growth proved to be the

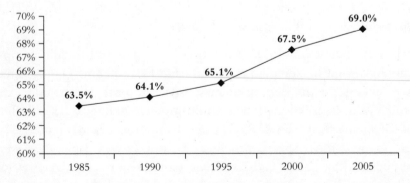

Figure 2.2   U.S. Home Ownership Rate: 1985–2005
SOURCE: U.S. Census Bureau. www.census.gov/hhes/www/housing/census/historic/owner.html.

straw that broke the camel's back. The extra 4 percent overstretched the financial capacity of marginal borrowers, leading to a large increase in subprime mortgages and subsequent defaults. By contrast, the home ownership level in 2005 was 44 percent in Germany, 58 percent in France, and 62 percent in Japan.[5] The major industrialized countries with higher home ownership rates than the United States in 2005 were Ireland and Spain, which both provide tax relief for certain mortgage payments and which both had housing bubbles burst in 2008.

Rising Quotas for Low-Income Housing

As the HUD Secretary raised the percentage of business Fannie Mae and Freddie Mac were required to devote to low and moderate-income housing, there were two significant responses. One was a relaxation of the criteria for meeting the housing goals. In 1995, HUD agreed to allow these two institutions to count their purchase of subprime mortgages toward meeting their goals for low- and moderate-income housing. In 2000, HUD said that the presence of these two institutions "in the subprime market could be of significant benefit to lower-income families, minorities, and families living in underserved areas."[6]

When setting its housing goals in 2000, HUD was warned by consumer advocates that subprime loans were starting to become more popular and that borrowers were being duped into accepting high priced mortgages by teaser rates, that is, low initial rates that ratchet up after a few years. In response, HUD officials informally indicated that it would not credit Fannie Mae and Freddie Mac for mortgages that were too costly or that were made without regard to the borrower's ability to pay. But that informal policy was never incorporated into HUD's rules or reporting requirements for either institution. According to Allen Fishbein of the Consumer Federation of America, HUD officials "chose not to put the brakes on this dangerous lending when they could have."[7]

As a result, Fannie Mae and Freddie Mac became the largest purchasers of MBS backed by subprime mortgages. The two institutions bought $81 billion in subprime MBS in 2003, $175 billion in 2004, $169 billion in 2005 and $90 billion in 2006.[8] "The market knew we needed those loans," said a spokeswoman for Freddie Mac. The higher

goals "forced us to go into that market to serve the targeted popula-
tions that HUD wanted us to serve."[9]

Lending Standards Fell

To fulfill their dual goals of meeting their low-income housing quotas and increasing their growth of annual earnings, the two institutions
gradually reduced their standards for buying loans. In 1999, for example,
Fannie Mae announced a program to loosen lending standards for
home owners with "slightly impaired" credit. At the time, Franklin
Raines, Fannie Mae's CEO, said the program was designed to provide
home ownership opportunities for "many borrowers whose credit
is just a notch below" qualifying for a loan.[10] In 2004, a risk officer
of Freddie Mac unsuccessfully opposed its practice of buying NINA
mortgages (no income/no assets); those mortgages were extended to
borrowers even though they had not verified their income or assets. In
2007, the chief risk officer of Fannie Mae wrote that it "has one of the
weakest control processes" he had ever seen in his career.[11]

When the two institutions tried to resist further erosion of their
mortgage standards, they were met with threats about moving business to private competitors less concerned with standards. For example,
Angelo Mozilo, the CEO of Countrywide, a large nonbank mortgage
lender, threatened to unravel its close partnership with Fannie Mae unless
it started buying Countrywide's riskier loans. Mozilo told Daniel Mudd,
the CEO of Fannie Mae, that Countrywide had other options. Wall
Street firms had started buying subprime loans, transforming them into
securities and selling the securities to investors. "You're becoming irrel-
evant," Mozilo told Mudd, according to two people with knowledge of
the meeting. Over half of Fannie's loan-reselling business had been lost
to Wall Street and other competitors in the previous year. "You need us
more than we need you," Mozilo said, "and if you don't take these loans,
you'll find you can lose much more."[12] Ironically, Countrywide was saved
from insolvency by Bank of America and Mozillo was charged with fraud.

Using Cheap Funding to Buy Back their Own Securities

The second disturbing trend was the increasing size of the debt obligations of Fannie Mae and Freddie Mac from the issuance of their own

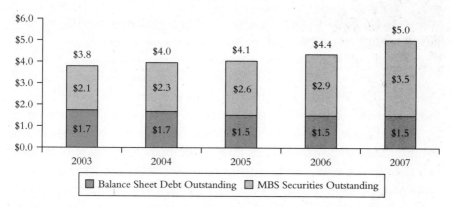

Figure 2.3   Fannie & Freddie Balance Sheet Liabilities and MBS Obligations (in $ trillions)
SOURCE: OFHEO 2008 Report to Congress.

bonds and their guarantees of MBS sold to investors. As Figure 2.3 shows, the total debt obligations for the two institutions increased from $3.8 trillion in 2003 to $5 trillion in 2007. That increase came from out-standing MBS, which jumped by 67 percent in that period. To put this number in perspective, the total U.S. Treasury debt held by the invest-ing public was just above $5 trillion at the end of 2007. In other words, the debt obligations of these two institutions grew to almost equal the total publicly held debt of the U.S. federal government.

Congress controls the aggregate debt limit of the U.S. government, which has been raised from time to time after considerable debate. By con-trast, Fannie Mae and Freddie Mac can create huge "moral" obligations of the U.S. government without any Congressional approval. The federal reg-ulator of these two institutions, the Office of Federal Housing Enterprise Oversight (OFHEO) under HUD, did not have the power to require them to maintain minimum capital levels or to limit their debt obligations. By contrast, the regulator of national banks has both these powers.

Fannie Mae and Freddie Mac could have fulfilled their housing mission at a much lower debt level if they had concentrated on pur-chasing mortgages, packaging them as MBS and selling the MBS to investors with guarantees. Instead, these two institutions held in their own portfolios large amounts of mortgages that they financed by sell-ing their own bonds to investors. At the same time, the two institutions guaranteed MBS they sold to investors, and then *repurchased for their own portfolios the MBS they guaranteed.* The mortgages and MBS in their portfolios peaked at $1.6 trillion in 2004 and subsequently declined in response to public criticism of holding such large portfolios of MBS.[13]

Why did Fannie Mae and Freddie Mac repurchase and hold their own guaranteed MBS? Because they were running a huge hedge fund for the benefit of their shareholders at the expense of the federal government. Fannie Mae and Freddie Mac borrowed money by selling bonds at very low interest rates due to the perceived moral obligation of the federal government to them, and then invested the bond proceeds in mortgages or their own MBS, which usually made payments one percent higher than those paid out by these institutions on their bonds. In 2004, for example, the interest income earned on the mortgage portfolios of Fannie Mae and Freddie Mac exceeded their borrowing costs by approximately $23 billion. This net portfolio income was much larger than the $4 billion in fee income they earned in 2004 from packaging, guaranteeing, and selling MBS.[14]

But this portfolio strategy involved two significant risks—credit defaults and mortgage prepayments. If the mortgages or MBS in their portfolios began to default, Fannie Mae and Freddie Mac would suffer major credit losses. In fact, they did suffer large credit losses in 2007 and 2008 when the significant portion of their portfolios representing substandard mortgages began to default.

The prepayment risk of this portfolio strategy depends on the likelihood of a future decline in mortgage interest rates, which would set off a wave of mortgage repayments and refinancing at lower interest rates levels. Yet, the fixed-rate bonds previously sold by these two institutions to investors would continue to require interest payments at the higher rate set before the decline. This potential mismatch between income from lower rates on refinanced mortgages in their portfolios and payment obligations on their higher-rate bonds held by investors could make a big dent in their earnings.

Complex Hedges Violated Accounting Rules

To reduce the adverse effects of this potential mismatch, Fannie Mae and Freddie Mac engaged in complex hedging transactions. In essence, these hedging transactions were designed to generate profits for these two institutions if interest rates declined, to offset the losses that would be incurred by the mismatch between the lower interest rate received on their portfolios and the constant interest rate payable to their bond investors. When any company engages in such hedging transactions, it must report its earnings in accordance with a lengthy and dense accounting standard. The errors of Fannie Mae and Freddie Mac in accounting for their hedging transactions led to financial restatements and intensified legislative review of both institutions.

In 2002, Freddie Mac fired Arthur Andersen because of its role as the outside auditor of Enron, and hired Pricewaterhouse Coopers (PWC) as its new outside auditor. After a careful review of the financial statements of Freddie Mac, PWC found serious errors in the institution's accounting for its hedging transactions. Admitting that it had understated its income because of hedging and other measures designed to smooth out its year-to-year earnings, Freddie Mac agreed to increase its income by $5 billion over several prior years. It also fired its CEO, Leo Brendsel, and sued him; this case was settled in 2007 with Brendsel agreeing to give up $13 million of deferred compensation.[15]

Days before PWC announced the accounting errors of Freddie Mac, OFHEO issued a report saying that Freddie Mac's internal controls were "accurate and reliable." Embarrassed by this report, OFHEO launched a review of Fannie Mae's accounting. In September of 2004, OFHEO released a lengthy report finding that Fannie Mae had failed to recognize $200 million of relevant hedging expenses for 1998, thereby allowing the payment of $27 million in bonuses to its executives. This report prompted an investigation by the SEC, which forced Fannie Mae to restate its prior earnings by $9 billion over several prior years. The CEO, CFO, and Comptroller of Fannie Mae were replaced and sued by OFHEO; they settled their cases in 2008 by paying $3 million in fines and giving up another $20 million in potential benefits.[16]

In his 2008 letter to shareholders, Warren Buffett had the following to say about derivatives and OFHEO:

> Derivatives are dangerous. They have dramatically increased the leverage and risks in our financial system. They have made it almost impossible for investors to understand and analyze our largest commercial banks and investment banks. They allowed

Fannie Mae and Freddie Mac to engage in massive misstatements of earnings for years. So indecipherable were Freddie and Fannie that their federal regulator, OFHEO, whose more than 100 employees had no job except the oversight of these two institutions, totally missed their cooking of the books.[17]

Congress Takes a Closer Look

These accounting scandals intensified the legislative scrutiny of Fannie Mae and Freddie Mac, which had always been lightly regulated by OFHEO. It was supposed to ensure that the two institutions were operating in a safe and sound manner. However, as mentioned earlier, OFHEO's regulatory powers were much more limited than those of the federal agency overseeing national banks.

In 1999, a collection of large banks formed a lobbying group called FM Watch, which pushed for stricter regulatory requirements to constrain the aggressive expansion of Fannie Mae and Freddie Mac. In response, Fannie Mae dismissively labeled the group as "fat-cat bankers," and hired several powerful lobbying firms just to keep them from working for FM Watch.[18] In 2003, several Republican Senators introduced a bill to replace OFHEO with an independent agency with new powers, including the authority to increase the capital of these two institutions and restrict the expansion of their activities. The bill also would have allowed the new regulator to put these two institutions into receivership if they were critically undercapitalized. When the House Banking Committee passed a substantially weaker bill on this same subject, it was opposed as inadequate by the Treasury Department and was never enacted.

In 2005 and 2007, Republican Senators introduced similar legislation to increase government oversight of Fannie Mae and Freddie Mac. Neither bill was enacted because the two institutions mobilized a mammoth lobbying effort and they were defended by liberal Democrats who supported more modest reforms. In the summer of 2005, for example, Democratic Minority Leader Harry Reid stated, "While I favor improving oversight by our federal housing regulators to ensure safety and soundness, we cannot pass legislation that could limit Americans from owning homes and potentially harm our economy in the process."[19]

Studies Find Little Public Benefit

The legislative process, however, elicited important new information. Testifying before the House Financial Services Committee in February of 2005, Fed Chairman Alan Greenspan stated that there was "no reasonable basis" for the portfolios of Fannie Mae and Freddie Mac to exceed $100 billion or $200 billion. In his view: "If [Fannie and Freddie] continue to grow, continue to have the low capital they have, continue to engage in the dynamic hedging of their portfolios, which they need to do for interest rate risk aversion, they potentially create ever-growing potential systematic risk down the road."[20]

The legislative debate also led to two studies estimating the value of the federal government's support of these two institutions, and the portion of that support benefiting shareholders rather than home owners. A study by the Congressional Budget Office estimated that the federal subsidies to Fannie Mae and Freddie Mac totaled almost $20 billion in 2003. Of that total, $6.3 billion was retained by these two institutions for their shareholders.[21] By contrast, a study by a Fed economist estimated the present value of the *implicit* federal subsidies to the two institutions in 2003 at $143 billion. The economist concluded that roughly half of these subsidies went to the shareholders of these two institutions, and that these subsidies reduced mortgage rates to home owners by only 7 basis points (7/100 of 1 percent).[22]

Paulson Takes Out the Bazooka

Only in the summer of 2008, when the stock prices of both institutions plummeted to almost nothing, did Congress finally act. At the end of July 2008, Congress passed the Housing and Economic Recovery Act, which established a new independent regulator for Fannie Mae and Freddie Mac. The new regulator has the power to set capital requirements, establish standards for internal controls and risk management, restrict asset growth and limit dividend distributions. The Federal Reserve also was given authority to monitor these mortgage-related institutions to prevent systemic risks. Most importantly, Congress authorized the U.S. Treasury until the end of 2009 to offer Fannie Mae and Freddie Mac an unlimited line of credit and make equity investments in these two institutions. In a Senate Banking Committee hearing on July 15, 2008, Treasury Secretary Paulson maintained that having these broad powers is like carrying a "bazooka" in your pocket: "If you've got a squirt gun in your pocket, you may have to take it out. If you've got a bazooka, and people know you've got it, you may not have to take it out . . ."[23]

On September 6, 2008, Paulson did reach into his pocket and used his bazooka to put Fannie Mae and Freddie Mac into a federal conservatorship. While the holders of their common and preferred stock were virtually wiped out, their bondholders were protected because of potential risks to the global financial system. The bondholders of these institutions include many financial institutions not only in the United States but also across the world. Thus, this bailout vindicated the widely held perception that the bonds of Fannie Mae and Freddie Mac were indeed the moral obligations of the federal government.

What Should Be Done with Fannie Mae and Freddie Mac?

In the short term, most executives and directors of Fannie Mae and Freddie Mac were replaced with new candidates by the U.S. Treasury, which has faced great difficulties in retaining CEOs for both institutions. The new CEOs must operate under a tight leash from the new federal regulator, which must approve every significant decision of the two institutions. In addition, the regulator has been directing them to purchase more mortgages and grant foreclosure holidays as part of the federal government's efforts to bolster the mortgage market.

Given the existing guarantees and holdings of Fannie Mae and Freddie Mac, it will take several years to implement any decision on how, if at all, they should operate in the future. Nevertheless, Congress should make that decision soon in order to start taking steps in the right direction. The Obama Administration has committed to studying a range of future alternatives for both institutions.[24] In conducting such a study, the administration should consider what functions these two institutions currently perform, and whether those functions could be reasonably performed by other public and private institutions. The four key functions are:

1. Subsidizing mortgages for low and moderate income families
2. Guaranteeing packages of mortgages sold as securities to investors
3. Raising mortgage capital for homes below the area median
4. Helping stabilize the MBS trading market in times of financial turmoil

Figure 2.4 delineates which public and private institutions might perform some of those functions, and what roles might be played by Fannie Mae and Freddie Mac in the future.

Subsidizing Mortgages Through a Government Agency

The first function—subsidizing certain mortgages—can take various forms: reduced interest on mortgages, tax credits for first-time buyers, or insurance on mortgages. Interest subsidies on mortgages are provided by HUD. Insurance on certain types of mortgages for eligible borrowers is provided by the FHA and the Department of Veteran Affairs (VA), as well as the Agriculture Department's Rural Housing Service and HUD's Office of Public and Indian Housing.

Since the function of subsidizing certain mortgages involves no profits, it is best performed by one of these federal agencies. By legislation or delegated authority, Congress can define the class of home owners and types of mortgages eligible for these subsidies. Through the appropriations process, Congress can also decide how large these subsidies should be every year.

Guaranteeing MBS Through Ginnie Mae and the Private Sector

The second function, guaranteeing MBS, can be performed by a federal agency, or a financial institution in the private sector to the extent necessary. Ginnie Mae offers guarantees for the loans insured under the FHA, VA, and other federal programs; all these programs are dedicated to home owners below certain income levels and/or mortgages below certain sizes. Unlike Fannie Mae or Freddie Mac, Ginnie

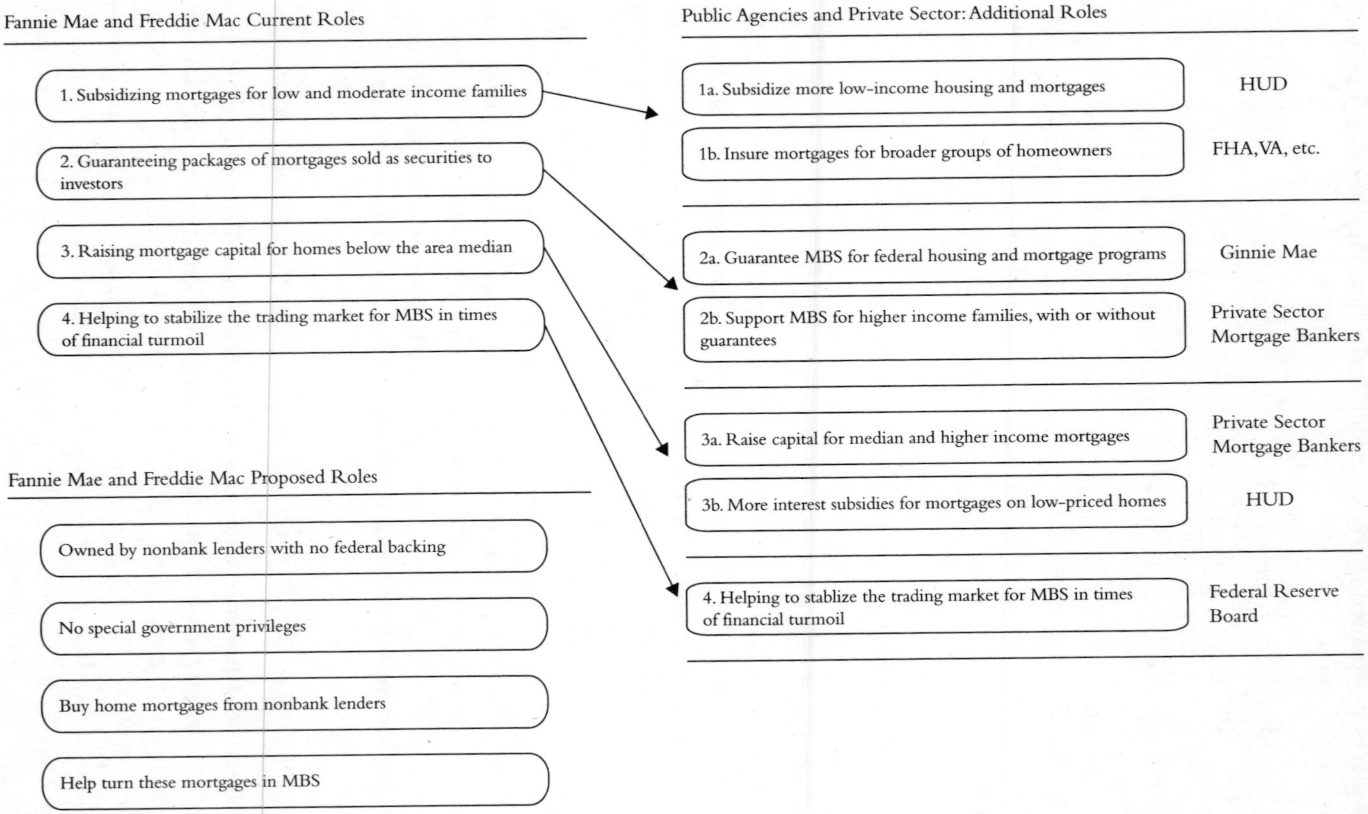

Figure 2.4 Reorganization of Functions for Fannie Mae and Freddie Mac

Fannie Mae and Freddie Mac Current Roles

1. Subsidizing mortgages for low and moderate income families

2. Guaranteeing packages of mortgages sold as securities to investors

3. Raising mortgage capital for homes below the area median

4. Helping to stabilize the trading market for MBS in times of financial turmoil

Fannie Mae and Freddie Mac Proposed Roles

Owned by nonbank lenders with no federal backing

No special government privileges

Buy home mortgages from nonbank lenders

Help turn these mortgages in MBS

Public Agencies and Private Sector: Additional Roles

1a. Subsidizing more low-income housing and mortgages — HUD

1b. Insure mortgages for broader groups of homeowners — FHA, VA, etc.

2a. Guarantee MBS for federal housing and mortgage programs — Ginnie Mae

2b. Support MBS for higher income families, with or without guarantees — Private Sector Mortgage Bankers

3a. Raise capital for median and higher income mortgages — Private Sector Mortgage Bankers

3b. More interest subsidies for mortgages on low-priced homes — HUD

4. Helping to stabilize the trading market for MBS in times of financial turmoil — Federal Reserve Board

Mae is a government agency within HUD; it is not a shareholder-owned corporation.

Ginnie Mae has been an effective agency for promoting government-insured mortgages by facilitating the securitization process and should continue to play that role. The mortgages backing MBS guaranteed by Ginnie Mae are originated in the private sector by mortgage bankers, savings and loans, commercial banks, and others. Ginnie Mae's functions are limited to helping form pools of similar mortgages from pre-approved lenders and guaranteeing for a fee the timely payment of principal and interest on these mortgages. The Ginnie Mae guarantee, backed by the full faith and credit of the U.S. government, allows lenders to sell their government-insured loans at attractive prices to investors so that these lenders can use the sale proceeds to make new government-insured loans to home owners eligible for these programs.

In contrast to Fannie Mae and Freddie Mac, Ginnie Mae does not purchase mortgages or MBS to hold in its investment portfolio. Therefore, Ginnie Mae does not need to sell bonds to finance these purchases or adopt hedging strategies to manage interest-rate risk. Nor is there a strong case for organizing Ginnie Mae as a government chartered company, rather than as a federal agency.

While Ginnie Mae caters to smaller mortgages and lower income families, its guarantee function for securities backed by jumbo mortgages or mortgages from higher income families could be performed by private financial institutions. The guarantee fee would presumably be set by the market based on loss experience in different categories of jumbo mortgages and home owner income. Investors may not insist on a 100 percent guarantee, if the quality of the mortgages in these categories were high enough. **There is no compelling reason for the guarantee function for these two groups to be performed by a federal agency or federally chartered corporation.**

Raising Mortgage Capital for Homes Below the Area Median

The third function is more complex: It entails raising capital to provide more mortgages at lower rates for homes priced below the median for the area. Some commentators would leave the allocation of mortgage capital to the normal workings of the financial markets. In their view, capital would be attracted to making mortgages to the extent doing so would be more profitable than competing uses. But other commentators would argue that mortgages are special because the country's goals include the promotion of home ownership. In their view, the market left alone might not allocate enough capital to support that goal, especially for homes below the area median.

The latter view underlies the case for Fannie Mae and Freddie Mac as shareholder-owned corporations, with special privileges tied to serving the U.S. mortgage market. By selling securities to the public and purchasing mortgages, these institutions bring more capital to bear on making mortgages eligible for purchase by these two institutions. However, pushing home ownership beyond a certain percentage of the American population is likely to be counterproductive: Some families cannot afford monthly mortgage payments, while others may prefer renting if they move frequently.

Even if Congress decides to promote home ownership for all Americans by increasing the amount and lowering the price of mortgage capital available for homes priced below their area's median, Fannie Mae and Freddie Mac have proven to be highly inefficient vehicles for achieving this goal. As explained earlier in this chapter, the reduction in mortgage rates attributable to Fannie Mae and Freddie Mac has been estimated at only 7 basis points (7/100 of 1 percent). Empirical studies show that one-third to one-half of the special government privileges afforded these two institutions benefit their shareholders, rather than home owners.

To reduce these benefits to shareholders, some have suggested that Fannie Mae and Freddie Mac be turned into public utilities with the rate of shareholder returns set by a regulator. The history of rate regulation in industries like airlines and electric utilities, however, is not encouraging. Regulators found it very difficult to calculate reasonable rates of returns, and the utilities managed to engage in risky activities outside of the regulated envelope.[25] Due to these drawbacks, the public utility format is usually reserved for industries that have the characteristics of natural monopolies. In other words, avoid rate setting by a regulatory commission if prices can reasonably be set by a competitive market.

In the mortgage market for homes priced near their area's median, Fannie Mae and Freddie Mac are not natural monopolies. Indeed, many private-sector firms already compete

head-to-head with these two publicly chartered institutions. If Congress takes away the public privileges of these two institutions, more private-sector firms would enter this portion of the home mortgage market.

By contrast, there is not much of a private mortgage market for low-income homes. The purchasers of these homes do not usually qualify for prime mortgages. When HUD told Fannie Mae and Freddie Mac to buy a certain quota of mortgages from purchasers of such homes, the two institutions generated a huge demand for high-yield, subprime mortgages. The response was predictable: Lenders frenetically originated subprime mortgages with high default rates to feed the two mortgage giants.

If Congress decides to allocate more capital at lower prices to families that would qualify only for subprime mortgages, it should provide them with interest subsidies or other forms of financial assistance from a federal agency. Then, all the government subsidy would go directly to the low-income families meeting the legislative criteria. This would be a much more efficient and targeted approach than providing governmental privileges to Fannie Mae and Freddie Mac and asking them to meet quotas on purchasing home mortgages for low-income families.

Stabilizing the Mortgage Market in Tumultuous Times

The fourth function is the most relevant to the current situation, namely, helping to stabilize the trading market for mortgages in times of financial turmoil. When there are no other buyers of mortgages, Fannie Mae and Freddie Mac continue to buy mortgages and MBS for their own portfolios. However, these purchases necessarily entail substantial risks. If these two institutions buy mortgages and MBS during a time of falling housing prices, they are likely to experience losses from credit defaults. If they issue fixed-rate bonds to finance purchases of mortgages or MBS, and then rates for mortgages decline sharply, they will suffer losses as home owners refinance at lower rates.

If the top officers of Fannie Mae and Freddie Mac manage these risks well, their shareholders are likely to profit. On the other hand, if they do not manage these risks effectively, the two institutions can easily become insolvent, as they have recently. Their insolvency imposes large costs not only on their own shareholders but also on all U.S.

taxpayers, who are forced to pay for their bailouts to avoid major blows to the global financial system. Therefore, Congress should consider whether Fannie Mae and Freddie Mac are the best organizations to serve as the mortgage buyer of last resort.

A better option would be to ask the Federal Reserve to perform the function of stabilizing mortgage markets during times of turmoil. In 2009, the Fed made huge purchases of MBS and other asset-backed securities to promote stability in those markets. (See Chapter 7.) All taxpayers bear the risk of losses from those purchases by the Federal Reserve. But they also reap the profits if those purchases turn out well, so there will be a symmetry of economic interest.

Becoming Coops Without Public Guarantees

Of course, Congress could shrink Fannie Mae and Freddie Mac over the next few years and then sell them as totally private entities to the highest bidders. However, these two institutions may be needed to support the mortgage market when credit becomes tight. During this financial crisis, mortgage bankers and nonbank lenders have faced great difficulties in finding short-term financing to hold loans before they could be securitized.[26] **Therefore, Congress could transform Fannie Mae and Freddie Mac over time into one cooperative, owned by relevant groups of nonbank lenders, to buy mortgages and help turn them into MBS.[27] To meet these needs, this cooperative would help provide short-term financing to nonbank lenders who have the strongest interest in maintaining an active secondary market for mortgages and MBS. However, the cooperative should *not* have special public privileges, and its debt should *not* be treated as the moral obligation of the federal government.** Accordingly, if the cooperative provided credit support for MBS, or took on interest rate risk in purchasing mortgages or MBS, its members would reap the benefits or suffer the losses from its strategic choices.

Summary

Fannie Mae and Freddie Mac started as federal agencies and became corporations owned by shareholders. Yet, they retained their public mission to promote low and moderate-income housing, as well as their corporate objective to obtain high earnings for their shareholders. The conflict between these two goals became more intense after 1995, as HUD increased their quotas for low-income housing. In 1995, HUD also ruled that purchases of subprime mortgages would count toward meeting their quotas of low-income housing.

Fannie Mae and Freddie Mac were lightly regulated by OFHEO, which did not have the power to set minimum capital levels or limit their debt loads. Without these regulatory constraints, these two institutions took on $5 trillion in debt supported by relatively little capital.

To fulfill their housing mission while still reporting high earnings, Fannie Mae and Freddie Mac greatly expanded the size of their investment portfolios and then had to hedge these portfolios to reduce potential losses from mortgage refinancings at lower mortgage rates. Their errors in accounting for these hedging strategies precipitated major scandals, which resulted in increased legislative scrutiny. To meet their dual objectives, Fannie Mae and Freddie Mac also became the dominant buyers of subprime loans with high yields and high risks. The rising defaults on these subprime loans contributed to their insolvency in September of 2008, when they were placed in a federal conservatorship.

So what functions, if any, should Fannie Mae and Freddie Mac perform in the future? The function of subsidizing mortgages for low and moderate income families (underserved families) is best performed by a federal agency. In fact, federal agencies already provide interest subsidies and mortgage insurance to promote home ownership for underserved families.

Similarly, Ginnie Mae already guarantees FHA-insured mortgages as well as other types of insured mortgages for underserved families and helps the lenders for these insured mortgages sell them as MBS to investors. Guarantees of prime mortgages or jumbo mortgages could easily be provided by the private sector at competitive rates.

The function of attracting more capital to the mortgage market is performed by Fannie Mae and Freddie Mac as shareholder-owned corporations. However, they perform that function inefficiently; one-third to one-half of the significant public subsidies to these two institutions accrues to the benefit of their shareholders instead of home owners. This function could be performed more efficiently by a federal agency for low-income mortgages and the private sector for median-priced homes.

The purchases of mortgages and MBS by Fannie Mae and Freddie Mac have served the function of stabilizing these markets in times of financial turmoil. However, if these purchases are successful, most of the profits go to the shareholders of these two institutions. If these purchases generate huge losses due to credit defaults or mortgage pre-payments, these losses are borne not only by their shareholders, but also by taxpayers who are obliged to finance their bailouts. Thus, this function would be better performed by the Federal Reserve, which already has authority to purchase MBS and other asset-backed securities in order to bolster the stability of those markets.

Of course, Fannie Mae and Freddie Mac could be shrunk down and sold off as totally private entities to the highest bidder. But a better approach may be to transform them into one cooperative, owned by relevant groups of mortgage lenders, without any special governmental privileges. These lenders have a strong interest in maintaining a deep and liquid secondary market for mortgages. As owners of the cooperative, they would reap the benefits or incur the losses of the strategies it pursued.

Chapter 3

Mortgage Securitization in the Private Sector

The Wall Street banks saw the great profit potential in securitizing mortgages and in 2002 started to take market share away from the three government-related sponsors: Fannie Mae, Freddie Mac, and Ginnie Mae. In 2002, mortgage-backed securities (MBS) from sources not related to the government represented 15 percent of the total MBS outstanding. That percentage rose to 23 percent in 2004, 31 percent in 2005, and 32 percent in 2006.[1]

But Wall Street banks did not have the moral backing of the U.S. government, so their borrowing costs were higher than those of Fannie Mae and Freddie Mac. Furthermore, if Wall Street banks had themselves borrowed monies to finance the purchase of mortgages, they would have been subject to much higher capital and disclosure requirements than Fannie Mae and Freddie Mac, which were lightly regulated. To be

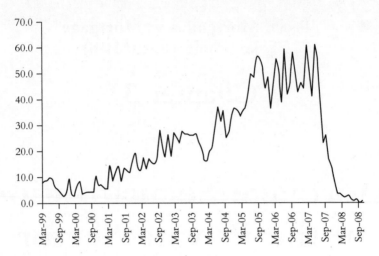

Figure 3.1 U.S. Nonagency Mortgage Backed Security Issuances (in $ billions)
SOURCE: Federal Reserve Bank of Boston 2008.

competitive, every Wall Street bank financed the purchase of mortgages through shell companies, called special purpose entities (SPEs), to avoid these capital and disclosure requirements.

The Wall Street banks were spectacularly successful in selling MBS through these SPEs. As Figure 3.1 shows, the nonagency issuance of MBS (not issued by Fannie Mae, Freddie Mac, or Ginnie Mae) went from less than $10 billion per month in March of 1999 to almost $60 billion per month in March of 2007.[2] However, as defaults on subprime mortgages increased, investors lost confidence in the market for nonagency MBS, which totally collapsed at the end of 2008.

In order to revive the mortgage market, the United States must find a new approach to mortgage securitization in the private sector. This chapter will describe in more detail how SPEs work, explain how they were designed to exploit loopholes in accounting rules, and evaluate proposals to improve the securitization process in the future. In addition, the chapter will review the conflicts of interest faced by credit rating agencies, assess the new regulations applied to these agencies, and suggest a more fundamental reform of the credit rating process.

From Mortgages to Mortgage Backed Securities (MBS)

To securitize mortgages, every Wall Street bank set up SPEs, shell corporations that were technically separate from the bank under legal and accounting rules. These SPEs would purchase pools of mortgages from mortgage lenders (mortgage brokers, regional banks, or thrifts), repackage the mortgages as MBS, and sell the MBS to institutional investors across the globe. Each SPE would sell several different types of MBS, called tranches, representing different claims on the mortgage pool. For instance, one high-risk, high-yield tranche of a MBS might absorb the first loss on mortgages in the pool, while another low-risk, low-yield tranche might receive the first payments of interest and principal from these mortgages. The Wall Street bank would also hire a credit-rating agency, which analyzes and rates bonds, to obtain high ratings for several tranches of the MBS so they would be competitive with the top-rated debt securities issued by Fannie Mae and Freddie Mac.

Figure 3.2 is a rough diagram of the mortgage securitization process. Several types of lenders originate mortgages to various borrowers, and then sell those mortgages to a SPE set up by the sponsoring bank. The SPE finances the purchase of those mortgages by selling different tranches of MBS (i.e., T1, T2, T3, etc.) to various investors; these tranches are actually sold by the bank sponsor as marketing agent for the SPE. The attractiveness of MBS to investors is enhanced by their top ratings, provided by a credit-rating agency hired by the bank sponsor. The bank sponsor also hires a mortgage servicer to collect interest and principal payments from the borrowers on the mortgages underlying the MBS and to direct the payments to holders of the appropriate tranche.

The Why and How of Off-Balance Sheet Financing

A balance sheet of a company lists all its current assets on the left side, and all its current liabilities plus its equity or capital on the right side. When a Wall Street bank borrows money to buy mortgages, both its

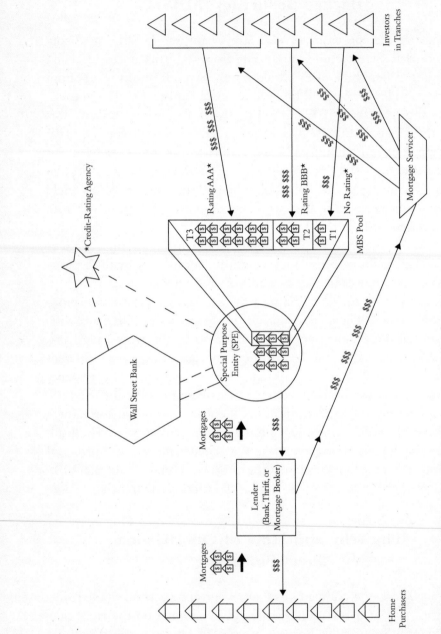

Figure 3.2 Mortgage Securitization Process in the Private Sector

assets and liabilities are increased by equal amounts. The additional assets must be supported by a certain amount of capital specified by the regulators. Thus, Wall Street banks have every incentive to buy assets through SPEs, which can pay for those assets by borrowing from investors through the sale of MBS. Because the assets and debt of SPEs are *off the balance sheet* of the Wall Street bank, they are not generally counted for purposes of calculating its capital requirement.

A SPE is a legitimate method for any company to finance the purchase of assets. The SPE should not be put on the balance sheet of the company if most of the risks related to the assets and liabilities in the SPE are assumed by other investors in the SPE. However, this device can easily be abused, so the Financial Accounting Standards Board (FASB) has established rules for when a SPE may be kept off the balance sheet of the sponsoring bank or other type of company. In the late 1990s, FASB allowed a SPE to be kept off the balance sheet of the sponsor only if at least 3 percent of the voting equity of the SPE were held by a party not affiliated with its sponsor. When Enron set up SPEs in the late 1990s, it violated that FASB requirement.

After the failure of Enron, FASB in 2003 adopted new rules on when most types of SPEs could be kept off the balance sheet of their sponsor. Unfortunately, it took Wall Street only a few months to figure out how to avoid the constraints in the FASB's new two-step rules. First, under the FASB's new rules, any investor holding 10 percent or more of the SPE's voting shares had to place the SPE on its balance sheet. But the sponsors of almost every type of SPE made sure that no one ever held more than 5 percent of its voting shares.

Second, if no one met the voting test, any party holding the majority of the SPE's risks and rewards had to put the SPE on its balance sheet. However, the risks and rewards of these SPEs were widely dispersed among holders of its various tranches. As a result, the assets and liabilities of most SPEs did not appear on the balance sheet of anyone: They were effectively accounting orphans.[3]

Bringing SPEs on Balance Sheets

Then an amazing thing happened in November of 2007: Banks suddenly started to put SPEs back on to their balance sheets. These banks included some of the biggest names in the world, including HSBC, Societe Generale, and Standard Chartered. In the United States, Citigroup had over $1 trillion in off balance sheet assets, of which at least $100 billion in assets came back on its balance sheet during 2007 and 2008.[4]

Why did the sponsoring banks take billions of dollars of assets back on their balance sheets in 2007 and 2008? In part, they wanted to avoid the reputational damage of having affiliated SPEs fail so publicly. More importantly, sponsoring banks were obligated on at least $300 billion of credit guarantees and liquidity puts for these SPEs.[5]

Credit guarantees mean that the sponsoring banks promise, under specified circumstances, to buy or replace certain defaulting mortgages in the pool supporting the SPE's mortgage-backed securities. If enough mortgages in the pool start to default, then the sponsoring bank becomes effectively obligated to provide most of the payments to the holders of the SPE's mortgage-backed securities. In that case, the bank sponsor might as well take the SPE's assets along with its liabilities on to its balance sheet.

A liquidity put is more complex. When a bank issues a put to investors, it promises to buy their securities at a specified price under certain conditions. Suppose investors bought three-year bonds from a bank at $100 per bond. The bank might promise to buy back these bonds at the same price from these investors if they could not find other buyers of these bonds at reasonable prices for the first year after purchase. This is called a liquidity put because it will be exercised by investors only when the bond markets are illiquid. In other words, if there are no other buyers of these bonds at reasonable prices during the first year after purchase, the investors have the right to "put" these bonds to the bank.

Liquidity puts were important to many investors in SPEs that intentionally set up a mismatch between the long-term maturity (final due date) of their assets and the short-term maturity of their liabilities. Most assets of SPEs were mortgages with maturities of 5 to 30 years. By contrast, many of the debt securities issued by SPEs were in the form of short-term commercial paper with maturities of 60–180 days, so they had to be resold (rolled over) frequently. (Commercial paper is a form of corporate borrowing with maturities from 1 to 270 days.) This mismatched structure was chosen by the sponsoring bank because the SPEs paid investors less interest on commercial paper with a maturity of 60 to 180 days than on 5-year or 30-year bonds.

When a bank sponsored a SPE, the bank sometimes agreed to a liquidity put, that is, an obligation to buy up any of the SPE's short-term commercial paper (e.g., with a maturity of 180 days) that could not be resold to the same investors by the SPE. This obligation did not seem important as long as investors regularly rolled over their short-term commercial paper in SPEs. Even Robert Rubin, former Treasury Secretary and Vice-Chairman of Citigroup, said in 2007 that he had never heard of a liquidity put until Citigroup's SPEs got into trouble.[6] However, when the default rate on subprime mortgages surged in late 2007 and 2008, investors no longer were willing to buy short-term commercial paper based on mortgage pools of SPEs. Because the sponsoring bank had issued a liquidity put to the SPE, the bank was forced to buy up all of the short-term commercial paper of the SPE as it became due (e.g., every 180 days).

When the sponsoring banks took billions of dollars from SPEs onto their balance sheets, institutional shareholders in these banks were surprised. Under FASB's rules adopted after Enron,[7] bank sponsors were supposed to disclose any significant obligations they had to their SPEs. But these disclosures were thin and cryptic until the end of 2007. In limiting their disclosures, the sponsoring banks maintained that the credit guarantees and liquidity puts were not significant because they believed that these contingent obligations were unlikely to be drawn upon.

The Search for the Right Accounting Rules

In response to the circumvention of its 2003 rules, FASB adopted revised rules in 2009 that would effectively force all financing of mortgages by banks on their balance sheets.[8] Under the revised rules, an SPE will be put on the balance sheet of its primary beneficiary, which will be determined by a qualitative analysis of two questions:

1. What party has the power to direct matters that significantly impact the activities of the SPE?
2. Does that party also have the right to receive potential benefits or absorb potentially significant losses from the SPE?

The answer to the first question will almost always be the sponsoring bank, which will also meet one of the criteria in the second question.

The revised FASB rules are based on the mistaken assumption that the bank is solely liable for all the risks associated with securitized assets sold by an SPE sponsored by the bank. However, this is not an all-or-nothing situation. In fact, the bank has shifted to investors most, but not all, risks of the securitized assets sold by the SPE. For example, the investors typically assume the risk that interest rates will decline and some of the mortgages held by the SPE will be refinanced at lower rates.

Despite the actual shift of significant risks to investors in the SPE's bonds, the bank will be required to commit capital in support of the SPE as if the bank had retained all the risks of the securitized mortgages.[9] This full capital requirement would undermine the profitability of the securitization process to banks, which would receive little benefit from the time and expense involved with creating and selling securitized loans. Therefore, FASB should reconsider its revised rules because they will dramatically reduce the volume of lending available for purchases of homes, autos and consumer goods through credit cards.

A similar form of regulatory overkill is reflected in the proposal to prohibit mortgage originators from booking any profits on the sale of a loan to a SPE for securitization.[10] **The adoption of this proposal to defer profit recognition would substantially and unfairly decrease the volume of business from mortgage originators. If the originator is required to absorb a 5 percent pro rata share of all losses on mortgages that it makes and sells to third parties, then the originator should be allowed to book a profit on 95 percent of the sale proceeds, perhaps with a loan loss reserve.**

To replace off-balance-sheet securitization, former Treasury Secretary Paulson and others have advocated "covered bonds," that is, bonds backed by specific assets on the balance sheets of banks.[11] He cited as precedent the favorable experience of European banks with covered bonds.[12] In the typical situation, the European bank puts a group of mortgages in a special account within the bank and issues bonds covered by the payments from those mortgages. If any of the mortgages in that account get into trouble, the bank is obligated to substitute a good mortgage for the bad one. As a result of this structure, covered bonds in Europe usually receive top ratings from the credit rating agencies.

However, the FDIC has prohibited U.S. banks from using more than 4 percent of their assets to support covered bonds,[13] so this technique is not a viable replacement for securitizing assets through SPEs. When a bank becomes insolvent, the FDIC takes control of its assets and would normally get paid first as the bank's most senior creditor. But the FDIC may not be the most senior creditor of an insolvent bank if that bank has sold a covered bond. In that case, the holders of the covered bond effectively have senior liens on all the assets of the bank since, under the terms of most covered bonds, the bank is obligated to replace with a good mortgage any defaulting mortgage supporting its covered bonds. In other words, if the holders of the covered bonds are the most senior creditors of the bank, they will be paid out first from the bank's assets if it becomes insolvent, and the FDIC would be left to try and collect on the remaining assets of that bank.

A better solution than covered bonds would be to allow a bank to keep a sponsored SPE off its balance sheet, but to require the bank to specify every obligation, formal or informal, to the SPE and then to impose a capital requirement reasonably related to every obligation. The bank should disclose the specific amount of any credit guarantee, liquidity put, or other continuing or contingent obligation to the SPE, the conditions that would trigger the contingent obligations and the likelihood that these obligations will be drawn upon. Based on these specific disclosures, the bank regulators would determine how much capital was needed by the sponsoring bank to support its continuing and contingent obligations to the SPE. For instance, suppose the bank sponsor agreed to replace mortgages once the default rate on the SPE's pool exceeded 6 percent. This replacement obligation might require the bank to put up capital equal to 3 percent of the SPE's assets. In this manner, the U.S. financial system could enjoy the benefits of a much larger volume of loans through securitization without the problems of hidden obligations to SPEs or inadequate bank capital supporting these obligations.

SPEs Should Increase Their Public Disclosures

Such an off-balance sheet SPE, with enhanced disclosures and capital support, would meet the other major concerns of investors. Most investors are put off by the complexity and nontransparency of the mortgage securitization process. A broad survey of market participants on this subject concluded that their highest priorities were enhanced disclosures and more standardization of information.[14] **These priorities would be best served by maintaining an SPE as a separate accounting and reporting entity from the sponsoring bank. If the SPE's assets and liabilities are commingled with those of the sponsoring bank on its balance sheet, shareholders of the bank would have great difficulty in getting an accurate picture of a specific SPE's financial status.**[15]

At the same time, the Securities and Exchange Commission (SEC) should increase the disclosure obligations of the SPE as a separate entity when it makes an initial offering and then files its annual reports. In an initial public offering, the SEC currently requires only aggregate statistics on the assets held by the SPE. **The SPE should also include in the offering statement data at the individual loan level so that investors can better evaluate the offering.**[16] The SEC currently permits a reporting entity to stop filing annual reports if its securities become held by fewer than 300 investors. This out is often used by SPEs to stop filing annual reports within a year after the initial offering.[17] But the information of the ongoing status of most SPEs is important not only to their investors but also to shareholders of the bank sponsors of the SPEs. **Therefore, the SEC should not allow SPEs to opt out of filing annual reports unless the total of their investors and their sponsors' shareholders drop below 300.**

Limited Utility of Danish Models

A more interesting European precedent than covered bonds would be the Danish model for securitizing mortgages.[18] In summary, mortgages in Denmark may be issued only by mortgage credit institutions (MCIs), which are limited to that function. All mortgages must follow a standardized format and comply with strict standards. For instance, no mortgage may exceed 80 percent of the value of a home. The documentation and appraisal for mortgages are verified by an independent Mortgage Institute. There are two critical features of the Danish model.

First, when an MCI issues a mortgage, it is required to sell a bond in the same amount with a maturity and cash flow matched to the underlying mortgage's payments. The other terms of the bond are standardized to create a large and liquid trading market. The bonds are attractive to investors because they have reasonable yields and each MCI must retain the risk of most losses on the mortgages underlying the bonds. This feature avoids the perverse incentive of U.S. lenders to skimp on due diligence of mortgages because they can be sold without liability to the secondary market.

The Danish model has another critical and innovative feature. Holders can retire their own mortgages by purchasing the same face amount of mortgage bonds at the prevailing market price. To prepay a mortgage by purchasing bonds, the home owner must give advance notice of several weeks to the MCI, which designates by lottery the specific bonds to be purchased. Thus, if rising interest rates or other factors cause mortgage bonds to trade at a discount, home owners can reduce the principal or retire the whole mortgage by purchasing an appropriate mortgage bond at a discount. In the United States, by contrast, when the mortgage bond market craters, few investors are prepared to buy these bonds even at discount. Although many home owners would love to pay down their mortgage by purchasing bonds trading way below their face value, they have no practical way to do so in the United States.

George Soros, star investor and noted philanthropist, has been promoting the adoption of the Danish model in the United States. He wrote: "The U.S. can emulate the Danish system with surprisingly few modifications from our current practices. What is required is transparent, standardized securities which create large and fungible pools."[19] **Unfortunately, to adopt the Danish model would involve significant modifications to the American mortgage system, such as substantial increases in down payments, extensive liabilities for mortgage originators and mandatory securitization of all mortgages. As explained in Chapter 1, however, the United States. does not yet require all mortgages to be supported by down payments of at least 5 percent of a home's value and does not yet impose liability on all mortgage originators for even 5 percent of losses on the mortgages they originate. Nevertheless, the**

United States should begin to emulate the Danish model by standardizing the documentation for most home mortgages and the terms of most MBS.

The Conflicted Position of
Credit-Rating Agencies

In selling the debt securities of SPEs, bank sponsors pushed hard to obtain the highest ratings from the credit-rating agencies for as many of the SPE's tranches as possible. Some institutional investors were legally limited to buying highly rated debt securities. Other institutional investors were limited to buying debt securities with certain ratings specified by their clients or directors. Moreover, in selling MBS backed by private pools of mortgages, banks needed top ratings to compete with the MBS issued by Fannie Mac and Freddie Mae because of their triple-A ratings and moral backing from the U.S. government.

Revenues Soar from Structured Deals

The growth of privately sponsored MBS was a boon to the credit-rating agencies. Historically, the big three—Moody's, Standard & Poor's, and Fitch—had received a substantial portion of their income from various publishing businesses as well as ratings. By 2000, however, more than 90 percent of their revenue came from rating fees paid by issuers. And these agencies received much higher fees for rating complex MBS than for rating municipal or corporate bonds. For corporate bonds, rating fees range from $30,000 to $300,000 depending on the size and complexity of the bond offering. For structured finance deals like MBS, the fee range was twice as high, with fees for very complex transactions exceeding $2 million per debt offering.[20]

The aggregate revenue of the big three credit-rating agencies rose from under $3 billion in 2002 to over $6 billion in 2007, as illustrated in Figure 3.3.[21] Similarly, the rise in their net income was dramatic. For example, the net income of Moody's rose from $159 million in 2000 to over $750 million in 2006. In September, 2005, the market capitalization

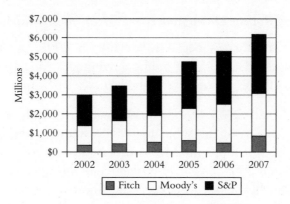

Figure 3.3 Revenue of Big Three Credit-Rating Agencies: 2002–2007
SOURCE: House Committee on Oversight and Government Reform 2008.

of Moody's was more than $15 billion—a price multiple of 30 times its earnings per share—and its profit margins were consistently above 50 percent.[22] Jerome S. Fons, a former managing director for credit quality at Moody's, testified before Congress: "In my view, the focus of Moody's shifted from protecting investors to being a marketing-driven organization. Management's focus increasingly turned to maximizing revenues. Stock options and other incentives raised the possibility of large payoffs."[23]

The business model of the credit-rating agencies came under increasing pressure as the quality of mortgages underlying the MBS began to deteriorate. As investors sought higher yields from MBS, bank sponsors included larger and larger portions of subprime mortgages in the mortgage pools of their SPEs. To deliver top ratings to MBS based on such pools, the credit-rating agencies became actively involved in negotiations with bank sponsors to structure these pools. For example, a credit-rating agency might suggest that a pool could receive a top rating if it was sufficiently over-collateralized with mortgages, obtained guarantees from its bank sponsor, or bought protection against defaults. For complex or innovative deals, the largest agencies developed an ancillary practice consulting on MBS design; this practice operated in tandem with their core ratings business.

The Flood of Rating Downgrades

As subprime mortgages began to default in 2007, the credit-rating agencies unleashed a flood of credit downgrades for MBS backed by subprime mortgages. According to the SEC:[24]

- As of February 2008, Moody's had downgraded at least one tranche of 94.2 percent of the subprime MBS issues it rated in 2006, and 76.9 percent of subprime MBS issues it rated in 2007.
- As of March 2008, S&P had downgraded 44.3 percent of the subprime tranches it rated between the first quarter of 2005 and the third quarter of 2007.
- As of December 2007, Fitch had downgraded 34 percent of the subprime tranches it rated in 2006 and in the first quarter of 2007.

This torrent of downgrades precipitated a major government review of the credit-rating agencies. As one Moody's executive said in an internal memo about these downgrades: "These errors make us look either incompetent at credit analysis, or like we sold our soul to the devil for revenue."[25]

The agencies face a fundamental conflict of interest because they are paid by the MBS issuers, but their ratings are supposed to help investors decide whether to buy these same MBS. If an issuer begins discussions with one rating agency that appears to be leaning against a top rating, the issuer can simply take its business to another agency. As Dean Baker, an economist, explained: "The agencies want to get hired, and they're well aware of the fact that if they're not giving acceptable ratings, they may not be called back."[26]

This conflict of interest is especially acute when one arm of the credit-rating agency is hired to structure a complex deal, and another arm is later paid to rate the deal. How likely is the agency to withhold a top rating if the issuer designs the deal according to the advice given by the same agency's consulting arm? By contrast, accounting firms are prohibited by the Sarbanes-Oxley Act from providing most consulting services to a company for whom they serve as its auditor.

Bad and Good Regulatory Responses

In response to growing public concerns about credit-rating agencies, Congress in 2006 passed legislation requiring the SEC to increase the number of credit-rating agencies it recognized for regulatory purposes. The legislative rationale was that the competitive market was not working because the rating industry was dominated by three large firms. If there were more SEC-recognized agencies, so the argument went, then there would be more competition, which would produce higher quality ratings. Accordingly, the SEC expanded the number of recognized agencies from 4 to 9 by June 2008.[27]

This initial response was misguided: By increasing the number of recognized credit-rating agencies, the SEC facilitated forum shopping among issuers. Now if each of the big three refuses to provide a top rating, the issuer can find other agencies willing to award a top rating. This point was driven home by an empirical study of what happened when Fitch began to make inroads on the rating markets dominated by Moody's and S&P (the two organizations controlled over 80 percent of the industry). The result was a deterioration in the quality of ratings at the two incumbents. They became more accommodating to the wishes of bond issuers in an effort to defend their market share.[28]

The SEC's next response in 2009 was more useful: It adopted prohibitions against some of the most serious conflicts confronting credit-rating agencies and increased their disclosures about their record of ratings. Rating agencies may no longer rate a debt offering that they helped structure. Nor may analysts involved in ratings participate in fee negotiations. The new rules also require rating agencies to disclose statistics on upgrades, downgrades, and defaults for each asset class they rate over periods of 1, 3, and 10 years. Further, rating agencies must disclose on their web sites a random sample of 10 percent of their ratings within 6 months after they were issued.[29]

Despite these recent rules, the most fundamental conflict of interest for credit-rating agencies still remains—that they are paid by issuers instead of investors. Before 1970, ratings were paid for mainly by investors. This changed in 1973 when the SEC began to build into its regulations a top rating by SEC-recognized credit-rating agencies in an effort to find a readily available proxy for high-quality securities. Since then, the SEC has relied heavily on credit-rating agencies in many of its rules, such as rules allowing money market funds to invest only in commercial paper with the top two ratings.

Four Groups of Ratings Users

In 2008, the SEC proposed to eliminate its heavy reliance on ratings from recognized agencies,[30] but the proposal has met with considerable resistance. This resistance reflects the four different groups of investors that utilize credit ratings. The first group of investors is legally limited by statute or regulation to investments with certain specified ratings. For example, some pension funds may be allowed by state law to invest only in investment-grade bonds. As Table 3.1 shows, investment grade bonds are rated Baa (Moody's), BBB (Fitch/S&P), or higher.[31] A second group of institutional investors may face similar limits on bond investments because of restrictions imposed by their clients, supervisory boards, or offering documents. Such limits are quite prevalent in the United States and Europe.[32] A third group are investors, who do not have sufficient resources to analyze and monitor bond investments, so they rely heavily on credit ratings as a practical matter. This group includes, for instance, some county and municipal treasurers.

The fourth group of investors includes most of the largest financial institutions of the world: the global banks, the multinational insurers, the biggest corporate pension funds, and the largest mutual fund complexes. In contrast to the other groups, this fourth group does not rely much on the work of credit-rating agencies. These large investors have the resources and expertise to do their own analysis of bond offerings and monitor the financial status of the entities issuing bonds. This group is especially critical of the slowness of credit-rating agencies to drop an investment grade rating for a company facing financial challenges. These agencies have often maintained investment grade

Table 3.1 Bond Ratings

S&P/Fitch	Moody's	Grade	Quality
AAA	Aaa	Investment	Highest Quality
AA	Aa	Investment	High Quality
A	A	Investment	Strong
BBB	Baa	Investment	Medium Grade
BB, B	Ba, B	Junk	Speculative
CCC/CC/C	Caa/Ca/C	Junk	Highly Speculative
D	C	Junk	In Default

ratings on doomed companies such as Enron until shortly before it went bankrupt. For example, Figure 3.4 shows how S&P maintained an investment grade rating on Bear Stearns until March 14th of 2008, a mere two days before its collapse and acquisition by J.P. Morgan.

Given these disparate views among investors about rating agencies, it would be difficult to obtain a consensus on proposals to purge SEC rules of all references to credit-rating agencies. Many smaller institutions depend on these references to define the parameters of their permissible investments. At most, the rating agencies may by forced by the SEC to adopt a different set of grades for structured products like MBS from the rating scheme just described for corporate bonds.[33] So let us consider other approaches to reforming the role of credit-rating agencies.

Sensible and Impractical Reforms

Some have suggested that credit ratings be based on the spreads between a specific bond and U.S. Treasuries, the amount by which the interest rate on the bond exceeds the interest rate on U.S. Treasuries with similar maturities.[34] Spreads would be more objective than the subjective factors now used by rating agencies. Spreads also change

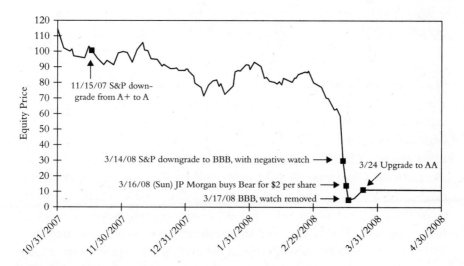

Figure 3.4   Bear Stearns Equity Price and S&P Ratings Actions
Source: Bloomberg.

continuously, avoiding the sharp decline in a bond's price when it is downgraded by a rating agency. However, it is unclear how much value would be added by credit-rating agencies if ratings were based mainly on spreads since they are publicly available. Moreover, spreads on bonds can widen or narrow because of general factors having little to do with the specific bond, such as the market reaction to the September 11th terrorist attack on the World Trade Center.

A better proposal would be to impose some type of civil liability on credit agencies if they failed to follow material aspects of their own methodologies for rating bonds or if they failed to comply with material aspects of the new SEC rules on conflicts and disclosures. In the past, rating agencies have been relatively successful in arguing for legal immunity on two grounds. Their ratings contain broad disclaimers that they should not be relied upon by investors. But these disclaimers should be given limited effect by the courts; a rating agency should not be allowed to disclaim responsibility for knowingly committing material violations of its own methodologies or applicable SEC rules. Credit-rating agencies have also argued that their ratings should be protected as free speech under the First Amendment.[35] However, the courts have recognized the government's right to regulate commercial speech in order to prevent fraud or other deceptive practices. If a rating agency is paid for its ratings, they should fall squarely within the definition of commercial speech.

It bears emphasis that the credit-rating agency would still choose its own methodology for evaluating bond issues. By contrast, the U.S. House of Representatives has seriously considered a bill delineating which factors could and could not be taken into account by a rating agency in evaluating a municipal bond.[36] For instance, in rating a general obligation bond of a state or city, an agency could take into account only the risk of nonpayment in accordance with the terms of the issuance. **Congress should reject all proposals by governmental bodies to mandate methodologies for credit-rating agencies to follow. These proposals would simply substitute one set of inappropriate influences on the ratings process with another.**

A more radical proposal would be to force investors, rather than issuers, to pay for all credit ratings.[37] This could be accomplished if Congress levied special fees on all bond trades or all bonds registered with the SEC. But such fees would be strongly opposed by the largest financial institutions, which do their own in-depth analysis of bonds and claim to make little use of credit ratings. In theory, it might be possible to impose a fee only on investors relying heavily on credit ratings for certain types of bonds. In practice, this would be a nightmare. Most investors do not know in advance whether they will buy into a bond offering until they see its exact terms. And once a rating is given, it becomes a public good that can be utilized by all investors—even by those who disdain the rating agencies and refuse to pay for their ratings.

For these reasons, Congress should insert third parties into the rating process, while continuing to have issuers pay for ratings. An effective third-party approach for the rating process should have two characteristics. First, the third party should be a knowledgeable person, independent of both issuers and credit-rating agencies. For example, they could be retired executives of companies, government agencies, or institutional investors appointed by a neutral public entity such as the SEC or a securities self-regulatory organization. Second, the functions of the third party should be limited to selecting a rating agency for a bond offering and negotiating the ratings fee. These functions would prevent the two worst abuses in the current rating process: The issuer shopping around for the agency promising the best rating, and the issuer paying especially high fees to obtain a better rating. These two targeted functions could be performed by an independent expert at a modest cost, paid as part of bond offering expenses; the issuer would continue to pay the fees of the rating agency negotiated and selected by the independent expert. Although this third-party approach is not perfect, it would be feasible for larger bond offerings and a big step in the right direction.

Summary

The private process for securitizing mortgages was subject to many abuses. The Wall Street banks sponsoring SPEs to securitize mortgages were able to circumvent the accounting rules to keep the SPEs off their balance sheets. As a result, these banks were able to avoid capital requirements and limit disclosures about their obligations to the SPEs. In fact, sponsoring banks had often had contractual commitments to replace defaulted mortgages held by the SPEs. They might also have formal and informal obligations to buy the short-term commercial paper issued by these SPEs if investors stopped reinvesting in this paper every three, six, or nine months. When investors became wary of the subprime mortgages and other assets held by SPEs, the sponsoring banks were obliged to support this paper and ultimately took many SPEs on to their balance sheets.

In response to these abuses, the FASB adopted revised accounting rules that would effectively force all securitizations of mortgages and other assets to be done on the balance sheet of the sponsoring bank. These new rules go too far, however, by incorrectly assuming that the sponsoring bank actually retains all the risk when mortgages are securitized. As a result, the new rules will dramatically reduce the volume of lending in the United States, at a time when the country desperately needs more lending.

Covered bonds would not be an adequate substitute for mortgage securitizations through off-balance sheet entities. The FDIC has limited covered bonds to no more than 4 percent of a bank's assets in order to protect the FDIC's position as the most senior creditor in the event of a bank's insolvency.

A better approach would be to allow banks to securitize mortgages through off-balance sheet entities, subject to two conditions. First, banks would have to publicly disclose all their continuing and contingent obligations to these entities, such as credit or liquidity support. Second, banks would have to back up these obligations with an appropriate level of capital as determined by the regulators, tailored to their actual projected obligations to the entities. These two conditions would ensure that the actual risks retained by the sponsoring bank would be recognized and supported with capital.

The U.S. should also study the Danish models where every mortgage is promptly transformed into a standardized security with matching cash flows. If these securities decline in value because of increases in interest rates or problems in the real estate market, home owners may purchase these securities and thereby reduce or eliminate their mortgages. Unfortunately, the Danish model would require major changes to the U.S. mortgage system. Nevertheless, the United States should begin to move toward that model by standardizing the terms of mortgages and MBS to the maximum extent feasible.

The role of credit-rating agencies in the mortgage securitization process was deplorable. They gave top ratings to many securities backed by mortgages that soon began to default at above average rates. In part, this may have been because the agencies did not fully understand the new products. But, more importantly, the agencies were paid by the issuers of these securities, which pressured them to give these high ratings. In some situations, one arm of a credit rating agency served as a paid consultant to design a bond offering, which was then rated by another arm of the same agency. This was a thicket of conflicts of interest.

To promote competition, Congress directed the SEC to expand the number of SEC-recognized rating agencies. However, this expansion was misguided because issuers are now able to shop for the most favorable rating among an even larger number of approved agencies. More sensibly, the SEC in 2009 adopted rules to prohibit significant conflicts of interest by credit rating agencies and require them to make more disclosures about their rating records. Material violations of these rules should be enforceable not only by the SEC but also by private parties. Although the credit-rating agencies have argued that their ratings are constitutionally protected as free speech, the courts have long recognized antifraud and other limits on commercially related speech.

In theory, investors should pay for credit ratings instead of bond issuers. This would eliminate the most fundamental conflict of interest in the rating industry. However, the largest investors have refused to pay for ratings, which they do not view as particularly valuable. If other investors paid for ratings, they would become public goods that could be utilized by everyone. As a practical approach, the SEC or another public body should develop a cadre of independent experts who could choose the rating agency and negotiate its fees for every major bond offering. The performance of these two functions by an independent expert would correct the worst abuses of the mortgage securitization process while having issuers continue to pay for credit ratings.

Chapter 4

Credit Default Swaps and Mathematical Models

I n Chapter 3, we described how bank sponsors put together pools of mortgages in special purpose entities, which then issued several tranches of mortgage-backed securities with different interest rates for different risk levels. To protect against potential defaults on these tranches of mortgage-backed securities, the holders of the tranches and other investors in turn often bought a kind of protection called credit default swaps (CDS) from highly rated insurance companies as well as other financial institutions. CDS are contracts to protect against potential default of a bond or other type of debt security. The buyer of CDS pays insurance-like premiums on a regular basis to the seller (the insurance company), who agrees to pay the buyer the full principal of the bond if it defaults in exchange for the defaulted bond. Figure 4.1 depicts

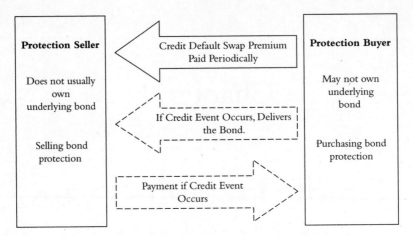

Figure 4.1 Common Credit Default Swap Transaction
SOURCE: Credit Derivatives and Synthetic Structures, 2001.

a common CDS transaction, with the protection buyer on the right side and the protection seller on the left side.[1]

This chapter will begin by reviewing the extensive use of CDS by bond investors, especially those buying mortgage-backed securities. Then it will explain the similarities and differences between CDS and traditional insurance. This section of the chapter will end by showing how CDS was left in a regulatory vacuum in 2000, and suggesting how CDS should now be regulated.

This chapter will also address the mathematical models that drove the expansion of mortgage-backed securities and CDS. In criticizing the mathematical models supporting new types of investments, Warren Buffet wrote that Americans have too frequently been in awe of a "nerdy-sounding priesthood, using esoteric terms such as beta, gamma, sigma and the like. Our advice: Beware of geeks bearing formulas."[2] This chapter will discuss why so many brilliant experts made the wrong assumptions in constructing their financial projections for the U.S. mortgage market. It will suggest that nonexperts, including senior officers and outside directors, need to review and question these assumptions on a common sense basis.

How Bond Investors Use Credit Default Swaps

The total amount of CDS outstanding increased dramatically from less than $1 trillion in 2001 to more than $60 trillion in 2007,[3] as shown

Figure 4.2   Credit Default Swaps: Notional Amounts Outstanding
SOURCE: International Swaps and Derivatives Association, Fall 2008.

in Figure 4.2. In part, the growth of CDS was attributable to the great utility of its core innovation: the separation of credit default risk from interest rate risk on bonds and other debt instruments. Most bonds have both types of risks. If interest rates rise generally, the price of a fixed-rate bond declines because investors can now purchase similar bonds paying higher interest. A bond's price will also decline if the chances of a default on that specific bond increases. This usually occurs if there is a decline in the financial condition or credit rating of the company issuing that bond. Although there are many ways for bond investors to hedge against increases in interest rates, the invention of CDS gave investors an easy way to hedge against increases in credit defaults separate from interest rate risk.

In part, the growth of CDS can be attributed to their extensive use for default protection on the tranches of mortgage-backed securities. As explained in Chapter 3, a bank sponsor would set up a special purpose entity to hold a pool of mortgages, which would then issue tranches of mortgage-backed securities to investors. The lowest-risk tranche would have the right to receive the first payments of principal and interest from the mortgage pool. The highest-risk tranche would receive any leftover principal or interest payments only if and when all obligations to all other tranches were satisfied.

Holders of a tranche of a mortgage-backed security could purchase protection against a default on that tranche by entering into a CDS with an insurance company. The holder of the tranche would pay regular premiums to the insurance company in return for the full repayment of the tranche's principal in the event of default. The premium level for the

CDS would depend on the priority of the tranche in the payment flow and the projected default rate for the pool of mortgages supporting the tranche. For example, the annual premium might be $30,000 for a CDS on a $10 million senior tranche of senior notes (lower risk) and $600,000 for a $10 million junior tranche of preferred shares (higher risk) based on the same pool of mortgages.

CDS Are Different from Insurance Contracts

Like insurance contracts, the availability of CDS encouraged many investors in MBS to take on more risk by their very existence. Just as flood insurance encourages people to build houses on flood plains, so bond default protection increased the willingness of investors to buy complex mortgage-backed securities even if they did not fully understand the risks involved. However, the counterparties in CDS operated under very different rules than the buyer and seller of a normal insurance contract.

After signing the CDS agreement, the value of both sides of the CDS would fluctuate, based on the actual payments from the mortgages in the underlying pool as compared to the initial projections for that pool. When the pools with subprime mortgages began to default at unexpectedly high rates in 2007, the value of the CDS to the buyers increased as the value to the insurance companies decreased. Because of these high default rates, the buyers often exercised their right to demand that the insurance company transfer to them large amounts of cash to ensure payment on the CDS. In addition, the buyers were typically allowed to demand cash payments from the insurance company if the company's rating from the credit-rating agencies dropped significantly. The lower rating implied that there was more risk that the insurance company might not be able to pay the CDS in the event of default.

Specifically, CDS are different from normal insurance contracts in three key respects. First, unlike the buyer of car insurance who must own a car, a CDS buyer does not have to own the underlying bond. In insurance parlance, the buyer does not need to have an insurable interest. As a result, CDS were often purchased by hedge funds and other investors making speculative bets that the bond's default risk would actually materialize. Second, since neither buyers nor sellers had to own the debt securities that were the subject of the CDS, the notional value of the CDS on any security could be a very large number. In fact, the CDS on a bond issued by a particular company were sometimes higher than the actual value of all outstanding bonds of that type from the company. Third, while standard insurance policies protect against events that are beyond anyone's control (such as hurricanes), buyers of CDS can actively undermine the position of the insurer so that it is obliged to give them more cash collateral. For example, hedge funds could bid up the price of a CDS on a bond, thereby implying that the issuer of the bond would probably default. With this evidence in hand, the hedge funds could then demand more cash collateral from the insurer that sold the CDS on that bond.

The Higher Risks in CDS on More Complex Mortgage-Backed Securities

Credit default swaps were used often to protect against defaults on more complex forms of mortgage-backed securities, which involved more risks than most of the writers of CDS understood. One such complex form was the collateralized debt obligation (CDO). In a common type of CDO, the bank sponsor would put together a special purpose entity with a pool of mortgage-backed security tranches, rather than a pool of actual mortgages. Then the entity would issue various tranches of CDOs, including senior tranches with a high priority for receiving payments from the underlying tranches of mortgage-backed securities, and junior tranches with a low priority for receiving payments from the underlying tranches of mortgage backed-securities. In other words, CDOs were one more step removed from the actual payment flows of those mortgage pools. Figure 4.3 shows an example of a hypothetical CDO offering, detailing its payments structure based on a cascading hierarchy of risk and return (the so-called waterfall).

The CDO example in Figure 4.3 captures the core concept of tranches behind the securitization process: The rank order of securities is based on the seniority of each tranche's claims on the CDO's underlying assets and cash flows. Although the average overall yield for investors who buy the CDO's $100 million in securities is 6 percent or $6 million, the allocation to the respective tranches is far from equal. The $65 million in senior notes are the tranches with the highest priority

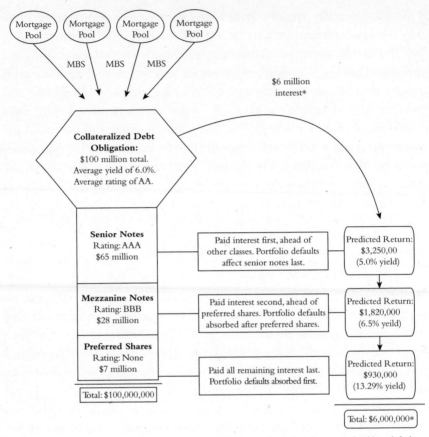

Figure 4.3   Collateralized Debt Obligation

claims. They would get paid ahead of all others and thus assume the least amount of risk. For this lower risk, they settle for a lower yield of 5 percent or $3.25 million. The $28 million in mezzanine notes are second in the claim line and thus assume additional risk. For this higher risk, they get a higher yield of 6.5 percent or $1.82 million. Finally, the $7 million of preferred shares issued by the CDO (the equity tranche) are last in the claim line and thus assume the greatest risk. For this highest level of risk, they are rewarded with the highest expected return of $13.3 percent or $930,000.

The popularity of CDS created another opportunity for new products called synthetic CDOs. When buyers agreed to pay premiums for CDS in order to protect against defaults on tranches of CDOs, the investment bankers would then quickly package these CDS into even more complex securities. They didn't need actual homes, borrowers, or lenders to create new financial products to sell. For this purpose, premiums from a CDS buyer were the functional equivalent of mortgage payments from a borrower. The investment bankers could create pools of CDS and issue tranches of debt securities, based on the premium payments from the buyers of CDS in these pools.

Ultimately, the value of such multilayer products depended on the actual payment record of the mortgage pools underlying the tranches of mortgage-backed securities, because that record measured the default risk that was being insured against by the CDS. However, debt securities based on CDS were several steps removed from the actual mortgages. When these mortgages were subprime loans of dubious quality, the layering helped to obscure the weak credit foundation of these products. Steve Eisman, a professional investor, characterized the tranches of such multilayer products as "the equivalent of three levels of dog [feces] lower than the original bonds."[4] As explained through an example in the Appendix at the end of this chapter, the vulnerability of these multilayer products soars when the default probability of the original mortgage pool is even slightly underestimated. For example, an increase from 5 percent to 7 percent in the default rate on the mortgage pool underlying a multilayer CDO product could increase by 100 times the default probability on the top layer of the CDO.

To revive the securitization process, the bank regulators should strongly discourage the offering of multilayered CDO products, except to extremely sophisticated institutions. These multilayered products embody the worst fears of investors about securitization, namely, these products are not transparent and their risks are very difficult to understand.

Credit Default Swaps Bring Down the Monoline Insurers and AIG

The two biggest writers of CDS were the so-called monoline insurers and the insurance giant AIG. Yet, as mentioned previously, CDS does not require the CDS buyer to own the bond being protected by the CDS. Without such an "insurable" interest, CDS did not constitute an "insurance contract" according to an opinion dated June 16, 2000 from the General Counsel of the New York State Insurance Department[5]—the primary regulator of most of the large U.S. insurers. Hence, for eight years, CDS were written out of nonregulated affiliates of these insurance companies, without the usual reserve and capital requirements for the insurance business imposed by the Insurance Department. After the federal bailout of AIG in September, 2008, the New York State Insurance Department announced its intention to regulate CDS issued by insurance companies doing business in New York, but withdrew the announcement within a week because federal officials were supposed to regulate CDS on a national basis.[6]

Unlike traditional insurance companies with diversified lines of business, monoline insurers write protection for only one line of business: guaranteeing bonds against default to bond investors. In mid-2008, the monolines guaranteed against default an estimated $2.4 trillion in outstanding debt. Of this amount, approximately 70 percent was written by the three largest monolines: MBIA, Ambac, and FSA.[7]

Before 1990, the monolines concentrated on protecting municipal bonds against defaults. This was a stable business with a reasonable cash flow. After 1990, the monolines became increasingly involved with structured finance deals. In particular, the monolines are estimated to have sold up to 50 percent of the CDS purchased to protect against default in mortgage-backed securities and collateralized debt obligations backed by subprime mortgages. Consequently, the stocks of Ambac and MBIA dropped by over 90 percent from mid-2007 to mid-2008, and their ratings were downgraded from triple A to double A in June of 2008.[8] And the bleeding continued for Ambac and MBIA. In 2009, Ambac reported a negative net worth,[9] and MBIA tried to save its municipal bond business by splitting it off from its structured finance products division, which has been crippled by guarantees on mortgage-backed securities.[10] Several smaller monolines (e.g., CIFG, FGIC, and Syncora) were downgraded from investment grade to junk bond status, which effectively put them out of the insurance business.[11]

These downgrades had broader consequences for the municipal bond market and the Wall Street banks. The liquidity of the municipal bond market has been substantially reduced, partly because investors are no longer so comfortable with bonds insured by MBIA, AMBAC, or lower rated monolines.[12] To fill the void, Warren Buffett has started a new municipal insurer, and one of the big three monolines (FSA) has announced plans to exit the structured finance business. Because of decreased competition, Buffett's new insurer and FSA have been able to raise prices in the municipal bond business.[13]

The virtual collapse of the smaller monolines also created large potential losses for the Wall Street banks, which purchased from these monolines CDS protecting tranches of collateralized debt obligations in their portfolios. Since these monolines could no longer be counted on to provide credit protection in the event of defaults on these collateralized debt obligations, the value of these CDS would have to be marked down substantially on the books of the Wall Street banks. To reduce the impact of these markdowns, Merrill Lynch settled CDS totaling $3.74 billion for a payment of $500 million from a smaller monoline called XLCA.[14] Similarly, Ambac paid Citigroup $850 million to terminate its guarantee of collateralized debt obligations with a par value of $1.4 billion, which were already in distress.[15]

The Fed Bails Out AIG Because of Its Huge CDS Exposures

The exposure of AIG to subprime loans through CDS was much larger than the potential liabilities of the monolines. Over several years, AIG had generated large profits by writing protection against credit defaults on collateralized debt obligations, but its fatal mistake was to write CDS protection in 2005 and early 2006 on $60 billion of collateralized debt obligations based mainly on subprime loans. As Barron's reported in November, 2008:

> The premiums on these CDOs were somewhat fatter than for other classes of credit risk, but AIG's risk models indicated that there was no chance of any loss claims being filed on them. After all they were insuring only the super senior triple-A portion of the securitization, and many risk layers below that would have to be burned through before any loss reached AIG.[16]

In early 2007, when prices on triple-A tranches of collateralized debt obligations based on subprime mortgages declined sharply, AIG was forced to recognize losses on over half of the $60 billion in these CDS from 2005-2006. Starting in August of 2007, counterparties such as Goldman Sachs also demanded that AIG transfer more cash to cover its CDS exposure. By August 2008, AIG had made $16.5 billion in cash payments to back its CDS. When AIG's credit rating was cut to single A on September 15 of 2008, the additional calls for cash payments from CDS were estimated to total $18 billion. Unable to meet these escalating demands on its liquidity, the giant insurer was rescued from insolvency by a $85 billion loan from the Federal Reserve.

After the Fed's rescue of AIG in September, 2008, the demands for more cash payments from AIG to holders of CDS surged—eating up most of the Fed's $85 billion loan. At the end of 2008 and again in early 2009, the federal assistance package was restructured and expanded to over $170 billion.[17] In March, 2009, AIG disclosed that it had agreed to pay $62 billion in cash to settle CDS contracts with multiple counterparties in return for mortgage-backed securities marked down to less than $30 billion.[18] These exchanges were made with the express approval of the federal government, which largely financed the exchanges.

As shown in Figure 4.4, the counterparties benefiting the most from these exchanges included not only Goldman Sachs and Merrill Lynch but also four large foreign banks: Société Générale, Deutsche Bank, Barclays, and UBS. It seems inappropriate for the United States to bail out large foreign banks. Of the two largest U.S. recipients from AIG, Goldman Sachs stated that its exposure to AIG was fully protected, collateralized or hedged before being paid by AIG.[19] Thus, these exchanges constituted unjustified gifts by the U.S. government to the most sophisticated investors in the world, who had made bad judgments about whether this AIG subsidiary could deliver on its promised credit protection. This is exactly the type of counterparty risk that financial firms must address every day in choosing their trading partners. Even the Vice Chairman of the Federal Reserve admitted that by paying 100 cents on a dollar to the large firms on the other side of CDS contracts, the federal government allowed these sophisticated investors to avoid losses and as a result "will reduce their incentive to be careful in the future."[20] These sophisticated investors would have been thrilled to accept 70 or 80 cents on the

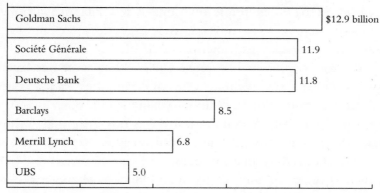

These values include AIGFP CDS Collateral Postings, Maiden Lane III Payments to AIGFP CDS Counterparties and use of Direct Support to AIG from September 16 to December 31, 2008.

Figure 4.4   Largest CDS Payouts by AIG After the Bailout
SOURCE: AIG.

dollar if AIG had threatened to put this subsidiary into bankruptcy since it would then be allowed to renege on its CDS contracts.

Despite the payments in Figure 4.4, AIG reportedly had another $1.6 trillion in "notional derivatives exposure" as of March, 2009.[21] **To minimize further exposure for the federal government, the one AIG subsidiary writing CDS should promptly file for bankruptcy, which would allow only this subsidiary to break its contracts.[22] Because the U.S. Treasury now knows the list of remaining counterparties to AIG contracts, it could alert them in advance to the bankruptcy threat and negotiate a settlement far below 100 cents on a dollar.** Although some individuals with AIG life insurance policies may become concerned if one AIG subsidiary declares insolvency, the insurance regulators should help AIG explain that its life insurance companies are separate and financially sound.

Credit Default Swaps Left in a Federal Regulatory Vacuum

As the New York State Insurance Department avoided jurisdiction over CDS until late 2008, so too did the Commodity Futures Trading

Commission (CFTC) on the federal level. The CFTC has jurisdiction over a broad range of swap agreements along with futures and forward contracts on financial instruments. In 1993, the CFTC issued an exemption for swaps, which covered CDS if they were not based on an agreement with standardized terms and were not traded "through a multilateral transaction execution facility."[23] In other words, the exemption was available to customized CDS that were traded through the over-the-counter (OTC) market. For many years, most CDS were traded in OTC markets, and not on established exchanges.

Brooksly Born, the CFTC chair in 1998, became concerned about this regulatory void in light of the huge growth in swaps contracts and other types of privately negotiated derivatives. But her views were curtly dismissed by then Federal Reserve Chair Greenspan as well as then SEC Chair Arthur Levitt and then Treasury Secretary Robert Rubin. As Michael Greenberger, a senior CFTC official at the time, explained: "Greenspan told Brooksly that she essentially didn't know what she was doing and she'd cause a financial crisis. Brooksly was this woman who was not playing tennis with these guys and not having lunch with these guys. There was a little bit of the feeling that this woman was not of Wall Street."[24]

On May 7, 1998, the CFTC issued a concept release raising questions about whether certain types of OTC derivatives should be regulated. Although the release did not actually propose any rules, it was met on the same day with a highly unusual joint statement by Greenspan, Levitt, and Rubin expressing "grave concerns" about the release and its possible consequences. On June 5, 1998, the trio publicly called on Congress to prevent the CFTC from acting in this area until other senior regulators developed their own recommendations.[25] On July 30, 1998, the Senate Agriculture Committee held a hearing to extract a promise from Born to cease her efforts to regulate OTC derivatives. If not, the Committee threatened to impose a moratorium on further CFTC actions. When Born defended the need for CFTC regulation, Greenspan responded with ideological fervor: "Regulation of derivatives transactions that are privately negotiated by professionals is unnecessary . . . Regulation that serves no useful purpose hinders the efficiency of markets to enlarge standards of living."[26]

In the fall of 1998, a large hedge fund called Long-Term Capital was rescued by a group of Wall Street firms at the behest of the Federal Reserve Bank of New York. The fund's problems included highly leveraged bets on OTC derivatives. Nevertheless, Congress froze the CFTC's regulatory authority for six months, and Born left the CFTC in 1999. Shortly afterwards, Congress specifically excluded any security-based swap agreement from the definition of *security* in the Securities Act of 1933 and also confirmed the exemption of privately negotiated CDS from CFTC regulation.[27] Though unheeded at the time, Born's foresight was recognized a decade later; in 2009, she received the John F. Kennedy Profiles in Courage Award.

With the CFTC and the SEC sidelined, the main response to the collapse of Long-Term Capital was a legislative rider, passed as part of the 2000 Commodity Futures Modernization Act, calling for a clearinghouse that would process trades and hold cash collateral for OTC derivatives.[28] But no clearinghouse for OTC derivatives was approved until January of 2009.[29] In response to prodding by central banks, a group of Wall Street executives published a report in 2005 with recommendations for reducing risk in processing OTC derivatives, and launched a successful campaign to clean up the backlog of unsigned paperwork for such derivatives.[30]

One Clearinghouse for CDS Is Needed

After the failure of AIG in September, 2008, the SEC, the Federal Reserve, and the CFTC signed a memorandum of understanding to expedite the regulatory approval of a clearinghouse for CDS. By then, all regulators agreed that such a clearinghouse was needed, to ensure the completion of CDS contracts, to make margin calls as CDS prices fluctuated, and to net multiple exposures among firms involved with many CDS contracts on different bonds. Nevertheless, because of squabbling among three approved sponsors[31] as well as regulatory delays, most CDS were not traded through a U.S. clearinghouse as of September 1, 2009.

In April 2009, the International Swaps and Derivatives Association introduced a standardized protocol for CDS on corporate and sovereign debt. **That standardized protocol should be extended to**

CDS on mortgage-backed securities. Then Congress should require all standardized CDS to be traded through a clearinghouse. But Congress should recognize that there is a legitimate need among industrial companies for customized CDS contracts that are not appropriate for a clearinghouse.[32] These customized CDS should be permitted to be offered in privately negotiated transactions by financial institutions, subject to a substantially higher capital charge than standardized CDS.

Treasury Secretary Geithner has supported the establishment of clearinghouses for CDS as a high priority. This is where the biggest risk lies for the U.S. financial system: Sooner or later a significant player in the CDS market will fail and its failure will have adverse ripple effects on many firms. A clearinghouse can reduce these ripple effects by requiring margin deposits and establishing a guaranty fund. Having one U.S. clearinghouse for CDS, rather than three, would greatly increase the operational efficiency of the clearinghouse and maximize the netting of multiple contracts among trading partners. Such a merger of all the back offices of the U.S. stock markets in the late 1970s has been a huge success. The risks and costs of trade clearance are uniformly low, while competition continues in the front office on physical and electronic trading venues.

The Treasury has also suggested that all standardized CDS and other derivatives be traded on established exchanges, rather than through OTC dealers.[33] Exchange trading of CDS and other derivatives is a worthy initiative. Although this would result in better transparency and lower transaction costs, exchange trading of CDS and other derivatives is strongly opposed by banks and other U.S. dealers, who would lose profits.[34] **It would be unfortunate to slow down the drive toward a centralized CDS clearinghouse because of a fierce political fight over exchange trading of CDS. These two issues should be kept separate to the extent feasible.**

In the meantime, the SEC has brought an enforcement case alleging insider trading with regard to CDS.[35] But this antifraud theory will have to be tested in the courts because, as mentioned earlier, CDS contracts are excluded from the definition of *security* in the Securities Act of 1933, and remain exempt from much of CFTC regulation. **Congress should quickly adopt the Treasury's proposal to repeal these exceptions for CDS.[36]**

All Models Have Significant Limits

In developing and buying mortgage-backed securities, collateralized debt obligations, and CDS, financial firms relied heavily on mathematical models formulated by their brilliant quantitative analysts—referred to in the industry as "quants." But many of these models turned out to be wrong. Why did so many bright and hard-working people get it wrong? We attempt to answer this question by looking at nine characteristic mistakes in modeling, in each case, providing an illustration and drawing out a lesson.

Most of these mistakes were not technical in nature; they happened because people did not apply sufficient common sense in building their models. **To reduce the number of such mistakes, outside directors and senior executives should ask for the key assumptions behind the significant models used by a financial institution. Directors and executives should critically review these assumptions on a common sense basis.**

Mistake 1: Simple Extrapolations of the Past Are Dangerous

Models are built on historical data, which are then projected into the future. When the historic trend line is strongly positive, models tend to be overly optimistic with insufficient weight given to the downside. Models also tend not to fully integrate recent changes in the underlying factors undermining historical trends. In his annual letter to shareholders published in 2009, Warren Buffett wrote, "The stupefying losses in mortgage-related securities came in large part because of flawed, history-based models used by salesmen, rating agencies, and investors. These parties looked at loss experience over periods when home prices rose only moderately and speculation in houses was negligible. They then made this experience a yardstick for evaluating future losses. They blissfully ignored the fact that house prices had recently skyrocketed, loan practices had deteriorated, and many buyers had opted for houses they couldn't afford."[37]

A good illustration is the typical projection for housing prices in the United States around 2004. Because the trend line was positive for the decade before 2004, the models gave short shrift to the likelihood of a drop in U.S. housing prices. When Steve Eisman, a professional investor, asked his contact at Standard & Poor's what would happen if real estate prices fell, the man's reply was that his "model for home prices had no ability to accept a negative number."[38] More systematically, a detailed study by four economists from the Federal Reserve found that analysts generally understood that a fall in housing prices would have disastrous consequences for the mortgage-backed security market, but assigned a very low probability to such a fall.[39]

In prior periods, particular regions in the United States had experienced severe downturns in housing prices, although national downturns were relatively rare. Of course, the U.S. housing market was becoming more national through higher rates of job mobility and mortgage securitization. However, the risk models of Citigroup, like many Wall Street banks, did not account for the likelihood of a national slowdown.[40]

The lesson: **Do not simply extrapolate past trends into the future. The differences between the past and future trend lines are as important as the similarities.**

Mistake 2: Estimates for New Products Are Especially Dicey

Projections for new products are especially difficult; by their very nature, new products have no or little historical data to work from. When I was president of Fidelity Investments, we regularly made projections of asset growth for new mutual funds. We estimated $500 million in assets after three years for each of four new funds, of which three went nowhere. But the fourth new fund reached $10 billion in assets in less than three years. So much for the science of projections!

Similarly, the projections for default rates on subprime mortgages were based on very few years of data. Subprime mortgages of recent years were effectively new products. If you went back a few decades, you were looking at prime loans, or much different types of substandard loans. In prior years, there were few mortgages with no down payment, and the demographic profiles of the subprime borrowers were different.

Moreover, although a new product can be successful at one scale, it often faces more challenges as the scale expands. The initial round of subprime mortgages tended to go to those families who had almost enough resources to obtain a home mortgage. As the volume of subprime mortgages multiplied, lenders began to attract borrowers who were nowhere close to being in the financial position to afford a home mortgage, and home ownership rates rose to historically unprecedented levels.

The lesson: **Be especially careful about models for relatively new products. Their histories are inherently short and their performance is likely to change significantly as they scale up.**

Mistake 3: The Tails on the Distribution Curve Are Fatter Than You Think

The two ends of a normal distribution curve are called the tails (see Figure 4.5). In a normal distribution curve, the first and second standard deviations together encompass 95.4 percent of the probable events. Although the two tails cover the remaining 4.6 percent, they may include truly horrendous events with very low probabilities. For instance, there may be only a 2 percent chance of an earthquake hitting downtown Los Angeles, but the results would be terrible.

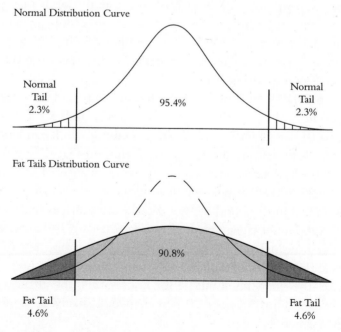

Figure 4.5   Normal Distribution vs. Fat Tails

Most people tend to underestimate the likelihood of abnormal events occurring in the financial markets. For example, mathematician Benoît Mandelbrot showed that if the Dow Jones Average moved in accordance with a normal distribution curve, it would have moved by more than 4.5 percent on only six days between 1916 and 2003. In fact, it has moved that much 366 times during that period.[41]

Thus, the normal distribution curve may not accurately describe many financial situations. Instead, the probability of future events may be better portrayed by a distribution curve with fat tails. Figure 4.5 shows both a normal distribution curve and one with fat tails. In the former, the two tails cover only 4.6 percent of possible events; in the latter, the two tails cover 9.2 percent of possible events—twice as high as normal.

Most large financial firms use a computerized system called Value at Risk (VaR), developed by a team of scientists and mathematicians working for J.P. Morgan, to measure the aggregate risk of their portfolio over short time periods.[42] For example, if a firm has $20 million of weekly VaR in its $1 billion bond portfolio, there is a 96 percent chance that its maximum loss in that portfolio over the next week will not exceed $20 million. Although VaR is a useful tool, it may provide too much comfort because it does not cover the events in the tails, or the events that may occur over longer time periods. It is these events— for example, a tripling of mortgage defaults over the next year—that can bring down a financial firm.

In the physical world of earthquakes, tornados, and hurricanes, the low probability events in the fat tails tend to be independent of each other. In the financial world, by contrast, seemingly independent events may be linked, thereby multiplying the likelihood that they will occur. Suppose hypothetically, there was a 2 percent chance of U.S. housing prices falling by over 30 percent during any one year in the absence of any problems in the bond market. But housing prices might also fall if the market for mortgage-backed bonds froze up for reasons unrelated to the housing market (e.g., a new and confusing tax ruling on such bonds). If there is a problem in the mortgage-backed bond market that reduces the financing available for houses, then the chances of U.S. housing prices falling by over 30 percent would likely be significantly higher than 2 percent.

The lesson: **Identify any low probability event that could put you out of business over the next five years, especially the**

possible linkage among these events. Then insure or hedge against these events to the extent feasible.

Mistake 4: Soft Information Is as Important as Hard Data

The modeling section of financial firms is dominated by scientists and quantitative analysts who are often seen as math geeks. Many of them come from academia. They feed reams of data into computer-driven models to assess financial risks. But human behavior is more complex. A managing director of Goldman Sachs, who initially was a physicist, wrote: "To confuse the model with the world is to embrace a future disaster driven by the belief that humans obey mathematical rules."[43]

A paper by several economists analyzed data on securitized subprime loans issued during the period 1997–2006. Their findings: "interest rates on new loans relied increasingly on hard information characteristics—interest rates become increasingly sensitive to a borrower's FICO scores and loan-to-value ratio . . ." (FICO scores are numerical credit scores).[44] But quantitative indicators underpredicted defaults by subprime borrowers in the latter half of the period studied. Why? As the demand for securitized mortgages surged, lenders had less incentive to collect soft information about borrowers—for example, their job stability, family ties, and ethical standards.

When financial models are based on quantitative data without a practical feel for the situation, the result is often misinterpretation of the data. According to Fortune magazine, the models for subprime securitizations were too optimistic in part because subprime defaults appeared to drop between 2002 and 2005, "but the models didn't take into account the fact that many borrowers were financing their payments with new loans. The borrowers' debts were growing, not shrinking, but the calculations didn't reflect that."[45]

The lesson: **The results of models depend on the quality of their inputs. Although quantitative measures are important, they must be combined with soft information based on experiences in the field.**

Mistake 5: Omit Liquidity Risk at Your Peril

Most models focus on two risks for debt securities: the risk of credit defaults and the risk of interest rate movements. But the financial crisis of 2008 drove home the importance of liquidity risk, that is, the ability to raise cash to meet current obligations. Even if a financial firm has assets that can be sold over time, it may lack the ability to turn them into cash immediately when the debt markets freeze up as they did in 2008.

To illustrate, AIG relied heavily on elaborate models developed by Wharton Professor (now Yale) Gary Gorton to evaluate the risk of credit defaults for CDS. CDS, however, exposed AIG not only to credit default risk but also to liquidity obligations in the event that the collateralized debt obligations protected by AIG dropped in value, or if the agencies dropped AIG's own credit rating. In either event, the other side of the CDS had the right to demand cash collateral from AIG. Neither event was included in Professor Gorton's models, as AIG was reportedly told.[46]

Liquidity risks are closely linked to the level of leverage present in the financial system. When the debt levels of financial firms are high relative to their equity capital, they will be forced to sell assets if losses erode their equity capital. As more firms try to sell assets, it becomes increasingly difficult to find buyers even at discounted prices.

The lesson: **Include liquidity risk as a key factor in financial models. The weight assigned to liquidity risk should increase as leverage increases in the financial system.**

Mistake 6: Be Ready to Question the Experts

As AIG relied too much on the expertise of Professor Gorton, so many firms relied too much on the ratings of mortgage-backed securities and collateralized debt obligations by the credit-rating agencies. Many financial institutions held in their portfolios the triple A–rated tranches of mortgage-backed securities and collateralized debt obligations, while selling lower rated tranches to investors. The risk of these triple A tranches defaulting was supposed to be 1 in 10,000 over a 10-year period, according to Moody's. In fact, by the end of 2008, 50 percent of the triple A tranches of mortgage-backed securities and almost 100 percent of triple A tranches of collateralized debt obligations had partially defaulted.[47]

Thomas Maheras, the head of fixed-income trading at Citigroup from 2005 to 2007, was one of the people who put considerable faith in top ratings on mortgage-backed securities and collateralized debt obligations.

According to published news reports, his team told SEC examiners in the summer of 2007 that the probability of a default on Citigroup's senior tranches of securitized subprime loans "was so tiny that they excluded them from their risk analysis." A slide used at a Citigroup meeting later that summer said these senior tranches were "viewed by the rating agencies to have an extremely low probability of default (less than .01 percent)." Around the same time, Maheras assured his colleagues that Citigroup "would never lose a penny" on these senior tranches.[48]

Yet, ironically, these very same financial executives knew about the many conflicts of interest faced by the credit-rating agencies, the ratings shopping that was taking place, and the magical transformation of subprime mortgages into triple-A rated securities. A bank sponsor would take a group of subprime mortgages rated as junk bonds, put them into a special purpose entity, and then create multiple tranches based on the cash flows from these lowly rated subprime mortgages. Then, in a modern version of alchemy, many of these tranches would be rated triple A based on the benefits of diversification and default assumptions built into the models of the credit-rating agency.

The lesson: **Understand the limitations of your expert's advice on modeling including the factors not covered by the expert. Be especially skeptical of advice from experts like credit-rating agencies with significant conflicts of interest.**

Mistake 7: Financial Incentives Lead to Rosy Projections

Just as the revenue of the rating agencies depended on their ability to give out the highest ratings to tranches of mortgage-backed securities and collateralized debt obligations, so also many of the employees of the financial institutions had substantial compensation incentives to make optimistic projections with their own models. As the securitization of prime mortgages accelerated, the modelers were under tremendous pressure from their bosses to approve as many deals as possible. Further, modelers and their bosses had limited time horizons because the financial rewards for both were mainly in the form of annual bonuses that did not take into consideration actual losses in future years.

At Citigroup, Thomas Maheras was one of the highest paid employees, earning as much as $30 million per year. One member of the team in charge of collateralized debt obligations at Citigroup said: "I just think senior managers got addicted to the revenues and arrogant about the risks they were running. As long as you could grow revenues, you could keep your bonus growing."[49] Similarly, the senior officials at AIG had huge financial incentives to support Professor Gorton's models despite the fact they did not include liquidity risks, as they were aware. In December of 2007, Martin Sullivan, the CEO of AIG, told investors concerned about mounting losses in its CDS business that Professor Gorton's models helped give AIG "a very high level of comfort."[50] Mr. Sullivan's total compensation for 2007 was $13.9 million.[51]

The best practice in financial firms is to award bonuses on performance measured over at least three years to encourage a consistent approach over a longer term. It is too easy for someone to have spectacular performance in one year simply because they happened to work in the hottest corner of a rising market, or they took huge short-term risks. In addition, a portion of a large bonus should be deferred for one or two years, with a potential clawback if the deals from the bonus year later start to fall apart. (For more on compensation incentives, see Chapter 11)

The lesson: **Insulate your modelers from sales pressures as much as possible. Base yearly bonuses on multiyear performance with a portion of the bonuses deferred for one or more years.**

Mistake 8: Don't Be So Impressed with Technology

There is a tendency among many people to be overly impressed by the technology behind models as well as the experts designing these models. For example, many outside directors and senior executives of major banks did not actually understand the financial derivatives used by their traders. Yet this technology was so dazzling that these directors and executives assumed that these derivatives were helping to limit the overall risk of their banks. In fact, while derivatives reduced the risks of some banks that used them, they dramatically increased the risks of other banks.

To take a simple example, if a bank owned a volatile stock, it could reduce that risk by buying a put option on that stock at its current market price. The put option gives the bank the right to sell the stock at that price even if the price of that stock later plummets. By contrast, the same bank would be increasing its risk if it sold a naked put option on the same stock without owning the underlying stock. In this case, the put option is simply a bet that the stock's price will remain above the strike price of the put option before it expires. If the stock's price nosedives before the put expires, the bank will incur a large loss.

Directors and executives at banks found their confidence in the technology of derivatives supported by then Federal Reserve Chairman Greenspan. In a 2004 speech, he asserted that the technology of derivatives would reduce not only the specific risks of individual banks but also the macro risks to the whole financial system. In retrospect, his comments could not have been more off base.

> No discussion of better risk management would be complete without mentioning derivatives and the technologies that spawned them and so many other changes in banking and finance. Derivatives have permitted financial risks to be unbundled in ways that have facilitated both their measurement and their management. Because risks *can* be unbundled, individual financial instruments can now be analyzed in terms of their common underlying risk factors, and risks can be managed on a portfolio basis. Concentrations of risk are more readily identified, and when such concentrations exceed the risk appetites of intermediaries, derivatives and other credit and interest rate risk instruments can be employed to transfer the underlying risk to other entities. As a result, not only have individual financial institutions become less vulnerable to shocks from underlying risk factors, but also the financial system as a whole has become more resilient.[52]

The lesson: **Do not be snowed by technology; its impact all depends on how a specific technological advance is used by humans. Understand the basic workings of the technology underlying derivatives before using them or approving their use by others.**

Mistake 9: Don't Be Swept Away by Popular Trends

Americans have seen the bubble mentality twice over the last decade—in Internet companies and in real estate. In both cases, the prices rose much higher than was justified by the economic fundamentals. Why? Because investors see others making large profits despite the weakness of their economic analyses. At first, investors hesitate, but as the bubble continues, they begin to capitulate: Maybe real estate prices always do go up!

In the late 1990s, the marketing folks at Fidelity Investments were pushing hard to launch an Internet fund. I resisted this push because I couldn't understand the Internet as an investment concept. My doubts were shared by Fidelity's Chairman Ned Johnson. But the Internet stocks continued to rise in 1999, despite the general absence of profits among Internet companies. Only in 2000 and 2001 did Internet stock prices collapse. This time lag makes it very difficult to stand up to a financial bubble; no one can know exactly when it will burst.

Once a bubble does burst, investors inevitably overreact in the opposite direction. Between 2004 and 2007, investors gobbled up the most complex mortgage-backed securities and collateralized debt obligations based on the very dubious projections for subprime loans. After the bubble burst in 2008, however, most investors refused to buy any type of asset-backed securities, even those backed by only prime mortgages and yielding over 10 percent. Instead, investors flocked to short-term U.S. Treasury bills paying close to zero interest.

The lesson: **Economic fundamentals will win out over time, but investment bubbles can last for years. Revise your models to incorporate the actual trends in fundamentals and wait patiently for the bubble to burst.**

Summary

Like many financial innovations, CDS offer substantial benefits, but can be utilized in problematic ways. Credit default swaps provide an easy way for investors to buy protection against default risk on bonds, as distinct from the risk of interest rate movements. However, the writers of CDS did not fully understand the range of factors impacting potential defaults of highly rated tranches of collateralized debt obligations. They also did not fully understand the important differences between CDS and traditional insurance, namely, that the buyers did not have to hold an insurable interest and that buyers could influence the outcome of the contract.

In particular, the writers of CDS did not take into account the demands for cash payments by CDS holders in the event that the value of the relevant tranche of a collateralized debt obligation declined, or the insurance company writing the CDS was downgraded. Nor did they fully appreciate that even the most senior tranches of collateralized debt obligations were heavily dependent on cash flows from subprime mortgages of dubious quality. As a result, AIG failed and the monoline insurers were impaired: Their problems exacerbated the financial turmoil in 2008.

The problems of CDS writers were facilitated by regulatory abdication at the state and federal levels. In 2000, the New York State Insurance Department declared CDS not to constitute "insurance contracts" and did not revisit that position until late in 2008. In intervening years, subsidiaries of insurance companies could write CDS in unregulated affiliates without normal capital or reserve requirements.

On the federal level, the CFTC exempted CDS if the contracts were customized and not traded on an established marketplace. The structure of this exemption encouraged the development of a private market without any formal clearing mechanism. When one chair of the CFTC raised the possibility of regulating CDS, the CFTC's authority in this area was suspended by Congress, which also excluded CDS from the definition of *security* in the Securities Act of 1933.

After AIG blew up in September of 2008, the Federal Reserve, the SEC, and the Treasury agreed to work toward the establishment of a voluntary clearing corporation to increase transparency and reduce risk in the CDS market. But Congress should go further by requiring most CDS contracts to be standardized and traded through one centralized clearing corporation. Congress should also repeal the exemption of most CDS from CFTC regulation and from the definition of securities in the Securities Act of 1933.

The huge defaults in collateralized debt obligations and the related calamities in the CDS market for these securities were not predicted by the mathematical models developed by brilliant PhDs. The critical components of any model are its assumptions, which are ultimately human judgments rather than scientific facts. In general, these judgments should be reviewed regularly on a common sense basis by nonexperts, such as outside directors or senior executives.

Many of the errors made by modelers for collateralized debt obligations and CDS were typical of projections made during a rising market. These mistakes can be limited or avoided in the future by keeping in mind nine specific lessons:

1. Do not mechanically extrapolate favorable trends from the past. Focus on the differences between the driving factors in the past and those in the future.
2. Take special care when making projections about new products. The relevant past experience is sparse, and the future will be influenced heavily by the actual volume of the product after launch.
3. Identify the low probability events that would be disastrous for your business, especially if they might be correlated. Insure against these events to the extent feasible.
4. Broaden your data inputs to include qualitative as well as quantitative factors. Soft information is often as important as hard numbers.
5. Include liquidity risk, as well as interest rate and credit risk, in your models. Liquidity risk becomes more important as firm debt rises relative to equity capital.
6. Understand the limitations of every model, including those developed by experts. Be especially skeptical of experts with significant conflicts of interest.
7. Compensation incentives can undermine modeling efforts. Use a multi-year horizon to judge performance and defer a substantial portion of annual bonuses.
8. Understand the technology underlying derivatives before using them or approving their use. Remember impressive technology can be applied wisely or poorly by humans.
9. Economic fundamentals will ultimately win out over investment bubbles. However, the timing of the burst of any bubble is impossible to predict, so be very patient.

Appendix to
Chapter 4

The CDO described in this example is set up as follows: There are 100 mortgages that pay $1 or $0. They are pooled and 100 $1 tranches are issued; tranche 1 defaults if any mortgage defaults, tranche 100 defaults only if all 100 mortgages default. If the tranches all have default probability of 5 percent and defaults are independent, tranche 10 will have a default probability of 2.82 percent. Now suppose we take tranche 10 from 100 of these pools, repool these 100 tranches, and issue 100 new prioritized claims. This is effectively a CDO. Tranche 10 of the CDO will have a default probability of 0.05 percent. Tranche 10 defaults every 10,000 years and gets rated AAA+.

If, however, the default probability on the original mortgage pool turns out to be 6 percent instead of 5 percent, the default probability would jump to 7.75 percent on the 10th tranche of the mortgage-backed

Note: The example is taken from Professors Joshua Coval, Jakub Jurek, and Erik Stafford, "Structured Finance." Presentation given at Harvard Business School, February 6, 2009.

security and 24.71 percent on the 10th tranche of the collateralized debt obligation. And if the default probability on the original mortgage pool turns out to be 7 percent instead of 5 percent, the default probability soars to 16.20 percent on the 10th tranche of the mortgage-backed security and 97.19 percent on the 10th tranche of the collateralized debt obligation.

In sum, as products based on mortgages get further and further away from the original pool of mortgages, a seemingly small margin of error in the default probability on that pool—from 5 percent to 7 percent in this example—can mean the difference between very low and very high levels of default risk on the different products. The key to this example is its focus on the tenth tranche of both the mortgage-backed security and the collateralized debt obligation. As the probability of default on the underlying mortgages increases, the probability of default on the tenth tranche of the mortgage-backed security increases at a faster rate, and the probability of default on the tenth tranche of the collateralized debt obligation increases even faster.

Part Two

IMPACT ON STOCK AND BOND MARKETS

In Part I, we reviewed the rise and fall of housing prices in the United States, and their implications for the global process of mortgage securitization, from 1995 through 2008. In Part II, we will cover in more depth a much shorter time period, from early 2007 through the end of 2008, in discussing the adverse impact of declining prices in U.S. housing and mortgage-backed securities (MBS) on the U.S. stock and bond markets.

During the spring of 2007, the consistent response by U.S. officials to the housing slump was that it was "contained." As Chairman Bernanke stated, "At this juncture, however, the impact on the broader economy and financial markets of the problems in the subprime market seems likely to be contained. In particular, mortgages to prime borrowers and fixed-rate mortgages to all classes of borrowers continue to perform well, with low rates of delinquency. We will continue to monitor this situation closely."[1] Despite Bernanke's optimism, the housing slump was actually spreading to financial institutions that held mortgages or MBS in their own portfolios or in funds managed by these institutions. From

March of 2007 to July of 2008, the institutions with the largest exposures to subprime mortgages either went bankrupt or were rescued on the verge of bankruptcy. For example, in the spring of 2007, New Century Financial, the second largest subprime lender in the United States, restated its financials and soon filed for bankruptcy. At the start of 2008, Countrywide Financial, the nation's biggest mortgage lender, was saved from insolvency when it was acquired by Bank of America. In March of 2008, Bear Stearns was so weighted down with mortgage-related losses that it agreed to be acquired at a nominal price by J.P. Morgan with federal assistance. In July of 2008, Indy Mac, a large California-based thrift and mortgage lender, was taken over by the FDIC.

By the end of the summer of 2008, the securities markets were actively responding to the mortgage crisis. The stock prices of many financial institutions plummeted, as the prices of their bonds fell sharply. Between September 7 and September 22, 2008, six unprecedented events occurred:

September 7, 2008—The U.S. Government put Fannie Mae and Freddie Mac into conservatorship.

September 15, 2008—Lehman Brothers declared bankruptcy, having received no assistance from the federal government.

September 15, 2008—Merrill Lynch, as its stock nosedived, was acquired by Bank of America (with federal assistance before the acquisition closed).

September 17, 2008—The Federal Reserve bailed out AIG with an $85 billion loan (later increased to $173 billion and restructured).

September 19, 2008—The Securities and Exchange Commission (SEC) banned all short selling of financial stocks (which lasted until October 8, 2008).

September 22, 2008—The last two large investment banks standing, Morgan Stanley and Goldman Sachs, were allowed to convert from broker-dealers to banks.

On October 3, 2008, President Bush signed the Economic Stabilization Act of 2008, authorizing $350 billion immediately for a financial bailout, with another $350 billion to come. Yet the securities markets continued to swoon: stock prices took a deep dive after October 3, as the trading markets in most bonds dried up.

Part II will explore the ramifications of all these events of the U.S. stock and bond markets in four chapters:

- Chapter 5 will explain why the governmental actions to limit short selling have been misguided, and why we need more federal oversight of hedge funds, which are the most active short sellers.
- Chapter 6 will critique the SEC's adoption of alternative capital requirements for the five largest investment banks, and will advocate major changes in the capital requirements for banks.
- Chapter 7 will outline the measures taken by the Federal Reserve and the FDIC to stimulate short-term lending, and discuss their adverse implications for controlling inflation and monitoring financial risk.
- Chapter 8 will argue against the expansion of federal guarantees for bank deposits from $100,000 to $250,000 per account, and against any federal insurance for money market fund accounts.

Chapter 5

Short Selling, Hedge Funds, and Leverage

Executives of many financial institutions allege that short sellers, investors who bet that stocks will decline in the future, were key players in bringing about the downfall or forced restructuring of their institutions. Financial executives have lashed out particularly at hedge funds, which are the biggest short sellers in the United States. In response, the SEC banned short selling in all financial stocks for three weeks in late September and early October of 2008. However, as this chapter will demonstrate, this ban did not prevent the further decline in financial stocks yet produced other adverse effects on the trading markets.

Of course, the steep fall in the U.S. stock market during 2008 was caused in large part by fundamental problems with the U.S. economy, especially in the financial sector. On the other hand, were there significant nonfundamental factors behind this market downturn? If so, the

U.S. government should adopt measures to reduce the impact of those nonfundamental factors in the future.

In addressing these issues, we begin by reviewing Figure 5.1, which shows the relationship during 2007 and 2008 between the U.S. stock market as represented by the S&P 500 index, and the U.S. market for the triple A portion of MBS based on subprime mortgages as represented by the ABX index.[2] Although the stock market is usually a leading indicator of the country's economic prospects, it lagged the mortgage market through all of 2007 and the first half of 2008. The ABX index fell from par or 100 in June of 2007, below 90 in October to 80 by the end of 2007. By contrast, the S&P 500 index rose throughout most of 2007, peaking in October of 2007. Between the start of 2008 and June 2, the ABX dropped by almost 30 percent. During the same period, the S&P 500 index declined by only 4 percent.

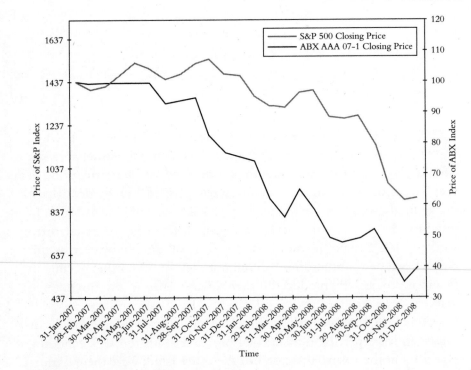

Figure 5.1   S&P and ABX AAA Levels
SOURCE: Markit Financial Information Services.

During the summer of 2008, the stock market finally became a leading indicator of the financial crisis. In June of 2008, the S&P 500 declined sharply from 1,400 to 1,278. Then the S&P 500 stayed above 1,200 until mid-September when it dropped below that number due to the bankruptcy filing of Lehman Brothers and the federal takeover of AIG.

On September 29, 2008, the S&P 500 fell by 8.5 percent, reportedly because the U.S. House of Representatives initially rejected the $700 billion TARP bill. Yet, on October 3, 2008, when the president actually signed the TARP legislation, the S&P 500 fell again by 5.3 percent. From October 3 onward, the S&P 500 declined until it reached the year's low of 741 on November 20, before rising to 903 by the end of 2008. In other words, the stock market paradoxically fell the farthest and the fastest *after* Congress authorized the Treasury to spend billions of dollars on resolving the financial crisis.

For the entire 2008, the S&P 500 lost 38.5 percent, the biggest annual loss since the Great Depression in the 1930s. Although a steep fall in the stock market historically had a negative psychological effect on most American consumers, it now has more of an actual negative impact on the 92 million Americans who own equities directly or through mutual funds.[3] When U.S. stocks lost $10.4 trillion in market value from the market high in October of 2007 to the market low in November 2008,[4] the roughly 50 million Americans with 401(k) accounts lost $1 trillion, or 29 percent of the value of these accounts.[5]

This chapter will begin by evaluating the allegation that short sellers were the main culprits in driving financial institutions to the brink of failure. It will show that the SEC's ban on short selling of financial stocks was ineffective in stopping the decline of these stocks, and will support certain of the current SEC proposals to constrain short selling. Second, this chapter will assess the role played by hedge funds, and funds of hedge funds, during this financial crisis. It will advocate stricter net worth tests for investors in hedge funds, and some form of regulatory oversight for managers of hedge funds. Third, this chapter will argue that the recent period with the steepest sell-off in U.S. stocks (from October 3 to November 20 of 2008) was driven in large part by deleveraging, that is, the selling of assets by financial institutions to maintain their ratios of average assets to capital. The obvious solution, to be discussed in Chapter 6, would be to increase the amount of capital cushion required of financial institutions.

The Realities of Short Selling

Short selling a stock means betting that a stock's price will decline in the future. As shown by the simple example in Figure 5.2, a short sale is effected by selling shares of a stock at Time 1 (May 1) by a seller who does not own the stock at Time 1 (May 1); instead, the seller borrows shares of the stock at Time 1 (May 1); and promises to return them at Time 2 (July 1) when she will actually buy the shares of the stock. A short seller hopes that the price of a stock will decline between Time 1 (May 1) and Time 2 (July 1) so that the price received for selling the shares at Time 1 (May 1) exceeds the price to be paid when buying the shares at Time 2 (July 1). In the example illustrated by Figure 5.2,

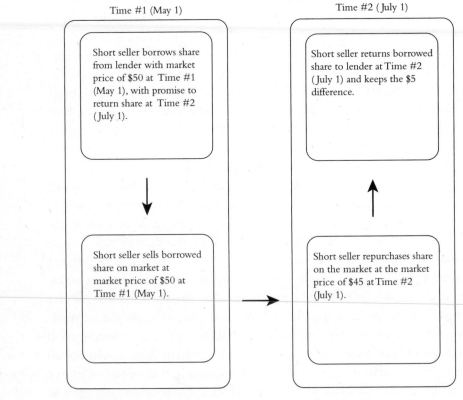

Figure 5.2   Typical Short Sale

the investor makes a profit of $5 by selling a borrowed share of a stock at $50, and later repurchasing a share of that same stock at $45 to return the borrowed share.

The Positives and Negatives of Short Selling

Short selling has positive functions as well as potential abuses. Most importantly, short sellers act as investigative reporters by ferreting out negative information about a company, which raises questions or directly challenges its financial reports. For example, David Einhorn, a controversial short seller, charged that Allied Capital, a business development corporation in Washington, DC, was cooking its financial books. The company, of course, retorted that Einhorn was spreading lies so that he could profit from his short sales of Allied Capital stock. In June, 2007, the SEC decided that Einhorn was right—finding that the financial statements of Allied Capital violated the applicable rules.[6]

Similarly, Jim Chanos, another prominent short seller, claimed to have questioned Enron's financial statements and business practices long before the scandal broke.[7] During the collapse of Enron in late 2001, CEO Ken Lay and CFO Jeff Skilling repeatedly blamed short sellers and negative press coverage for the firm's difficulties. In October of 2001, Lay told employees that Enron was under attack by short sellers "just like America is under attack by terrorism."[8] Ultimately, widespread illegal activity and fraud were uncovered at the company.

Short selling has other positive functions like hedging the stocks in an investor's portfolio. Suppose an investor owns shares of IBM and wants to receive her dividends, but she is concerned about a potential fall in IBM stock over the next six months. To guard against this possibility, she can short sell a specific number of IBM shares, while retaining the same number of IBM shares in her long portfolio. In addition, short selling helps arrive at the right price by expanding the ways an investor can take a negative stance on a stock. A traditional long manager, who has a very negative view of a stock, can only sell what she holds or refuse to buy the stock; a hedge fund can implement this negative viewpoint more forcefully by shorting the stock. In this manner, short sellers can help deflate small investment bubbles before they become large ones.

On the other hand, short selling can create a downward momentum in a stock's price, which may gain a life of its own—accidentally or intentionally. This is called a bear raid, which the SEC described as follows:

> A "bear raid" involves the active selling of a security short to drive down the security's price in the hopes of convincing less informed investors of a negative material perception of a security, triggering sell orders. Falling prices could trigger margin calls and possibly forced liquidations of the security, depressing the price further. This unrestricted short selling could exacerbate a declining market in a security by eliminating bids, and causing a further reduction in the price of a security by creating an appearance that the security's price is falling for fundamental reasons.[9]

Did Short Sellers Bring Down Financial Institutions?

In the current financial crisis, several executives claimed that their institutions were the victims of bear raids by short sellers. Let's begin with the role of short sellers in the failure of Bear Stearns. Andrew Ross Sorkin, a *New York Times* reporter, wrote about the rumors he personally heard on the Friday morning before Bear Stearns failed in March of 2008.

> On Friday morning, when there still seemed to be a glimmer of hope that the stricken Bear might survive, William C. Repko, former chairman of J.P. Morgan's restructuring group and now senior managing director at Evercore Partners, was already writing Bear's obituary.
>
> "Bear failed," Mr. Repko was telling me. "Bear is gone." He seemed so sure. "This is a run on the bank," he said. "It's what happened to Enron." Bear's demise, it seemed, was a foregone conclusion.
>
> The run on Bear began around midday on Wednesday, when a series of banks and hedge funds started a whisper campaign against the firm. The firm was doomed, they said. It was almost broke. But some of the money managers were clearly talking their book. They were obviously shorting Bear's stock betting it would decline.[10]

Later in the financial crisis, a number of CEOs attributed their declining stock performance partly to short sellers. In an internal memo to employees, John Mack, CEO of Morgan Stanley, said, "What's happening out there? It's very clear to me—we're in the midst of a market controlled by fear and rumors, and short sellers are driving our stock down."[11] In the case of Morgan Stanley, the volume of short selling in the stock consistently increased in the two months prior to the adoption of short-sale restrictions by the SEC on September 22, 2008. This increase in short selling was significantly correlated to a proportional decrease in Morgan Stanley's share price over the same time period. It is therefore reasonable to conclude that short sellers are likely to have placed substantial negative price pressure on the firm's stock.

In Congressional testimony, Dick Fuld, then CEO of Lehman Brothers said, "The naked shorts and rumor mongers succeeded in bringing down Bear Stearns. And I believe that unsubstantiated rumors in the marketplace caused significant harm to Lehman Brothers."[12] Fuld seems to have been right. Leading up to his firm's September 15 bankruptcy filing, not only did short selling consistently increase in volume, but a burst of short selling on September 9 also coincided with a 45 percent decrease in the firm's share price on that day alone. Since this decrease occurred in the absence of new material information, a bear raid is a likely explanation.

John Thain, the CEO of Merrill Lynch, contended that short sellers bet against Merrill as its share price fell and credit became harder to come by, creating a vicious downward spiral.[13] However, the evidence does not support Thain's contention. Ahead of the September 14 announcement of Merrill Lynch's acquisition by Bank of America, short selling had gradually increased over the preceding two months, but at a relatively slow pace. There was also a low correlation of short sale volume to the share price of Merrill Lynch during this period.

Similarly, the failures of Fannie Mae and Freddie Mac on September 8, 2008, seem to have been caused more by long-standing fundamental factors (discussed in Chapter 2), than by short selling. The high daily levels of short selling in both stocks in early September coincided with the release of material adverse information regarding the future of these two corporations, while the longer-term correlation of short-selling volume to the price movements in both stocks was weak.

In short, while the CEOs of most companies with falling stock prices vociferously blame short sellers, some are right and others are wrong. This is ultimately an empirical issue.

The Three Responses of the SEC

In response to widespread complaints about short selling, the SEC in the fall of 2008 adopted three new rules:

First, the SEC required short sellers to secure borrowed shares in advance of making their sales. **This securing of borrowed shares is a good idea since it eliminated the potential for short sellers failing to deliver when they were obligated to buy shares to cover their short positions.**

Second, the SEC required all managers of $100 million or more in assets to file weekly reports of their daily short positions, which would be made public several weeks after filing.[14] **This reporting requirement is another sensible measure because the market should be informed of significant short positions, though on a lagged basis to prevent copycatting.**

Third, the SEC temporarily banned all short sales in 799 financial stocks (upped quickly to almost 1,000 stocks) from September 19 through October 8, 2008. **The SEC's temporary ban on short selling was misguided and should not be utilized again.** Prior to the ban, these financial stocks performed better than the stock market as a whole, but fell along with the market during the ban. Further, the stock market as a whole dropped far more during the ban than before.[15]

At the same time, the temporary ban had other adverse effects. The liquidity of these financial stocks decreased as their trading volume declined sharply. The cost of trading these financial stocks increased substantially as the spread widened between the bid (buy) and ask (sell) prices offered by their market makers.[16] Long-term holders of these financial stocks complained that they could not hedge their risks by selling short. The ban also closed down legitimate investment strategies of hedge funds, such as trying to profit from the small price differences between convertible preferred shares and the common stocks into which those preferred shares converted.

The Uptick Rule Was Repealed Without
Adequate Empirical Support

In the past, the SEC's uptick rule constrained downward spirals by allowing a stock to be sold short only after an increase (an uptick) in its last sale price from its prior price. For example, if a stock's price fell from 50.3 to 50.1, it could not be sold short at 50.1. On the other hand, if the stock's price rose from 50.1 to 50.25, it could then be sold short.

Adopted in 1938, the uptick rule was repealed by the SEC on July 3, 2007. The SEC based its decision on a brief pilot during 2005, a year in which the stock market was rising and its volatility was very low. As one commentator pointed out, "the effects of an unusually rapid and large market decline could not be measured or analyzed during the pilot because such decline did not occur during the period studied."[17]

The SEC compared pilot stocks no longer subject to the uptick rule—943 randomly selected stocks from the Russell 3000 (an index of the 3000 most actively traded stocks)—with the remaining stocks in the Russell 3000 that were still subject to this rule. The pilot began on May 2, 2005, and the SEC study ended on October 30, 2005. This six-month period was far too brief to draw conclusions about a rule that had been in effect for 70 years. Professional traders never had time to develop sophisticated techniques to take full advantage of the repeal of the uptick rule.

During these six months, the SEC found that the pilot stocks (without the uptick rule) showed 2 percent lower returns than the control stocks (with the uptick rule). The SEC dismissed this 2 percent difference in six-month returns as statistically insignificant relative to the standard deviation of the Russell 3000 during the pilot period. However, if we eliminate a small number of outliers in the Russell 3000 with returns over 100 percent and use a normal distribution fitted to the remaining stocks, the standard deviation of the Russell 3000 during the pilot decreases enough to make the 2 percent difference statistically significant. More fundamentally, return differences of 2 percent within 6 months are economically important because nominal annual returns in the U.S. stock markets since World War II average in the range of 6 to 8 percent.

This statistically significant difference of 2 percent implies that removing the uptick rules goes further than the SEC's apparent goal of promoting a neutral environment for stocks. As explained by an independent analyst of the pilot, researcher Min Zhao, "lifting the tick-test rule goes beyond correcting stock overvaluation and is associated with stock undervaluation, suggesting that the SEC's recent decisions of removing tick-test restrictions for all U.S. exchange traded securities may not be considered an optimal policy if such undervaluation is driven by predatory short sellers' price manipulation."[18]

The downward acceleration of stock prices occurs in a bear raid, when short sellers drive down a stock's price in the hopes of scaring other investors into dumping the stock or triggering margin calls, leading to forced liquidation. Two individual investors opposed the SEC's repeal of the uptick rule because it prevented bear raids. In response, the SEC approvingly noted other commentators who felt that bear raids "are highly unlikely to occur in today's markets which are characterized by much smaller spreads, higher liquidity, and greater transparency than when the rule was adopted 70 years ago."[19] These other commentators did not factor in an important new development since 1938, namely, the managers of $1.8 trillion in hedge funds who were allowed to short stocks.

The SEC Proposes Two Approaches to Reinstating the Uptick Rule

In April, 2009, the SEC proposed for comment two approaches to reinstating the uptick rule on short selling.[20] One approach would apply a price test across all U.S. securities markets at all times. Short selling would be permitted if it happened after the stock's price met a test specified in the SEC's rules. A short sale would be allowed only at a price above the current national best bid to buy that stock.[21] **This price test approach to reinstate the uptick rule should be adopted, although the SEC is debating exactly how that price test should be formulated. This price test approach to reinstate the uptick rule seems sound.**

The second approach would apply the uptick rule to short selling only after a stock's price had dropped by a large percentage within a day.[22] **This "circuit breaker" approach should not be adopted: By the time the rule applies, the downward spiral of a stock's price is likely to have started and will be very difficult to halt.**

Do Fast Growing Hedge Funds Need More Regulatory Oversight?

In its narrowest form, a hedge fund is a collective investment pool that hedges its bets. For instance, a hedge fund with a long-short strategy is typically hedged against the general ups and downs of the market. It has roughly half of its assets invested in stocks that the manager favors (called long positions) and the other half invested in stocks that the manager disfavors (called short positions). The fund aims to make money whichever way the general market moves—by picking better-than-average winners on the long side and worse-than-average losers on the short side.

In practice, many hedge funds are not hedged against general market movements, so the label is a misnomer. Indeed, there is a mind-boggling array of investment strategies utilized by the pools labeled as "hedge funds." These investment strategies include convertible arbitrage, merger arbitrage, distressed securities, macroglobal, and multistrategy. Some of these strategies are very risky; others are relatively conservative. Nevertheless, hedge funds as a group are the main short sellers in the U.S. market because this investment strategy is prohibited or severely restricted for many other types of large institutional investors such as life insurers, mutual funds, and pension plans.

In sum, hedge funds have six main characteristics that differentiate them from other collective investment pools like mutual funds.

1. They are offered to a limited number of institutions and wealthy individuals—historically under 100 "accredited investors" meeting net worth tests, and more recently under 500 "qualified purchasers" with $5 million or more in their investment portfolios.
2. Hedge funds make private offerings to their investors, who usually are locked in for a year or so and subsequently must ask to redeem 60 to 90 days in advance.
3. By not making public offerings and staying below a specified number of investors, hedge funds do not have to register with the SEC or any other regulatory agency.
4. Hedge funds are free to offer any investment strategy they choose with relatively high degrees of leverage—for example, they can

raise $100 million in capital, borrow $400 million, and invest $500 million.

5. With relatively short investment horizons, most hedge funds are very active traders; they regularly account for over one-fifth of the daily trading volume on the New York Stock Exchange, and a majority of trading in credit default swaps.[23]

6. The managers of most hedge funds are typically paid a base fee of 2 percent of assets per year, plus an incentive fee equal to 20 percent of the fund's annual capital gains (but they do *not* reduce their fees by 20 percent of its annual capital losses).

The Rapid Growth of Hedge Funds

Hedge funds have grown dramatically: from less than $250 billion in assets in 1995 to $1.8 trillion at the end of 2007, as shown by Figure 5.3. Similarly, the number of hedge funds rose from around 2,000 in 1995 to almost 8,000 in 2007.[24] This phenomenal growth was driven in part by the burst of the dot–com bubble in 2000–2002, when stock prices fell by one-third and hedge-fund performance was generally still in the positive territory. In part, this growth was driven by the greed of managers

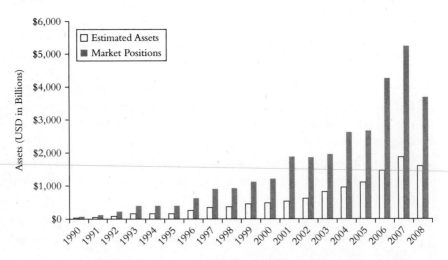

Figure 5.3 Hedge Fund Assets and Market Positions: 1990–2008
SOURCE: Andrew Lo before U.S. House of Representatives Committee on Oversight and Government Reform.

who loved the standard fee structure of hedge funds—a base fee of 2 percent of assets plus an incentive fee equal to 20 percent of the annual capital gains—versus most stock mutual funds that charge a management fee of .5 to 1 percent without any incentive fee. As Charlie Munger, Warren Buffett's partner, commented on hedge fund managers: "Never have so many people made so much money with so little talent."[25]

Further, the growth of hedge funds was fueled by the growth of funds of hedge funds (FOFs). As shown in Figure 5.4, a FOF is a top-level fund that invests in anywhere from 5 to 30 hedge funds. Funds of funds provide investors with diversification among hedge funds and expertise in selecting hedge funds of high quality. On the other hand, FOFs add a second layer of fees to be paid by investors. FOFs usually charge an annual base fee of 1 percent plus 10 percent of the upside annual capital gain in addition to the 2 percent base fees and 20 percent incentive fees charged by all the hedge funds underlying the FOF.[26]

As the number and assets of hedge funds grew so quickly, it became increasingly difficult to achieve outstanding performance. As the traditional hedge fund strategies were exhausted, managers abandoned their core areas of expertise in an effort to exploit new opportunities like

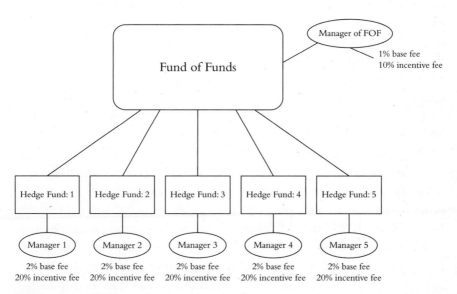

Figure 5.4   Structure of a Fund of Funds

collaterized debt obligations. To stand out in a crowded room, hedge funds took more risk and became more image oriented. As Seth Klarman, one of the best and longest-serving hedge fund managers, explained: There was a "change in the very nature of hedge funds—from nimble vehicles focused almost exclusively on investing to marketing organizations with well-staffed investor relations teams."[27]

In 2008, the hedge fund bubble burst. The average hedge fund lost over 20 percent, despite promises to make money in any type of market; the total net outflows were $200 billion, most of which was concentrated in the last quarter of the year.[28] Accordingly, the assets of hedge funds were roughly $1.2 trillion by the end of 2008, down from $1.8 trillion at the end of 2007. FOFs averaged a negative return of almost 17 percent in 2008. With negative performance and large redemptions, the assets under management by FOFs fell by 30 percent during 2008—from slightly over $1 trillion to $700 billion.[29]

Do the Clients of Hedge Funds Need More Protection?

Currently, hedge funds in the United States are virtually unregulated, except for generally applicable laws like antifraud and antitrust statutes. In considering more government oversight of hedge funds, lawmakers should focus on two very different objectives: first, to protect clients of hedge funds, and second, to monitor the material risks posed by hedge funds for the financial system.

In 2004, the SEC adopted a rule requiring the managers of most hedge funds to register under the Investment Advisers Act of 1940. Despite the Act's exemption for advisers with 15 or fewer clients, the SEC's new rule looked through pension plans and other institutional clients of hedge funds in calculating the number of their investors. However, a federal court of appeals invalidated this new SEC rule because it reversed many of the SEC's prior decisions against looking through the institutional clients of an investment adviser.[30] Although U.S. Representative Barney Frank introduced a bill in Congress to reverse the court's decision, it met with opposition from the strong lobby for hedge funds. Instead, the SEC adopted a specialized antifraud rule aimed at preventing any deceptive or manipulative act or course of conduct by any investment adviser, even if exempt from SEC registration.[31]

Do the types of clients in hedge funds need the registration protections of the federal securities laws? Historically, a hedge fund could use a private offering to attract "accredited investors" who have incomes of $200,000 or more or net worths of $1 million or more. A subsequent SEC rule allowed hedge funds to make private offerings to fewer than 500 "qualified purchasers" with at least $5 million in investable assets. By following either set of rules, a hedge fund is able to avoid SEC registration of the offering under the Securities Act of 1933 (which applies to initial public offerings) and to avoid registration of the hedge fund under the Investment Company Act of 1940 (which applies to mutual funds).[32] Given the inflation of income and assets over the last few decades, these historic limits are now too low to serve as a rough test of financial sophistication.

In 2006, the SEC proposed the addition of a third test for accredited investors in private pools like hedge funds—those with at least $2.5 million in investable assets.[33] If the third test were adopted and increased periodically to reflect inflation, the SEC should let accredited investors meeting all three tests accept or reject private offerings of hedge funds without SEC registration of the offering or the fund. These are presumably sophisticated investors who can evaluate the pros and cons of such offerings by hedge funds. **In addition, the SEC should allow any investor meeting both of the two prior tests for an accredited investor—those with $200,000 in income and $1 million in net worth—to qualify for exempt offerings if he or she is represented by a qualified financial adviser. The adviser should help the investor be considered sophisticated for this purpose.**

Nevertheless, the managers of all hedge funds over a specific size should register under the Investment Advisers Act. Such registration would not limit the investment strategies or borrowings of these hedge funds. Nor would such registration force any changes in the structure of their incentive compensation as long as all their clients had at least $750,000 invested with that investment adviser.[34] However, registration would mean regular SEC inspections of the books and records of hedge fund managers as well as more disclosures by these managers to their clients. Thus, such registration would provide a window on the policies and practices of most hedge funds, about which we know very little. In fact, over one-third of all hedge fund managers are already registered under the Advisers Act since that regulatory status helps them attract pension funds and other institutional clients. The Treasury has proposed legislation requiring registration for all advisers to hedge funds with more than $30 million of assets under management.[35]

The Treasury has gone further by proposing registration under the Investment Advisers Act for all managers of "other private pools of capital, including private equity funds and venture capital funds."[36] In contrast to hedge funds, private equity and venture capital funds do not trade in securities, nor are they active short sellers; instead, they buy large stakes directly in operating companies in many industries. **To the extent that they invest in operating companies through privately negotiated transactions, there is little reason for private equity or venture capital funds to be supervised by the SEC.** If these funds acquire 10 percent or more of the shares of a bank or financial institution, they must submit a detailed application and be approved by the Federal Reserve or other appropriate regulator.

Do the Clients of Funds of Hedge Funds Need More Protection?

In contrast to the high net worth clients of hedge funds, investors in funds of hedge funds (FOFs) may need more protections. Funds of funds often sell interests of $100,000 or less to a large audience of less sophisticated investors. **Some FOFs make only private offerings to sophisticated investors. These should meet the income and net worth tests as well as the third proposed test of $2.5 million in investable assets, as described earlier.** Other FOFs make broader public offerings to investors. These offerings are registered with the SEC under the Securities Act of 1933, although the FOF itself is usually exempt from registration under the Investment Company Act of 1940.

In these publicly registered offerings by FOFs, investors are already informed about the qualifications of the FOF's managers and their material conflicts of interest, as well as the range of strategies and redemption restrictions on the FOF and the underlying hedge funds. **In addition, investors in FOFs should be provided with con-crete illustrations of how both layers of fees are calculated—the**

2 percent base fee plus 20 percent incentive fee of the underlying hedge funds as well as the 1 percent base fee plus 10 percent incentive fee of the FOF. In particular, investors should be told whether this FOF has in the past generated enough additional return to justify its second level of fees, since most FOFs have not been able to jump this hurdle.[37]

Small institutions like state pension funds or college endowments frequently invest in FOFs because these institutions seek diversified exposure to hedge funds and lack the in-house expertise to choose the best ones. This approach is naïve because significant due diligence is required to select good FOF managers. David Swensen, the distinguished head of Yale University's endowment fund, articulated his concerns about FOFs:

> Funds of funds are a cancer on the institutional investor world. They facilitate the flow of ignorant capital. If an investor can't make an intelligent decision about picking managers, how can he make an intelligent decision about picking a fund-of-fund manager who will be selecting hedge funds? There's also more fees on top of existing fees.[38]

Most importantly, neither managers of FOFs nor other investors can currently make a fair comparison of performance among the thousands of hedge funds. Princeton Professor Burton G. Malkiel and Analysis Group manager Atanu Saha have shown that between 1994 and 2003 the voluntary reporting services of hedge funds exaggerated their returns on average by over 5 percent per year.[39] This is a huge overstatement, as compared to the average nominal returns of the U.S. stock markets of 6 percent to 8 percent per year. Why? These reporting services have no consistent methodology for performance reporting. For instance, they allow a fund that began in 2000 to start reporting in 2002 to make its performance look better. Moreover, the existing reporting services have a serious survivor bias: Any hedge fund with a terrible record can simply shut down and reopen a year later under a new name. The performance statistics of the shut-down fund will be eliminated from the database.

As in most areas, some hedge funds will perform well, others will perform poorly, and still others will be average. Even sophisticated investors need an accurate and consistent way to compare performance among hedge funds. **Working with investor groups and the trade associations for hedge funds, the SEC should take the lead in developing a precise definition of hedge fund performance and a uniform format for reporting such performance. This format should show the hedge fund's performance from its actual start date, before and after all fees, as well as the performance of any predecessor hedge fund.**

Very Large Hedge Funds Should Submit Confidential Reports to the Systemic Risk Monitor

Besides the protection of clients, the other goal of regulating hedge funds should be to reduce the likelihood of their creating adverse effects on the general financial system. In 1998, a large hedge fund called Long-Term Capital Management achieved extraordinary levels of risk by investing huge sums of borrowed money; it invested over $110 billion, of which less than $5 billion was equity capital and the rest was debt.[40] With over $110 billion, the fund made large bets based on historic correlations among various markets, which had been studied extensively by two Nobel Prize economists who worked for the fund. But these bets went wrong when Russia devalued its currency and reneged on its ruble debt in August of 1998. By September, the fund was on the brink of failure. Concerned that the fund's failure would impose substantial losses on its lenders and trading counterparties, as well as further undermine the tumultuous markets at that time, the New York Federal Reserve Bank called together in one room the commercial banks and investment banks that were the primary lenders and counterparties of the fund. Pressured by officials at the Federal Reserve Bank, all but Bear Stearns agreed to inject new capital into the fund and take it over, without any financial assistance from the Federal Reserve Bank or any other governmental agency.

In 1999, the President's Working Group on Financial Markets issued a lengthy report on the lessons of Long-Term Capital Management.[41] The report included recommendations for more international coordination with offshore financial centers to achieve compliance with international standards for hedge funds, since Long-Term Capital was formally based in the Cayman Islands. There have been modest steps in this direction, though most hedge funds are still located legally in offshore havens to limit their U.S. tax exposure, as explained later. The report included recommendations for expanded risk assessment authority over nonregulated affiliates of broker-dealers. But efforts in this area were totally ineffective. (See Chapter 6.) Finally, the report included recommendations for more frequent and meaningful publication of information on hedge funds and the exposure of financial institutions to hedge funds. However, these recommendations were not implemented.

In 2007, Timothy Geithner, then President of the Federal Reserve Bank of New York, publicly warned that Wall Street lenders were not receiving enough information from hedge funds with high leverage ratios (the ratio of a fund's average assets to its capital).[42] Looking at the balance sheet of most hedge funds, their assets were in the range of 2–6 times capital.[43] In the summer of 2008, when Wall Street banks began to recognize large losses in mortgage-backed securities, the banks called in the margin loans of some highly leveraged hedge funds, which also were faced with rising redemption requests from their clients. To raise cash, these hedge funds sold securities, contributing to the glut of debt securities on the market and to the rapid drop in the prices of more liquid stocks.

Called before a Congressional committee in mid-November of 2008, the heads of five large hedge funds offered to provide data on their activities directly or indirectly to the Federal Reserve, so it could monitor their systemic risk. But these managers had one condition: that their data not be released to the public so that they could continue to pursue their proprietary trading strategies.[44]

Congress should require all large hedge funds (e.g., over $25 billion in assets) to submit regular confidential reports to the SEC, which should pass them onto the Federal Reserve (or whatever agency is designated to monitor systemic risk. See Chapter 14.) A requirement for such reports was endorsed by Treasury Secretary Geithner.[45] But what information should these reports contain?

- **Fund Borrowing:** The most important piece of information is the amount of the Fund's borrowings relative to its capital. While the Fed could attempt to put together all the loans to one hedge fund by combing through reports from many banks, it would be more efficient to receive reports on aggregate loans from the hedge fund.
- **Implicit Leverage:** The fund should also report its implicit leverage in the swaps or futures market. The Fed's main concern should be the extent of a fund's obligations to sell assets in a down market.
- **Illiquid Assets:** The fund should report the composition of its investment portfolio and its percentage of illiquid assets. Liquidity could be measured by the number of days estimated to sell out the fund's position in a security—for example, without selling more than one-half of the security's average daily volume.
- **Valuation Methods:** The fund should report its method of valuing investments for which there is no actively traded market. For instance, this could be discounted cash flow or asking market professionals for quotes.
- **Asset Concentration:** The fund should report on its concentration of assets. These should cover investments that comprise a significant portion of its portfolio, as well as any large positions relative to the outstanding securities of a particular company.
- **Redemption Requests:** The fund should report its redemption policies and any recent change in these policies. This report should include any client request for substantial redemptions in the near future.
- **Trading Counterparties:** The fund should identify who its main counterparties are for trading in various types of assets, including derivatives. This report should divulge how large the fund's exposure is to its main counterparties.
- **Risk Assessment:** The report should describe policies and procedures for risk assessment. The report should include any significant deficiency in these policies or their implementation.

In reviewing this information, the Federal Reserve should evaluate whether a large hedge fund, like Long-Term Capital, is so overstretched that a small loss in its portfolio is likely to force it to dump a lot of assets quickly. In such a case, the Fed should ask the large banks with outstanding loans to the hedge fund to reconsider their exposures to the fund. The Fed should also work with the SEC to take other appropriate steps with that hedge fund.

The Compensation of Hedge Fund Managers Should be Taxed as Ordinary Income

A typical hedge fund is organized as a corporation in a tax haven like the Cayman Islands or Bermuda to avoid corporate taxes in the United States. The fees of a hedge fund manager are often deferred through what is called a nonqualified plan and reinvested in the hedge fund. As a result, the hedge fund manager would not pay any U.S. tax on such fees until they were actually distributed to him or her in the United States. For example, the manager of one large hedge fund deferred more than $1.7 billion in fees between 1990 and 2007.[46]

In the Economic Stabilization Act of 2008, Congress prohibited the deferral of fees by hedge fund managers for more than 12 months in offshore corporations not subject to U.S. tax, unless the deferred fees are subject to a substantial risk of forfeiture.[47] In other words, once the hedge fund manager earns the fees, they cannot be deferred for more than a year in a corporation located in a tax haven unless the manager could actually lose the fees by failing to meet a condition related to future employment.

A second and larger issue for hedge fund managers is whether their incentive fees are taxed as capital gains or ordinary income, since incentive fees constitute the bulk of their income. Under current law, their incentive fees are generally taxed at the top capital gains rate (presently 15 percent) rather than the top ordinary income rate (presently 35 percent). This tax result is achieved by allocating to the manager 20 percent of the fund's income, which mainly takes the form of capital gains.

This tax result is putting form over substance. The incentive fees go to the manager of a hedge fund because he or she is performing a service, namely, investing the securities of the fund. The manager is not receiving incentive fees as a return on his or her capital invested in the hedge fund (although the manager may separately invest their own capital in the fund). **In the United States, we usually tax service-related compensation as ordinary income, rather than**

capital gains, so incentive fees of hedge fund managers should be taxed as ordinary income. The Obama Administration proposed in 2009 that incentive fees of hedge fund managers be taxed as ordinary income,[48] but Congress has not made a decision on this proposal as of September 1, 2009.

How Deleveraging Pushed Down Stock Prices

As mentioned earlier, the sharpest sell-off in the U.S. stock market during this financial crisis was between October 3 and November 20, 2008. This presents an apparent paradox: The stock market plummeted the day the federal government authorized $700 billion for the bailout and kept falling until November 20. Why did the stock market react so negatively to what appeared to be a big step in the right direction?

The answer seems to lie in a process known as deleveraging. As financial institutions experienced losses in their portfolios of MBS, they were forced to sell assets to maintain their leverage ratios—the ratio of average assets to capital. At the same time, in response to deteriorating financial conditions, banks were calling outstanding loans of hedge funds and other institutional investors, which were also forced to sell assets. Since the markets for corporate bonds and asset-backed securities were frozen, the sellers turned to their most liquid holdings—publicly traded stocks.

Leverage within the financial system has increased markedly over the past five years, particularly among investment banks and hedge funds. The ratio of average assets to capital for the five largest U.S. investment banks exceeded 30 to 1 at its peak in late 2007.[49] Leverage ratios for hedge funds are difficult to calculate due to sparse public information, but their market positions rose sharply above their estimated assets as shown by Figure 5.3, suggesting a doubling of hedge fund debt from 2003 to 2007.[50]

These estimates do not fully capture the significant leverage built into derivative investments, which have grown rapidly in recent years—more than tripling to a market value of almost $34 trillion between December, 2006 and December, 2008.[51] Purchasers of most derivatives are much more leveraged than investors buying stock on margin. Before the stock market crash in 1929, investors could buy stock with up to 90 percent in borrowed money called margin debt. But now margin debt is limited to 50 percent of a stock's purchase price.[52] By contrast, an investor can usually purchase a future or swaps contract with a deposit equal to 5 percent or less of the contract value.

Once the financial crisis hit, leverage decreased rapidly in the financial sector. As Dick Fuld, the former CEO of Lehman Brothers, remarked in 2007, whereas credit grows arithmetically, it shrinks geometrically.[53] Deleveraging was driven partly by higher costs of debt; during the crisis, credit became scarce and interest rates soared on short-term debt. Large banks became reluctant to lend, and investors became unwilling to buy short-term commercial paper. At the same time, deleveraging was driven by losses on MBS, which forced financial institutions to sell assets in order to maintain required leverage ratios. Suppose a bank needed to have $10 million of capital for every $100 million in assets (or 10 percent of assets). If the bank lost $4 million on its MBS, its capital would decrease to $6 million. To maintain a leverage ratio of 10 percent, the bank would need to raise more capital or sell down its assets to $60 million (10 percent of $60 million = $6 million). In addition, many banks were hanging onto assets in the hope that the Treasury Department would purchase them. In October, 2008, when Treasury announced that it would be recapitalizing banks, rather than purchasing toxic assets, many banks dumped bonds on the market.[54]

The pace of deleveraging is reflected in Figure 5.5 on the volume of overnight repurchase agreements (called repos), which are used by sophisticated investors to borrow cash in exchange for securities. Overnight borrowing in the repo market declined 31 percent between October 1, 2008, and the end of that year. Leverage in the bond market and borrowing by primary dealers both also declined appreciably during 2008. Although declines in borrowing through these channels were somewhat offset by a rise in Federal Reserve lending, it is clear that widespread deleveraging occurred.

The deleveraging process can create a vicious cycle, as the sale of assets to meet leverage and margin requirements can depress asset prices, triggering further selling. As losses mount, additional collateral is required, pushing firms to sell as the market deteriorates. As firms sell assets, prices decline in response to the increased supply, creating further losses and potentially requiring additional selling. This cycle can easily spread throughout the financial system. A wave of selling by

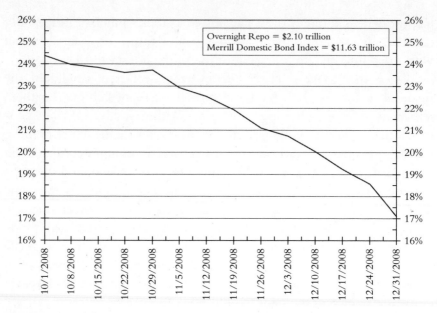

Figure 5.5   Overnight Repo as a Percent of the Market Value of the Merrill
Domestic Bond Index
SOURCE: Fritz Handler, Bianco Research LLC.

relatively weak firms can quickly cascade to create losses and trigger
selling at healthier firms.

The pace of deleveraging on asset prices can be exacerbated by
two distinct factors: illiquidity and correlation. In a down market, the
immediate need for capital can concentrate selling in the most liquid
of assets, such as publicly traded stocks. The number of investors put
into positions in which such sales are necessary is determined largely by
correlation among their portfolio holdings. If investors hold similar types
of assets, this increases the likelihood that a large number of investors
will simultaneously need to sell liquid assets quickly in response to losses.

In 2005, MIT Professor Andrew Lo raised concerns that hedge
funds exhibited both of these properties: Many had portfolios that were
quite illiquid, and their investment strategies were increasingly correlated.[55] He showed that the relatively even annual returns of hedge
funds resulted from a marked increase in the illiquidity of their investments. Since a manager of a hedge fund had no way to measure the
fluctuations of those investments, the manager assumed that their value

was rising steadily. He also found that the correlation of 13 different hedge fund strategies had increased significantly between 1994 and 2000. This increased correlation was likely driven by the rapid flow of capital into hedge funds during this period, making differentiation of strategies ever more difficult as market positions increased in size. Therefore, it seems likely that, during October and November of 2008, hedge funds were heavy sellers of the liquid stocks in their portfolios in order to meet collateral obligations and investor redemptions.

Summary

The U.S. stock market plunged by over 38 percent in 2008, inflicting heavy damage on firms and families. The majority of this plunge resulted from fundamental problems in the American economy and financial institutions. But some part of this plunge was likely the result of three related nonfundamental factors: short selling, hedge funds, and deleveraging.

Short sales involve betting that a stock's price will decline. Short sales have constructive functions such as ferreting out adverse information and hedging a long portfolio of securities. But they can be subject to abuses, notably, bear raids in which short sellers create artificial pressures designed to reduce a stock's price.

In response to the burst of short selling in September, 2008, the SEC adopted two sensible rules. One required short sellers to line up borrowed shares before making their sales. A second required short sellers to submit weekly reports on their short positions. The third measure, a temporary ban on all short selling of financial stocks, was ineffective in preventing further declines in stock prices; it also reduced liquidity and raised trading costs for these stocks.

Instead of temporary bans, the SEC should reinstate the uptick rule, which was repealed in the summer of 2007 based on a pilot study of questionable validity. The SEC has proposed two different approaches to reinstating the uptick rule. One would be triggered only if the price of a stock drops precipitously within a day. But this is likely to be too late; the downward spiral has already begun. The better approach would be to permit short selling if a specified price test were met. A short sale could occur only at a price above the highest national bid to buy the stock.

Hedge funds are the most important and most active short sellers in the United States. They are unregulated pools of capital, raised from institutions and wealthy individuals, that can employ any investment strategy with any amount of leverage. Their managers are typically paid a base fee of 2 percent of assets per year plus 20 percent of the fund's capital gains. Hedge funds assets are supplied to a significant degree by funds of hedge funds (FOFs), which often sell interests of $100,000 or less. Funds of funds select a diversified portfolio of hedge funds and are usually paid an additional base fee of 1 percent of assets per year plus 10 percent of the FOF's aggregate capital gains.

Hedge funds should be allowed to make private offerings to institutions and wealthy individuals if these investors meet appropriate tests. Specifically, the SEC should adopt its proposal requiring individual clients of privately offered hedge funds to have at least $2.5 million in investable assets as well as to meet the current income and net worth tests. By contrast, many clients of FOFs are small or less sophisticated investors who need extensive SEC-mandated disclosures. More generally, the SEC should take the lead in developing a uniform methodology and consistent format for reporting the investment performance of hedge funds.

As hedge funds have grown larger and taken on more leverage, many have pointed out the need for more governmental oversight of very large hedge funds to prevent adverse effects of their failures on the financial system. But little has been done until recently, when the leaders of major hedge funds offered in principle to submit nonpublic reports on their activities to the Federal Reserve. Such reports, which should be filed only by the largest hedge funds, should focus on the amount of leverage taken by hedge funds, and the related issue of their ability to sell assets quickly at current prices. These reports should also highlight any concentrated long or short positions in the hedge fund's portfolio, and identify its main counterparties for trading.

More broadly, managers of hedge funds above a certain size (expressed in terms of assets under management) should be registered under the Investment Advisers Act, as the U.S. Treasury suggests. Registration would not limit their investment strategies or incentive fees, but it would subject these managers to regular SEC inspections. Nevertheless, this registration requirement should not generally be extended to managers of all other pools of capital, such as private equity and venture capital funds.

In 2008, Congress stopped hedge fund managers from deferring for more than 12 months the recognition of income on their fees by keeping them invested in offshore vehicles. Congress should go further, as the Obama Administration has proposed, and tax the incentive fees of hedge fund managers at ordinary income rates rather than lower capital gains rates. Incentives fees are a form of compensation for investment services, rather than a form of capital appreciation.

Excess leverage was a key factor in aggravating the financial crisis in general and pushing down stock prices in particular. The ratio of average assets to capital rose significantly between 2004 and 2008 at large banks, investment houses and hedge funds. The steep decline in overnight repurchase agreements during the fourth quarter of 2008 shows a huge wave of deleveraging occurred at that time.

Deleveraging was driven by two main factors. As the financial crisis continued, credit became scarce and collateral requirements increased. Hedge funds and other borrowers were forced to sell assets to raise more collateral or pay back their loans. Similarly, as financial institutions experienced heavy losses related to home mortgages, they were forced to sell assets to maintain leverage ratios set by their regulators. As these institutions sold assets, prices declined in response to increased supply, creating further losses and triggering additional asset sales. This cycle can easily spread from weak institutions to healthy ones, as widespread selling creates price declines in all asset categories.

In late 2008, the debt markets were frozen. Therefore, as they were forced to delever, hedge funds and other institutions sold their most liquid holdings—publicly traded stocks. In addition, hedge funds needed to sell liquid assets to meet rising redemptions. This selling spree was a major factor in pushing down stock prices so dramatically in October and November of 2008.

Chapter 6

Capital Requirements at Brokers and Banks

The ratio of average assets to capital (called the leverage ratio) is the most critical component of any regulatory system for commercial banks or investment banks. If a financial institution is allowed to maintain a high leverage ratio, it can greatly expand the amount of loans it can make and securities it can buy while keeping the same amount of capital on hand. When the economy is booming, these additional assets will generate high profits for the institution. However, if the economy goes into a recession, a highly leveraged institution will likely incur losses that will substantially erode its capital. Then the institution will be forced to sell some of its additional assets into weak markets and incur further losses.

The dangers of high leverage were vividly illustrated in this financial crisis: the demise or restructuring of the five largest investment banks in the United States. Bear Stearns, reeling from mortgage-related losses, was forced to accept a merger with J.P. Morgan at a nominal share price in March of 2008. Lehman Brothers filed for bankruptcy on September 15, 2008. On the same day, Merrill Lynch—pressed by rising losses and a falling share price—agreed to be acquired by Bank of America. A week later, the Federal Reserve allowed Morgan Stanley and Goldman Sachs to convert quickly from broker-dealers to bank holding companies. As a result, both companies now are subject to the capital requirements of the Fed rather than the Securities and Exchange Commission (SEC). For a diagram of a bank holding company, see Figure 6.1.

Because the remaining large investment banks are now banks or parts of banks, the capital requirements for banks are even more crucial to the U.S. financial system. In 1988, an international committee of regulators based in Switzerland issued Basel I, which divided bank assets into a few broad risk categories (e.g., mortgages, corporate loans, and government bonds) for the purpose of calculating a bank's capital requirements. Basel I applied to U.S. banks for the decade before 2008. Recognizing the need for more refined categories, international bank regulators spent many years developing Basel II. which became effective for U.S. banks in April, 2008.[1] The capital requirements of Basel II are more complex and customized than those of Basel I, allowing banks to rely heavily on their own internal risk models as well as credit ratings for their bond portfolios.

As Basel II was being finalized, the SEC moved in 2004 toward a more bank-like approach to the capital requirements for the five

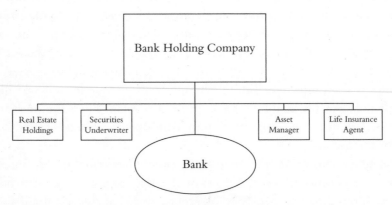

Figure 6.1   Activities of a Bank Holding Company

largest investment banks—Bear Stearns, Goldman Sachs, Lehman Brothers, Merrill Lynch, and Morgan Stanley (collectively known as the Five Investment Banks). In contrast to the Federal Reserve, which had broad powers over the parent holding companies of banks, the SEC had minimal authority over the parent holding companies of these Investment Banks (which were all SEC-registered broker-dealers at that time). In 2004, these Five Investment Banks agreed to consolidated SEC supervision of their parent holding companies as well as other affiliates. In exchange, the SEC permitted these Five Investment Banks to utilize an alternative method of calculating their capital requirements based roughly on Basel II.[2] Under this alternative method, the ratio of average assets to net capital at these Five Investment Banks more than doubled.[3]

This chapter will focus on capital requirements for the Five Investment Banks and commercial banks. First, it will explain why the alternative method of calculating the capital requirements for the Five Investment Banks contributed to their demise. Then it will argue for the establishment of an effective consolidated regulator for each type of U.S. financial institution. Second, it will explain why the 1999 repeal of the Glass Steagall Act, which expanded the securities activities of commercial banks, was not a major cause of the financial crisis. Instead, it will argue that a commercial bank with securities activities has important funding advantages over a free-standing investment bank. Third, it will explain how the crude risk categories in Basel I's capital rules contributed to the financial crisis. Then it will argue for less reliance on credit ratings and internal risk models in the capital standards of Basel II. Finally, it will explain how Basel II is detrimentally procyclical. Therefore, it will suggest an anticyclical approach, encouraging banks to build up excess capital and loan loss reserves in good times.

The Demise of the Five Large Investment Banks

During the decade before 2008, the Five Investment Banks were masters of the universe. Their assets grew rapidly as did their stock prices. Their CEOs were lavishly paid and heralded as inspiring leaders. Yet by the end of 2008, none of the Five Investment Banks existed in their prior form. Two effectively failed (Lehman and Bear Stearns), another two converted to bank holding companies (Goldman and Morgan Stanley), and the fifth (Merrill Lynch) was acquired by a bank holding company.

How did this abrupt reversal of fortunes occur? As will be explained below, the SEC in 2004 allowed each of the Five Investment Banks to more than double their leverage ratio. Although the SEC simultaneously took on the supervision of the parents of the Five Investment Banks, it did not properly implement this new model of consolidated supervision.

The SEC Allows Too Much Leverage

The Five Investment Banks led the charge for a reduction in the SEC's capital requirements with a battle cry of deregulation; they complained about burdensome rules at a time of rising global competition. In addition, the Five Investment Banks were concerned about a threat by the European Union to regulate their holding companies and affiliates unless they were subject to consolidated regulation by one U.S. agency.[4] The Europeans were accustomed to this model of consolidated supervision from their historic oversight of their own universal banks, which engaged in a broad range of securities activities as well as traditional banking functions. With one set of new SEC rules adopted in 2004, the Five Investment Banks achieved both goals: They were granted an alternative method of calculating their leverage ratios, and they agreed to subject their parent holding companies to consolidated SEC supervision.

At an open meeting in 2004 to approve the new rules, the head of the SEC's Division of Trading and Markets characterized the alternative calculation method as conservative. Although she admitted that the new method might result in a 20–30 percent reduction in net capital, she emphasized that it would apply only to the Five Investment Banks.[5] "We've said these are the big guys," commented SEC Commissioner Harvey Goldschmid, "but that means if anything goes wrong, it's going to be an awfully big mess."[6]

According to a 2008 report by the Office of the Inspector General (OIG), the ratio of average assets to net capital for Bear Stearns was 33 to 1 at the time of its demise.[7] At that time, Bear Stearns was apparently in compliance with the new alternative method. Figure 6.2 shows the increase in the leverage ratio for the Five Investment Banks between August 31, 2006 and February 29, 2008.

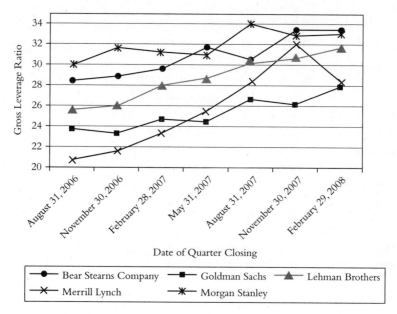

Figure 6.2 Major Investment Banks Gross Leverage Ratios
SOURCE: OIG Report September 25, 2008.

A high leverage ratio is a recipe for disaster for any financial institution, despite a diversified portfolio of loans and long-term investments. A high leverage ratio means that the financial institution will have a thin capital cushion against losses from a large volume of assets. If some of those assets experience significant losses, the capital cushion will be eroded. With a 33 to 1 leverage ratio, Investment Bank B could make $33 million of loans for every $1 million in capital. An $800,000 loss (after-tax) in its portfolio would reduce its capital from $1 million to $200,000. Then, as shown in Table 6.1, Investment Bank B would have to sell $25.6 million in loans (and pay off $25.6 million in borrowings) in order to maintain a leverage ratio of 33 to 1 ($32.2 million − $25.6 million = $6.6 million in loans relative to $200,000 in capital or 33 to 1).

When capital is depleted, the institution has two main choices to get back to the required leverage ratio: It can raise more capital or sell assets. Because financial institutions often experience significant losses during times of financial crisis, they will find it almost impossible to raise new capital at that time. Instead, they typically are forced to sell assets in difficult

Table 6.1 Leverage Ratio Effects

	Assets (Loans, Bonds, etc.)	Liabilities (Plus Capital)	Leverage Ratio (Assets to Capital)
T#1 – Start	$33 m in loans	$32 m borrowing $1 m capital	33 to 1
T#2 – Losses of $800,000	$32.2 m in loans	$32 m borrowing $200,000 capital	
T#3 – Sells $25.6 m in loans and pays back borrowers	(–$25.6 m sold loans)	(–$25.6 m paid to borrowers)	
T#4 – Finish	$6.6 m in loans	$6.4 m borrowing $200,000 capital	33 to 1

markets. Such forced sales not only result in unfavorable prices for the selling institution, but also can trigger a downward spiral for the whole market as multiple institutions are faced with the same dilemma. This downward spiral occurred with a vengeance during the latter half of 2008.

The Need for a Consolidated Regulator

At that same SEC meeting in 2004, Mr. Goldschmid asked: "Do we feel secure if there are these drops in capital [that] we really will have investor protection?" A senior staff member replied that the SEC would hire the best minds with quantitative skills to implement this Consolidated Supervised Entities (CSE) program. In fact, the SEC assigned only seven people to examine the parents of the Five Investment Banks, which had combined assets of more than $4 trillion in 2007.[8]

In exchange for greater flexibility on leverage ratios, the Five Investment Banks agreed to have sophisticated systems for risk management, and to allow the SEC more frequent access to these systems, as applied to the parents of the Five Investment Banks as well as their other affiliates. This group-wide SEC supervision "would impose reporting (including reporting of a capital adequacy measurement consistent with the standards adopted by the Basel committee on Banking Supervision)."[9] Like Basel II, the new consolidated supervision program at the SEC relied heavily on the internal risk models of the Five

Investment Banks in determining the riskiness of their investments in order to determine their own risk-based capital requirements.

The OIG report concluded that the CSE program was never properly staffed, did not pay close enough attention to the important issues, and did not have a formal automated process to ensure that issues were resolved. According to the report's executive summary on Bear Stearns:

> Thus, it is undisputable that the CSE program failed to carry out its mission in its oversight of Bear Stearns because under the Commission and the CSE program's watch, Bear Stearns suffered significant financial weaknesses and the FRBNY needed to intervene during the week of March 10, 2008, to prevent significant harm to the broader financial system.[10]

Although the SEC poorly implemented the 2004 CSE program, it is no longer the consolidated regulator of the Five Investment Banks, which have all become parts of bank holding companies under the Federal Reserve. Nevertheless, if properly staffed, the SEC can be an effective consolidated regulator of smaller investment banks and broker-dealers.[11] Without a consolidated approach, it is virtually impossible for any regulator to form a true picture of a financial institution's overall risk level and of how the activities of one subsidiary might impact the well-being of another. Before 2004, the SEC had jurisdiction over just 7 of the 200 subsidiaries of the holding company for Lehman Brothers.[12] In many cases, the riskiest activities of the Lehman group were carried out in unsupervised subsidiaries. This statutory vacuum put the SEC in a weak bargaining position to obtain relevant information about Lehman as a consolidated entity. To obtain supervisory jurisdiction over all affiliates of the Five Investment Banks, the SEC offered them an overly generous alternative method of computing their capital requirement.

To avoid this problem in the future, Congress should grant the SEC supervisory powers over all holding companies and affiliates of broker-dealers that are not already subject to supervision by a competent regulator. For instance, if a broker-dealer firm is a subsidiary of a bank holding company, the Federal Reserve is already its consolidated regulator, so the SEC need not play that role for that firm. **Every financial institution should have a consolidated regulator to make sure risks are not shifted to unsupervised entities and to monitor transactions among the different parts of a diversified financial conglomerate.**

In principle, the consolidated regulator should usually be the one with primary jurisdiction over the most important financial institution in the conglomerate. In practice, what should Congress do about large financial conglomerates where the dominant institution is an insurance company? Currently, all global insurance companies based in the United States are chartered by one state and regulated by most of the other states. Yet, as the AIG case illustrates, the demise of such a global insurance company can have dramatic ripple effects on U.S. and foreign credit markets.

To address these systemic risks, and to reduce the administrative expense of dealing with 50 state regulators, Congress should allow a handful of U.S.-based global life insurance companies to obtain federal charters under a new federal insurance agency.[13] In that event, the new federal agency could also serve as the consolidated supervisor of the insurance conglomerate. Although a federal life insurance charter will be strongly opposed by the states, they would still regulate most life insurers and all property-casualty insurers. The focus of property-casualty insurers is mainly on local auto and real estate markets, whereas a life insurer applies the same actuarial tables across the United States.

The Artificial Distinction Between Advisers and Brokers

The SEC's inadequate supervision of the holding companies of the Investment Banks was not an isolated event. As the case of Bernie Madoff illustrates, the regulators failed to uncover a $50 billion fraud in two inspections, even after being tipped off by a whistleblower. Madoff ran a broker-dealer, which executed stock trades for customers, and also purported to run an investment adviser with a thriving business managing other people's money through a hedge fund. His investment record of 10 to 12 percent per year was remarkably consistent through up and down markets over more than a decade—so consistent that it couldn't be true, as documented by a whistleblower named Harry Markopolos.

Beginning in 1999, Mr. Markopolos tried several times to educate SEC officials about Madoff's Ponzi scheme, but none of them took notice.[14]

The Financial Industry Regulatory Authority (FINRA), the self-regulatory organization for broker-dealers, performed a full-scale investigation of Madoff's broker-dealer in 2007. The result: minor violations of technical rules. At the time of the 2007 inspection, the chair of FINRA was Mary Schapiro, who was appointed chair of the SEC in January of 2009. In the Senate hearings confirming her nomination, she explained FINRA's failure to detect Madoff's Ponzi scheme as a result of "the stove pipe" approach, in which issues can slip through the cracks because different regulatory authorities have jurisdiction over different activities.[15] FINRA had the right to inspect Madoff's broker-dealer, though not his investment adviser. But FINRA's jurisdiction does extend to associated persons of a broker–dealer, which would include Madoff personally and his investment adviser.[16]

In any event, the SEC clearly had the right to inspect both entities. The SEC did an inspection of Madoff's broker-dealer in 2005 and found only technical violations.[17] When Madoff registered his adviser in 2006, the SEC reportedly did not conduct the usual review of his adviser in the first year after it registered.[18] The SEC presently has 400 staffers to inspect approximately 11,000 financial advisers, who are growing rapidly in number.[19] In addition, the SEC has proposed to perform a surprise exam every year for any investment adviser who retains custody of its clients' assets.[20] **Because the SEC needs help in this area, Congress should either establish a new self-regulatory organization or ask FINRA to help perform inspections of investment advisers—at least those affiliated with broker-dealers.**

The Madoff debacle also points out the need to eliminate this artificial distinction between investment advisers and brokers offering advice. Technically, an investment adviser may not execute trades without a brokerage license, though an investment adviser may use the brokerage platforms provided by Fidelity or Schwab. Under an SEC exemption from the Investment Advisers Act, a broker was historically allowed to provide investment advice as an ancillary service to trade executions and receive special compensation for the advice. But this exemption was invalidated by a federal court of appeals in 2007.[21] In fact, most customers have no idea whether they are receiving recommendations from a representative of a brokerage firm or an employee of an investment adviser. Yet the legal rules for customer protection are quite different in these two organizational contexts.[22] **The solution: The SEC should figure out appropriate customer protection rules for financial professionals paid by customers to provide investment advice (as distinct from the execution of transactions) and apply the same rules to such financial professionals whether they work for brokerage firms or investment advisers.**[23]

Should the Glass Steagall Act Be Reinstated?

Several commentators have argued that the repeal of Glass Steagall was a major cause of the current financial crisis because it increased the riskiness of the securities activities of banks and the associated conflicts of interest. Therefore, these commentators argue for a reinstatement of the restrictions of Glass Steagall on the securities activities of banks.[24] But these arguments are weak from both empirical and policy perspectives.

The New Securities Activities of Banks Were Not Their Main Problems

Most of the securities activities performed by banks and their affiliates after the repeal of Glass Steagall were permitted before its repeal. Under Glass Steagall, banks were allowed to engage in agency trades of stocks and bonds on the order of customers.[25] These included, most importantly, acting as a securities broker in executing stock trades on the New York Stock Exchange. Banks were also allowed for many years to trade as principal, that is, as a market maker or underwriter, in a broad range of bonds including U.S. Treasuries, Fannie Mae and Freddie Mac bonds, as well as municipal and state bonds. Over a decade before the repeal of the Glass Steagall Act, the Federal Reserve allowed any nonbank affiliate of a bank holding company to derive from 5 percent (in 1986) to 25 percent (in 1997) of its revenues from underwriting and dealing in all equity and debt securities, including mortgage-backed securities (MBS).[26] The main power added by the repeal of Glass Steagall was the ability of the bank, rather the bank holding company, to underwrite MBS.

Some banks took advantage of these expanded securities powers, and others did not. As a result, academics were able to perform comparative analyses on this subject. Professor Alex Tabarrok, of George Mason University, cited several studies as supporting the proposition that large, multifunctional financial institutions were in fact stronger than their single-focus counterparts.[27] Based on historical evidence, for example, Professor Eugene White found that national banks with security affiliates were much less likely to fail than banks without such affiliates.[28] According to Professors Kroszner and Rajan, securities underwritten by universal banks turned out to be of higher quality than those underwritten by investment banks.[29] Moreover, of the 25 U.S. commercial banks that became insolvent in 2008, only one was a significant player in selling MBS.[30] According to an SEC report, the failures of these 25 commercial banks were mainly related to their large credit losses on their loans—the core of traditional banking activities.[31]

The Wall Street banks have suffered major losses on the MBS held in their investment portfolios. But commercial banks have long been allowed to invest in MBS. It could be argued that their new power to underwrite these securities magnified the losses of Wall Street banks to the extent they were stuck with MBS underwritten by them. If this argument were valid, we would expect to see the portfolios of money-center banks populated mainly by low-rated MBS that could not be easily sold in their underwritings. However, the most significant losses suffered by large banks engaged in securities underwriting were concentrated in their holdings of the most highly rated type of MBS, the senior and supersenior tranches.[32]

The inherent riskiness of investment banking was *not* demonstrated by the demise of the Five Investment Banks in 2008. As explained earlier in the chapter, the fundamental problems of these Investment Banks resulted primarily from the SEC's decision in 2004 to allow them to more than double their leverage ratio, combined with the SEC's ineffective efforts to implement the consolidated supervision of these Investment Banks. Indeed, the repeal of the Glass Steagall Act allowed two of the Investment Banks to be rescued by becoming part of large banking complexes—Merrill was acquired by Bank of America, and Bear Stearns was merged into J.P. Morgan. To stem attacks on their stocks and increase their sources of liquidity, Goldman Sachs and Morgan Stanley were also allowed to convert quickly to bank holding companies.

As these conversions show, the universal banking format has a significant advantage over the separate investment bank format in terms of financing sources. A universal bank can finance its daily activities from more sources than an investment bank: commercial paper and repurchase agreements with sophisticated investors as well as insured deposits at the bank level, and loans from the Federal Reserve. In particular, the insured deposits from retail depositors are a more stable source of funding than commercial paper (short-term loans) from sophisticated investors. These multiple sources of funding help explain why universal banks, with powers to underwrite securities, have been the favored format in most countries.

One remaining question is why Lehman Brothers was not allowed to convert to a bank holding company when its CEO reportedly asked to do so in the summer of 2008.[33] Neither was Lehman Brothers bailed out by the Federal Reserve, as were Bear Stearns and AIG. Although it may be unfair to second-guess such real-time decisions in the relative calm of hindsight, it is critical to impose a framework upon those decisions. Indeed, if Bear Stearns and AIG had been traditional banks, we would know whether the steps taken by the federal government were the least costly means of preventing their failure. **In 1991, Congress passed a law requiring that federal regulators follow special procedures before an emergency bailout of a bank. These procedures include a supermajority vote by the FDIC and Federal Reserve boards, an explicit rationale from the Treasury Secretary and an audit by the Comptroller General after the bailout.[34] Therefore, Congress should extend the 1991 bailout law for banks to all financial institutions.** In the absence of such a law regarding other financial institutions, it is impossible to determine whether the government made the best decisions on financial bailouts.

Why Glass Steagall "Lite" Does Not Make Sense

Although the repeal of Glass Steagall was at most a minor factor in causing the current financial crisis, some commentators have suggested that banks be prohibited from engaging in specified types of risky activities in the future. This is usually referred to as Glass–Steagall "lite."[35]

The first suggestion would be to prevent banks from engaging in proprietary trading of financial instruments for the bank's own account.

Although proprietary trading may be risky if viewed in isolation, it is often part of a larger strategy to hedge portfolio investments of the bank to lock in funding or currency rates for future transactions. A second suggestion is to prohibit banks or their affiliates from managing hedge funds and private equity funds. But many of these funds are quite profitable. They are also designed to reduce risk by providing absolute returns, regardless of whether the securities market is going up or down. A third suggestion is to prohibit banks from managing mutual funds to prevent "the blurring of boundaries between buy side and sell side, and the mingling of client funds with those of a bank or its employees."[36] However, mutual fund assets are held in segregated accounts and their management fees provide banks with a stable flow of income, as compared with the volatile revenue and principal risk associated with lending and other traditional bank operations.

In addition, critics have complained that the repeal of the Glass-Steagall Act expanded the potential conflicts of interest between securities underwriting and lending activities of large banks. Such potential conflicts are regulated by federal statutes that prohibit or limit transactions between banks and their affiliates. For example, Section 23B of the Federal Reserve Act prohibits any bank from making an extension of credit to a borrower at below-market terms when an affiliate, including an underwriting affiliate, is a participant in the transaction or when the proceeds of such an extension of credit are used for the benefit of an affiliate.[37] These statutes have been fairly effective in the past, though they could be applied to a broader range of transactions between a bank and its affiliates such as hedge funds and private equity funds advised by bank affiliates.[38]

Finally, critics have claimed that certain commercial banks are guilty of tying arrangements, such as conditioning loans to companies on winning their securities underwriting business in the near future. The empirical studies on this claim reach different results,[39] perhaps because tying arrangements are not usually formalized in writing. One study found tying arrangements, but concluded that companies often benefited from these arrangements through lower costs for both loans and underwriting.[40] Federal statutes prohibit banking institutions from using tying arrangements to engage in anticompetitive behavior. For example, Section 106 of the Bank Holding Company Act prohibits any bank or bank holding company from requiring any borrower to buy any other service from the same institution or its affiliates as a condition of a loan.[41] Nevertheless, corporate executives continue to complain that they are pressured by bankers to buy additional services in connection with obtaining loans. **Because many of these pressures are exerted in oral conversations, the bank regulators should take a more proactive approach with the business community to uncover and prevent improper tying arrangements.**[42]

The Myth of Revenue Synergies

More broadly, despite the repeal of Glass Steagall, bankers should be skeptical about the alleged benefits of launching or maintaining financial supermarkets, that is, offering securities, insurance, and other financial services together with banking functions. In advocating for the repeal of the Glass Steagall Act, Citigroup argued that it could achieve revenue synergies by offering mutual funds and life insurance as well as banking services to its clients.[43] Citigroup believed that its high-net-worth customers would want the convenience and comfort of buying multiple financial services with the Citigroup brand.[44] By 2006, however, Citigroup had sold both its insurance unit (Travelers) and its asset management unit (Smith Barney funds).

Why was Citigroup not able to realize these revenue synergies? In part, high-net-worth customers want the best quality and price for each financial service, rather than the convenience and comfort of the Citigroup brand. In part, the customers and the regulators would be suspicious if Citigroup's banking clients bought mutual funds primarily managed by Smith Barney and life insurance primarily issued by Travelers. With the flood of product information and the ease of Internet transactions, Citigroup's high net worth customers did not want to be pressured to buy from Citigroup's affiliates.[45] Instead, these customers preferred open architecture, where financial advisers choose the best product in each category regardless of affiliation. This customer preference led Citigroup to sell its fund management and insurance units, and to concentrate instead on being a distributor of many products from multiple unaffiliated providers.

I had a similar experience at Fidelity when the company launched a credit card bank in the 1990s. We all thought that, with millions of loyal mutual fund clients, Fidelity could easily build a successful credit card business. But Fidelity's core clients for mutual funds were the worst credit card customers. They refused to pay an annual fee on a credit card, and almost always paid their balances on time, so they rarely incurred interest charges. To earn profits, the executives at the Fidelity bank started to distribute credit cards to non-Fidelity customers. Because Fidelity could not achieve enough scale as an independent card provider, however, it soon sold the credit card bank and put Fidelity's name in bold letters on another company's credit card. So much for revenue synergies!

Bank Capital Requirements Need to Be Reformed

Since the large investment banks have converted to bank holding companies, the capital requirements for banks have become even more important. During the build-up to the financial crisis from 2000 to 2007, U.S. bank capital requirements followed the model of Basel I.[46] Basel I creates perverse incentives due to its crude risk categories for bank assets, such as government securities, unsecured corporate loans or bonds, and MBS. Any asset within that broad category has the same risk rating for purposes of calculating capital, regardless of actual risk. For example, Basel I treats all unsecured corporate bonds as equally risky. Accordingly, it encourages banks to sell corporate bonds with low actual risk and to hold on to corporate bonds with high actual risk, because the capital requirements are the same for both types of bonds, but the riskier bonds usually have higher yields and higher expected returns.

Basel I Assumed Low Risks for All Residential Mortgages and MBS

More specifically to the financial crisis, Basel I effectively allowed the reduction of a bank's minimum capital requirement for all first-lien mortgages on residential homes. Although a bank was normally required to hold capital equal to 8 percent of its risk-weighted assets (4 percent of Tier 1 capital + 4 percent of Tier 2 capital—see Table 6.2), the capital requirement for residential mortgages was effectively only 4 percent of such assets. Again, Basel I allowed this reduction in a bank's

Table 6.2   Capital Tiers

Tier 1 Capital "Core"	Tier 2 Capital "Supplementary"
• Equity (common and perpetual preferred stock)	• Revaluation reserves
	• General provision/loan-loss reserves
• Preferred stock (bought by Treasury)	• Hybrid debt capital
• Retained post-tax earning	• Subordinated term debt

capital requirements regardless of the actual riskiness of the mortgages.[47] Thus, a prime mortgage with a 30 percent down payment and a subprime mortgage with a minimal down payment would both have the same 4 percent capital requirement. Further, the capital requirement for a highly rated tranche of MBS was effectively only 2 percent of risk-weighted assets, even if these securities were backed by a pool with a substantial portion of subprime loans!

Basel II Depends Too Much on Credit Ratings and Internal Risk Ratings

Basel II maintains the same minimum capital requirement of 8 percent of a bank's risk-weighted assets (4 percent in Tier I capital and 4 percent in Tier 2 capital), but it attempts to customize this requirement to the actual riskiness of a bank's assets. Large, internationally active U.S. banks must use the so-called advanced approach,[48] which bases their capital requirements primarily on inputs from a bank's own internal risk models, as well as credit ratings of bonds and other claims. **The advanced approach of Basel II has three main flaws, which need to be remedied quickly, because Basel II is in the process of being phased into practice from 2008 through 2010.**

First, until credit-rating agencies are reformed, Basel II should give very little weight to their ratings in calculating capital requirements for MBS or securities backed by other types of assets such as car loans or credit card receivables. The ratings of many asset-backed securities were downgraded shortly after they were issued, as explained in Chapter 3. These downgrades are symptomatic of the serious issues confronting credit-rating agencies. As Columbia Professor Charles Calomiris commented on credit-rating agencies: "Incentives were not properly aligned, as those that measured risk profited from underestimating it and earned large fees for doing so."[49]

Second, Basel II should not rely so heavily on the internal risk models of banks because they are too complex and subjective; they may also be based on unrealistic assumptions. (See Chapter 4.) FDIC Chair Sheila Bair remarked about the assumptions employed in the internal risk models of banks: "To say the assumptions turned out to be wrong would be an understatement."[50] Although a bank examiner does have the power to override these models under Basel II, many are very difficult to understand, especially for structured finance deals like the issuance of MBS. Former FDIC Chairman William Isaac had the following to say about the models built into Basel II:

> I've been in the business for nearly 40 years and I don't understand these models. It takes a mathematician and that is one of my principal objections to the models is that bank boards of directors and senior management, even senior regulatory people cannot understand these models.[51]

Third, although Basel II expanded the scope of capital analysis to include operational risk as well as interest rate and credit default risk, it should have also imposed some type of capital charges for liquidity risk. Liquidity risk means the chance that a bank cannot sell securities at a reasonable price because the trading volume in those securities has been reduced to a trickle. During the current financial crisis, many banks faced severe liquidity crunches. For example, at the end of 2008 banks could not sell short-term commercial paper at a reasonable price because the trading markets for such paper were effectively frozen. International bank regulators have recently proposed principles for consideration of liquidity risks by bankers.[52] For example, these principles say that banks should create strategies and managerial processes to address liquidity risks, and regularly disclose their liquidity risks to the market. However, these principles are qualitative in nature; they have no express capital charges for banks with significant liquidity risks.

Two Practical Approaches to Bank Capital

The broader challenge is to make Basel II less dependent on internal risk models and credit ratings, while moving toward capital requirements that are more refined than those of Basel I. **One sensible approach would be to create a set of capital rules with many subcategories based on objective factors: Each subcategory would have its own standard risk rating.** Home mortgages, for instance, could be divided into fixed rate and variable rate, and then into maturities of 5, 15, or 30 years. Residential mortgages could then be further subdivided within each category according to other factors, such as the loan-to-value ratio and insurance by third parties. This solution is similar to the standardized approach for calculating capital, proposed by regulators for banks with less than $250 billion in assets.[53] Unfortunately, the proposal would not permit this approach to be utilized by large banks because the regulators prefer the customization of the advanced approach.

A second sensible approach would be to combine a relatively simple leverage ratio based on average assets with a minimum requirement of subordinated debt. A simple leverage ratio would mean that a bank had to maintain Tier 1 capital at a specified percentage (e.g., 3 percent) of its quarterly assets *without* any reductions in assets due to their risk ratings. In other words, a bank would total its assets without regard to whether they were mortgages, commercial loans or corporate bonds. Then it would hold the specified percentage of Tier I capital relative to its total assets. Such a leverage ratio would have the virtue of simplicity, but it would lack a refined analysis of the composition of a bank's assets. That function could be performed to a significant degree by the investors in the bank's subordinated debt.

A bank would be required to have subordinated debt, capable of absorbing losses and equal to a specified percentage of its capital.[54] Subordinated debt is a form of a bond typically bought from banks by sophisticated investors. They usually receive a relatively high interest on subordinated debt because it ranks so low in priority that it would be virtually worthless in the event the bank became insolvent. **The mandatory inclusion of subordinated debt in a bank's capital would provide an independent and market-based monitor of its riskiness.** The trading price of a bank's subordinated debt would move up or down depending upon the market's perception of the bank's risk of default. Such a requirement for subordinated debt at large banks was studied in 2000 by the Federal Reserve, which concluded that significant evidence exists to support subordinated debt as an effective means of encouraging market discipline.[55] However, the Federal Reserve's position was opposed by the banking industry and was never implemented.

The Need for Anticyclical Measures

Many commentators have pointed out that Basel II is procyclical—that is, it reinforces the prevailing economic trends. In fact, Basel II does allow banks to expand in good times, but requires banks to raise more capital in bad times as they increase the risk ratings on their assets and incur loan losses. Of course, during these bad times, it is very difficult for banks to raise capital or replenish loan losses. But many bankers tend to delay increases in their loan loss reserves until the economy is already deteriorating.[56] **The solution: Regulators should use their supervisory powers under Basel II to require that banks adopt anticyclical measures, building up contingent loan loss reserves and excess capital in good times to provide more cushion to absorb the shocks of bad times.** (The effects of fair market value accounting will be addressed in Chapter 12.)

Banks Should Establish Contingent Reserves in Good Times

Anticyclical measures were introduced in Spain in 2000. Spanish banks were required to increase loan loss reserves when lending was increasing rapidly, and allowed to draw down reserves when lending cooled.[57] As a result of these measures, Spanish banks recorded loan loss reserves equal to 255 percent of nonperforming loans in 2006 at the height of the credit boom, as compared to 55 percent in the United Kingdom.[58] At the end of March, 2009, the two largest Spanish banks had not received any government capital.[59] Nonetheless, recent evidence suggests that even these increased loan loss reserves were insufficient. Heading into the credit crisis, Spanish banks reportedly held loan loss reserves equal to 1.5 percent of risk-weighted assets, while many major banks in Europe and the United States incurred loan losses over 10 percent of risk-weighted assets.[60]

In the United States, unfortunately, excess loan loss reserves have been strongly discouraged by the SEC, together with related accounting and tax rules. As an investor protection agency, the SEC is mainly concerned with making sure that banks accurately present their income for each reporting period. Specifically, the SEC has been worried that banks are allocating excess reserves for loan losses in good times as a way to manage their incomes. If a bank allocates large amounts to its loan loss reserves in good times, it can downplay its reported net income by subtracting these amounts as expenses. Later, in bad times, it can exaggerate its net income by reducing additions to its loan loss reserves and quietly absorbing its actual losses through the excess reserves built up in good times.

The SEC drove home its position in 1998 by questioning the size of the loan loss reserve of SunTrust Bank, when it tried to clear a registration statement in connection with a stock acquisition of a smaller bank.[61] To obtain SEC clearance of its registration statement, SunTrust was effectively forced to reduce its loan loss provision by a total of $100 million for three prior years. The SunTrust case was reinforced by a statement from a senior SEC official suggesting "that allowances for loan losses reported by some U.S. banks may be overstated."[62] The banks got the message; they kept loan loss reserves down to the minimum necessary to cover probable losses.

The SEC's position on loan loss reserves has long been criticized by the banking regulators. They want to see large loan loss reserves, calculated on the most conservative basis, to protect the safety and soundness of the banking system. Basel II encourages banks to maintain relatively large loan loss reserves by counting them as Tier 2 capital.[63] However, this will not happen if the SEC brings enforcement actions against banks with large reserves for misrepresenting their income. United States Treasury Secretary Geithner has called for a revision of current rules to create sufficient loan loss reserves to cover significant losses in a downturn.[64]

The federal regulators should allow banks in good times to establish a contingent reserve, in addition to its normal loan loss reserve, up to a total of three or four times its normal reserves.

To satisfy the SEC, banks should be required to prominently display the contingent reserve as a separate item excluded from the calculation of its current net income.[65] Furthermore, the bank regulators could develop various indicators of good times; in those periods, banks would be required to set aside some minimum to fund contingent reserves. For instance, banks could be told to establish a contingent reserve equal to 100 percent of the normal reserve if annual GDP growth exceeded 3 percent, and up to 200 percent of the normal reserve if annual GDP growth exceeded 4 percent per year. In this manner, banks could build up loan loss reserves in good times without misleading investors.

Anticyclical Capital Requirements to Cope with Excess Leverage

Excess leverage, together with Basel II, is a strong exaggerator of cyclical effects, expanding too much in good times and contracting sharply in bad times. In good times, individuals and corporations borrow and spend more on consumer goods. Individuals and corporations may also spend borrowed money on income-producing assets like real estate. Similarly, in good times, the capital of banks is rising under Basel II. Consequently, banks are prepared to lend more money and buy more assets. If enough money chases the same assets, asset bubbles can form—such as our recent housing bubble.

The negative procyclical effects of borrowed money happen when economies decline. During economic recessions, unemployment increases and asset values decrease. Both factors increase loan losses at banks because unemployed individuals are less able to make debt payments, and falling asset values mean banks receive less at auction for repossessed loan collateral. Under Basel II, rising losses at banks reduce their capital, making them curtail their lending. As a result, it becomes more expensive for businesses to finance expansion projects. Consumers also decrease their spending, because they are worried about the economy, and they are feeling poorer because their home and investment portfolios have just declined in value.

To illustrate the negative procyclical effects of borrowed money on financial firms, consider the example of Bear Stearns. Prior to its forced acquisition by J.P. Morgan in March of 2008, Bear Stearns had less than

$12 billion of tangible equity backing assets of $395 billion, translating into a leverage ratio of more than 33 to 1.[66] This meant that just a 3 percent decline in asset value would have been enough to wipe out almost all of the firm's equity capital. Even worse, a large portion of Bear's assets were funded by short-term borrowed money. This meant that if enough short-term lenders asked for their money back at once, Bear would have to raise cash by selling assets quickly at a loss.

Because too much financial leverage causes procyclicality, the solution is to mandate greater buffers of equity capital. Specifically, banks should build up a substantial capital cushion during good times to ensure an adequate margin of safety during bad times. As recommended by former Fed Chairman Paul Volcker and the Group of 30, regulators should accomplish this goal by raising the regulatory range for being well-capitalized during good times.[67] In those times, financial institutions should operate at the top of the range, because the worst loans are typically originated during good times. **Furthermore, very large financial institutions should generally hold more capital than smaller institutions. Because these institutions are likely to be bailed out at the taxpayers' expense, the United States should reduce their risk of failure by asking them to hold more capital than usual.**[68] In good times, for example, a bank might be classified as well-capitalized if its Tier 1 capital relative to risk-based assets was in the 8–10 percent range, instead of 6 percent as currently. Similarly, a bank might be classified as well-capitalized if its total capital (Tier 1 plus Tier 2) relative to risk-based assets was in the 12 to 14 percent range, instead of the current 10 percent. During good economic times, banks would be expected to maintain capital levels near the top of these ranges to act as a buffer against subsequent downturns.[69]

Summary

The five largest investment banks in the United States—Bear Stearns, Goldman Sachs, Lehman Brothers, Merrill Lynch, and Morgan Stanley (the Five Investment Banks)—were transformed during 2008. Two failed, one was acquired, and two converted to bank holding companies. The SEC facilitated the transformation of these Five Investment Banks by allowing them to more than double their leverage ratios. In addition, the SEC's new program for consolidated supervision of the Five Investment Banks was ineffective.

Nevertheless, the concept of consolidated supervision is critical to a viable regulatory system for diversified financial conglomerates. Because each of the financial services is regulated by a different agency, one government body needs to have supervisory authority over the consolidated group to prevent regulatory gaps and to monitor transactions within the group. The Federal Reserve plays this role for banking groups, and the SEC should play this role for any broker-dealer not within a banking group. A state can serve as the consolidated supervisor for most insurers, which are currently chartered and regulated by the states. However, Congress should authorize a federal charter for a small number of U.S.-based, global life insurers with a new federal agency to supervise the consolidated group of each such insurer.

The repeal of the Glass Steagall Act was at most a minor factor contributing to the current financial crisis. A decade before its repeal, federal regulators allowed banks and bank holding companies to deal and underwrite in most stocks and most bonds. The recent problems of the banking industry are mainly due to credit losses on loans and bonds, rather than their underwriting activities. Moreover, universal banks are superior formats to stand-alone investment banks because the latter rely primarily on commercial paper and repurchase agreements for short-term financing, whereas the former have two more sources of short-term financing: insured deposits and Federal Reserve loans.

Because all the Five Investment Banks have become parts of banking organizations, the capital requirements for banks have become even more important. Basel I, which was in effect until the beginning of 2008, encouraged a bank to hold subprime mortgages because they were subject to only half the normal 8 percent capital requirement, and highly rated MBS because they were subject to only one-fourth the normal 8 percent capital requirement. Basel I also did not address many of the capital market transactions in which banks participated.

Although Basel II provides a more refined set of capital rules than Basel I, the new rules are too dependent on the rating of bonds by credit-rating agencies and assessments by internal bank risk models. In addition, the new rules are devilishly complex and give too little attention to liquidity risk. One solution would be to create 10 to 20 categories and subcategories of bank assets, which would be linked to capital requirements by objective factors such as collateral types and loan-to-value ratios. Another solution would be for the bank examiners to enforce a simple leverage ratio together with market monitoring through a requirement for banks to have a specified percentage of their capital in the form of subordinated debt.

Finally, Basel II is procyclical, allowing banks to expand rapidly in good times and requiring them to raise capital or sell assets in bad times. In bad times, banks cannot usually raise capital, so they are forced to sell assets at inferior prices. As many banks in the same situation sell assets, this creates a downward spiral in asset prices. The logical solution would be to encourage banks to build up large loan loss reserves in good times. However, the SEC opposes the build-up of excess reserves as a potentially deceptive method of banks to manage their net income reported to investors.

Banking regulators should require banks to establish a contingent loan loss reserve, in addition to their normal reserves, up to three or four times the size of their normal reserves. This should be allowed only in good times as defined by the bank regulators, for example, if annual GDP growth exceeds a specified percentage. In such good times, the SEC should require these banks to disclose, specifically and prominently, that they have reduced their net income by allocating a specified amount of money to a contingent loan loss reserve. In this manner, banks will be better prepared for bad times without misleading investors.

Excess leverage is a powerful driver of procyclicality. Therefore, bank regulators should increase capital requirements in good times so that there will be a sufficient cushion to absorb losses in bad times. These capital requirements should be especially strict for very large banks, because they are the ones most likely to be deemed too big to fail.

Chapter 7

Impact on Short-Term Lending

$\mathbf{S}$hort-term lending is one of the engines that drive the American economy, through loans to small firms to run their businesses and through loans to consumers to finance their purchases of goods. As the crisis expanded during the summer of 2008, the market deteriorated for short-term loans and commercial paper, a form of corporate borrowing with maturities ranging from 1 to 270 days. But the saving grace was the federal government, which had protected all holders of bonds and commercial paper when it rescued Bear Stearns in March, 2008. Then the bomb exploded in the short-term lending market; the federal government allowed Lehman Brothers to fail and holders of its bonds to suffer heavy losses. A notable loser was the Reserve Fund, a money market fund that held $785 million in commercial paper of Lehman on the date of its bankruptcy.[1]

After Lehman's failure, investors no longer could count on the U.S. government to bail out all troubled financial institutions. Investors were surprised and scared, as explained by a financial guru named Colin Negrych:

> Folks were shocked to find the US government unwilling to throw good money after bad at Lehman. This discovery caused market participants to question whether the government would support other large financial entities which they knew to be, or strongly suspected of being, in financial distress, when this support had previously been taken as a given.[2]

As a result, few banks or money market funds were willing to buy commercial paper; or, looked at from the other side, few corporations or banks could borrow money for more than a week. In particular, banks developed an incredible aversion toward lending to each other. Consider Figure 7.1, which shows the difference between 3-month London Interbank Offered Rate (LIBOR) and the U.S. federal funds rate. LIBOR is the standard measure of the interest rate charged for a loan by one bank to another. The fed funds rate is the short-term interest rate target set by the Federal Reserve. Note that the difference between LIBOR and the U.S. policy rate was roughly 0.2 percent in January of 2008, but

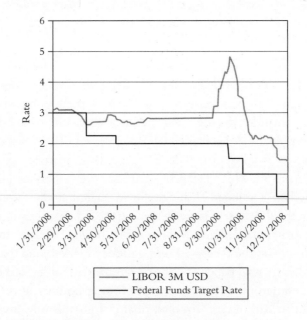

Figure 7.1   3–Month LIBOR vs. Fed Funds Rate
SOURCE: Federal Reserve, Bloomberg.

jumped to over 2 percent in October of 2008. In other words, U.S. banks demanded to be paid 10 times more to lend to other banks in October of 2008 than in January of 2008!

Why does this risk aversion among banks matter for the rest of the economy? First, if banks have to pay high interest rates to borrow from each other, they will probably charge even higher rates to companies seeking loans. This means some companies will cut back employment or production because they cannot obtain sufficient financing for their inventories or payrolls. Second, the rates on many credit cards and adjustable mortgages are pegged to LIBOR, so a higher LIBOR will translate into higher rates for consumers and homeowners. This means that more individuals will default on their credit cards or mortgages. Third, some banks and money market funds may need a lot of cash quickly to meet substantial withdrawals by customers. If they cannot borrow enough money in enough time to meet withdrawal requests, they may fail.

To encourage lending between banks and from banks to customers, the Federal Reserve has pursued its traditional strategy of cutting short-term interest rates. After bringing those rates down to zero by the end of 2008, the Federal Reserve went far beyond its traditional role by purchasing MBS in the open market, lending Treasury securities to a broad range of financial institutions, and purchasing commercial paper from industrial companies as well as money market funds. This chapter will outline the positive impact of these unprecedented steps by the Federal Reserve, and will then discuss the potential adverse implications for the Fed's ability to head off inflation in the future.

At the same time, the FDIC has guaranteed 100 percent of most debt issued by banks, thrifts, and their holding companies—originally in order to facilitate the refinancing of over $1 trillion in unsecured bank debt maturing before June 30, 2009.[3] This chapter will argue that the depth and breadth of these guarantees undermines the market discipline usually exerted by sophisticated investors on banks.

Cutting Short-Term Rates, but Worrying about Long-Term Inflation

When the economy slows down, the standard response of the Federal Reserve is to reduce short-term interest rates. Cutting interest rates usually stimulates the economy by increasing demand for loans from firms due to the lower costs of doing business. Lower rates also stimulate the economy by increasing consumer demand through the reduced cost of borrowing on credit cards and home mortgages. This is exactly what the Federal Reserve has done since September 2007, when it began to reduce its target rate for federal funds. The federal funds rate is the one used by banks when they lend or borrow excess reserves to or from each other on an overnight basis. Step by step, the Fed reduced its target rate to reach a range of 0–0.25 percent at the end of December, 2008, so further cuts in short-term interest rates are no longer possible. Table 7.1 shows the progression of the Fed's cuts in its target rate from the fall of 2007 through the end of 2008.

Cutting Interest Rates Has Its Limits

The Fed's cutting of short-term rates has not spurred economic growth in 2008 and 2009 because interest rates are not the main factors constraining short-term lending in this recession. As mentioned already, banks have not been lending because they fear defaults from even the largest borrowers and want to preserve their liquidity to deal with emergencies.

Table 7.1 Federal Funds Rates

| Date | Change (Basis Points) | | Level (percent) |
	Increase	Decrease	
2008			
December 16	...	75–100	0–0.25
October 29	...	50	1
October 8	...	50	1.5
April 30	...	25	2.00
March 18	...	75	2.25
January 30	...	50	3.00
January 22	...	75	3.50
2007			
December 11	...	25	4.25
October 31	...	25	4.50
September 18	...	50	4.75

SOURCE: www.federalreserve.gov/fomc/fundsrate.htm.

The prevailing mindset was, if Lehman failed, which institution will be next? Banks also have been husbanding their cash to cover mounting losses on existing loans and MBS already in their portfolios.

By reducing its target rate, the Fed can bring down short-term interest rates in the United States. However, the Fed normally has much less influence over long-term interest rates, which are critical to the mortgage market. To help decrease long-term mortgage rates, the Fed announced that it would purchase up to $1.45 trillion of outstanding bonds and MBS from Fannie Mae and Freddie Mac during 2009.[4] As a result, the rates on 30-year mortgages initially dropped below 5 percent, though they rose back above 5 percent in June of 2009. This initial drop in long-term rates allowed many homeowners to refinance their mortgages and make lower monthly payments.

As the recession lingers, despite interest rates close to zero, the Fed is legitimately concerned about the threat of deflation. Deflation means a widespread decline in prices—usually reflected in the consumer price index—that can build a downward momentum. Deflation typically occurs when there is a collapse in aggregate demand that is so severe that firms must cut prices to find buyers. As buyers see prices dropping across the board, they delay spending in the expectation that prices will drop further if they delay. The Fed has been trying to prevent deflation during this crisis by taking extraordinary actions (called quantitative easing). In addition to buying mortgage-related bonds, as mentioned earlier, the Fed announced that it would buy $300 billion in long-term U.S. Treasuries in order to reduce long-term interest rates.[5]

Why is the Fed so concerned about having a recession together with price deflation? These situations pose two serious risks, as elaborated by Fed Chairman Ben Bernanke:

> First, when the nominal interest rate has been reduced to zero, the *real* interest rate paid by the borrowers equals the expected rate of deflation . . . In a period of sufficiently severe deflation, the real cost of borrowing becomes prohibitive. Capital investment, purchases of new homes, and other types of spending decline accordingly, worsening the economic downturn.[6]

> Second, when prices are falling because of deflation, households and firms with existing debt must repay the principal in dollars of increasing

value. (This is just the opposite effect of inflation, when existing debtors can repay principal with ever-cheaper dollars.) If deflation occurs in the United States, existing debtors will default more often as they scramble to repay principal with more expensive dollars. Consequently, deflation would put more pressure on an already fragile U.S. banking system.

Investors Are Concerned about Inflation

Although deflation is a threat in the short term, in the long term a greater concern is run-away inflation. This concern is based mainly on the stubbornly high levels of budget deficits in the United States, together with the ballooning of the Fed's balance sheet discussed below. In 2008–2009, the federal budget deficit was about $1.6 trillion, over 11 percent of gross domestic product (GDP).[7] This is the largest budget deficit in the United States since World War II by a huge margin—the second largest budget deficit was 6 percent of GDP in the 1983 when it was only $442 billion in inflation adjusted dollars. Despite the best intentions of the Obama Administration, deficits are likely to be in the range of $1 trillion each year over the next decade, according to an independent analysis by the Brookings Institution.[8] The Obama Administration will try to raise the top tax rate on income from 35 percent to 39.6 percent for those with annual incomes of $250,000 or higher. But these revenue gains from the top earners are substantially less than the Obama Administration's continuation of the Bush tax cuts for middle and lower-income families.[9]

At present, inflationary forces are on hold in the United States because of the weak economy and lower energy prices. In addition, foreign investors have been flocking to U.S. Treasuries as a safe haven. However, these factors are likely to change as the economy picks up steam through the stimulus package, and foreign investors focus on the inflationary implications of huge U.S. budget deficits. Foreign investors will demand much higher rates on long-term Treasuries if they fear that the value of the U.S. dollar will decline because the U.S. government intends to print money to cover its huge deficits.

For instance, on March 13, 2009, Chinese Premier Wen Jiabao expressed concern about the safety of China's huge holdings of U.S. Treasuries, which was widely interpreted as concern about rising

U.S. budget deficits leading to inflation and a weaker dollar.[10] Responding to a question after a speech at Peking University, Treasury Secretary Geithner tried to assure the audience that "Chinese assets are very safe" in the U.S. His assurances were greeted with loud laughter from the crowd.[11] When Richard Fisher, President of the Federal Reserve of Dallas, went to China in the spring of 2009, he was asked repeatedly why the Fed was buying back long-term Treasury debt: "senior officials of the Chinese government grill[ed] me about whether or not we are going to monetize the actions of our legislature."[12] The officials were worried that the Fed would use its monetary powers to buy U.S. public debt created by large budget deficits in Congress.

Given these concerns, the Federal Reserve needs to make sure that it does not destabilize future expectations about inflation by rigidly sticking with low interest rates. Columbia Professor Frederic Mishkin, a former governor of the Federal Reserve, wrote: "It needs to communicate that it will be flexible in the opposite direction by raising rates quickly if there is a rapid recovery in financial markets, or if there is an upward shift in projections for future inflation."[13]

The Fed Should Adopt an Inflation Target

How can the Federal Reserve demonstrate that it will reverse directions by raising interest rates promptly after the threat of inflation materializes? By adopting an inflation target—an express policy to raise interest rates if core inflation (excluding food, energy, and seasonal factors) exceeds a specified percentage for a specified time period. This subject has been extensively debated by economists.[14] The opponents of inflation targets emphasize that the Fed's mandate includes two goals: keeping prices stable and maximizing employment. They worry because an inflation target might lead the Fed to raise interest rates to promote price stability at a time when unemployment is high. On the other hand, Canada, England, and Sweden have adopted inflation targets, which have effectively anchored expectations about inflation. In addition, supporters of inflation targets argue that the Fed's primary mission is to maintain price stability, with maximizing employment as a secondary goal.

In my opinion, the Fed should adopt an inflation target, expressed in terms of a range to permit the Fed a degree of

flexibility. And the Fed should move quickly because it is much easier politically to adopt an inflation target when rates are being lowered than when they are being raised. Although the Fed recently started to publish a longer term economic forecast, considered to be an informal constraint on inflation, its formal adoption would help defuse the concerns of foreign investors about the future of the U.S. dollar. Also, the adoption of an inflation target would help the Fed educate Congress and the American public about the rationale for its interest-rate decisions. For instance, the Fed could explain today's zero interest rates by pointing to today's very low rate of price inflation. Then, when inflation rears its ugly head, the Fed could explain that it is raising rates because consumer price increases exceed its inflation target.

Even if the Fed has an articulate rationale and the political will to raise interest rates, it needs sufficient tools to accomplish the goal. The Fed has flooded the financial system with dollars in a noble effort to expand liquidity and revive the economy. When price inflation becomes a serious threat, the Fed should be in a position to promptly drain a huge amount of dollars from the U.S. economy. As the economy improves, many of the Fed's short-term lending programs should naturally wind down. In addition, the Fed normally sells the Treasury securities in its portfolio to drain dollars from the financial system.

However, as explained later in this chapter, U.S. Treasuries comprised only 30 percent of the Fed's $2.1 trillion portfolio as of June 10, 2009. In helping to implement the bank bailout, the Fed has promised longer-term loans to partnerships to purchase troubled assets, and it has guaranteed against losses almost $400 billion in troubled assets. The Fed is also making from $200 billion to $1 trillion in longer-term loans to finance the purchase of newly issued asset-backed securities. These longer-term loans and asset guarantees cannot be easily withdrawn or sold to drain dollars from the economy.

To create an additional tool to influence the economy, the Fed should focus on the interest rate it pays on bank reserves maintained at the central bank. In the fall of 2008, Congress for the first time allowed the Fed to pay interest on such bank reserves, which have rapidly built up from $3 billion to close to $800 billion by June of 2009. This build-up of bank reserves has decreased funds currently available for lending by banks, which can earn a reasonable risk-free rate by maintaining large reserves at the Fed. On the other hand, if the economy starts to take off, these reserves can be easily withdrawn by banks to make loans, thereby fueling inflation. **Accordingly, the Fed should pay a very low rate on bank reserves in the present environment to encourage more lending. Later, as Chairman Bernanke recognizes, when price inflation becomes a threat, the Fed should hike the rate it pays on bank reserves to draw dollars out of circulation.**

The Fed Vastly Expands Its Lending Programs

Traditionally, the Federal Reserve has allowed member banks to borrow money from its discount window on an overnight basis. This borrowing facility was only utilized by banks when they were in serious financial trouble, and they were required to collateralize the borrowing with U.S. Treasuries or other government agency bonds. However, when the short-term borrowing market began to falter in late 2007, the Federal Reserve expanded its borrowing programs and removed the historical stigma associated with borrowing from the discount window. In addition, the Federal Reserve introduced new programs to buy commercial paper from industrial companies, finance the purchase of asset-backed securities and make dollar loans to foreign central banks. These expanded and new programs have been critical in keeping the U.S. economy afloat, given the sharp contraction in private-sector lending during 2008 and 2009.

Outline of the Fed's New Lending Programs

Table 7.2 outlines the new programs implemented by the Federal Reserve. In December of 2007, it started a facility to allow depository institutions to borrow monies from the Federal Reserve for a longer term and with a broader range of collateral than the normal requirements for the discount window.[15] On March 11, 2008, the Federal Reserve initiated another facility for primary dealers—the small group of big brokers and banks that help the Fed implement monetary policy—to exchange liquid Treasury bonds for illiquid MBS with an investment-grade credit rating.[16]

Table 7.2 Federal Reserve: New Lending and Purchase Programs

Program Name	Date Operational	Description and Purpose
Term Auction Facility (**TAF**)	First Auction 12/2007	Federal Reserve will auction "term funds" to depository institutions. All depository institutions that are eligible to borrow under the primary credit program will be eligible to participate in TAF auctions.
		All advances must be fully collateralized.
		Each TAF auction will be for a fixed amount, with the term loan's interest rate determined by the auction process (subject to a minimum).
Term Securities Lending Facility (**TSLF**)	3/2008–	Weekly loan facility that promotes liquidity in Treasury and other collateral markets and thus fosters the functioning of financial markets more generally.
		Program offers Treasury securities held by the System Open Market Account (SOMA) for loan over a one-month term against other program-eligible general collateral.
		Securities loans are awarded to primary dealers based on a competitive single-price auction.
Primary Dealer Credit Facility (**PDCF**)	3/2008	An overnight loan facility that provides funding to primary dealers, in exchange for a specified range of eligible collateral.
Asset-Backed Commercial Paper Money Market Mutual Fund Liquidity Facility (**AMLF or ABCP MMFLF**)	9/2008	Lending facility that provides funding to U.S. depository institutions and bank holding companies to finance their purchases of high-quality asset-backed commercial paper (ABCP) from money market mutual funds under certain conditions.
		Intended to assist money funds that hold such paper in meeting demands for redemptions by investors and to foster liquidity in the ABCP market and money markets more generally.

Money Market Investor Funding Facility (**MMIFF**)	11/20085*	MMIFF (authorized by the Board under Section 13(3) of the Federal Reserve Act) supports a private-sector initiative designed to provide liquidity to U.S. money market investors.
		New York Fed will provide senior secured funding to a series of special purpose vehicles to facilitate an industry-supported private-sector initiative to finance the purchase of commercial paper not backed by assets from participating money market funds.
Commercial Paper Funding Facility (**CPFF**)	10/2008	Created by the Fed to provide a liquidity backstop to U.S. issuers of commercial paper.
		Federal Reserve Bank of New York finances the purchase of highly rated unsecured and asset-backed commercial paper from eligible issuers via eligible primary dealers.
		Money market mutual funds and other investors had become reluctant to purchase CP, especially at longer dated maturities. An increasingly high percentage of outstanding CP had to be refinanced each day, interest rates on longer term CP increased significantly and volume declined.
		CPFF is intended to increase availability of term CP funding to issuers and to provide greater assurance to issuers and investors that firms will be able to roll over maturing CP.
Term Asset Backed Securities Loan Facility (**TALF**)	3/2009 – TALF financing also available for private-public partnerships to purchase toxic assets from banks. (see Chapter 10).	TALF is a funding facility that will help market participants by supporting new issuances of asset-backed securities (ABS) collateralized by student loans, auto loans, credit card loans, and loans guaranteed by the Small Business Administration (SBA).
		Federal Reserve Bank of New York (FRBNY) will lend up to $200 billion on a non-recourse basis to holders of certain AAA-rated ABS backed by newly and recently originated consumer and small business loans.
		FRBNY will lend an amount equal to the market value of the ABS less a haircut and will be secured at all times by the ABS. The U.S. Treasury Department—under the Troubled Assets Relief Program (TARP) of the Emergency Economic Stabilization Act of 2008—will provide $20 billion of credit protection to the FRBNY in connection with the TALF.

*Did not become operational by September 1, 2009.

On March 17, 2008, just after the fall of Bear Stearns, the Federal Reserve started to provide cash advances to primary dealers.[17] This was the first time in history that the Federal Reserve had loaned cash to institutions other than commercial banks. The CEO of Bear Stearns, Jimmy Cayne, was livid because the Federal Reserve waited to make this historic move until *after* Bear Stearns went down. Cayne berated the then president of the Federal Reserve Bank of New York, who did not believe Bear Stearns was sufficiently creditworthy to borrow cash from the Federal Reserve. "You're not an elected official. You're a clerk. Believe me, you're a clerk."[18] That clerk, Timothy Geithner, is now Secretary of the Treasury.

As banks and investors became reluctant to buy even highly rated commercial paper, money market funds could not easily sell such paper if they were faced with a flood of shareholder redemptions. Money market funds are a type of mutual fund whose investments are limited to highly rated commercial paper, certificates of deposits of banks, or government bonds with an average maturity of 90 days or less. To help money market funds meet redemption requests, the Federal Reserve in September of 2008 began lending to banks for the specific purpose of purchasing, from money market funds, commercial paper backed by assets.[19] Later in 2008, the Federal Reserve supported the establishment of a private-sector facility to buy, from money market funds, commercial paper not backed by assets or certificates of deposits of banks. The Federal Reserve plans to make loans to this facility so that it can buy up to $600 billion in eligible short-term paper from money market funds.[20]

After the failure of Lehman Brothers, large companies like AT&T struggled to issue highly rated commercial paper at reasonable rates for a term longer than 30 days. In response, the Federal Reserve took a great leap forward by creating a special vehicle to purchase commercial paper—both unsecured and asset backed—directly from nonfinancial companies. The facility has purchased only U.S. dollar-denominated commercial paper with the highest rating.[21]

Similarly, after Lehman's collapse, the trading market dried up for securities backed by consumer loans, such as auto, credit card, and student loans. In response, the U.S. Treasury in November of 2008 announced the creation of a new program that will make loans on very attractive terms to private investors to buy securitized assets. As detailed in Chapter 10, the Treasury has provided $20 billion in credit protection to the Federal Reserve to support $200 billion to $1 trillion in low-interest, nonrecourse loans to private investors to purchase new issues of securities backed by consumer and other loans.[22] The Fed has also committed to making low-interest, nonrecourse loans to partnerships between the Treasury and private investors to help find buyers for up to $1 trillion in toxic assets from banks. (A nonrecourse loan means the borrower will not be liable if the loan is not repaid).

In addition, the Federal Reserve actively participated in the bailout of several financial institutions during 2008. It made a $28.8 billion loan to a special fund set up to purchase $30 billion in troubled assets from Bear Stearns. The Federal Reserve loaned over $40 billion to a special vehicle to purchase AIG's troubled assets. When the federal government agreed to guarantee $301 billion in troubled assets for Citigroup, the New York bank was obliged to absorb the first $29 billion of losses but only 10 percent of the remainder. With respect to 90 percent of the losses above the $29 billion, the Treasury and the FDIC will together absorb $15 billion, leaving the Federal Reserve with a potential loss exposure of over $220 billion.[23] In a similar arrangement with Bank of America to guarantee against losses of $118 billion in troubled assets, the Federal Reserve could have a potential loss exposure of approximately $87 billion. (See Chapters 9 and 10.)

Finally, the Federal Reserve committed over $550 billion in currency swaps at the end of 2008 to the central banks of foreign countries to help them supply U.S. dollars to local businesses, which need to pay off their loans and finance international trade. For instance, the Fed made a $30 billion loan to each of the central banks of Brazil, Mexico, Korea, and Singapore.

The Fed's efforts to revive the short-term lending markets have been very helpful, though there is more to be done. The demand for commercial paper maturing in over 30 days has been rising, and the 3-month LIBOR has been declining as banks lend more to each other.[24] However, we are a long way from normal markets for short-term lending. As explained by Mervyn King, the Governor of the Bank of England: "But the age of innocence—when banks lent to each other unsecured for three months or longer only at a slight premium to expected policy rates—will not quickly, if ever, return."[25]

Has the Fed Compromised Its Independence?

All these programs have substantially increased the size of the Federal Reserve's balance sheet and its exposure to losses. The size of the Fed's balance sheet has ballooned from $859 billion in October, 2007 to $2.1 trillion on June 10, 2009. In October of 2007, over 90 percent of the Fed's portfolio was comprised of U.S. Treasury securities. As of June 10, 2009, U.S. Treasury securities comprised only 30 percent of the Fed's portfolio, which was now crammed with commercial paper, MBS, and other debt obtained through the facilities described earlier.[26] (These percentages do not include most of the Fed's guarantee of troubled assets in government bailouts, already outlined.)

The Fed's programs for buying and lending against corporate assets pose the risk of substantial credit losses, though so far the Fed has generally profited from its risky assets. The Fed has bought large amounts of commercial paper and financed purchases of asset-backed securities issued by private entities. Moreover, by participating in the bailouts of Bear Stearns, AIG, Citigroup, and Bank of America, the Federal Reserve has gained considerable exposure to truly troubled assets, such as commercial real estate holdings and credit default swaps.

The Fed's main job is to set and implement monetary policy: This job requires an independent agency. If the Fed incurs significant losses due to its large exposures to troubled assets, it would become subject to political criticism and might seek budget support from the U.S. Treasury.[27] If the Fed becomes vulnerable to political influences, it might not be able or willing to raise interest rates when economically necessary but politically unpopular.

By contrast, the Treasury is an integral part of the administration currently in power; it should be the main vehicle to set and implement fiscal policy. Charles Plosser, President of the Federal Reserve Bank of Philadelphia, has opposed the Fed's financing of toxic assets as crossing the line between its traditional role in implementing monetary policy and its unprecedented actions in supporting the government's fiscal policy: "We need to draw a bright line once again between monetary and fiscal policy. The recent crisis has muddied that separation considerably and we must restore it. The Fed must not be seen by the public or the Congress as a piggy bank that can substitute for difficult policy decisions."[28]

To protect the independence of the Fed, it should insist that the Treasury finance the purchase of corporate assets and provide loss guarantees for troubled assets in bailouts of financial institutions. Bailouts are complex political decisions by the President and executive branch, so the burden of these decisions should be borne by the U.S. Treasury rather than the Federal Reserve. If the Fed is the only available source of emergency loans in a financial bailout, these loans should be transferred to the executive branch as soon as practical. The Treasury has made a vague promise to acquire or otherwise remove from the Fed's balance sheet the toxic assets it acquires. However, this promise is open-ended and conditional—"in the long term and as authorities permit. . ."[29] Moreover, the Treasury is trying to link the bailout decisions of the executive branch more closely to the emergency lending powers of the Fed by requiring it to obtain advance approval from the Treasury before exercising any of these powers.[30]

The Fed's active participation in the bank bailout also raises fundamental questions about the role of Congress in controlling expenditures by federal agencies. Congress has appropriated $700 billion for the bank bailout, most of which has already been spent. To avoid going back to Congress for more monies, the Treasury has been relying heavily on the lending capacity of the Fed. As mentioned earlier, the Treasury provided $100 billion in credit support so the Fed could loan up to $1 trillion to private investors to buy asset-backed securities. Similarly, the Treasury guaranteed only a small portion of Citigroup's troubled assets; most of those assets were guaranteed against loss by the Fed. The Fed's maximum potential exposure to the financial bailout exceeded $7.3 trillion at the end of March 2009, although its actual exposure was almost $1.8 trillion.[31] As shown in Table 7.3, this $7.3 trillion included the Fed's commitments to purchase assets and make loans to various programs described in this chapter, as well as its guarantees of troubled assets.

So far Congress has implicitly acquiesced to the Treasury's avoidance strategy despite receiving relatively little information about the details of the Fed's involvement in the financial bailout. However, on two nonbinding resolutions, large majorities in the U.S. Senate have called on the Fed to release more information on its emergency loans, and so has one lower court.[32] In the U.S. House of Representatives, 208 Congressmen have co-sponsored a bill removing long-standing limits

Table 7.3 Maximum and Actual Exposure of Federal Reserve to the Financial Bailout ($Bn)

As of March 25, 2009	Maximum Exposure[a]	Actual Exposure[b]
1. Depository Institutions and Primary Dealers		
Term Securities Lending Facility (TSLF)	250.00	88.50
Term Auction Facility (TAF)	900.00	468.00
Primary dealer credit	94.00	20.00
2. Money Market Funds		
Asset-Backed Commercial Paper Liquidity Facility (AMLF)	24.00	7.00
Money Market Investor Fund Facility (MMIFF)	540.00[c]	0.00
3. Non-Recourse Loans to Buy Securities		
Term Asset Backed Loan Facility (TALF)	1,000.00[d]	5.00
Commercial Paper Funding Facility (CPFF)	1,800.00[e]	241.00
4. Commitments to Buy Long-Term		
Fannie-Freddie securities and MBS	1,450.00[f]	286.60
US Treasuries	300.00[f]	7.50[g]
5. Bailout of Institutions		
AIG loans	60.00	43.10
Maiden Lane I (Bear Stearns)	27.00[h]	26.20
Maiden Lane II (AIG)	20.00[h]	18.40
Maiden Lane III (AIG)	27.00[h]	27.00
Citigroup guarantee of troubled assets	220.40	220.40[i]
Bank of America guarantee of troubled assets	87.40	0.00[j]
6. Currency Swaps with Foreign Central Banks	554.00[k]	328.00
Fed Total ($Bn)	**7,353.80**	**1,786.70**

[a] Unless denoted otherwise, all figures in this column are based upon FDIC "Supervisory Insights" (Summer 2009). These figures represent the maximum potential exposure that could be taken on by the Federal Reserve, but do not represent the actual or probable exposures taken on by the Federal Reserve.

[b] Unless denoted otherwise, all figures in this column are based upon Federal Reserve Statistical Release H.4.1 (March 26, 2009). These figures represent the actual potential exposures taken on by the Federal Reserve as of March 25, 2009, but do not represent the actual or probable losses that may be incurred by the Federal Reserve.

[c] From "Report Pursuant to Section 129 of the Emergency Economic Stabilization Act of 2008: Money Market Investor Funding Facility"; did not become operational as of September 2009.

[d] Year-end balances from H.R.1; capacity from periodic report pursuant to EESA, "Update on Outstanding Lending Facilities Authorized by the Board Under Section 13(3) of the Federal Reserve Act," February 25, 2009, page 2.

[e] From "Report Pursuant to Section 129 of the Emergency Economic Stabilization Act of 2008: Commercial Paper Funding Facility."

[f] Announced commitments to purchase in 2009.

[g] Source: Pittman and Ivry, Bloomberg.com (March 31, 2009).

[h] Maximum loans to partnership.

[i] Actual guaranteed amount.

[j] Unclear if guarantee issued.

[k] Actual balances at end of 2008.

SOURCE: Federal Reserve March 26, 2009, Statistical Release H.4.1, Federal Reserve Press Releases, FDIC "Supervisory Insights" (Summer 2009), and "Financial Rescue Nears GDP as Pledges Top $12.8 Trillion." Bloomberg.com, (March 31, 2009).

on audits of the Fed by the General Accounting Office.[33] **Because the Fed is vulnerable to criticism that it has assisted the Treasury in circumventing the legislative appropriations process, the Fed should disclose to Congress the details of its ongoing exposure to the bailout program, except to the extent that disclosures on a specific financial institution would threaten that institution's solvency.** By making such disclosures, the Fed could hopefully move Congress from implicit acquiescence to express recognition of the Fed's large expenditures to support the bank bailout.

FDIC Broadly Guarantees Borrowings of Banks and Holding Companies

As the Federal Reserve helped financial institutions and industrial companies sell short-term commercial paper, so too has the FDIC helped insured institutions, their holding companies and affiliates (collectively known as "eligible institutions") sell bonds with longer maturities. In October, 2008, the FDIC announced a Temporary Liquidity Guarantee Program for guaranteeing senior unsecured debt issued on or before June 30, 2009, by any eligible institution;[34] the issuance period was later extended to October 31, 2009. The original guarantee was for three years, though the FDIC intimated that it may extend the term to ten years.[35] The amount of the debt covered by the FDIC guarantee may not exceed 25 percent of the institution's debt outstanding as of September 30, 2008. The guarantee is for 100 percent of the debt issued and the guarantee fee was originally .75 of 1 percent per year. In April, 2009 the FDIC began adding surcharges of either .25 or .50 of 1 percent for guaranteeing debt of longer maturities issued by certain institutions.[36]

The objective of this FDIC program is laudable—to facilitate the refinancing of large amounts of unsecured bank debt maturing during 2009. By the end of March 2009, the FDIC had guaranteed over $300 billion in debt under this program. However, the design flaws of the program will result in excessive costs to the FDIC and perhaps the federal government. Moreover, these design flaws have created problems of moral hazard, unfair competition, and covert public subsidies.

100 Percent Guarantees Create Moral Hazard

When the federal government guarantees 100 percent of any bond offering, it creates what is called moral hazard. This is an economic term meaning that bond buyers have no incentive to conduct due diligence on the issuing institution or to monitor its financial condition because, regardless of what happens to that institution, they will be repaid by the federal government. In turn, the bank issuing the debt does not need to take steps to improve its financial situation to make its debt more attractive to investors because they will look to the federal government for repayment.

Of course, the FDIC already provides insurance for small bank depositors because they need a safe haven for their savings and may not be in a good position to evaluate the bank's financial condition. (See Chapter 8.) But this FDIC guarantee is different. It benefits very large investors who are perfectly capable of evaluating a bank's condition. These large investors are also capable of negotiating changes in the bank's policies if necessary to ensure the repayment of the debt. By offering a 100 percent guarantee, the FDIC is effectively eliminating the assistance of large investors in policing the financial condition of FDIC-insured banks.

Moreover, these FDIC guarantees are not limited to banks or thrifts determined to have excess capital or those that received top grades in their last examination. The guarantee fee is the same regardless of the riskiness of the bank or thrift (though the new surcharges are higher for debt issued by their holding companies). **Charging the same insurance premium for all banks and thrifts, instead of a risk-based premium, is imprudent.** After seeing that the savings and loan crisis in the 1980s was made worse by the fact that deposit insurance fees were the same for all thrifts,[37] the FDIC switched to differential insurance premiums on deposits based on the risk rating of the bank. **Similarly, the FDIC should take a risk-based approach to its guarantee fees on borrowings by banks or thrifts.**

More critically, the FDIC guarantee should be limited to 90 percent of the debt issued. This would provide considerable comfort to investors, without creating a moral hazard that is likely to be very costly to the FDIC. In fact, Sheila Bair, Chair of the FDIC, resisted the idea of a 100 percent guarantee of unsecured bank debt and proposed a 90 percent limit as a compromise. But she was pressured into agreeing to a 100 percent guarantee by the U.S. Treasury and the Federal Reserve.[38]

By contrast, when the Obama Administration rolled out its program to help small business in March of 2009, it raised loan guarantee levels temporarily to 90 percent under the existing loan programs of the Small Business Administration (SBA). These programs had previously provided guarantees up to 85 percent for loans at or below $150,000 and up to 75 percent for larger loans. But the Obama Administration concluded that 75 percent to 85 percent guarantees were not high enough to persuade banks to lend to small businesses given the current economic conditions.[39] In the Obama Administration's view, a 90 percent guarantee—rather than a 100 percent guarantee—would be sufficient to persuade investors to participate in these SBA programs, although small businesses are generally considered riskier borrowers than large commercial banks.

The Scope of the FDIC Guarantee Is Too Broad

The FDIC has credible reasons for guaranteeing the debt issued by FDIC-insured banks and thrifts (S&Ls). As their insurer, the FDIC would not want them to fail because they could not refinance their debt coming due. The FDIC should also gain considerable comfort from the extensive regulatory powers of federal agencies over banks and thrifts.

It is less clear why the FDIC guarantees should extend to holding companies of banks and thrifts, although the FDIC is now charging higher guarantee fees to holding companies than their bank or thrift subsidiaries. Bank holding companies do not process payments and generally are not high-volume lenders. Instead, they are allowed to engage in a broader range of activities than banks such as real estate development, asset management, and venture capital. (See Figure 6.1 in Chapter 6 for a diagram of a bank holding company.) Bank holding companies are not insured by the FDIC, although they are regulated by the Federal Reserve, which expects them to be a source of strength for the underlying banks.[40] It may be more efficient for multiple banks under the same bank holding company to borrow collectively through the holding company. **But the FDIC should make sure that the**

monies raised by a bank holding company through selling FDIC-insured debt are promptly pushed down to the underlying banks, rather than deployed by the holding company to engage in nonbanking activities.

To assure that its special borrowing program is used for the benefit of the banking system, the FDIC should also avoid guaranteeing debt of bank holding companies with minimal banking operations. In September of 2008, the Federal Reserve allowed Goldman Sachs and Morgan Stanley to convert quickly into bank holding companies, so they could then meet their short-term financing needs through bank deposits and loans from the Federal Reserve as well as commercial paper. (See Chapter 6.) Yet in November of 2008, when their banks were barely operational, the parents of Goldman Sachs and Morgan Stanley were permitted to sell $5 billion and $5.75 billion, respectively, of FDIC-guaranteed bonds at below-market rates.[41]

The case for guaranteeing the debt of thrift holding companies is weakest. These are mainly industrial firms taking advantage of an exception from the general rule that industrial firms may not own FDIC-insured banks.[42] Although the FDIC may have good reasons for guaranteeing the debt of the underlying thrift, there is no good reason for the FDIC to guarantee the bonds of an industrial firm that happens to be a thrift holding company. Yet, the FDIC has agreed to guarantee up to $139 billion in debt for General Electric Capital, which happens to own an FDIC-insured thrift.[43]

Similarly, if a life insurance company gets into financial trouble because of its exposure to MBS, it could quickly buy a small FDIC-insured thrift and become a thrift holding company. Then the life insurance company would be eligible for an FDIC guarantee of its newly issued debt. Because some life insurers have experienced large losses on their bond holdings, they have applied to participate in the bank bailout programs. The availability of an FDIC guarantee has a large impact on how investors value life insurers. For example, on the day when Lincoln National (an insurer that owns a thrift) announced it had withdrawn its application for an FDIC guarantee of its debt, its stock fell by 38 percent.[44] On the other hand, Evan Greenberg, CEO of a large insurer, argued against federal assistance for the insurance industry.

In his view, insurers are not critical to American lending, and usually do not experience bank-like runs because they do not hold daily deposits.[45] **In any event, it is irrational to allow life insurers to participate in the bank bailout program only if they become the parent of a small thrift.** (This argument is elaborated in Chapter 9.)

Broad Government Guarantees Crowd Out Other Borrowers

Since the FDIC is now guaranteeing bonds issued by a broad swath of depository institutions and their holding companies, they are paying much lower interest rates than industrial firms with similar credit ratings. A good measure of this relative cost is the spread, that is, how much higher the interest rate is on a corporate bond than the interest rate on a U.S. Treasury bond of the same maturity. For example, at the beginning of December, 2008, the spread over U.S. Treasuries was twice as high for the bonds of Oracle and AT&T than for the FDIC-guaranteed bonds of Morgan Stanley, which became a bank holding company in late September, 2008.[46] By the end of the first quarter of 2009, Morgan Stanley had already sold $23 billion of FDIC-guaranteed bonds under this program.[47] On this amount of bonds, the difference in spreads means $40 million per year more in interest payments for Oracle or AT&T than for Morgan Stanley.

When General Electric Capital was authorized to issue up to $139 billion in FDIC-guaranteed debt, a General Electric spokesman said this would allow the company to source its debt "competitively with the other financial institutions eligible for [this program]."[48] But what about all the competitors to General Electric that did not own FDIC-insured thrifts? For instance, General Electric Capital provides leasing financing for many of its operating companies like the one that builds jet engines. FDIC-guaranteed bonds would constitute "unfair competition" from the perspective of the other firms in the leasing business and manufacturers of jet engines.

Similarly, government-guaranteed debt of financial institutions is crowding out other issuers of debt in Europe. In the fall of 2008, the three largest countries in the European Union announced large government programs for guaranteeing bank debt—over $430 billion in France and England, and over $540 billion in Germany.[49] Sweden launched a plan to guarantee up to $200 billion in bank debt, equivalent to half of its GDP.[50] Even countries like Canada, where the banks have been quite strong, have been obliged to offer debt guarantees for their banks so they would not be at a competitive disadvantage to American and European banks.[51]

FDIC Should Reprice and End Its Guarantee Fees

The FDIC's guarantee program provides a large implicit subsidy to all participating banks. In November, 2008, the FDIC's guarantee fee was a uniform 75 basis points (bps), .75 of 1 percent for a three-year bond. At that time, the average spread on credit default swaps (CDS) to buy default protection for three-year bonds of the five largest U.S. money center banks was 255bps (slightly over 2.5 percent).[52] The three-year CDS spread represents the cost of insuring that bank's unsecured debt, as valued by the capital markets. The implicit government subsidy is 180bps (1.8 percent), the difference between the 255bps average price for default protection from the private market and the 75bps guarantee fee charged by the FDIC at the time. Even if the FDIC's guarantee were 125bps because of surcharges, the implicit government subsidy would be 130bps (255bps – 125bps). Because these five money center banks sold over $164 billion in FDIC-guaranteed debt by April, 2009, the implicit FDIC subsidy to these five banks was between $2 and $3 billion per year.

To illustrate more concretely the size of the subsidy provided by the FDIC, compare the offering of Citigroup's bonds with and without an FDIC as of May 26, 2009. Of course, the two bond offerings are not exactly comparable because their maturities differ by less than two months. Nevertheless, the 4.75 percent difference in spreads over U.S. Treasuries (5.15 percent – 0.40 percent = 4.75 percent) between the two bond offerings demonstrates the enormous value of the FDIC guarantee for a troubled bank like Citigroup.

	With FDIC Guarantee	Without FDIC Guarantee [53]
Issuer	Citigroup	Citigroup
Maturity	April, 2012	February, 2012
Rate	40 bps (0.40 percent)	515 bps (5.15 percent)
	Over the 3-year U.S. Treasury	Over the 3-year U.S. Treasury

Accordingly, the FDIC should promptly increase its guarantee fee to a level closer to the market rate, with different rates based on the riskiness of the bank. FDIC should terminate its guarantee program for bank debt by the end of October 2009, when the program is slated to expire. The expiration date has already been extended once, so the FDIC will have to resist intense political pressure to continue guaranteeing bank debt after October 31, 2009. **If any bank redeems its preferred stock from the Treasury before then, the FDIC should immediately prohibit that bank and all its affiliates from utilizing FDIC guarantees to issue their debt, and should ask that bank with its affiliates to repay any outstanding FDIC-guaranteed debt as soon as practical.** However, the 10 large banks that redeemed the Treasury's preferred stock in June, 2009, were permitted to keep outstanding their debt with the FDIC's guarantee.[54] If these banks are healthy enough to return Treasury's capital contribution, why do they still need a generous interest rate subsidy from the FDIC? And if these banks are no longer subject to the burdens of the special restrictions on executive compensation, why should they enjoy the lucrative benefits of the FDIC's debt guarantees? Although Morgan Stanley and J.P. Morgan had sufficient capital to repay their federal preferred stock, they continued to rely on their FDIC-guaranteed debt with built-in interest subsidies of over $3 billion each.[55]

Summary

As the U.S. economy weakened in the summer of 2007, the Fed began to reduce its target rate for federal funds and continued reducing it until the end of 2008 when the target rate reached almost zero. Although cutting interest rates usually stimulates economic growth by encouraging more lending, it is unclear how effective this strategy has been because the main constraint on bank lending has been fear of loan defaults and a desire to preserve liquidity, both of which are not affected much by interest rates. Furthermore, the Federal Reserve began paying interest on bank reserves deposited at the Fed, which provided a new disincentive for banks to make loans.

In the short term, deflation is a threat in the current U.S. recession. If there is a collapse in demand, consumers and firms could decide to defer purchases in the expectation that prices will decline further. Deflation would impose a substantial burden on borrowers, who would be forced to pay off loans with more expensive dollars, just as inflation allows borrowers to pay down debt with cheaper dollars.

Over the next five to ten years, inflation is a more troublesome issue to the foreign investors who hold the majority of U.S. Treasury securities. Foreign investors are concerned that the United States will print a lot more dollars to finance its huge budget deficits. In order to limit the inflationary potential of a much larger supply of dollars, the Federal Reserve should announce an inflation target (expressed as a range to allow a degree of flexibility) and publicly commit to raise interest rates within a reasonable time after consumer prices exceed that range.

After the failure of Lehman Brothers in September, 2008, the short-term lending markets froze up. In order to provide liquidity to commercial banks and investment banks, the Federal Reserve initiated programs to allow these institutions to borrow cash or Treasuries with highly rated, but illiquid, securities as collateral. The Federal Reserve, working with money center banks, provided similar liquidity facilities for highly rated commercial paper held by money market funds. In addition, the Federal Reserve started to buy highly rated commercial paper directly from industrial companies.

Although these programs have increased liquidity and lowered rates in the short-term market for commercial paper, other initiatives potentially threaten the institutional independence of the Federal Reserve. It has made large nonrecourse, low-interest loans to private investors to buy newly issued asset-backed securities and toxic assets from banks. It has also guaranteed almost $400 billion in troubled assets at the weakest financial institutions. As a result, the central bank could become less independent and more vulnerable to political pressure. Therefore, the Treasury rather than the Fed should provide loss guarantees of troubled assets.

In addition, the funding of these programs through an expansion of the Federal Reserve's balance sheet arguably circumvents the legislative process. Congress has so far appropriated only $700 billion for the financial bailout, but the Fed's total potential exposure to the financial bailout was approximately $7.3 trillion in March, 2009. To make sure that

Congress does not later object to its new programs, the Fed should periodically provide Congress with a detailed report on all loans, guarantees,
and other expenditures relating to the financial bailout.

To help the refinancing of debt with a term longer than commercial paper, the FDIC has established a program to guarantee most debt
issued on or before October 31, 2009 by depository institutions and
their holding companies until mid-2012. The guarantee extends for up
to three years, and covers 100 percent of the debt issued by any eligible
institution; the fee schedule is the same regardless of the financial situation of such institution. By April, 2009, the FDIC had already guaranteed over $300 billion in debt issued by a broad range of banks, bank
holding companies, and thrift holding companies.

This FDIC program has three glaring defects. First, the 100 percent
guarantee creates a moral hazard, that is, large investors who buy the
debt have no incentive to scrutinize the financial situation of the issuing
institution, because they will be repaid by the FDIC even if the bank
becomes insolvent. Second, the FDIC has gone far beyond protecting
the special functions of banks by guaranteeing the debt of bank holding
companies lacking fully operational banks and thrift holding companies
engaged in industrial activities. Third, the broad swath of FDIC-guaranteed
debt has given many thrift holding companies an unfair competitive
advantage over industrial firms that do not happen to own a thrift.

To remedy these deficits, the FDIC should limit its guarantee to
90 percent of the debt of banks and thrifts. It should not guarantee the
debt of any bank or thrift holding company unless the consolidated
group is primarily engaged in banking, and it should charge differential
fees based on the financial situation of the institution.

The FDIC's guarantee program provides a significant government subsidy to the participating financial institution. Although banks
will lobby to extend this program, the FDIC should terminate its program for guaranteeing bank debt as scheduled by the end of October
2009. Before then, the FDIC should not guarantee the debt issued by
any bank or affiliate that redeems its preferred stock from the Treasury.
Finally, the FDIC should promptly increase its guarantee fees to a level
closer to market rates.

Chapter 8

Insuring Deposits and Money Market Funds

Bank deposits and money market funds are normally considered safe havens for American investors. However, even these safe havens were heavily impacted by the financial crisis. In 2008, the FDIC closed 25 banks including Washington Mutual, a large mortgage lender on the West Coast, which was closed at the end of September. To help Americans "maintain confidence in the banking system,"[1] Congress increased the limit on deposit insurance for all bank accounts to $250,000 from October 3, 2008 until the end of 2009. This period was later extended through the end of 2013.

In September 2008, the U.S. Treasury also launched for the first time an insurance program for money market funds, which was authorized to run for one year.[2] The Treasury was responding to the plight of the Reserve Fund, one of the oldest money market funds in the United States, which experienced large redemptions because of its large losses on the commercial paper of Lehman Brothers. More broadly, the problems of the Reserve Fund scared some investors into moving their monies to U.S. Treasury bills and funds holding only U.S. government securities.

This chapter will explain why the temporary increase to $250,000 on bank deposit insurance should not be continued past 2013, despite a predictable lobbying effort by depository institutions to make the new limit permanent. This increase will not help resolve the financial crisis; rather, it will raise the cost of bank failures by reducing the market discipline of weak banks. Similarly, the Treasury's insurance program for money market funds should not be extended beyond its scheduled expiration date on September 18, 2009. There are better ways to deal with potential redemptions from money market funds, which would allow them to pay higher rates to savers at relatively low risk levels.

How FDIC Insurance Works for Bank Deposits

Let's begin by understanding the operation of FDIC deposit insurance, which applies to deposits at thrifts (S&Ls) as well as banks. Suppose you have a family of four with a husband, a wife, a son, and a daughter. Under the 2007 rules, each of them may open an account at the same bank and receive $100,000 of FDIC insurance coverage. Each of the parents may also open an individual retirement account and receive an additional $250,000 in FDIC insurance coverage under a special higher limit for retirement accounts. Further, the parents may open a separate trust account for the benefit of each child; each of those accounts will be covered by $100,000 in FDIC insurance. Finally, the small business of the parents may open a transaction account at the bank and be insured up to $100,000.[3]

In sum, this one family could easily obtain $1.2 million in FDIC insurance by maintaining these nine deposit accounts in the same bank under the 2007 rules. Under the "temporary" higher limits between 2009 and 2013, this total would increase to $2 million for the eight bank accounts maintained by the family as individuals.[4] In addition, the transaction account of the family business would be entitled to FDIC insurance *on any amount* if the bank participates in the FDIC's Temporary Liquidity Guarantee Program.

Higher Insurance Coverage Is Not Needed to Protect Most Depositors

When Congress initially established insurance on bank deposits in 1934, it set the limit at $5,000 per account—"high enough to provide adequate protection to small depositors and low enough so that large depositors continue to act as a form of market discipline in depository institutions."[5] That limit was raised gradually over the years until it was jumped up to $100,000 in 1980. This last jump occurred during a period when banks were losing deposits because federal regulations set a ceiling on the interest they could pay, which was much lower than market rates at the time. But that increase proved costly to the federal government, because many savings and loan associations (S&Ls) failed during the late 1980s.[6] Perhaps due to the S&L experience, the $100,000 limit for deposit insurance was maintained until October of 2008.

The 2008 increase in FDIC insurance limits from $100,000 to $250,000 has been justified as catching up with inflation. It is true that the aggregate rise in consumer prices since 1980 has been close to 150 percent. On the other hand, the increase to $100,000 in 1980 went far beyond what would have been justified by inflation since deposit insurance began in 1934. On an inflation-adjusted basis, the $5,000 FDIC limit in 1934 should have risen to only $30,746 in 1980.[7] (See Table 8.1.) Using a consistent methodology based on the Labor Department's Consumer

Table 8.1 Actual and CPI Inflation-Adjusted Increases in FDIC Insured-Deposit Limit

Year	Limit	Inflation-Adjusted 1934 Limit
1934	$ 5,000	–
1950	$ 10,000	$ 8,993
1966	$ 15,000	$12,090
1969	$ 20,000	$13,694
1974	$ 40,000	$18,395
1980	$100,000	$30,746
2008	$250,000	$80,337

SOURCE: U.S. Department of Labor CPI Inflation Calculator www.bls.gov/data/inflation_calculator.htm.

Table 8.2   Statistics of Depository Institutions (June 2008)

	Average Account Balance ($)	Number of Accounts (Thousands)
Below Insured Threshold		
Deposits[a]	5,837	444,794
Retirement Deposits[b]	9,992	21,252
Total	6,027	466,046
Above Insured Threshold		
Deposits[a]	431,754	7,345
Retirement Deposits[b]	449,522	35
Total	431,839	7,380
All Accounts		
Deposits	12,756	452,139
Retirement Deposits	10,721	21,287
Grand Total	12,665	473,426
% of Accounts Fully Insured		
Deposits		98%
Retirement Deposits		100%
Total		98%

[a] "Insured threshold" for deposits is $100,000. Beginning June 2006, excludes retirement acounts for Call Reporters. Beginning September 2006, excludes retirement accounts for Insured U.S. branches of foreign banks (IBA). Beginning December 2006, excludes retirement accounts for TFR Reporters.

[b] "Insured threshold" for retirement account deposits is $250,000. Beginning in June 2006, includes retirement accounts for Call Reporters. Beginning September 2006, includes retirement accounts for Insured U.S. branches of foreign banks (IBA). Beginning December 2006, includes retirement accounts for TFR Reporters.

SOURCE: FDIC Statistics on Depository Institutions http://www2.fdic.gov/SDI/main4.asp.

Price Index from the beginning of the FDIC's deposit insurance program, the limit in 2008 should be approximately $80,000 per account.

Nor can these increases in FDIC insurance limits be justified as necessary to protect small depositors. In fact, according to an economist at the Federal Reserve Bank of Cleveland writing in 2000, over 98 percent of nonbusiness deposit accounts in commercial banks were under the $100,000 limit and the average balance in those accounts was below $6,000.[8] The percentage of insured accounts and the average account balance were quite similar in June, 2008 as shown by Table 8.2.[9]

The frequency of bank runs would also not be affected by permanently raising the deposit insurance limit to $250,000, because the

$100,000 limit already covers 98 percent of all bank customers. These customers have continued access to their deposits even if their bank is put into receivership by the FDIC. Moreover, if an FDIC-insured bank did face a run by insured depositors, it could quickly access liquid funds by borrowing from the Federal Reserve.

The rationale for extending the $250,000 limit until the end of 2013 was stated by the White House: "This will provide depository institutions with a more stable source of funding and enhanced ability to continue making credit available across the country."[10] However, there is no proven connection between higher FDIC insurance limits and increased lending by banks in the current recession. When FDIC-insured banks attracted more deposits because of higher insurance limits, they often used the extra cash to invest in government bonds, pay down outstanding advances, or bolster their loan loss reserves.

The protection of transaction accounts, which usually do not pay interest,[11] is more complex. Many small businesses use these accounts for payments of inventory, wages, and taxes, so these could easily exceed $100,000 or even $250,000. However, the FDIC's guaranty program has *no limit* based on the size of the business. Therefore, IBM or Cisco could use a bank account for millions of dollars of transactions every day, and that account would be fully insured by the FDIC. **If we want to protect transaction accounts of small businesses, the FDIC should limit eligibility for its unlimited insurance of transaction accounts to businesses with revenues in the prior year of less than some reasonable amount (e.g., $1 million).**

Higher FDIC Insurance Limits Raise Costs and Eliminate Market Discipline

Because higher FDIC insurance limits will probably attract more savings to bank deposits, it is probable that less savings will be directed to other financial vehicles. This means less savings, for example, to taxable money market funds that mainly purchase short-term commercial paper of American companies, or tax-free money market funds that buy mainly short-term paper from U.S. states or municipalities.[12] As explained later in this chapter, money market funds concentrate their investments in both types of short-term paper.

But we can say, for certain, that increasing deposit insurance limits will raise the cost of bank failures for the FDIC. The FDIC generally aims to finance the deposit insurance program totally from fees paid by banks, rather than legislative appropriations, although Congress had to appropriate over $100 billion to clean up the S&L crisis.[13] At the end of 2008, the FDIC's insurance fund was down to $19 billion, and its staff predicted $65 billion in losses over the next five years. In early 2009, the FDIC proposed to charge banks a one-time assessment fee of 20 cents on every $100 of domestic deposits, as well as doubling the normal premium paid by banks.[14] The combination would have meant $27 billion in insurance fees for 2009, nine times higher than 2008.[15]

In 2009, the small banks lobbied hard in Congress to prevent the FDIC from assessing the one-time fee of 20 cents on every $100 of domestic deposits. In response, Congress authorized the FDIC to borrow $100 billion immediately from the U.S. Treasury, and to later borrow another $400 billion with the consent of the Federal Reserve and the Treasury.[16] In the same legislation, Congress extended the $250,000 FDIC insurance on deposits through 2013. In response, the FDIC reduced the special assessment from 20 cents to 5 cents on every $100 of domestic deposits.[17]

With the insurance limits at $250,000 per account, the FDIC will lose much of the market discipline from the relatively small group of quite sophisticated investors who maintain large deposits at banks (just as the FDIC does when it guarantees 100 percent of a bank's debt). These are the investors who would otherwise avoid weak banks and criticize their financial condition. But if these large investors can spread their monies among FDIC-insured accounts at many banks, they will no longer bring to bear the discipline of the market. Instead, they will seek the FDIC-insured accounts with the highest interest rates, which are usually paid by the weakest banks. This is what happened during the S&L crisis and again in 2008–2009: The weakest banks attracted large inflows of deposits by offering high interest rates and advertising them nationally.[18] After the S&L crisis, bank regulators were given the authority to take "prompt corrective action" when a bank's capital fell below a specified level. That action typically involves a program for a bank to improve its financial condition over several months. However, weak banks fail quickly. Of the 25 FDIC-insured banks that failed in 2008, only one was subject to a "prompt corrective action."[19]

These concerns about the elimination of market discipline are especially relevant to the blanket FDIC coverage now provided to transaction accounts of businesses, which typically pay no interest. When FDIC insurance for a transaction account was limited to $100,000, the chief financial officer of any business would carefully examine the financial condition of the bank before using such an account for accepting payments and issuing checks. But once the FDIC coverage of these transaction accounts became unlimited, no business executive has any incentive to scrutinize the financial situation of the bank. Furthermore, banks participating in this FDIC program for unlimited insurance on transaction accounts pay a uniform premium, rather than a risk-rated premium.[20] In other words, the FDIC does not even force weaker banks to pay more to take advantage of unlimited governmental guarantees for transaction accounts.

For all these reasons, the FDIC should revert to its prior insurance limits of $100,000 per deposit account after December 31, 2013. However, the banks will lobby heavily for making permanent the $250,000 limit. **As a second best alternative, Congress should prohibit FDIC insurance without any limits for transaction accounts of businesses, except for truly small firms defined by objective criteria.**

More Deposit Insurance Spreads Across the World

This trend toward higher insurance limits and blanket coverage on bank accounts is spreading around the world. Ireland jumped out ahead of the European Union by quickly announcing a blanket guarantee of all bank deposits. In order to prevent local deposits from moving to Ireland, soon afterward many of the larger European countries like England and Germany offered higher or blanket guarantees of deposits at their banks.[21] This is a predictable nationalistic response, aimed at keeping local deposits in local banks.[22] However, the new EU members from the former Communist block could not afford such generous guarantees.[23] **Although international agreements are difficult to achieve, it seems feasible for the limited number of European countries with the Euro as their common currency to agree on a uniform policy on insuring bank deposits. If such an agreement cannot be reached within**

the Eurozone, there is no hope for financial agreements among a broader range of countries.

Even countries in Asia that had traditionally shunned deposit insurance jumped on the bandwagon. Australia and New Zealand jettisoned their purist stances and started insurance schemes for bank deposits.[24] Hong Kong announced a blanket guarantee of all bank deposits to prevent capital from fleeing to other Asian destinations.[25] In response, the chief of HSBC's Asian operations called upon Asian governments to abandon their broad guarantees of bank deposits because they risk imposing a costly burden on taxpayers for what amounts to inappropriate assistance to weak banks.[26]

In short, each country rushed to protect its own banks without the least bit of concern for other countries—the financial version of the destructive trade policy of beggaring thy neighbor.

Don't Regulate Money Market Funds as Banks

A money market fund is a type of mutual fund that is similar in some respects to a bank deposit. Both pay income regularly, both do not typically fluctuate in value, and both are relatively safe. But there are crucial differences between a money market fund and a bank deposit. Most importantly, a bank deposit is insured by the FDIC up to a specified amount, whereas a money market fund is not generally insured by any federal agency (except for the period from September 19, 2008 thru September 18, 2009). Instead of being insured by the FDIC, money market funds are subject to strict limits on their investments, established by the Securities and Exchange Commission (SEC).

The SEC imposes three main types of restrictions on taxable money market funds (as opposed to tax-free money market funds). First, at least 95 percent of the money market fund's assets must be invested in the highest quality money market instruments, and the other 5 percent or less must be invested in issuers of the second highest rating.[27] Second, a money market fund may not invest more than 5 percent of its assets in any single top-rated issuer (other than the federal government), and no more than 1 percent of its assets in any second-rated issuer. Third, the average maturity of the money market fund's assets may not exceed 90 days.[28] Because of these strict limits on their investments, together with certain accounting conventions, shares of money market funds usually maintain a net asset value (NAV) of $1 per share.

During the 1980s, money market funds grew quickly because they could make distributions at the then-current high rates, while federal rules set a low ceiling on the interest that bank accounts could pay. Even after the federal regulators lifted the ceiling on interest paid by bank deposits, money market funds continued to grow. They offered competitive rates for short-term investments, as well as the transparency of daily pricing and the convenience of withdrawals by check. At the end of 2008, the United States had 784 money market funds with total assets of $3.8 trillion.[29]

What It Means to Break the Buck

Money market funds must calculate and publish every day their net asset value or NAV (the current value of the fund's portfolio divided by the number of shares of the fund outstanding). Money market funds generally distribute all of their net income as it is earned and use an accounting technique called amortized cost to maintain a constant dollar value for each share, rather than a fluctuating value, as do the shares of stock and bond funds.[30] By adhering to its investment restrictions, distributing all income as received and using amortized cost, a money market fund will almost always be able to maintain a NAV of $1 per share.

A money market fund must calculate its NAV using actual valuations on at least a weekly basis and compare that NAV to its $1 NAV to determine if there is a significant difference. This process is called shadow pricing. If a money market fund were to incur losses of .5 of 1 percent or more on its portfolio securities based on actual valuations rather than amortized cost, the fund would need to take prompt action to reinstate the NAV to $1 or its NAV would be rounded down to 99 cents per share. This is called breaking the buck. Thus, even a small loss—$5 million on a $1 billion fund—can theoretically force a money market fund to break the buck. Such losses could occur in the event of a credit default on a substantial position in one issuer held by a money market fund or, less likely, in the event of a severe movement in interest rates for a money market fund with a particularly long average maturity.

The managers of money market funds are very reluctant to let a money market fund break the buck because its investors might rapidly redeem their shares of the fund. On the other hand, these managers are very reluctant to make prospective promises that they will always bail out their money market funds.[31] Under SEC rules, money market funds (like other mutual funds) must generally allow their shareholders to redeem their shares at the NAV set at 4 P.M. on every business day, and redemption proceeds must be paid within seven days.[32] For this reason, when a money market fund has come close to breaking the buck, its manager has almost always bailed it out, usually by buying at face value the fund's investments that had incurred the loss. In 1995, for instance, several advisers bailed out their money market funds for losses they sustained on securities issued by Orange County in California.[33] In 2007 and 2008, several managers again bought at face value questionable commercial paper from the money funds they managed.[34]

In the early 1990s, one money market fund in Colorado actually did break the buck, but this incident did not lead to a general wave of redemptions of money market funds. Rather, there was a flight to quality, as investors flocked to the money market funds with the most conservative investments and the managers with the best reputations for integrity. In fact, the Colorado fund's shareholders were mainly institutions, which recovered over 95 percent of their investments in the fund.[35]

On Tuesday, September 16, 2008, the money market industry was shaken up when the Reserve Fund, run mainly for institutional investors, broke the buck because of losses on its holdings of Lehman bonds. The Reserve Fund had $62.6 billion in total assets, of which $785 million was invested in Lehman bonds, or only about 1.3 percent of its assets.[36] The Reserve Fund was one of the oldest money market funds, run by a veteran manager with a previously conservative reputation. During the same week, however, institutions tried to redeem most of their monies from the Reserve Fund.[37]

On Wednesday, September 17, 2008, the trustees of the Putnam Prime Money Market Fund, another institutional fund with $12.3 billion in assets, suddenly voted to close the fund and distribute its $12.3 billion in assets to investors.[38] Putnam said that the Fund had no investments in the bonds of Lehman Brothers or AIG. Nevertheless, the Fund had experienced a wave of redemption requests. According to Putnam, serious liquidity constraints on the Fund's investments created the risk that, in selling these investments to meet redemptions, the Fund would realize substantial losses.[39]

During the rest of that week, investors withdrew a record $133 billion from money market funds invested in commercial paper (prime funds), as opposed to money market funds investing in U.S. Treasuries and other securities of federal agencies (government funds). These withdrawals constituted almost 4 percent of the money market fund industry, which held $3.34 trillion in assets at that time.[40] Because the U.S. Treasury feared a run on prime funds, a few days later it offered an emergency federal program for insuring against losses to all money market funds that chose to participate. Although the program was initially launched for three months, it was later extended to September 19, 2009.[41]

The Insurance Program for Money Market Funds Was Limited

The insurance program for money market funds was narrowly designed to allay the fears of bankers as well as fund executives about large-scale transfers from bank deposits to money market funds.[42] The maximum amount of insurance was limited to the amount in a shareholder's account at a money market fund at the end of the day on September 19, 2008, a date prior to the initiation of the insurance program. If a shareholder decreased the amount in his or her account at the money fund after September 19, 2008, the insurance coverage for that account was automatically reduced to the lower amount. On the other hand, a shareholder could not increase insurance coverage above the September 19th amount by increasing the amount in his or her account at the money market fund or setting up new accounts at that fund.[43]

Furthermore, the insurance would pay off only if the money market fund actually was liquidated and the shareholders incurred losses in the liquidation. Most notably, the insurance would not be paid if a money market fund broke the buck and continued to operate. For this limited form of insurance for three months, a money market fund paid in advance to the Treasury a premium of either 1 basis point (.01 of 1 percent) if the fund was not close to breaking the buck, or 1.5 basis points if the fund's NAV was within .25 of 1 percent of breaking the buck. Any fund that had already broken the buck was not allowed to participate in the insurance program.[44]

All major mutual fund complexes agreed to participate in the Treasury's insurance program,[45] though some did not believe that the program was really needed. In fact, the insurance was useful only to cover potential losses in high-quality commercial paper held in prime money market funds. There was no risk of loss in money market funds investing mainly in U.S. Treasuries or other debt securities of the federal government. Investors, led by institutions, moved their monies quickly to government money market funds. In the twelve months ending November 30, 2008, the assets in government money market funds rose by 150 percent to $750 billion.[46] In the weeks following the failure of Lehman in September of 2008, close to $500 billion moved from prime money market funds to government money market funds.[47]

By the end of 2008, money market funds in the United States had climbed to $3.8 trillion in assets, a 20 percent increase from the end of 2007, as shown by Table 8.3.[48] The assets of money market funds exceeded those of stock funds in the United States for the first time in many years.[49] Although the shift from stock funds to money market funds may have been partly attributable to the federal insurance program, a more critical factor was probably the enormous drop in stock prices during 2008. In fact, the majority of money market funds did not renew their federal insurance before April 30, 2009, without any significant shareholder response.[50]

The Treasury's insurance program for money market funds should expire as scheduled on September 18, 2009, and should *not* be established on a permanent basis for several reasons. First, it is unclear how important federal insurance was to money market fund investors. The federal insurance did not cover any new shareholders in a money market fund after September 19, 2008 or any existing shareholders to the extent they increased the size of their money market accounts after September 19, 2009. Yet shareholders made initial investments in money market funds, or increased their account size, after September 19, 2009. Furthermore, as mentioned earlier, shareholders did not redeem money market funds that let their federal insurance lapse in the spring of 2009.

Table 8.3   Money Market Funds' Assets and Net New Cash Flows

All Money Market Funds
Total Net Assets

Year	Total	Government	Non-Government	Tax-Exempt
1996	$ 901,807	$ 217,912	$ 544,077	$139,818
1997	1,058,886	244,978	653,105	160,803
1998	1,351,678	302,792	860,375	188,512
1999	1,613,146	325,911	1,082,820	204,415
2000	1,845,248	352,468	1,254,748	238,033
2001	2,285,310	437,235	1,575,676	272,399
2002	2,271,956	447,673	1,549,500	274,784
2003	2,052,003	403,535	1,360,095	288,373
2004	1,913,193	372,440	1,230,407	310,346
2005	2,040,537	382,493	1,324,046	333,998
2006	2,338,451	405,822	1,566,225	366,404
2007	3,085,760	726,084	1,894,602	465,075
2008	3,832,244	1,450,340	1,890,444	491,460

Net New Cash Flow (millions of dollars, annual)

Year	Total	Government	Non-Government	Tax-Exempt
1996	$ 89,422	$ 20,759	$ 58,427	$10,236
1997	103,466	18,513	69,533	15,420
1998	235,457	43,155	169,346	22,956
1999	193,681	8,680	174,146	10,855
2000	159,365	16,510	116,339	26,515
2001	375,291	81,623	267,447	26,221
2002	−46,451	−4,586	−57,601	15,735
2003	−258,401	−51,508	−216,211	9,318
2004	−156,593	−36,481	−138,429	18,318
2005	63,147	10,305	32,607	20,234
2006	245,236	16,286	203,959	24,990
2007	654,476	309,431	261,224	83,821
2008	636,832	691,800	−69,048	14,078

NOTE: Data for funds that invest primarily in other mutual funds were excluded from the series. Components may not add to the total because of rounding.

SOURCE: Investment Company Institute *2009 Investment Company Fact Book,* Tables 37 and 38.

Second, the federal insurance applied only if the money market fund was liquidated and its shareholders lost money. Most money market funds have not come close to breaking a buck and, in those rare instances in which a fund broke the buck, it almost always was rescued by its manager. The three instances in which the manager did not rescue its money market fund involved funds that were dominated by institutional investors, who should be able to fend for themselves without federal insurance.

Third, the SEC almost certainly will adopt stricter rules for money market funds.[51] As will be described later, the new rules will reduce the average maturity of all money market funds, prohibit these funds from investing in second-tier commercial paper, and increase the liquidity buffers of the funds. As a result of these new restrictions, chances of a money market fund breaking a buck will become even lower.

Money Market Funds at Zero Yields

Unfortunately, the yields on government money market funds dropped to almost nothing when the Federal Reserve reduced its target rate to close to zero. For example, the average monthly return for Treasury money market funds was .013 percent at the end of 2008, as compared to over 2 percent in 2007.[52] As Treasury bills matured after December 2008, their yields dropped further, and the total returns for government money market funds came close to zero; they did not drop below zero only because their managers absorbed most of their expenses. At the beginning of 2009, a number of well-known managers (e.g., Fidelity, Schwab, and Vanguard) stopped accepting new investors into their government money market funds.[53]

Let's consider the implications of a zero policy rate for a retail money market fund holding 30-day U.S. Treasury bills with a gross yield before expenses of 10 basis points (10/100 of 1 percent). The manager of a retail money market fund on average charges 35 basis points to manage the fund. In addition, the fund has other expenses—custodial, audit, and registration fees, as well as check writing, reporting, and other service expenses—that usually cost another 15 basis points. So the total expenses of a retail money market fund could easily be 50 basis points (35 for management and 15 for other expenses).

Even if the manager waives its management fee, the fund will still have 15 basis points of expenses with only 10 basis points of gross yield. In other words, in order to attain a zero rate of return for the money market fund, the manager will not only have to waive its management fee but also will have to subsidize 5 basis points of expenses (15 basis points of other expenses minus a gross yield of 10 basis points on 30-day U.S. Treasury bills). In a government money market fund with $10 billion in assets, this means that the manager is paying fund shareholders $5 million per year for the privilege of running the fund for free.

Money Market Funds Need Tighter SEC Restrictions

The Group of 30, a nonprofit association of financial experts from around the world, has proposed that all money market funds should become "special-purpose" banks. "If money-market funds provide bank-like services, then they should be organized like banks," said the executive director of the Group of 30.[54] In their view, money market funds should be subject to similar capital and reserve requirements as banks; and like banks, money market funds should be insured by the FDIC.[55]

With all due respect to the Group of 30, money market funds should not be regulated like banks. Instead, the federal government should try to preserve competition by offering savers different types of vehicles for short-term investing. Money market funds promote competition by offering savers higher interest rates for certain maturities in certain economic environments. For example, a taxable money market fund could pay an annualized interest rate of 3 percent, when monies kept in various types of savings accounts with limited or no checking could pay 1 percent or 2 percent interest. Indeed, on a nightly basis, many banks sweep excess cash from low-interest transaction accounts to higher paying money market funds. Investors, provided they receive fair disclosure of the risk, may well prefer to incur the remote risk of breaking the buck in order to realize that higher return.

Tax-exempt money market funds provide a unique way for savers to receive interest income that is exempt from income taxes at the federal, state, and city levels. In places like New York or California, these double or triple tax-free funds are especially attractive to investors. By contrast, bank deposits cannot offer tax-exempt income to investors because bank deposits do not pass through the tax-exempt feature of any of the bank's own portfolio holdings. To obtain tax-exempt income in a

Table 8.4   Selected Money Market Instruments (December 2008)

	Total	Money Market Fund Holdings	
	Billions of Dollars	Billons of Dollars	Percentage of Total
Agency securities[a]	$ 1,748	$ 774	44%
Commercial paper	1,599	629	39
Treasury securities[b]	2,473	591	24
Repurchase agreements[c]	2,381	552	23
Certificates of deposit[d]	2,192	353	16
Eurodollar deposits[e]	1,489	132	9
Total Taxable Instruments	$11,882	$3,031	26%
Total Tax-Exempt Instruments[f]	750	491	65

[a] Debt issued by Fannie Mae, FreddieMac, and the Federal Housing Finance Board due to mature by the end of December 2009: category excludes agency-backed mortgage pools.
[b] Marketable Treasury securities held by the public due to mature by the end of December 2009.
[c] Repurchase agreements with primary dealers: category includes gross overnight, continuing, and term agreements on Treasury, agency, mortgage-backed, and corporate securities.
[d] Certificates of deposit are large or jumbo CDs, which are issued in a amounts greater than $100,000.
[e] Category includes claims on foreigners for negotiable CDs and non-negotiable deposits payable in U.S. dollars, as reported by banks in the U.S. for those banks or those banks' customers' accounts. Values for customer accounts are for September 2008.
[f] Category includes VRDNs, ARSs, TOBs, and other short-term debt. Category does not include long-term fixed-rate debt due to mature by the end of December 2009.

SOURCE: Report of the Money Market Working Group to Board of Governors of the Investment Company Institute (Figure 2.3, p. 19).

bank context, a saver would have to establish a trust or other investment account to invest in municipal bonds.

In their current form, money market funds are important suppliers of short-term capital to both companies and local governments in the U.S., as shown by Table 8.4. At the end of 2007, mutual funds held 47 percent of the U.S. commercial paper market, the largest share of this corporate borrowing market by any type of financial institution. Mutual funds also held 32 percent of all tax-exempt debt issued by U.S. municipalities, a critical source of short-term financing for these local governments.[56] Money market funds provide much more capital to meet these short-term needs of companies and municipalities than banks. Banks can invest in short, medium, and long-term bonds as well as real estate and commercial loans, whereas money market funds must hold highly liquid assets with an average maturity of 90 days or less.

If money market funds were permanently insured by the FDIC, this insurance would discourage large investors from bringing to bear market discipline on these funds. In the past, large investors have looked carefully at the holdings and strategies of prime money market funds to avoid situations that would come anywhere near breaking the buck. Large investors also have given serious consideration to the quality and financial soundness of the managers of these funds. If large investors are willing to accept lower returns in return for no risk of credit losses, they do not need insured money market funds; they can easily shift their monies to government money market funds.

Instead of continuing an insurance program for money market funds, the federal government should tighten the regulations for holdings by prime funds. Under current SEC rules, a prime fund may hold a debt security with a maturity of slightly more than one year, and the fund's average maturity may not exceed 90 days. These relatively loose maturity limits *increase* the risk of credit losses to a prime fund's portfolio, which can break the buck with only .5 of 1 percent in losses. **Therefore, the SEC should decrease the maturity limit for an individual debt security in a prime fund from over one year to 6 months, and decrease the average maturity for any prime fund from 90 to 60 days.**[57] **In addition, the SEC should eliminate the ability of prime funds to invest 5 percent in second-tier-rated commercial paper.**

Money Market Funds Should Authorize Special Measures for Heavy Redemptions

Despite those tighter maturity limits, a prime fund could still face a flood of redemption requests if investors became panicked about potential corporate bond defaults and fled to Treasury securities. In those situations, prime funds have a number of potential tools that should be put at their disposal. **The charters and prospectuses of prime funds should authorize their independent directors to suspend redemptions for up to five business days. On a more targeted basis, if an institutional investor wants to redeem 10 percent or 20 percent of a prime fund in one day, the fund should employ a technique called a redemption in kind.** Under that technique, the prime fund would not pay cash to the institutional investor because that would require a large sale of commercial paper in a relatively illiquid market. Instead, the prime fund would transfer to the institutional investor a portfolio of securities representing the investor's proportionate share of the fund's current holdings.

In addition, a prime fund should be authorized in its charter and prospectus to borrow up to one-third of its assets to meet redemption requests.[58] **As another backstop, a prime fund should obtain an SEC exemption to establish an interfund lending facility, which allows one fund to borrow from another fund within the same mutual fund complex under specific conditions.**[59]

The Investment Company Institute, the trade group for mutual funds, has also proposed that the SEC adopt stricter rules for liquidity of money market funds.[60] **The SEC should adopt the Institute's proposed requirements for:**

- Taxable money market funds (excluding Treasury funds) to meet certain daily liquidity standards;
- All money market funds to meet weekly liquidity standards; and
- All fund advisors to regularly stress test their portfolios to demonstrate their ability to meet anticipated levels of credit risk, shareholder redemptions, and interest-rate changes.

Although the Treasury supports all the aforementioned restrictions, it remains concerned about possible future runs and money market funds. Therefore, the Treasury has called for a study on "fundamental changes to address systemic risk more directly," such as moving from a stable NAV of $1 per share to a fluctuating NAV for money market funds.[61] However, the Investment Company Institute has opposed such a shift from a constant dollar NAV to a fluctuating NAV, because it would obviously make money market funds less attractive to many investors. The Institute pointed out that in countries like France, where money market funds have a fluctuating NAV, they still experienced heavy redemption requests during this financial crisis.[62]

In my view, it is not necessary to move from a stable $1 NAV to a fluctuating NAV for money market funds. After the SEC adopts all the tighter restrictions described earlier for money

market funds, the chances of any well-managed fund breaking the buck would be quite low—though not zero. Investors should be able to take the low risk in return for higher return in a money market fund as long as they are provided with prominent and understandable warnings that they will not be insured or protected if the fund breaks the buck. In addition, to deal with short-term liquidity problems, money market funds should (for an appropriate fee) be allowed to make short-term exchanges of their highest quality commercial paper for U.S. Treasuries at the Fed, as was allowed during late 2008 and early 2009.

Finally, during the first few months of the financial crisis, the SEC permitted money market funds to apply shadow pricing to any portfolio security within 60 days or less of maturity by using its amortized cost rather than available market quotations.[63] The amortized cost of a debt security is its original purchase price, plus or minus a prorated charge applied daily until the debt security reached its face value at maturity.[64] Unfortunately, this permission expired on January 12, 2009. Although I generally support mark-to-market accounting for financial instruments, I believe that **such shadow pricing should be allowed on a permanent basis for money market funds, as well as for other financial institutions, for a high-quality debt security with 30 days or fewer left to maturity, subject to certain conditions.[65] It makes little sense for a fund to search out market quotations for pricing debt securities that will most likely be paid back by the corporate issuer in such a short time period.**

Summary

The deposits of banks have long been insured by the FDIC to provide a safe haven for small savers, who are not in a good position to compare the financial conditions of competing banks. The level of FDIC insurance coverage has been gradually raised to $100,000. Then in October of 2008, Congress temporarily increased the insurance level on most bank deposits to $250,000 until the end of 2009, and provided unlimited insurance coverage for transactional accounts used by businesses. This $250,000 limit was later extended through 2013.

However, higher insurance levels are not needed to protect small depositors, whose average account balance falls below $6,000. For the same reason, raising the level of FDIC insurance above $100,000 will not affect the frequency of runs on banks. Even in that event, FDIC-insured banks can borrow quickly from the Fed's discount window to deal with withdrawals. There is also no evidence that raising the FDIC's insurance limit from $100,000 to $250,000 has produced more lending by banks.

Protected by higher insurance limits, weak banks can attract more deposits by offering very high interest rates, leading to more costly bank failures. Further, higher insurance limits undermine the incentives of large sophisticated investors to monitor the financial conditions of banks. Similarly, unlimited deposit insurance on transaction accounts allows businesses to ignore the threat of a potential insolvency of their main relationship banks.

As a result of increasing FDIC insurance on deposits from $100,000 to $250,000 through 2013, the costs of bank insolvencies will rise substantially. Although the FDIC has generally tried to finance deposit insurance from fee assessments on banks, Congress had to appropriate over $100 billion to clean up the S&L problems. In 2009, Congress authorized the FDIC to borrow $100 billion immediately from the Treasury, and to borrow another $400 billion if approved by the Federal Reserve and the Treasury.

Money market funds are the type of mutual fund most similar to bank accounts. They pay interest on short-term investments and allow withdrawals by check. But accounts at money market funds are generally not insured by any federal agency. Instead, they are subject to a strict set of SEC regulations, which allow these funds to maintain an NAV of $1 per share in normal times. During highly abnormal times, the NAV of a money market fund can break the buck if it sustains losses of .5 of 1 percent on more of its assets.

When one prime fund, investing primarily in commercial paper, broke the buck in September, 2008, many investors redeemed shares of that fund and similar prime funds. In response, the U.S. Treasury offered a limited form of insurance on the lower amount in a shareholder's money market account on September 18, 2008, or on the actual account balance if the shareholder redeemed the fund's shares after that date. Yet, despite this insurance coverage, investors transferred large sums from prime funds to government money market funds. The gross yield on the latter was so low that they had to be subsidized by fund managers to reach a zero return for fund shareholders.

The federal insurance for money market funds should not be continued beyond September 18, 2009, when it is slated to expire. If money market funds were insured by the federal government, they would soon be regulated like banks in most respects. However, savers benefit from competition between banks and different types of short-term investment vehicles. Moreover, money market funds are the largest buyers of short-term notes from publicly traded companies and local governments.

Instead, the SEC should tighten its rules for prime funds by limiting the maturity of any individual security held to 6 months, and limiting the average maturity of prime money funds to 60 days. The SEC should eliminate the ability of prime funds to invest 5 percent of their assets in second-tier commercial paper. The SEC should also adopt the Investment Company Institute's proposals to bolster the liquidity of money market funds.

Part Three

EVALUATING THE BAILOUT ACT OF 2008

O n May 16, 2008, in a speech to business leaders, U.S. Treasury Secretary Paulson gave an optimistic view of the financial crisis: "But in my judgment we are closer to the end of the market turmoil than the beginning. Looking forward, I expect that financial markets will be driven less by the recent turmoil and more by broader economic conditions and, specifically, by the recovery of the housing sector."[1] However, the housing sector did not recover and the market turmoil became much worse.

By mid-September, 2008, the Treasury had put Fannie Mae and Freddie Mac into conservatorship, rescued AIG, and let Lehman Brothers fail. Instead of dealing with each financial emergency on an individualized basis, Paulson was looking for a more systemic solution. Federal Reserve Chairman Ben Bernanke put forward a suggestion: Ask Congress for the money and authority to bail out the banks. Paulson responded to Bernanke's suggestion: "Fine, I'm your partner. I'll go to Congress."[2]

So Paulson put together a Bailout Bill of only three pages, which broadly authorized the Treasury Secretary to spend up to $700 billion to purchase mortgage-related assets from any financial institution head-quartered in the United States. The $700 billion number was picked out of thin air. "It's not based on any particular data point," said a Treasury spokeswoman. "We just wanted to choose a really large number."[3] Yet the original version of the Bailout Bill provided that all decisions of the Treasury in spending the $700 billion would be "committed to agency discretion, and may not be reviewed by any court of law or any admin-istrative agency."[4]

On September 23, 2008, Paulson and Bernanke presented a plan for government purchases of troubled assets to the Senate Banking Committee, which quickly rejected the plan because it was so vague and offered so little to homeowners. Senator Dodd, a Democrat, declared: "This plan is stunning in its scope and lack of detail. It does nothing in my view to help a single family save a home."[5] Republican Senator Bunning shared similar sentiments: "The Paulson plan will not bring a stop to the slide in home prices. But the Paulson plan will spend $700 billion in taxpayer dollars to prop up and clean up the balance sheets of Wall Street."[6]

Through a week of negotiations, the Bailout Bill was expanded from 3 to 110 pages and put to a vote in the House on Monday, September 29, 2008. Despite endorsements by the Democratic and Republican leadership in the House, President Bush, as well as both presidential can-didates Obama and McCain, the Bill was defeated in a 228 to 205 vote. After the adverse House vote on the Bill, the stock market dropped 7 percent that Monday, a loss of $1.2 trillion in market value.

On Wednesday, October 1, 2008, the Senate approved 74 to 25 a revised Bailout Bill, along with an array of tax sweeteners and pet projects to win the necessary votes—for instance, extension of tax credits for alter-native fuels and capital improvements for bike paths. The revised Bill now covered 451 pages and cost $850 billion because of the tax sweeteners; it appropriated $350 billion immediately for the bank bailout with another $350 billion to come later. The revised Bill passed the House 263 to 171 on Friday, October 3, 2008, and was signed into law several hours later.[7]

Although the Bush Administration initially sold the $700 billion to Congress as necessary to buy toxic assets from banks, Paulson quickly found this strategy was unworkable, since these assets were not actively traded and had no reliable prices. On October 2, 2008, a day *before* the

House vote on the Bailout Bill, Paulson told his staff: "We are going to put capital into banks first."[8] But he did not inform Congress of this major shift in strategy on that day. On October 13, 2008, Paulson met with the CEOs of the eight largest U.S. banks to pressure them into accepting almost \$125 billion from the U.S. Treasury in the form of preferred stock. (Preferred stock is a form of capital that pays a pre-set dividend each year, as opposed to common shares where the directors have discretion to pay dividends or not each year.)

By January, 2009, the Bush Treasury had purchased almost another \$70 billion in preferred stock from an additional group of 309 banks. Further, the Bush Treasury purchased a second round of preferred stock from both Citigroup and Bank of America. At the urging of the outgoing Bush Treasury and the incoming Obama Treasury, Congress appropriated the other \$350 billion for the bank bailout. With these new funds, the Obama Administration announced programs in March, 2009, to modify home mortgages and buy toxic assets from banks. The Obama Treasury also bought preferred stock in other banks, raising the total of federally assisted institutions to over 600 by June of 2009.

In the Bailout Act of 2008, Congress imposed relatively loose restrictions on executive compensation for banks receiving federal assistance. In February of 2009, the Treasury proposed tighter restrictions on executive compensation only for banks receiving federal assistance in the future. Within a few days, however, Congress passed the Stimulus Act of 2009 with new restrictions on executive compensation, which applied to all banks receiving federal assistance in the past or future. In June of 2009, Treasury adopted rules implementing the Stimulus Act and appointed a Special Master to approve compensation arrangements at firms receiving extensive federal assistance, such as Bank of America and Citigroup.[9]

In the Bailout Act of 2008, Congress also directed the SEC to submit a report within three months on whether it should suspend fair-value accounting, which requires banks to use current market prices for bonds and loans in their trading accounts. However, the SEC's report concluded that fair-value accounting should not be suspended because it provides investors with more accurate financial information than historical cost accounting.

Part III will evaluate the main components of the Bailout Act of 2008 in four chapters.

- Chapter 9 will analyze why and how the U.S. Treasury recapitalized so many banks.
- Chapter 10 will assess the multiple programs to buy toxic assets and modify home mortgages.
- Chapter 11 will evaluate the restrictions on executive compensation and related director issues.
- Chapter 12 will review the main accounting issues that are important to the financial crisis.

Chapter 9

Why and How Treasury Recapitalized So Many Banks

When the federal government bailed out Fannie Mae and Freddie Mac in early September of 2008, it deemed the two institutions "too big to fail." The two institutions together owned or guaranteed half of the mortgages in the U.S., and their bonds were widely held by foreign institutions, which had relied on the moral backing of these bonds from the U.S. government. Thus, Fannie Mae and Freddie Mac seemed intuitively too big to fail, but the U.S. Treasury did not articulate any parameters for this vague doctrine. Then, in mid-September, 2008, the Treasury let Lehman Brothers fail, although it was twice the size of Bear Stearns, which Treasury had bailed out in March of 2008. The opposite decisions on Lehman and Bear Stearns, both large investment banks, highlighted the question: What should be the criteria for concluding that an institution is too big to fail?

From mid–October 2008, through mid–January 2009, the U.S. Treasury purchased almost $195 billion in preferred stock from 317 banks.[10] In addition, the U.S. Treasury gave "exceptional" assistance to Bank of America and Citigroup, buying more preferred stock and guaranteeing large amounts of troubled assets in each bank. In the spring of 2009, the Treasury and other holders of preferred stock in Citigroup converted some of their preferred stock into common shares of Citigroup.[11] At that time, the Treasury made clear that such conversions would be offered to other banks that did poorly on a series of stress tests. These recapitalizations raise the question: What should be the form of federal ownership of financial institutions?

This chapter will begin by proposing criteria for deeming a financial institution too big to fail. In light of those criteria, it will evaluate whether the federal government should have recapitalized the big investment banks, the small community banks, the life insurers, and other financial institutions. This chapter will also analyze the four different models of government ownership implicit in these bank recapitalizations: preferred stock, revised preferred stock, exceptional assistance, and majority ownership. It will argue that the U.S. should use only the revised form of preferred stock and majority ownership through common shares because the other ownership models are unfair to taxpayers.

What Are the Limits of Too Big to Fail?

When any insured bank gets into serious trouble, the federal government has a range of available alternatives. On one end of the range, the FDIC can place a bank into receivership, and liquidate it by selling all its assets. This is the procedure followed by the FDIC in resolving failures of most small banks. Less drastically, the FDIC can place a bank into conservatorship, place its bad assets in a separate entity and sell the remaining bank to other financial institutions or private investors. This is the approach the FDIC employed in resolving Indy Mac, a large thrift (S&L) that failed in 2008. On the other end of the range, the Treasury and the Fed can inject enough capital into a bank so it can continue to do business and meet its ongoing obligations. This is the route taken so far with Citigroup. The federal government may also provide assistance to one financial institution to acquire another. Such assistance was given to Bank of America when it acquired Merrill Lynch.

Why the United States Should Be Reluctant to Bail Out Troubled Banks

There are several good reasons why the federal government should be reluctant to bail out troubled banks by any method. First, to the extent that such bailouts protect private investors in large banks, bailouts undermine the incentives of private investors to bring market discipline to bear on large banks. If investors believe that large banks will always be bailed out by the federal government, they will not care if the banks expand into unprofitable lines of business or take on too much debt. The policing of these banks will be left entirely up to the bank regulators.

Second, any bank that receives public support because it is deemed too big to fail has an unfair advantage over its competitors. The bank receives cheap capital from the federal government, which implicitly backs the continuing businesses of the bank. The competitors of AIG, for example, have complained that it now has an unfair competitive advantage in attracting life insurance clients. Such unfair competition impedes the efficient workings of the market for financial services.

Third, if the federal government provides financial assistance to encourage acquisitions of troubled banks, it reduces competition in the financial sector. This has already happened in the United States; now there are fewer large investment banks that could underwrite global securities offerings, and the retail banking market is now dominated by a small number of mega banks (with assets over $100 billion). **It is probably impractical to break up existing mega banks into small enough pieces to achieve a competitive financial sector. But the Justice Department should reject any merger or acquisition that further increases the concentration at the top end of the financial sector. Moreover, federal officials should resist the urge to subsidize acquisitions of troubled institutions that create a mega bank or expand the size of an existing one.**

Finally, once the federal government opens the door to bailouts beyond mega banks or quasi-public institutions like Fannie Mae, the line of supplicants becomes very long and the slope becomes very slippery. In May 2009, for example, one of the largest trucking companies in the United States, named YRC Worldwide Inc., sought a $1 billion bailout from the U.S. Treasury. The reason? To help cover the company's $2 billion obligation to a multiemployer pension plan. According to the CEO of YRC, the plan unfairly forces the trucking company to help cover the costs of retirees from other trucking firms that are also members of the multiemployer plan.[12] Is YRC or the multiemployer pension plan too big to fail?

Only Two Valid Justifications for Bailing Out Banks

In my opinion, there are only two valid justifications for bailing out banks. **First, one of the key functions of the banking system is to process payments, such as checks and wires, through the Federal Reserve network.** Because payment processing is critical for the operation of the economy, the United States needs a set of banks that play that function. But that does not mean that the United States should protect all banks that perform that function—just a core group of payment processors. **Second, the United States should bail out a bank that is too interconnected to fail, that is, a bank whose obligations are so large to so many other financial institutions that its failure would cause widespread havoc throughout the financial sector.** But the regulators should analyze carefully how many other firms are likely to become insolvent—as distinct from sustaining substantial losses—as a result of that institution's failure. In evaluating the impact on the overall financial system, the regulators should also determine whether the customers and assets of that failing institution could be transferred quickly to a healthy firm.

Some may argue for bailing out banks because they have specialized knowledge about making loans, and lending is essential to economic growth. Although both propositions are true, they do not justify bailing out banks to maintain lending activity. As discussed in Chapter 10, the volume of lending in the United States is driven mainly by the loan securitization process, which is used extensively by nonbank lenders as well as banks. **So long as a reasonable number of banks and nonbanks are originating loans and selling them to be securitized, the federal government should not recapitalize a marginal bank to maintain its lending capacity.**

Others might argue that we should bail out banks to protect small depositors. But every bank depositor is currently insured up to $250,000 by the FDIC. As explained in Chapter 8, one family can easily obtain $1 million of FDIC insurance by registering the deposits in the name of the father, the mother, and two children. Although a bank failure does upset its insured depositors, they typically have full access to their deposits on Monday morning after the FDIC closes a bank over the weekend.

Adverse Impact of Lehman's Failure Could Have Been Reduced

It is simply untrue that the failure of any large financial institution would wreak havoc upon the entire financial system. For instance, the 1990 bankruptcy of Drexel Burnham Lambert, the most powerful bond house in the world at the time, did not lead to a widespread breakdown in the financial system, although there was some disruption in the corporate bond markets. Indeed, if we take the position that all large banks are too big to fail, we will create a self-fulfilling prophecy. For instance, in performing stress tests on the 19 U.S. mega banks, each with assets over $100 billion, federal regulators have publicly vowed that they will help supply more capital to any of those banks that fail the tests. This vow has been widely interpreted as meaning that all 19 banks "essentially have been labeled too big to fail."[13] If one of those 19 banks were later allowed to fail, its failure would have a big impact primarily because this event would violate the expectations of investors.

Some commentators would urge federal regulators to bail out all large financial institutions on the basis of the fallout from Lehman's bankruptcy filing in mid-September of 2008. On the other hand, Stanford Professor John Taylor has argued that the freezing of the credit markets was not caused by the failure of Lehman, but rather by the federal government's announcement of the initial TARP program later that week.[14] Taylor is clearly in the minority on Lehman. Most observers contend that investors will not buy the short-term commercial paper of any large financial institution if even one—like Lehman—is allowed to fail by the federal government. But this contention implicitly assumes that any federal takeover of a financial institution will automatically wipe out all its stock and bond holders. In fact, when the federal government takes over a financial institution and eliminates all its shareholders, the government can choose to protect some of the institution's uninsured creditors or bondholders, as it did for Bear Stearns in March of 2008.

The adverse repercussions of Lehman's failure resulted primarily from the implicit expectations created by the federal bailout of all bond holders in Bear Stearns earlier in 2008. If the federal government had let Bear fail, Lehman would have moved very quickly to bolster its financing sources and find an acquisition partner. Indeed, the Korean Development Bank offered to bail out Lehman as late as August of 2008 for $18 per share, but that offer was rejected by Lehman's CEO who reportedly believed that the U.S. Treasury would come to the firm's rescue if necessary. However, when the federal regulators bailed out Bear and did not articulate criteria for doing so, their silence was interpreted by many bond investors and certain Lehman executives as an implicit promise to bail out all bondholders in other large investment banks. When Lehman was allowed to fail, many of its bondholders felt that federal regulators had reneged on this implicit promise. These bondholders were surprised by the government's hands-off approach to Lehman, despite strong market signals in early September that the firm's demise was imminent.

In my view, the adverse repercussions of Lehman's failure could have been substantially reduced if the federal regulators had made clear that they would protect all holders of Lehman's commercial paper with a maturity of less than 60 days and guaranteed the completion of all trades with Lehman for that period. This combination of governmental measures would have been similar to the approach taken in 2009 by the Obama Administration toward Chrysler; the government gave advance notice of its possible bankruptcy, guaranteed car warranties to all Chrysler buyers, and offered temporary financing to the struggling car company.

The Rationale for Recapitalizing 600 Banks Is Unclear

Most of the federal recapitalizations of banks from October 2008 through February 2009, do not seem to have been based on the too-big-to-fail doctrine. Instead, they seem to have been part of a broad preemptive strike to prevent further deterioration in the financial sector. For example, the capital infusions of almost $125 billion into the eight largest U.S. banks in October of 2008 were not based on a finding that they were about to fail or that their payment processing functions were at risk. Although a few of these banks may have needed the capital, others clearly did not. For instance, J.P. Morgan reluctantly accepted $25 billion in federal preferred stock, but its CEO wanted to redeem that stock as soon as Congress imposed bonus restrictions in February of 2009.[15]

In June 2009, 10 financial institutions were permitted to redeem a total of $68 billion in preferred stock from the Treasury.[16] Although the Treasury touted these redemptions as showing that TARP was working, these redemptions after less than seven months showed that most of these 10 financial institutions probably did not need Treasury's preferred stock in the first place. Most of these 10 financial institutions were not close to failure in October of 2008. In response to heavy pressure from the Treasury, these institutions were prepared to accept cheap federal capital, until these benefits were outweighed by the new restrictions on executive compensation in February of 2009.

There is a better approach: Wait until the capital of a particular bank, or group of banks, approaches a level indicating even a remote risk of insolvency, and then evaluate what would be the appropriate response—including capital injections—in light of the specific circumstances. During the evaluation process, the bank or group of banks could continue to operate by obtaining low-cost loans from the Fed if needed.

Let us examine the rationales for three other types of federal infusions of capital into small banks, newly converted bank holding companies, and life insurers.

Small Banks Are Receiving Capital for Political Reasons

By the end of 2008, the Treasury had bought $200 million or less of preferred stock from each of over 160 small and midsized banks or their holding companies.[17] In May, 2009, Secretary Geithner announced that the Treasury would reopen the window for applications for federal capital from more banks with assets under $500 million.[18] These capital infusions cannot be justified as protecting the payment processing system or preventing systemic failures because these banks are too small. Nor are these banks on the brink of failure; they seem to be chosen because they are in relatively healthy condition. It appears that these capital infusions are a political concession to small bankers who were upset that so much federal assistance was going to the largest U.S. banks.

Moreover, the choice of certain banking organizations for federal infusions did not fit with the objective of increasing local lending. For example, the Treasury bought $154 million of preferred stock from a bank holding company called Boston Private Financial Holdings. It owns the Boston Private Bank & Trust Company, which caters to high net worth individuals for trust and other services. For this reason, it owns a dozen or so asset management firms across the country. Since the federal capital was injected at the level of the holding company, it could use this capital to buy another asset manager. Indeed, it was not even required to push this federal capital down to the Boston Private Bank, which could then make additional loans to its wealthy clients.

With the adoption of the restrictions on executive compensation and dividends on common shares, some small and midsized banks have redeemed their federal preferred stock. As of June 9, 2009, 22 small banks returned a total of $1.8 billion in capital to the Treasury.[19] Earlier in the year, at least 50 banks decided not to accept federal capital after taking the time and effort to obtain Treasury approval. The executive vice president at United Bankshares, Inc., of Charleston, West Virginia, explained its rejection of federal capital: "There is a provision that allows the government to unilaterally change the rules and that is of great concern to us."[20]

Conversions to Bank Holding Companies Should Be Allowed, but Not Capital Infusions

When Lehman Brothers pleaded with the Federal Reserve to become a bank holding company in August 2008, its plea was rejected. By contrast, when Goldman Sachs and Morgan Stanley asked to become bank holding companies in September 2008, both were promptly given approvals. Over the next few months, the Fed also approved conversions to bank holding companies of several other financial institutions: American Express, a credit card company; Discover Financial, another credit card company; and GMAC, an auto loan company. In all five cases, the Treasury committed to buy preferred stock in the newly minted bank holding companies within a month of their conversion.

The conversion of these five institutions into bank holding companies makes sense because it allows them to tap additional financing sources. In their prior form, all five companies could borrow money for periods of 8 to 270 days mainly by issuing commercial paper to large investors. But these large investors are demanding and risk averse; the commercial paper market was actually frozen for several months in the fall of 2008. (See Chapter 7.) As bank holding companies, these institutions could also borrow short-term funds by gathering FDIC-insured deposits in their subsidiary banks; these deposits are generally less costly and more stable than commercial paper. Further, their subsidiary banks could borrow on a short-term basis from the Fed.

Although the bank holding company designation opened up additional financing sources for these five institutions, they should *not* have received federal capital. They have no involvement in processing payments, and they have no obligation to increase their lending as a result of the capital infusion. Of course, Goldman Sachs and Morgan Stanley would argue that they are too big to fail. But there was little concrete evidence that either institution was on the brink of failure in October, 2008. Indeed, Goldman Sachs and Morgan Stanley wanted to redeem their preferred stock from the government as soon as practical to avoid the February, 2009 restrictions on executive compensation.[21]

American Express and Discover Financial are big issuers of credit cards that were allowed to become bank holding companies and supplied with billions of dollars of cheap federal capital. However, the failure of either would not have led to a widespread breakdown of the financial system. In contrast to AIG mentioned below, they did not have huge obligations to a limited group of very large financial institutions. They are credit card companies serving millions of customers and merchants, who would rapidly be picked up by Capital One, J.P. Morgan, and other card issuers.

GMAC's conversion to a bank holding company was particularly problematic. The Treasury purchased $5 billion in preferred stock from

GMAC, and it lent $1 billion to General Motors so that the parent company could participate in a rights offering by GMAC.[22] Although the Treasury can legitimately decide to bail out the car industry, it relied on TARP funding—authorized for financial institutions—because Congress would not appropriate additional funds to rescue the car companies.

In a sixth case, the federal government allowed CIT, a lender to small- and medium-sized businesses, to convert quickly to a bank holding company, and then bought $2.3 billion of its preferred stock in late 2008. In mid-2009, however, when CIT experienced a liquidity crunch, the federal government refused to guarantee its short-term debt. As a result, CIT reached an agreement with its bondholders to swap their bonds for equity.[23] The CIT case illustrates several points. First, as the 20th largest bank holding company with $75 billion in assets, CIT was clearly not too big to fail; its failure would not have brought down many other large financial institutions. Second, when the federal government balked at providing financial guarantees, CIT was able to work out a deal in the private sector. Third, the federal policy toward CIT was inconsistent. Why pump $2.3 billion into CIT in late 2008 if, with that extra capital, it was still not worthy of a federal debt guarantee?

The Case for Bailing Out Life Insurers Is Weak

The federal government bailed out AIG, the global insurer, because it was the largest seller of credit default swaps (CDS), which offered protection against the default of MBS and corporate bonds. Because there was no clearinghouse for CDS at the time, federal officials feared that AIG's failure would lead to the failure of an indeterminate number of counterparties. (The bailout of AIG is described in detail in Chapter 4.)

More generally, the Treasury has said that other life insurers will be eligible for capital infusions if they own a federally regulated bank or thrift.[24] Several insurance companies such as Genworth and Lincoln National have announced acquisitions of small thrifts to become savings and loan holding companies; other life insurers, such as Allstate and Prudential, already owned thrifts, and did apply to the Treasury to get capital infusions.[25]

In May, 2009, the Treasury agreed in principle to inject $22 billion into at least seven life insurers that own savings and loan associations.[26]

The life insurers argued for a federal capital infusion because they are significant investors in corporate bonds, real estate, and commercial MBS. They also provide unique long-term products—insurance promises to pay death benefits and annuity promises to pay retirement benefits. But the most articulate opponent of federal subsidies for the insurance industry is Evan Greenberg, CEO of an insurer called ACE Limited, who wrote:

> There is no evidence that insurers inhibit the availability of credit, or possess counterparty credit exposure, that threatens the financial system. Yes, insurers have been buffeted by the current financial market turmoil. But this is not a crisis, nor does it threaten a "run on the bank." Insurers are not generally lenders, and the availability of credit is not meaningfully affected by insurers' financial issues. Nor will delivering capital to insurers unfreeze any credit markets.[27]

Some of the largest life insurers such as New York Life and Northwestern Mutual, are not asking for assistance because they are financially sound.[28] Several insurers, including Prudential, that were approved for a federal capital infusion have decided to reject the government's offer.[29] **When the Treasury provides cheap capital to troubled life insurers, they obtain an unfair advantage over their healthy competitors that were more prudent managers of financial risk. Therefore, the Treasury should not have recapitalized life insurers. If they need short-term liquidity, they should be allowed to take advantage of the Fed's lending program and the FDIC's debt guarantees.** (See Chapter 7.)

How the U.S. Treasury Recapitalized the Banks

Shortly after the passage of the Bailout Act, Treasury Secretary Paulson brought to his office the CEOs of the eight largest U.S. financial institutions and pressured all of them into accepting substantial capital contributions from the Treasury in the form of preferred stock.[30] Although the CEOs of some of these banks said they did not need the government's capital, this was an offer they could not refuse. Paulson wanted all eight banks to accept the government's preferred stock to avoid any stigma being attached to the few banks, such as Citigroup, which really needed the capital infusion. According to documents obtained under the Freedom of Information Act, Paulson said: "We don't believe it is tenable to opt out because doing so would leave you vulnerable and exposed. If a capital infusion is not appealing, you should be aware that your regulator will require it in any circumstances."[31]

The Treasury had already decided on the amounts of capital to be received by each bank (see Table 9.1), and the uniform terms for the preferred stock.[32] Its preferred stock pays an annual dividend of 5 percent for 5 years, which then increases to 9 percent if not redeemed by the bank. The preferred stock carries warrants (similar to call options) for the Treasury to purchase a certain amount of the bank's common shares at a specified price. The bank may redeem the preferred stock at its face value, without penalty after three years, with a significant portion of the cash derived from a public or private offering. At any time, the Treasury may sell the preferred stock to a third party.

Table 9.1 Summary of Estimated Value Conclusions (Largest Eight Banks)

Purchase Program Participant	Validation Date	Face Value	Value	Subsidy %	Subsidy $
Capital Purchase Program					
Bank of America Corporation	10/14/08	$ 15.0	$12.5	17%	$ 2.6
Citigroup Inc.	10/14/08	25.0	15.5	38%	9.5
JPMorgan Chase & Co	10/14/08	25.0	20.6	18%	4.4
Morgan Stanley	10/14/08	10.0	5.3	42%	4.2
The Goldman Sachs Group Inc.	10/14/08	10.0	7.5	25%	2.5
The PNC Financial Services Group	10/24/08	7.6	5.5	27%	2.1
U.S. Bancorp	11/3/08	6.6	6.3	5%	0.3
Wells Fargo & Company	10/14/08	25.0	23.2	7%	1.8
Total		**$124.2**	**$96.9**	**22%**	**$27.3**

SOURCE: Congressional Oversight Panel.

If the Treasury holds only preferred stock of a participating bank, the Treasury has limited rights to nominate directors or vote for them. Its preferred stock is nonvoting with three exceptions. If the participating bank falls behind on its preferred dividend payments to the Treasury for six successive quarters, the Treasury may nominate two "preferred directors" to the bank's board. The Treasury also has the standard right to vote on any matters that could adversely affect the rights of its preferred stock. Finally, the Treasury retains the right to vote on any merger, as well as on any exchange or new issuance of bank shares.

The Terms of the Initial Preferred Omitted Key Conditions

The standard terms of the preferred stock are notable for what they do *not* contain. A participating bank may continue to pay dividends on its other shares at current levels, unless it misses dividend payments on the Treasury's preferred stock. But critics pointed out that $25 billion of the $125 billion contributed to the eight largest banks by the U.S. Treasury would be paid out as dividends to bank shareholders in the first year.[33] Nor were participating banks required to increase their lending; they were merely urged to try to "expand the flow of credit to U.S. consumers and businesses."[34] The loan volume for some of the largest recipients of federal capital declined from the third to the fourth quarter of 2008, and again in the first quarter of 2009.[35]

These quantitative trends are supported by anecdotal evidence from banks receiving capital infusions from the Treasury. For example, when the Independent Bank of Michigan received $72 million in Treasury's preferred stock, it shored up its financial situation by repaying short-term advances and tried hard to avoid making bad loans. The bank's chief lending officer explained: "It is like if you are in an airplane and the oxygen mask comes down. First thing you do is put your own mask on, stabilize yourself."[36]

Moreover, as Harvard Professors Coates and Scharfstein have pointed out, capital contributions were made by the Treasury to the holding companies of banks, rather than to their banking subsidiaries where most of the lending occurs.[37] The holding companies for banks may engage in a much broader range of venture capital, securities, and other financial activities than banks. (See Figure 6.1 in Chapter 6.)

By the end of 2008, less than 17 percent of the capital contributed by the Treasury to the four largest banks had been pushed down from the holding company to the bank level.[38] **The Treasury should invest capital in a bank holding company only if it commits to promptly push the capital down to its bank(s).**

The Treasury's Capital Contribution Was Substantially Undervalued

According to the Congressional Oversight Committee on TARP, the Treasury contributed $124.2 billion in cash in October and November of 2008 to the eight largest bank holding companies in the United States, but received only $96.9 billion in value, representing a 22 percent discount,[39] as illustrated by Table 9.1. The Committee's conclusions were based on detailed evaluations conducted by Duff & Phelps and an advisory committee of three distinguished finance professionals. The discount seems to have been the result of several factors, such as the relatively low dividend rate, the ability of the participating banks to buy back the preferred at face value without penalty and, perhaps most importantly, the Treasury's decision to offer preferred stock with the same terms to all participating banks. Because the Treasury wanted all of the largest banks, regardless of financial strength, to accept the same type of preferred stock, it had to offer attractive terms that effectively subsidized the weaker banks receiving federal assistance.

Another fruitful perspective on valuation is to compare the terms of the preferred stock bought by the Treasury in Goldman Sachs to the terms of the preferred stock bought by Warren Buffett in Goldman Sachs around the same time in late 2008. Consider Table 9.2, which summarizes five of the key terms of both transactions.

Because the Treasury bought twice the amount of preferred stock as Buffett did in Goldman Sachs, the Treasury should have obtained better terms than him, but Buffett got a much better deal. Buffett's initial dividend rate was 10 percent, as compared to 5 percent for the Treasury. He would receive a 10 percent premium above face value in the event his preferred stock is repaid early, whereas the Treasury would receive no premium. Buffett received warrants to purchase common shares equal to 100 percent of the face value of his preferred stock, whereas the Treasury received warrants to purchase

Table 9.2   Goldman Sachs (GS), Preferred Stock Terms: Buffett vs. Treasury

	Buffett	Treasury
Amount	$5 billion	$10 billion
Annual Dividend Rate	10%	5% for initial 5 years, and then 9%
Callability(Early Repayment)	Callable by GS at any time at 10% premium above face value	Callable by GS after 3 years at face value
Amount of Warrants	$5 billion	$1.5 billion
Exercise Price of Warrants	$115 per share; trading at $125 per share at time of purchase of preferred stock	Price per share at average price for 20 days before the purchase of preferred stock

only 15 percent of the face value of its preferred stock. Buffett's warrants would be exercisable at a price below the current market when he purchased the preferred stock; the Treasury's warrants would be exercisable at the current market price when it purchased the preferred stock.[40] **In the future, the Treasury should set the terms of its preferred stock at market rates. As of June 12, 2009, for example, the market rate for dividends on preferred stock was over 8 percent for J.P. Morgan and over 10 percent for Bank of America.**[41]

Treasury Plan Was to Promote Acquisitions

If the link between recapitalizing banks and increasing loan volume was weak, what was the rationale underlying the first phase of the Treasury's recapitalization plan? As mentioned earlier, this plan seemed to be designed as a preemptive strike to prevent further deterioration in the financial sector. As part of this strategy, Treasury supplied cheap capital to stronger banks that would be likely to acquire weaker ones. Although this strategy may reduce explicit costs of saving banks in the short run, the implicit costs in the long run will be less price competition and more systemic risk in a highly concentrated financial sector. This strategy, as University of Michigan Professor Whitman pointed out, "will both lessen competition and create more financial institutions that will be deemed too big to fail."[42]

In October of 2008, Treasury officials made clear that a plan to make acquisitions would help a bank obtain a federal contribution of capital. "If a healthy institution is making an acquisition, we would look very favorably on that," said a senior government official.[43] That official cue was picked up quickly by the banking community. A few days later, a J.P. Morgan senior executive said that the $25 billion in federal capital will make the bank "more active on the acquisition side or opportunistic side for some banks who are still struggling."[44] In December of 2008, J.P. Morgan bought the Canadian energy operations and global agricultural business of Swiss bank UBS.[45]

A key factor in promoting acquisitions of banks was a policy change on the tax treatment of net operating losses by the Internal Revenue Service (IRS), an agency that reports to the Secretary of the Treasury. For two decades, the IRS had severely limited the ability of an acquiring bank to offset its profits with the net operating losses incurred by the acquired bank *prior to the acquisition*. This limit was designed to prevent a profitable company from buying other firms primarily to benefit from their tax losses. Then on September 30, 2008, without public notice and opportunity for comment, the IRS issued a one-sentence ruling saying that the limit on using preacquisition losses would no longer apply to acquisitions of banks.[46] (The limit continued to apply to acquisitions in all other industries.)

The impact of the IRS ruling was immediate. Although Wells Fargo had apparently dropped its interest in buying Wachovia, Wells Fargo suddenly reversed its position and outbid Citigroup for the North Carolina bank. Under the old rule, Wells Fargo would have been limited to deducting $18.6 billion of Wachovia's losses over the next 20 years. Under the new IRS ruling, Wells Fargo would be able to utilize all of Wachovia's $74 billion in tax losses for an additional tax savings estimated at $19.4 billion by an independent tax analyst. By contrast, the total purchase price paid by Wells Fargo for Wachovia was $14.3 billion.[47]

Later in October of 2008, PNC Financial Services Group relied on the new IRS ruling, together with a $7.7 billion capital infusion by the Treasury, to help finance its acquisition of National City Corporation, a Cleveland bank. According to an independent tax analyst, the tax savings to PNC from the acquisition could exceed $5 billion.[48] In October of 2008, Banco Santander also reaped billions in tax savings under the new tax ruling, when the Spanish bank acquired the portion of Sovereign Bank that it did not already own.[49]

Helping to finance bank acquisitions through the new IRS ruling is terrible policy. These huge losses in future tax revenues are stealth costs, which fly below the public radar screen. Congress was not given an opportunity to approve this significant change in tax policy, although the billions of dollars of tax revenue lost from this new ruling circumvent the legislative ceiling of $700 billion on the bank bailout. In the Stimulus Act of 2009, Congress finally forced the IRS to revert to its old position on preacquisition losses, but only with respect to future bank transactions.

The Obama Administration Improved the Terms of the Preferred

In February 2009, the Obama Administration announced a Financial Stability Plan with new conditions applicable only to banks receiving preferred stock from the Treasury in the future.[50] These new conditions correct the main defects in the initial round of bank recapitalizations. The new conditions will prohibit banks from paying dividends to shareholders other than the Treasury. The new conditions will require participating banks to submit a plan detailing how the capital will be used, including a monthly report on new lending compared to prior lending volumes. But the recapitalized banks will *not* be required to increase their lending. Instead, they must commit to participate in the federal government's loan modification programs described in Chapter 10.[51]

Within a few days after the release of the plan, the Stimulus Act of 2009 restricted executive compensation by limiting bonuses to one-third of annual compensation. This legislative limit applies to any bank receiving federal assistance in the past or the future. As detailed in Chapter 11, this legislative limit will perversely weaken the link between pay and performance by increasing base salaries and decreasing performance bonuses.

Further, the Stimulus Act of 2009 permits banks to redeem their preferred stock from the Treasury at any time without raising new capital from public or private sources. This legislative change to the original terms for redeeming preferred stock is counterproductive, although federal regulators still control the actual timing of stock redemptions and have insisted that recapitalized banks sell stock to third parties before allowing these banks to redeem preferred stock from the Treasury. **The regulators should continue to insist that recapitalized banks raise capital from nongovernmental sources, rather than take the circular path of using federal capital to generate earnings in order to buy back preferred stock from the Treasury.**

The initial model for redeemable preferred stock should be replaced by the revised model delineated by the Obama Administration, except that the amount of warrants and the dividend level on the government's preferred stock should be set at market rates. When the ten institutions redeemed $68 billion in preferred stock in June, 2009, the value of their warrants was estimated to be in the $3.8 to $4.6 billion range.[52] However, if the warrants had been equal to the face value of the preferred stock, in accordance with normal market practice, these warrants would have been worth at least $20 billion to the Treasury. Moreover, in contrast to normal market practice, these financial institutions did not have to pay any premium for early redemption of the Treasury's preferred stock.

Majority Ownership Avoids One-Way Capitalism

After the initial round of recapitalizations, the Treasury decided to grant exceptional assistance to Bank of America and Citigroup. As will be explained below, both grants were ill-conceived; they grossly undervalued the federal assistance and unwisely guaranteed troubled assets against losses. In these situations, the U.S. Treasury should become the majority owner of the bank. This is the way that taxpayers will be treated fairly, because they would reap most of the benefits if the bank turns around, although they would also bear most of the losses if the bank fails. Table 9.3 compares the key features of the four models of federal ownership of banks.

Exceptional Assistance = One-Way Capitalism

On September 15, 2008, Bank of America agreed to acquire Merrill Lynch for $50 billion in "the deal of a lifetime" as perceived by the

Table 9.3 Comparing Four Models of Governance

	Original Preferred Stock	Revised Preferred Stock	Exceptional Assistance	Majority Ownership
Voting Rights of Federal Government	Non-voting preferred with three exceptions	Non-voting preferred with three exceptions	Non-voting preferred with three exceptions, plus minority interest in voting common shares	Own majority of voting common shares, plus public minority vote
Convertibility of Preferred to Common	No	No	Yes, at option of bank	Already converted to common
Dividend Restrictions	None	Max dividend payment of $0.01 per quarter	Max dividend payment of $0.01 per quarter	Max dividend payment of $0.01 per quarter
Lending Requirements	None	Report monthly on lending activity	Report monthly on lending activity	Report monthly on lending activity
Executive Compensation Restrictions	Yes	Yes, with enhanced restrictions	Yes, with enhanced restrictions	Yes, with enhanced restrictions
Acquisition Restrictions	None	Yes	Yes	Yes
Participation in Mortgage Loan Modification Program	No	Yes	Yes	Yes

Bank of America; Ken Lewis, the Bank's CEO, called the acquisition a "major grand slam home run."[53] However, when Merrill Lynch started to experience greater losses than expected toward the end of 2008, the Bank planned to walk from the deal under the material adverse condition (MAC) clause in the acquisition agreement. When Ken Lewis came to Washington, DC, on December 17, 2008, to explain this plan to Treasury Secretary Paulson and Fed Chairman Bernanke, they strenuously objected. According to an e-mail on December 19, 2008, from Tim Clark, a senior adviser at the Fed: "Ken Lewis' claim that they were surprised by the rapid growth of the losses [at Merrill Lynch] seems somewhat suspect. At a minimum it calls into question the adequacy of the due diligence process [Bank of America] has been doing…"[54] In another e-mail dated December 21, 2008, Chairman Bernanke urged Fed officials to explain to Bank of America why the invocation of the MAC clause "would be a foolish move and why the regulators will not condone it."[55] Yet when Lewis expressed concerns about shareholder suits, and "asked whether he could use as a defense that [government] ordered him to proceed [with the transaction] for systemic reasons. I said no," Bernanke declared in a subsequent e-mail.[56]

A spokeswoman for Paulson said that his discussions with Lewis centered on the opinion of the Fed's lawyers that Bank of America was not legally justified in invoking the MAC clause and Treasury's view that it would not let a systematically important institution like Merrill Lynch fail.[57] According to the minutes of the board meeting on December 22, 2008 of the holding corporation that owns Bank of America, "the Treasury and Fed stated strongly that were the corporation to invoke the material adverse change clause . . . The Treasury and Fed would remove the board and management of the corporation."[58]

Bank of America did not publicly disclose Merrill's mounting losses, the Bank's plan to walk away from the Merrill transaction, or the position taken by the federal officials. Why? Here is a verbatim transcript of questions from a representative of the New York Attorney General with answers from Mr. Lewis:[59]

> Q: Were you instructed not to tell your shareholders what the
>   transaction was going to be?
> A: I was instructed that "We do not want a public disclosure."

Q: Who said that to you?

A: Paulson . . .

Q: Had it been up to you would you (have) made the disclosure?

A: It wasn't up to me.

Q: Had it been up to you.

A: It wasn't.

Because Secretary Paulson wanted the acquisition to go through, the Treasury agreed to buy $20 billion in redeemable preferred stock from Bank of America (in addition to the $25 billion in the initial round) with an 8 percent dividend. The Treasury agreed to guarantee a pool of $118 billion in troubled assets, consisting 75 percent of assets acquired from Merrill and 25 percent of assets from Bank of America that it had owned before the Merrill acquisition. For a guarantee of $118 billion in troubled assets, with a deductible of $10 billion retained by Bank of America, the federal government received only $4 billion in redeemable preferred stock from the Bank of America.[60]

Federal officials gave this exceptional assistance to Bank of America in order to prevent the failure of Merrill Lynch, although they knew about the brokerage firm's payment of $3.6 billion in annual bonuses on December 29, 2008, just before the acquisition closed. Four of Merrill's top executives together received $121 million, and another 700 Merrill executives became millionaires.[61] In a proposed SEC settlement, Bank of America did not disclose to the shareholders voting on the acquisition that the acquisition agreement allowed Merrill to pay out bonuses of up to $5.8 billion in December of 2008.[62]

Similarly, Citigroup received an additional federal investment of $20 billion in preferred stock over and above the $25 billion received in the first round of recapitalizations.[63] That additional $20 billion in preferred was overvalued by 50 percent according to the Congressional Oversight Panel. The Panel concluded that the second round of capital infusions did not adequately reflect the significant increase in the riskiness of Citigroup's condition between the two rounds.[64]

The Panel did not attempt to value the federal government's guarantee against losses of $306 billion in Citigroup's troubled assets (later reduced to $301 billion). For this guarantee, the federal government received $7 billion in preferred stock from Citigroup, which retained the first $29 billion in losses as a deductible. The federal government has never provided a justification for its pricing of this mammoth guarantee of Citigroup's troubled assets.

This exceptional assistance model is unfair to U.S. taxpayers. After the second round of federal assistance at the end of January, 2009, the federal government's warrants were convertible into no more than 7.8 percent of Citigroup's common shares and no more than 6 percent of Bank of America's common shares.[65] Yet taxpayers had contributed $45 billion in capital to each bank and offered large guarantees of troubled assets. At the end of January, 2009, by contrast, Citigroup's total market capitalization was less than $20 billion and Bank of America's total market capitalization was less than $33 billion.

In short, the exceptional assistance model is a form of *one-way capitalism*. Taxpayers own most of the downside if Citigroup or Bank of America fails. However, taxpayers own a very small percentage of the upside if these banks turn around and become profitable. To provide taxpayers with the upside as well as the downside, the federal government should move from the exceptional assistance model to the majority ownership model for mega banks in serious trouble.

Majority Ownership of Troubled Banks Is Not Permanent Nationalization

In February of 2009, Citigroup went to Washington, DC a third time with another request for federal assistance. This request was precipitated by the announcement that banking regulators would conduct a comprehensive stress test of the 19 mega banks with assets in excess of $100 billion to determine how these banks would fare under two different economic scenarios.[66] The stress test would focus on the bank's ratio of tangible common equity to assets, a ratio used to measure each bank's ability to absorb loan losses with hard assets like cash, as opposed to intangible assets like goodwill. As of February of 2009, Citigroup had a ratio of tangible capital to assets of 1.5 percent, the lowest among the largest banks at that time.[67]

In order to increase Citigroup's ratio of tangible common equity to assets, the Treasury agreed to convert its initial $25 billion of preferred stock into common shares along with several private holders of

Citigroup's other preferred stock. After all these conversions of preferred stock to common shares, taxpayers owned approximately 34 percent of Citigroup's common shares.[68] But this is a gross understatement of Treasury's economic interest in Citigroup. The federal government did not convert to common shares the $27 billion in redeemable preferred stock it acquired in its second capital contribution to Citigroup ($20 billion of preferred stock plus another $7 billion for the asset guarantee). If all this federal preferred stock were also converted to common shares, the federal government would own close to 80 percent of Citigroup's common shares.

The Obama Administration is reluctant to recognize its full owner-ship interest in the 9 or 10 large banks that needed more capital after the stress tests;[69] it does not want to play a role as an activist shareholder.[70] Similarly, many federal officials have publicly emphasized that they want "a privately held banking system," rather than "nationalization,"[71] by which they mean wiping out all bank shareholders in favor of govern-ment ownership of 100 percent of a bank's equity. To avoid holding a majority of a bank's voting shares, the Treasury has indicated that it will not convert its redeemable preferred to common shares in banks other than Citigroup. Instead, the Treasury's redeemable preferred will become mandatorily convertible preferred, a unique security that counts as com-mon shares for bank capital purposes but has voting rights similar to those of redeemable preferred.[72] Shares of mandatorily convertible pre-ferred can be converted to a bank's common shares at any time by the bank, and will convert automatically to common shares at the end of seven years.

Let us consider the arguments for and against nationalization of banks. Advocates of nationalization emphasize that it allows the FDIC to take over troubled assets and dispose of them over time, without objec-tions from the bank's shareholders because they would have been elimi-nated. These advocates point to the positive experience of the Resolution Trust Corporation, which centralized and managed troubled assets for S&Ls that had been placed into receivership during the 1980s and 1990s. Advocates mention Continental Illinois Bank, which was successfully nationalized, cleaned up, and ultimately sold off in 1994. They also point to the success of Sweden in nationalizing its banks during the 1990s when they faced a serious financial crisis.

However, the Resolution Trust Corporation dealt with a much smaller set of troubled assets than the current crisis, which involves anywhere between $2 trillion and $5.5 trillion of troubled assets. Continental Illinois held only 2 percent of the assets of the U.S. banking system at the time, while the current group of troubled banks holds a majority of the nation's banking assets. Similarly, Sweden's largest bank at that time held the equivalent of only 10 percent of the assets held by either of the two largest banking organizations in the United States today.[73]

Critics of nationalization emphasize that it would mean a bureaucratic approach to bank management. Regulatory officials would have a veto over significant decisions by bank executives, and elected officials might be tempted to pressure banks to take politically attractive but economically risky actions like lending to distressed auto companies. In addition, banking executives would be subject to strict limits on executive compensation. For all these reasons, it may be difficult to attract the most talented managers to run nationalized banks.

On the other hand, any bank receiving exceptional federal assistance would already be subject to the new limits on executive compensation and bonuses described in Chapter 11. Senior officers at Citigroup already must obtain advance approval of any significant decision from federal regulators. For example, regulators have suggested certain acquisitions to Citigroup and directed it not to proceed with other acquisitions.[74] Politicians have also been critical of banks with federal capital for holding conferences for top clients or employees at swanky resorts. For instance, Wells Fargo cancelled a Las Vegas conference in early 2009 for its most productive mortgage brokers in response to Congressional criticism.[75]

So what makes the most sense? **To avoid one-way capitalism, the federal government should take a majority ownership interest in seriously troubled banks, of no more than 80 percent of its common shares, on a temporary basis. That percentage would provide taxpayers with most of the upside if the bank turns around, as well as most of the downside if the bank fails. Maintaining private ownership of at least 20 percent of the bank's common shares would allow for grants of restricted shares to recruit qualified bank executives, and would make it easier for the government ultimately to exit by selling its shares. The fiduciary duties**

of bank executives to public shareholders would also help these executives fend off political pressures.

Pressures to pursue unprofitable objectives would be the biggest threat to the majority-owned model for banks. **The Treasury should protect majority-owned banks from Congressional interference by setting clear profit objectives for these banks and providing them with explicit subsidies to carry out any other goals.** For example, if a majority-owned bank were asked by Congress to invest in bonds with below-market yields, it should receive from the Treasury cash subsidies equal to the yield differential. Unless political goals are accounted for separately from profit objectives, taxpayers will not be able to hold executives of these banks accountable for rehabilitating them, and it will be more difficult for the government to sell its shares at attractive prices. Having well-run, majority-owned banks is critical to recouping the government's investment in them.

How to Facilitate an Exit from Government Ownership

The exit from government ownership of banks will be challenging. It may be difficult for the government to find a financial institution willing and able to buy all of a mega bank like Citigroup, so it might have to be sold in pieces, by geographic area or by function. Alternatively, a public offering of the whole government position might be hard for the market to absorb at a reasonable price, so the government might have to sell down its position in stages over time. Another possibility would be for the government to sell all or some of its shares to private equity funds.

To attract private equity funds as potential buyers of troubled banks, the Federal Reserve has already liberalized its rules for noncontrolling investments in banking organizations; that is, investments that do not result in the investor becoming a bank holding company.[76] These rules are necessary because financial services holding companies are not permitted to engage in most nonfinancial businesses because of long-standing Congressional concerns about mixing commercial and banking activities.

In brief, an investor will generally not be deemed to have control of a banking organization if the investor appoints just one of its directors, as long as the investor does not own above 15 percent of the voting power and above 33 percent of the total equity of the organization. Alternatively, an investor will be able to appoint two directors if they do not exceed 25 percent of the board seats and another shareholder controls the banking organization. In both situations, the Federal Reserve will treat as voting securities any preferred stock that converts into common shares at a certain date or at the option of the stockholder.[77] To comply with these restrictions, several private equity funds in 2009 each had to buy a limited stock position in an insolvent bank.[78]

To attract investments by private equity funds in troubled banks, the Federal Reserve may have to liberalize its rules further. For example, a private equity fund organized for the sole purpose of acquiring and running troubled banks should be able to buy controlling interests in such banks subject to existing statutory restrictions and additional conditions—designed to prohibit any material transactions between the bank and any nonfinancial affiliate of the private equity fund. However, the FDIC has adopted new barriers to private equity investments in insolvent banks, such as much higher capital requirements for banks controlled by any private equity fund as well as cross-guarantees against certain FDIC losses at other banks controlled by the same fund.[79]

At the same time, the U.S. government should be more receptive to large investments in troubled banking organizations by sovereign wealth funds (SWFs). In the early days of the financial crisis, several SWFs made substantial investments in U.S. financial institutions—for example, the $5.9 billion investment by a Singapore SWF in Merrill Lynch.[80] By my estimates, the value of these past investments in U.S. financial institutions by SWFs has decreased by more than 50 percent. Each of those SWF investments represented less than 10 percent of the equity of the relevant financial institution because larger SWF investments in U.S. companies of strategic significance are subject to a special inter-agency review. This review process, conducted through the Committee on Foreign Investment in the United States, examines foreign acquisitions of 10 percent or more of any U.S. company with national security or strategic implications.[81]

If the United States wants SWFs to invest in troubled banks in the future, the United States should treat them the same as private equity funds under the Federal Reserve's liberalized guidelines summarized earlier. SWF investments in banking organizations should not have to undergo a special review by the Treasury, since they are already subject to extensive scrutiny by the Federal Reserve Board. In addition, given the outcry against other SWF investments in large American companies, such as when a Chinese oil company tried to acquire Unocal Corp., the Treasury should publicly announce that it would welcome SWF investments in U.S. financial institutions.

Summary

The Treasury should limit the too-big-to-fail doctrine to financial institutions that are critical to the payment process or that would probably wreak havoc on the financial system if they failed—for example, by likely causing the insolvency of many other large institutions. The Treasury should not recapitalize all mega banks in a preemptive move to prevent deterioration in the financial sector. Nor should the Treasury recapitalize small banks as a political concession: They are not big processors of payments, and they are not likely to be too interconnected to fail. Such bailouts impose large direct costs on taxpayers and undermine market incentives to monitor financial institutions.

In particular, the federal government should stop infusing capital into financial institutions recently converted to banks, unless they are on the brink of failure and meet one of the two justifications for a federal bailout. By allowing these nonbanks to become banks, the Fed has already expanded their financing sources to include insured deposits and short-term loans from the Fed's discount window. Nor should the federal government be purchasing preferred stock in weak insurance companies, which happen to own or buy a savings and loan association. If insurance companies need short-term liquidity, they should be permitted to obtain loans or loan guarantees from the Fed and the FDIC to the extent necessary.

If the federal government decides to bail out relatively healthy banks, it should utilize the preferred stock model of government ownership as revised by the Obama Administration, if the dividend rates and warrant levels on the Treasury's preferred stock are based on market indicators. The revised rules already limit the payment of dividends on other shares by participating banks, and they require detailed reporting by those banks on how they are deploying the federal capital. However, the case for federal investments in relatively healthy banks is weak because, by definition, they are not anywhere close to insolvency. A better approach would be for federal regulators to wait until the yellow light starts blinking for a bank or a set of banks, and then decide whether to contribute capital or pursue a different strategy.

The Stimulus Act of 2009 implicitly revised the preferred stock model by adding two counterproductive provisions—unlinking pay from performance by limiting executive bonuses to one-third of annual compensation, and allowing participating banks to redeem the Treasury's preferred stock without raising any new capital. Pursuant to the second provision, 10 financial institutions redeemed $68 billion in preferred stock from the Treasury within less than seven months of the original purchase. Such quick redemptions strongly suggest that these institutions were not close to failure at the time the Treasury purchased the preferred. These redemptions left the Treasury with warrants estimated to be worth between $3.8 and $4.6 billion. However, if the Treasury's preferred stock had warrants equal to the face value of the preferred, as is the market practice, the Treasury's warrants in these 10 financial institutions would have been worth at least $20 billion.

The exceptional-assistance model was developed in connection with the additional capital contributions and asset guarantees provided to Bank of America and Citigroup. This model does not accurately reflect the ownership interest of the federal government in both banks—for example, potentially 6 percent of Bank of America's common shares for a capital contribution of $45 billion and a possible guarantee of $118 billion in troubled assets (with a $10 billion deductible). By understating federal ownership, the exceptional-assistance model gives taxpayers a small portion of the bank's upside if it becomes profitable, as compared to almost full exposure to huge losses if the bank becomes insolvent. Therefore, if a bank needs exceptional assistance, the federal government should adopt the majority-ownership model.

The majority-ownership model means letting the Treasury own up to 80 percent of the common shares of the troubled bank. This equity interest would give taxpayers most of the upside if the bank becomes profitable, as well as most of the downside if the bank becomes insolvent. The 20 percent or higher float of public shares allows for incentive stock awards needed to attract executive talent, and will also make it easier for the Treasury ultimately to exit by selling its shares to investors.

Although "majority ownership" does not have the stigma of "nationalization," the Treasury will still have to protect majority-owned banks from political interference, such as pressures to make below-market loans. After all, if these banks do not return to profitability, their losses will be absorbed by taxpayers. To help fend off political pressures, the Treasury should insist that Congress supply explicit subsidies for majority-owned banks if they are asked to undertake unprofitable activities. The Treasury should also emphasize that the executives at majority-owned banks have fiduciary duties to their public shareholders to generate reasonable profits.

Chapter 10

Increasing Lending Volumes and Removing Toxic Assets

I n order to help end the current recession, the United States needs to increase the volume of lending, which has decreased sharply over the last year. Many business executives complain that they are being turned down for loans needed to finance their payrolls or inventories. However, as was explained in Chapter 9, the Bush Administration did not impose any lending or reporting requirements on recapitalized banks. Nor will the Obama Administration require more lending by banks receiving federal assistance, although recapitalized banks will have to file special reports on their loan volumes.[1]

The unwillingness of federal officials to impose lending requirements probably represents a realistic assessment of the pressures confronting most recapitalized banks. Some banks say they are prepared to make more loans, but they cannot find enough creditworthy borrowers in the current economic situation. Others say they need to apply the new federal capital to maintain the bank's liquidity or increase its loan loss reserves.

More fundamentally, banks provide only 22 percent of the credit extended in the United States;[2] the rest is supplied through nonbanking lenders such as mortgages brokers, money market funds, and car companies. The dramatic reduction in lending volume is mainly due to the collapse of the loan securitization process, on which many of the nonbank lenders rely. In that process, loans are bought from banks as well as nonbank lenders, aggregated into pools and sold as asset-backed securities.[3]

Therefore, this chapter will begin by explaining the importance of loan securitization to lending volumes. It will then evaluate the Fed's programs for supporting asset-backed securities, and it will suggest more fundamental reforms to the process of securitizing loans.

This chapter will then address the various efforts of the federal government to relieve U.S. banks of their toxic assets: the MBS and related derivatives that are not easily traded because no one can accurately price them. Senior government officials have asserted that banks are not going to increase their lending unless toxic assets are removed from their books.[4] However, it is unclear what portion of a bank's toxic assets would have to be sold before it would materially increase its lending. When banks received cash from the Treasury through its purchase of preferred stock, they tended to use the money to bolster their loan loss reserves and expand their liquidity in case of future problems.

In any event, there are various ways to remove toxic assets from the books of banks. The Obama Administration has announced private-public partnerships with generous subsidies in an attempt to persuade private investors to bid for toxic assets.[5] This chapter will raise questions about both the effectiveness and fairness of these subsidies. Given the tremendous disagreement between buyers and sellers on the prices of toxic assets, do these subsidies constitute an effective use of taxpayer dollars? And is it fair to taxpayers for the federal government to subsidize aggressive investors in highly leveraged deals similar to those that helped bring about the financial crisis?

Because the partnership programs may be ineffective and/or unfair, this chapter will end by considering two alternative strategies for dealing with toxic assets. First, if no one can accurately price toxic assets at the present time, should they be isolated into one or more "bad" banks that would gradually try to sell them over several years? Second, during those years, should the federal government facilitate mortgage modifications because the value of toxic assets will ultimately be determined by the losses incurred on the mortgages underlying these assets?

Loan Securitization Is the Key to Lending Volumes

The value of new bank lending has declined precipitously. For example, Harvard Professors Ivashina and Scharfstein demonstrated that new lending fell by 47 percent during the peak period of the financial crisis (September–November of 2008) relative to the prior three-month period, and by 79 percent relative to the peak period of the credit boom (March–May of 2007).[6] On the other hand, economists at the Minneapolis Federal Reserve documented that the value of total outstanding loans and leases of U.S. commercial banks stayed relatively constant during 2008, after growing steadily since 2002.[7] During 2009, banks with the largest capital infusions showed modest declines in the value of their loans outstanding. For example, the total amount of loans for 15 large U.S. banks declined by 2.8 percent from the first to the second quarter of 2009.[8]

These ostensibly opposing perspectives on lending can be reconciled. The volume of new lending did decline sharply from 2007 to 2008. But the outstanding loan book of commercial banks slipped only modestly, as many businesses drew down on their existing lines of credit to borrow cash so they would be sure to have enough on hand.[9] In other words, the monthly *flow* of loans—mainly new loans—declined sharply, though the *level* of outstanding loans, including existing loans and loan commitments, dipped only slightly.

Increasing the flow of new loans is much more important to reviving the U.S. economy than maintaining the level of outstanding loans at banks. The flow of new loans, in turn, depends mainly on the pace of loan securitization. For example, a bank can make one loan for $400,000, sell it to investors as part of a pool supporting an asset-backed security, and then use the sales proceeds to make a new $400,000 loan. If this cycle happens multiple times, then the volume of new loans created during any year will be much larger than it would be without securitization.

The issuance of asset-backed securities plummeted from $100 billion per month in mid-2006, to $40 billion per month in mid-2007, and then to nearly zero by the end of 2008.[10] The sharp drop-off in the issuance of asset-backed securities, as shown in Figure 10.1, reflects fundamental flaws in the loan securitization process and a dramatic decline in confidence by investors in this process. As explained below, the Fed is trying to restart this process by buying asset-backed securities and providing favorable financing for investors to buy securities backed by consumer loans. Although the Fed's efforts are helpful, the United States needs major reforms to restore the loan securitization process on a permanent basis.

The Fed Has Two Programs to Revive Securitized Loans

The Federal Reserve has two programs aimed at reviving the market for asset-backed securities. The first is an effort to reduce interest

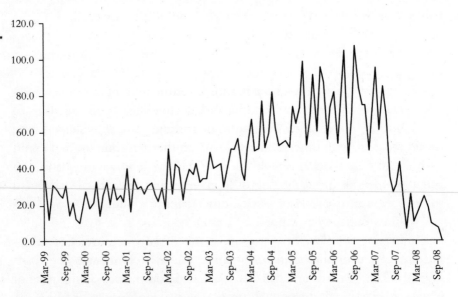

Figure 10.1   U.S. Asset Backed Security Issuance ($Bn)
SOURCE: Federal Reserve Bank of Boston.

rates on fixed-rate mortgages. The Fed announced it would buy $1.45 trillion of outstanding bonds and MBS of Fannie Mae and Freddie Mac during 2009. **This program has been helpful: The fixed rate on 30-year mortgages fell below 5 percent in April, 2009, and the number of mortgage refinancing applications tripled from the year before.**[11] Lower mortgage costs from 2009 refinancings could put as much as $18 billion in the pockets of consumers.[12] However, fixed rates on 30-year mortgages rose above 5 percent in June, 2009 as the interest rates on long-term Treasuries climbed. **It is unclear how large an amount of Fannie Mae and Freddie Mac bonds the Fed would have to buy in order to keep fixed-rate mortgages below 5 percent. This is not a viable long-term strategy to increase the volume of mortgage lending.**

The second Fed program is more complex; it was originally aimed at reviving the market for newly issued, asset-backed securities based on consumer loans—auto, credit card, equipment leases, and student loans. Under this program, the Federal Reserve is making low-interest loans, initially up to $200 billion with the hope of going to $1 trillion, to private investors if they buy newly or recently issued securities backed by such assets.[13] Eligible investors are U.S. companies, banks, and asset managers; hedge funds and private equity funds are likely to be the most active buyers.

Figure 10.2 lays out the mechanics of how the Term Asset-Backed Securities Loan Facility (TALF) program works under a hypothetical situation. This program is a bonanza for investors who put down only $5 to $14 in equity for every hundred dollars they receive in low-interest Fed loans to buy securities backed by consumer loans.[14] Furthermore, these Fed loans are nonrecourse, meaning that the borrowers cannot lose more than their equity if they default on loan payments. In the event of loan defaults, the Federal Reserve will own these securities backed by consumer loans and will be effectively indemnified by the U.S. Treasury up to the first $20 billion in losses on these securities.[15]

In May, 2009, the Fed expanded the TALF program to finance securities backed by commercial real estate loans.[16] Under intense pressure from politicians and lobbyists, the Fed further expanded the TALF program to include securities backed by motor homes, recreational boats, motorcycles, and snowmobiles.[17] There is no end to the line for

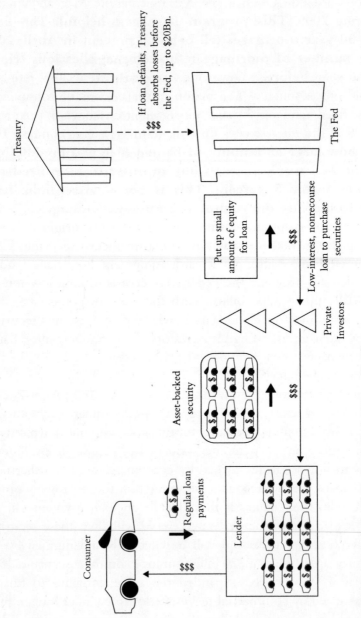

Figure 10.2 The Term Asset-Backed Loan Facility

a financing subsidy as lucrative as the one provided by the TALF. To maintain its independence and objectivity in setting interest rates, the Fed should not become vulnerable to such partisan politicking and industry jockeying for position.

Although these nonrecourse loans are helping to restart the market for newly issued securitized loans, this is a very expensive program that is not a viable long-term vehicle for reviving asset-backed securities. One of the government's major goals for this program is price discovery, that is, setting a market price for asset-backed securities that have not traded in months. However, this program will not set an indicative price for a normal market in these asset-backed securities, because low-interest, nonrecourse federal loans will not be available to buyers on a regular basis. Moreover, the program suffers from investor concerns about the current restrictions on hiring foreign workers by firms participating in this program and possible retroactive legislation to tax their profits.[18] To revive loan securitization, we need a more permanent solution.

Reforming Loan Securitization

As explained earlier in this book, the loan securitization process was filled with abuses, both at the origination stage, with brokers pushing over-priced loans to naïve or complicit buyers (Chapter 1), and at the securitization stage, with Wall Street firms obscuring their liabilities through off-balance sheet vehicles (Chapter 3). **To revive the loan securitization process, we need major reforms at each stage of the process in order to regain investor confidence. Below is a brief outline of such reforms, which have been discussed in prior chapters.**

Borrowers (Chapter 1)

- They need to provide complete and accurate documentation relating to their ability to pay back mortgage loans.
- They need to make significant down payments for mortgages and other large loans so they have skin in the game.
- They should sign standardized documents providing clear procedures for effecting loan refinancing or modifications if their loan is sold to the secondary market.

Loan Originators (Chapter 1)

- They need to provide borrowers with a concise summary with understandable disclosures on all material loan terms.
- They should not receive bonuses for selling high-cost loans.
- They should retain at least 5 percent of loans sold to the secondary market so they have skin in the game.

Bank Sponsors (Chapter 3)

- They should be allowed to use off-balance sheet entities to securitize loan pools, which would be described in standardized disclosure documents.
- They should be required to make specific disclosures to investors of all current and contingent obligations to support these off-balance sheet entities.
- They should also be required to back those obligations with adequate capital, as set periodically by bank regulators.

Credit-Rating Agencies (Chapter 3)

- They should be selected by an independent expert representing investors, who will come from a panel chosen by the SEC.
- They should comply with the limits on conflicts of interest and other procedures in the new SEC rules.
- They should be liable for material violations of these rules (without legal immunity under the First Amendment).

Toxic Assets Are Very Difficult to Price

There is no precise definition of "toxic assets." A narrow definition would be confined to mortgage backed-securities and related derivatives; these have been estimated in the vicinity of $2 trillion. A broader definition would encompass all troubled assets held by American banks, including toxic assets and all other loans in default; these were estimated to exceed $5 trillion in January, 2009.[19] This chapter will use the broader definition of troubled assets, because they include all sources of loan-related losses to banks regardless of whether they are related to MBS.

In asking Congress for $700 billion in October 2008, Treasury Secretary Paulson emphasized that those funds were needed for the federal government to buy troubled assets from banks. However, he quickly decided to recapitalize banks instead of buying their troubled assets. In part, recapitalization was viewed as quicker to implement; more importantly, no one could figure out how to determine a right price for the troubled assets.

Here is a simple illustration of the pricing challenge presented by troubled assets. In 2007, a bank bought $1 million of a highly rated tranche of a collateralized debt obligation (CDO), based on various kinds of MBS. Since October of 2008, neither this CDO nor any similar one has traded because it was largely supported by cash flows from subprime mortgages of uncertain quality. In response to pressures from the bank's external auditor, its executives have marked down the CDO on its books to an estimated current value of $500,000. But the executives believe that if they wait until the financial crisis is over, they would be likely to collect $650,000 on this CDO. In fact, no one will know for a few years whether the right price is $650,000, $500,000 or less.

Reverse Auctions for Toxic Assets Are Unworkable

When Treasury Secretary Paulson originally proposed to buy toxic assets with federal monies, government officials talked about using the pricing technique called a reverse auction so that banks would receive a right price and taxpayers would not overpay. In a reverse auction, a cash buyer announces it will purchase a certain dollar amount of a particular security. Various holders of that security submit secret offers to sell specific amounts of that security at a specific price. The buyer accepts the offers, with the lowest prices, up to the announced dollar limit.

Reverse auctions can be an effective way to buy homogeneous assets with many holders such as IBM bonds. But reverse auctions do not work well for mortgage-backed securities because that market is much more fragmented than the market for corporate bonds. During the last decade, thousands of mortgage pools have been formed to sell MBS to investors, and these pools typically issue several separate tranches, each with a different claim on interest and principal payments. To make sure that all bids at a particular auction would be on the same MBS, the Treasury would have to run literally thousands of reverse auctions. When the Treasury realized that reverse auctions were unworkable for toxic assets, it publicly switched its main strategy to recapitalizing banks.

The Partnerships Are Too Favorable to Private Investors

The most recent programs for buying toxic assets are the private–public partnerships financed by the federal government, namely, the program for legacy loans and the program for legacy securities.[20] (Legacy means that these assets and loans were acquired by troubled banks before 2009). Table 10.1 lays out the key elements of each of these two programs. In the legacy loan program, a bank selects a pool of loans that it wishes to sell. The FDIC indicates how much in nonrecourse, low-interest debt it will guarantee for the buyer of these loans, up to six times the equity in the partnership buying these loans. The FDIC then holds an auction to find the highest bidder for the loans, subject to the FDIC's indicated financing terms. The bank is free to accept or reject the highest bid. If the bank accepts, the highest bidder contributes half of the equity to the partnership and the Treasury contributes the other half.

In the legacy securities program, the Treasury has selected nine investment managers who will be permitted to raise equity for a private-public partnership. The Treasury will match the equity in the partnership raised by the investment manager. The partnership will be controlled by the investment manager, who will be paid by the partnership to purchase MBS issued before 2009 from any financial institution. Most importantly, the Treasury will consider requests by the investment manager for low-interest, nonrecourse loans up to 50 percent or possibly 100 percent of the equity of the partnership. To increase the leverage of the partnership, the investment manager may apply for additional low-interest, nonrecourse loans from the Federal Reserve under the program described above for financing asset-backed securities.

These Public-Private Investment Programs (PPIP) seem to be designed with two political objectives in mind. First, the Fed and the FDIC are providing the bulk of the financing for PPIP so the Treasury does not have to go back to Congress for another appropriation. But Congress may become upset if they understand how overly generous

Table 10.1 Side-by-Side Summary of Legacy Loans and Legacy Securities Program

Topic	Legacy Securities Program	Legacy Loan Program
Public–Private Investment Fund (PPIF)	Treasury expects to establish at least nine PPIFs	FDIC will establish a PPIF for each pool of loans of a selling bank or thrift (Seller)
Eligible assets	Commercial and residential MBS issued before 2009, originally rated AAA or equivalent by two organizations and secured directly by loans or mortgages	Loans satisfying criteria to be issued by the FDIC, selected by the Seller after consultation with its banking supervisor
Eligible sellers of assets to PPIF	FDIC-insured banks and thrifts and apparently U.S. branches and agencies of foreign banks not controlled by foreign governments	FDIC-insured banks and thrifts not controlled by foreign banks or companies
PPIF structure	Treasury and a vehicle controlled by the fund manager in which private investors invest ("Vehicle") will be sole investors in PPIF	Separate PPIF for each Seller pool of loans with equity capital from Treasury and private investors
Eligible investors	No apparent restrictions in Vehicle except that PPIF cannot purchase from (i) an affiliate or other managed entity of the PPIF's Fund Manager or (ii) an investor that has committed 10% or more of the PPIF's capital	No apparent restrictions, but private investor groups subject to FDIC approval and PPIF cannot purchase from (i) an affiliate or (ii) an investor that has committed 10% or more of the PPIF's capital
Fund managers	Prequalified upon application to the Treasury, which expects that there will be at least nine fund managers	FDIC is manager and Seller is servicer

(Continued)

Table 10.1 (*Continued*)

Topic	Legacy Securities Program	Legacy Loan Program
Equity of PPIF	Provided by the Treasury and Vehicle, with no relative amounts specified	Target is 50% of equity to be provided by the U.S. Treasury, but investors may take less
Debt funding of PPIF	Fund manager may obtain secured nonrecourse loans from Treasury in amount up to 50% of PPIF's total equity, with possibility of obtaining 100% subject to certain restrictions; TALF funding also available	PPIF may issue secured nonrecourse debt guaranteed by FDIC based on third party valuation firm's estimate of value of loans, with amount determined by FDIC, but leverage no greater than six to one
Warrants	Treasury will obtain warrants from each PPIF	Treasury will obtain warrants from each PPIF
Fees	Fund managers may charge Vehicle investors fees in their discretion, subject to Treasury review	Fees payable to FDIC for administration and for guarantee of debt issued by PPIF
Servicing of PPIF assets	Fund manager	Seller
Asset purchase/liquidation	Subject to fund manager control	Purchase to be determined by auction conducted by FDIC, with prices determined by investor bids for the loan pool; no specification on liquidations
Reporting by PPIF	Monthly to the Treasury on assets purchased and disposed of as well as valuations	Monthly to FDIC with copy to the Treasury
Term of PPIF	Subject to fund manager proposal but no longer than 10 years subject to extension with U.S. Treasury consent	Not specified

SOURCE: Shearman & Sterling LLP.

these programs are to private investors by providing loans without any recourse—that is, loans for which the borrowers would not liable if they fail to repay these loans. Consider the following example from Barron's Magazine:[21]

> Under the PPIP, there are two classes of investors, a junior and a senior. The senior investor, hereinafter known as Uncle Sugar, provides 84 percent of the total. The junior investors are the government again and private asset managers, each contributing 8 percent.
>
> Assume that the assets are purchased at 50 percent of face value and that, in five years, they either fall to zero or return to 100 percent of face value. Under the downside scenario, both the private investors and the taxpayers lose all their money. But under the recovery scenario, the private investors will reap a 625 percent return—nearly 50 percent a year. Uncle Sugar's annual return in the upside scenario is unlikely to climb much above 10 percent—it depends on how low the senior financing rate is set.

Nevertheless, some investors are unwilling to participate in these private-partnerships because of concerns about legislative backlash. The Treasury has announced that it will not apply the new restrictions on executive compensation to investors in these partnerships. This makes sense because the investors are the buyers of toxic assets; these investors are not the ones who are responsible for the problems. However, investors are worried that Congress will later impose a special tax on their profits from these partnerships or it will enact retroactive restrictions on their compensation. In addition, the Stimulus Act of 2009 limits the hiring of foreign employees by any firm receiving TARP monies, including firms participating in the private-public partnerships.[22]

Second, this approach appears designed to provide political protection for the Treasury against accusations of overpaying for troubled assets. That accusation will be tough to make because all prices will be set by private investors trying to maximize their returns. In theory, sweetheart financing should allow hedge funds to make higher bids on troubled assets. In practice, it seems unlikely that the banks would be willing to sell their troubled assets at prices that are attractive to hedge funds. To go back to our basic example, if the bank believes the CDO is worth $650,000 in terms of future cash flows, why would it sell the CDO for $500,000 today and turn a paper loss into a real loss? On the other hand, would the hedge fund pay $650,000 today for a CDO with a current trading value of $500,000, in the hope that next year it could be sold for a price above $650,000? **In practice, the cheap federal financing will probably lead private investors to ferret out the relatively sound loans and MBS among the troubled assets of banks. If cherry-picking of relatively sound assets at banks begins to occur, the federal government should not continue to provide such generous financing to these partnerships.**

The likelihood of private investors and banks agreeing on prices for truly troubled assets was further reduced by the new accounting rule approved in early April 2009, which allowed banks to mark more of these assets to an internal bank model rather than a current market price.[23] As explained in Chapter 12, this new accounting rule will allow banks to value their illiquid assets at higher prices on their books. Because banks will not want to sell assets below their book values and take additional losses, investors will have to make higher bids to reach mutually agreeable prices with the banks.

Capital Certifications Could Be Used to Bridge the Pricing Gap

No one will know for several years whether the $500,000 price in our example results from the currently illiquid market for the CDO, or the reduced cash flow that it may generate in the future. **So here is a practical solution to this pricing dilemma, which could be employed with or without private-public partnerships.** The partnership buys the CDO for $500,000 in cash, and delivers a capital certificate for $150,000 to the bank. That certificate would count as $150,000 in bank capital for regulatory purposes until the CDO is sold by the partnership. That certificate would also entitle the bank to 70 percent of any sale proceeds above $500,000.[24]

For example, if the partnership sold the CDO for $650,000 three years later, then the bank would receive $105,000 (0.7 × $150,000) and the partnership would receive $45,000 (0.3 × $150,000). If the partnership sold the CDO for $480,000 three years later, the bank would receive nothing and the partnership would lose $20,000. In both cases, once the partnership sold the troubled asset, the capital certificate would expire. The purpose of the certificate is to buy time so everyone can see what the actual sale price of the troubled asset will be.

Moving Toxic Assets to Bad Banks Is a Better Solution

Because of the difficulties of pricing troubled assets, some commentators have suggested that the federal government bring together all of the troubled assets from all of the troubled banks into one aggregator "bad" bank. These commentators, like former Comptroller of the Currency Eugene Ludwig, point to the success of the Resolution Trust Corporation, which was established to sell off the troubled assets of many savings and loans associations (S&Ls) during the 1980s.[25] However, the assets handled by the Resolution Trust were much smaller in size than the troubled assets in today's financial crisis. The Treasury should not concentrate $2 trillion to $5 trillion of troubled assets in the hands of one or two Resolution Trust Corporations. More critically, the Resolution Trust Corporation took over troubled assets of S&Ls that had already been put into receivership by the FDIC, so the government already owned 100 percent of those assets. The FDIC is not likely to put into receivership five or ten of the largest banks in the country. So long as they have stockholders or bondholders, these banks would have to agree with the federal government on a price for any assets transferred to the new version of the Resolution Trust.

The U.S. financial system would be better off with an approach designed to avoid the challenge of pricing troubled assets, while allowing them to be worked out by private experts in multiple entities. Specifically, the federal regulators should divide every large troubled bank, with the government as the majority owner, into a "bad" bank and a "good" bank. The pricing challenge could be avoided if all the shareholders and bondholders of the troubled mega bank would have the same interest in both the bad and good bank.[26] For instance, if an investor owned 1 percent of the common shares of the troubled mega bank, the investor would own 1 percent of the common shares of both the bad and good bank. Similarly, a holder of $200 million out of $2 billion in bonds of the troubled mega bank would hold 10 percent of the bonds in both the bad and good bank.

This splitting approach would allow the bad bank to sell its troubled assets gradually as the trading market for such assets revives. The bad bank would be run by work-out experts, who would not quickly dump assets on the market; they would take several years to fetch decent prices for asset-backed securities and real estate loans. The financing of the bad bank would be supplied by a pro rata share of the stocks and bonds from the mega bank, plus loans from the Federal Reserve and/or bonds guaranteed by the FDIC. (See Chapter 7.)

Without the management distraction of troubled assets, the good bank would be run by commercial and residential lending officers, who would make loans and sell them to be securitized, so the bank could make new loans. The good bank would be financed by a pro rata share of the stocks and bonds from the mega bank, together with FDIC-insured deposits as well as commercial paper.

This splitting approach should be employed when a mega bank needs so much federal assistance that it becomes majority owned by the Treasury, as explained in Chapter 9. In the case of such a troubled mega bank, we as taxpayers already own most of its losses if it becomes insolvent, so we should also own most of its gains if it does well. This objective can be accomplished if the Treasury's ownership share of the large bank is carried over to both the bad and good banks. For example, if the Treasury owned 79 percent of the common shares of the large troubled bank, it would own 79 percent of both the bad bank and good bank. If 21 percent were owned by private investors, banks could award restricted shares to recruit bank executives and the Treasury would have a market into which to sell its shares at a later date.

Loan Modifications Are the Key to Salvaging Toxic Assets

Even if troubled assets are placed in a bad bank, their value will ultimately depend on the default rates on the underlying loans. The number of mortgages with higher balances than their current home prices—that is, underwater borrowers—has risen sharply. At the end of June, 2009, over 32 percent of all holders of home mortgages in the United States were already underwater, and another 5 percent were close to having negative equity in their homes.[27]

Therefore, we need to understand the federal programs developed to help mortgage holders avoid default. In the Bush Administration, there were many programs, but they were voluntary and had minimal impact. In the Obama Administration, two programs offer significant incentives to lenders and servicers to participate, but both are geared to reducing monthly payments rather than mortgage balances.

The Problems with the Bush Administration's Loan Modification Programs

Although the Bush Administration talked a good game about helping homeowners to avoid foreclosure, its actual programs were voluntary and ineffective. For example, in February of 2008, the Bush Administration announced a new program called Project Lifeline. It was a statement of intent by six major lenders to delay foreclosures for 30 days for borrowers who were considered by the lenders to be good candidates for loan modification. *BusinessWeek* said that Project Lifeline "exemplifies [the Bush administration's] hands-off approach to the workings of the market. In fact, it's not a government program at all."[28]

In April 2008, Federal Reserve Governor Kroszner testified before the House Committee on Financial Services about the federal government's effort to help struggling homeowners avoid foreclosure. He pointed to the Homeowner's HOPE Hotline as a prime example of the positive steps being taken by the Bush Administration. He also praised the Hope Now Alliance, a broad-based coalition of banking groups, mortgage servicers, Fannie Mae, and Freddie Mac that was working to find ways to help troubled borrowers through loan modification programs.[29]

By far the most effective program of the Bush Administration was the one introduced by the FDIC after it took over Indy Mac, an FDIC-insured thrift that became insolvent during the summer of 2008. Under this program, the FDIC modified more than 8,500 loans, and had almost another 9,500 modifications in the pipeline, by January 2009.[30] Instead of going through the time-consuming process of making customized modifications to home mortgages, the FDIC sought to achieve a standard objective of reducing total monthly housing payments to 38 percent of the homeowner's pretax income. The FDIC tried to reach that objective by lowering the interest rate and/or lengthening the term of the mortgage.

In November, 2008, James Lockhart, the federal official in charge of Fannie Mae and Freddie Mac, announced a new plan to expedite mortgage modifications. Homeowners would be eligible for this plan if they were at least three months behind on their payments and their mortgage balances represented 90 percent or more of their home's current value. The interest rate on their mortgages, plus other housing expenses, would be reduced to 38 percent of their pretax income, and their mortgages could be extended from 30 to 40 years.[31] Lockhart called the plan "a bold attempt to move quickly in defining a nationwide program that can quickly and easily reach many of the troubled borrowers."[32]

By contrast, the *New York Times* reported that the plan "would have virtually no impact on the millions of people who took out expensive subprime loans and who are at the heart of the nation's foreclosure crisis."[33] The article went on to explain that the plan fell short of the one advocated by FDIC Chair Sheila Bair, who was frustrated because she had been "close to an agreement with the Treasury Department on a plan to spend as much as $50 billion to modify mortgages and keep people in their homes."[34]

The Economic Stimulus Act of 2008 authorized HUD to insure up to $300 billion in mortgages under a voluntary refinancing program called Hope for Homeowners or H4H. The program became operative on October 1, 2008. Later in October, HUD Secretary Preston spoke enthusiastically about H4H:[35]

> Right now lenders are signing up. We've seen a lot of them begin to work through the process . . . It's specifically designed for the most urgent cases, people who have a loan greater than the value of their home.
>
> Many of the large lenders have told us they will take an important slice of their portfolio and put them into H4H. We urge anyone who thinks they may have a problem paying their loan to get to a counselor quickly. Talk to your lender about your options. Potentially go see other lenders about refinancing.

By December 17, 2008, the H4H program had received only 312 applications and was widely viewed as a failure because of its excessive costs and administrative complexities. Nevertheless, this program is worth fixing because it is aimed at the heart of the housing problem, namely, reducing mortgage balances for underwater borrowers. In May of 2009, Congress enacted legislation with three improvements to the H4H program.[36] It permitted a reduction of the program's fees, made more flexible some of the requirements for eligibility, and provided mortgage servicers with some legal protection.[37] Engaging in loan modifications if they are consistent with the Obama Administration's programs, as described in the following section.

The Obama Plan Puts Dollars behind Loan Modifications

In March of 2009, the Obama Administration announced a two-part effort to reduce monthly payments for mortgage holders.[38] The first part allows any homeowner with a mortgage owned or guaranteed by Fannie Mae or Freddie Mac to refinance without penalty, even if the outstanding mortgage balance exceeds 80 percent of the current market value of the home, which was the normal maximum for Fannie Mae and Freddie Mac. The new program permitted these two institutions to refinance a mortgage if its outstanding balance was no more than 105 percent of the home's current estimated value (increased to 125 percent). In addition, the homeowner must be current on his or her mortgage payments and must prove the ability to afford the new mortgage debt. Although there is no income limit on borrowers, the mortgage must be a conforming loan, that is, no more than $417,000 except in high-cost areas.

The program, which will be in effect until June 2010, is projected to help up to 5 million homeowners; it should lead to a higher volume of refinancings. The main drawback is that this new program is being funded by a $200 billion increase in federal capital—$100 billion more each for Fannie Mae and Freddie Mac, which are already insolvent and reporting huge losses. (See Chapter 2.) This drawback is aggravated by the decision to raise from 105 percent to 125 percent the maximum mortgage balance relative to a home's current value. As explained below, such "underwater" mortgages are highly likely to default even after refinancing.

The second part of the plan is much bolder. It offers loan modifications to any homeowner who has already missed mortgage payments, is at imminent risk of doing so, or who has a mortgage that is underwater. In those cases, the homeowner must show that his or her monthly mortgage payments exceed 31 percent of his or her pretax income, and that their outstanding mortgage balance is $729,750 or less. In addition, the program is limited to mortgages originated on or before January 1, 2009, and for single-family homes that constitute the borrower's primary residence.[39] Figure 10.3 lays out some of the key qualification criteria for the loan modification and loan refinancing programs.

Because this loan modification program is voluntary, the Obama Administration has provided financial incentives totaling $75 billion for mortgage holders, servicers and borrowers to participate. For the mortgage holder, the program has three key elements:[40]

1. The lender first will have to reduce interest rates on mortgages to a specified affordability level (specifically, bring down rates so that the borrower's monthly mortgage payment is no greater than 38 percent of his or her income).
2. The program will match further reductions in interest payments dollar-for-dollar with the lender, down to a 31 percent debt service-to-income ratio for the borrower.
3. To ensure long-term affordability, lenders will maintain modified payments in place for five years. After that point, the interest rate can be gradually stepped-up to the conforming loan rate in place at the time of the modification.

The mortgage servicer also will potentially receive three different kinds of fees.[41]

1. An upfront fee of $1,000 for each eligible modification meeting guidelines established under this program.
2. Pay-for-success fees, awarded monthly as long as the borrower stays current on the loan, for each such loan, up to $1,000 each year for three years.
3. Separate incentives to deal with homes subject to first and second mortgages.

Loan Modification

For homeowners who have already missed mortgage payments, are at imminent risk of doing so, or who have a mortgage that is "underwater."

Qualify	Do Not Qualify
Payments exceed 31% of pretax income and can demonstrate hardship	Are not about to default
Occupy a single family home	Are investors with a home that is not occupied by the owner
Can show the home to be primary residence	Have a home that is vacant or condemned
Have unpaid principal balance of $729,750 or less on a first lien mortgage	Have an unpaid principal balance of more than $729,750 on a first lien mortgage
Have a mortgage originated on or before January 1, 2009	Have a mortgage included in securities whose rules explicitly forbid modification
Make all modified payments over three month (or more) trial period	Have loan servicer who will not consider modification or cannot be reached

Loan Refinancing

For borrowers who aren't able to refiance due to such factors as a decrease in the value of their home.

Qualify	Do Not Qualify
Have loans owned or guaranteed by Fannie Mae or Freddie Mac	Have loans owned or guaranteed by companies other than Fannie Mae or Freddie Mac
Are up to date on mortgage payments	Have been more than 30 days late on a payment in the last 12 months
Can demonstrate the ability to afford new mortgage debt	Cannot prove ability to afford new mortgage debt
Balance of mortgage is no more than 125% of the current estimated value of the home	Balance on mortgage now exceeds more than 125% of the current estimate value of the home

Figure 10.3   Qualifying for Loan Modification or Refinancing

Furthermore, because loan modifications are more likely to succeed if they are made before a borrower misses a payment, the program will offer an incentive payment of $500 to mortgage servicers and $1,500 to mortgage holders for loan modifications made while a borrower at risk of default is still current on his or her payments.

This is an attractive offer for the three to four million borrowers who should qualify for the loan modification program. They will have their monthly payments reduced to 31 percent of pretax income for five years. More importantly, if the borrower stays current on his or her monthly payments, his or her mortgage balance can be reduced by a total of $5,000 ($1,000 per year for five years.)[42] **Unfortunately, the program's incentives for lenders or servicers to reduce mortgage balances are quite weak; rather, they will almost always decrease monthly payments by lowering interest rates and stretching out payment periods. Without substantial reductions in mortgage principal, however, there is a high likelihood that homeowners with shaky finances will default again on their modified loans.**

In the past, the default rate has risen sharply if a mortgage is underwater, that is, if the outstanding mortgage balance exceeds the current value of the home.[43] In such situations, it is simply too easy for homeowners to walk away from a mortgage because they have no equity to lose. As Figure 10.4 shows, negative equity in a home is by far the most

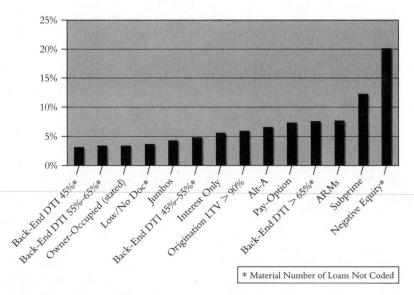

Figure 10.4   Percentage of Loans 60–89 Days Delinquent
SOURCE: Congressional Hearings (March 6, 2009) p. 27.

important factor associated with mortgage defaults; it is more important than having a low-quality loan of any type.

The studies on this subject have shown mixed results at best. For example, a study released in April, 2009, concludes that homeowners receiving monthly payment reductions of 10 percent or more had re-default rates of 26 percent after nine months, as compared to 50 percent for those whose monthly mortgage payments increased or stayed the same.[44] In July of 2009, however, analyst Mark Hanson published data showing re-default rates of 34 percent to 59 percent within 10 months on loan modifications for homeowners current on their payments. Hanson's explanation: "Loan mods are designed to keep the unpaid principal balances of the lender's loans intact while re-levering the borrower."[45]

Moreover, the combination of negative equity in a mortgage and a subprime loan is a recipe for disaster. For instance, if the balance on a subprime adjustable rate mortgage is the same as the current value of the home, there is a close to 50 percent likelihood that the mortgage will become more than 60 days delinquent during the next year.[46] According to a Fitch Report released in May, 2009, "a conservative projection was that between 65 percent and 75 percent of modified subprime loans will fall 60 days or more delinquent within 12 months of the change."[47] There are two main reasons for this exceptionally high default rate: the public pressure to modify loans for weak borrowers, and the tendency of borrowers to walk away from underwater mortgages.

Several distinguished economists have called for a newly formed federal housing corporation to buy underwater mortgages and issue new ones at 95 percent of the home's value.[48] The difference between the old and new mortgage balances could be financed by the new housing corporation in various ways, for example, setting an interest rate on the new mortgage 2 percent above the 10-year U.S. Treasury bond, sharing the losses with the lender, and/or providing the corporation with a share of the home's profits on resale. Even if the federal government had to support these mortgage exchanges with cash payments, subsidies targeted at reducing mortgage balances below current home prices may very well be the best long-term use of the $75 billion in the loan modification program.

Federal financing of principal reductions should be pursued despite the political backlash from families who were more prudent in buying their homes. To illustrate, suppose the Jones family put down $60,000 and obtained a $140,000 mortgage to buy a $200,000 house. The Smith family put down only $10,000 and obtained a $190,000 mortgage to buy the home next door for the same purchase price of $200,000. If the market value of both houses drops to $170,000, the Smith's mortgage is underwater by $20,000, whereas the Jones family has $30,000 in house equity remaining. The Jones family is likely to resent the idea that their neighbors are able to get a bailout due to irresponsible lending on the part of the mortgage broker, or imprudent behavior on the part of the Smith family. Nevertheless, the Jones family will probably be better off if the Smith family's mortgage balance is reduced and the Smiths continue to live in the house next door. If the Smiths abandoned their house, that would likely bring down the value of all houses on the block.

Allowing Bankruptcy Judges to Modify Mortgages Is a Close Call

As part of its program for mortgage relief, the Obama Administration has backed a legislative proposal that would allow bankruptcy judges to reduce interest and principal payments for home mortgages when borrowers file for bankruptcy. In a bankruptcy proceeding, debtors can develop a reorganization plan, approved by the judge, to reduce some debts and extend the repayment period. According to judges and lawyers, about half of bankruptcy filers lose their home: "That's because debtors often have to make higher monthly mortgage payments than they did before bankruptcy, in part because their bankruptcy reorganization plans must include the payments they already missed, plus financial penalties."[49]

The "cramdown" proposal, as it is called by its opponents, has generated strong objections from most lending groups, who appear to have blocked the legislation for now in the U.S. Senate. They claim that it would provide a windfall to bankrupt homeowners, and raise mortgage costs for future homeowners because lenders will now build into mortgage pricing the chances of a bankruptcy cramdown. They point to a staff study by the Federal Reserve that the rate on car loans dropped by over 2.5 percent after Congress eliminated the power of bankruptcy judges to modify auto loans in 2005.[50] In addition, this new power would place another burden on the relatively small number of bankruptcy judges, who handled 900,000 bankruptcy filings between March 2007 and March 2008.[51]

The supporters of the proposal emphasize that bankruptcy judges have for years been authorized to modify many other types of loans, such as loans for vacation homes, investment properties, yachts, and planes. They also stress that mortgages could not be reduced below the market value of the home at the time of bankruptcy. They point to studies supporting their position; for example, a study by a Georgetown law professor and an economist found that "permitting unlimited strip-down had no effect on origination rates or the number of bankruptcy filings."[52] Other supporters, like the CEO of Citigroup, justify the legislation in terms of today's "exceptional economic environment."[53]

In my view, application of the proposal to future mortgages would raise the prices of mortgages, because they would have to take into account the risk of cramdown in bankruptcy. **However, this financial crisis is an emergency situation, which was created during several years when the federal rules on mortgage practices were quite lax. (See Chapter 1.) Because these rules were substantially improved at the end of 2008, the legislation should apply only to mortgages issued on or before December 31, 2008. Such a retrospective approach should minimize the impact on mortgage rates in the future. Nevertheless, mortgage bankers argue that Congress will predictably apply cramdown in every emergency situation. To counter this argument, Congress should build into this legislation a requirement for a two-thirds vote of both the House and the Senate before cramdown could be applied to any future period.**

Summary

Contrary to popular opinion, banks supply only 22 percent of all credit extensions in the United States; the large majority are provided by non-bank lenders like mortgage brokers and money market funds. Although the outstanding loans on the books of large banks have slipped a little, new U.S. lending has plummeted. This is mainly due to the collapse of the secondary market for securitized loans. If we want to reignite the U.S. economy by increasing lending, the United States must revive the process of loan securitization.

The Fed has purchased over $1 trillion in Fannie Mae and Freddie Mac securities. These purchases have helped drive fixed-rate mortgages below 5 percent, leading to a tidal wave of refinancings. Lower monthly mortgage payments will put billions of dollars in the pockets of American consumers. But it is unclear how much the Fed needs to purchase for how long to keep fixed-rate mortgages at that level. This Federal program is a form of short-term economic stimulus.

The Fed has also provided nonrecourse loans at low rates to investors under a special program to encourage purchases of newly issued securitized loans. However, this is too expensive to be more than a short-term, starter program. To revive loan securitization on a permanent basis the U.S. needs to fundamentally reform the process at all levels, from the borrower to the loan originator to the credit rating agency. Most importantly, we need to allow banks to sponsor off-balance entities to issue securitized loans, subject to strict requirements for detailed disclosures of continuing or contingent bank obligations and capital backing those obligations.

It is unclear whether the sale of troubled assets by banks would lead them to substantially increase their loan volumes in the United States. In any event, such sales are unlikely until we figure out the right price for these assets. It may take several years before it becomes clear whether the currently depressed prices of troubled assets are the result of temporarily illiquid markets, fundamental credit problems, or some combination of both. This pricing challenge undermines all creative proposals for the federal government, alone or together with private investors, to buy troubled assets from banks.

The Treasury has rolled out two public-private partnership programs, one to purchase legacy loans and the other to purchase legacy asset-backed securities. The legacy loan program is financed by guarantees from the FDIC, which will auction a bank's loans for sale. However, the bank can reject the highest bidder. The legacy securities program is financed by the Fed and the Treasury, which have chosen nine investment managers to run partnerships, but it is not clear whether these bidders or managers will be able to agree with the banks on a mutually acceptable price for most troubled assets. Moreover, the low-interest, nonrecourse loans in these two programs are too generous to the private investors.

Instead, federal regulators should divide each of the large troubled banks, with the government as the majority owner, into a "good" and "bad" bank. The good bank could get back to business as usual, and the bad bank would gradually work out the troubled assets over several years. This approach would avoid the problem of pricing troubled assets if the shareholders and bondholders of the large bank maintained their same proportionate interest in both the good and bad banks. In particular, the Treasury should have a majority ownership in the good bank as well as the bad bank to obtain the lion's share of the upside as well as the downside.

The value of troubled assets will ultimately depend on the default rate on the underlying mortgages and the losses incurred on these defaults. The Bush Administration unsuccessfully promoted loan modification on a voluntary basis. The Obama Administration backed its loan modification programs with substantial incentive payments to lenders and servicers, so it is likely to help several million families with shaky finances decrease their monthly mortgage payments to 31 percent of their pretax income.

However, the evidence shows that participants in loan modification programs are very likely to default again if they are underwater: Their mortgage balances are greater than the current value of their homes. Therefore, the Obama Administration would probably obtain a better result for its $75 billion investment if it bought up underwater mortgages and issued new mortgages at 95 percent of home values. The difference between the old and new loan balances could be financed by a combination of mortgage rates above federal borrowing costs, cost sharing with lenders, and profit sharing with owners on the sale of their homes.

In addition, the Obama Administration backed a legislative proposal to allow mortgages to be modified in bankruptcy proceedings. This proposal is designed to produce customized mortgage modification only for those in deep financial distress. However, the proposal is bitterly opposed by bankers as undermining the sanctity of contract.

In my view, a general application of this proposal will increase future mortgage rates for financially pressed families, since bankers will assume that some of them will obtain mortgage modifications in bankruptcy. This proposal makes sense only as an exceptional measure applicable to mortgages issued before December 31, 2008, when the improved federal rules on mortgage practices were not yet effective. To address concerns that similar legislation will be passed again in every recession, Congress should include a provision requiring a two-thirds vote before this exceptional measure could be applied to mortgages in the future.

Chapter 11

Limiting Executive Compensation and Improving Boards of Directors

E xecutive compensation was a hot topic in the United States well before the current financial crisis because of the recent and rapid rise in executive pay throughout this century. The ratio of the average Chief Executive Officer's (CEO) pay to the average worker's pay has gone from 20 to 1 for much of the twentieth century to 400 to 1 in 2007.[1] The median total direct compensation for CEOs at the largest U.S. companies was approximately $14 million in 2007.[2] Critics were particularly outraged by huge severance payments given to CEOs when they were asked to leave for poor performance. For example, Hank McKinnell, the former CEO at Pfizer, received $34.2 million in severance payments out of a total exit package of almost $200 million, after the company's stock lost about $137 billion of its market value during his tenure as CEO.[3]

The current financial crisis has shone a harsh spotlight on the huge payments to CEOs at financial institutions, many of which have subsequently failed and needed money from the federal government to survive. According to one study by the *New York Times*, executives at seven major financial institutions that have either failed or been propped up with federal aid received $464 million in performance pay from 2005 until their collapse in 2008.[4] Richard Fuld, the former CEO of Lehman Brothers, which filed for bankruptcy in 2008, received about $466 million in total compensation between 1993 and 2007.[5] As a result of the rising chorus of public criticism, most CEOs of large financial institutions in the United States agreed not to receive any bonus in 2008.

In response to this public fury over executive compensation, the federal government adopted three new sets of restrictions on executive compensation since the fall of 2008. (For a chart of these three sets of executive compensation restrictions under the Bush and Obama administrations, see Table 11.1.) In summary:

1. In October of 2008, Congress and the Treasury Department under President Bush established certain executive compensation restrictions at financial institutions receiving federal assistance under the Troubled Asset Relief Program.[6] These compensation restrictions were described by the first head of the this program as "quite reasonable" and "a pretty modest hindrance."[7]

2. In mid-February of 2009, Congress imposed tougher restrictions on executive compensation for all financial institutions that received federal assistance in the past or will do so in the future. Most importantly, these restrictions included limits on the amount of any bonus or incentive pay of top executives, and required an annual advisory shareholder vote on the company's executive compensation practices ("say on pay").[8]

3. In June of 2009, the Obama Administration issued rules with further restrictions on executive compensation for recipients of federal aid, such as prohibiting them from paying taxes due on any executive compensation items and requiring more disclosures on

Table 11.1 Federal Compensation Restrictions for Recipients of Federal Assistance

	Programs Under President Bush TARP & Treasury Restrictions[a]	Programs Under President Obama	
		The Stimulus Bill[b]	Treasury Regulations[e]
Which companies do restrictions apply to?	Any entity that (in)directly sells troubled assets or receives equity capital	Any entity that has received or will receive financial assistance	Any entity that has received or will receive financial assistance
For how long?	Until December 31, 2009 or as long as the Treasury holds an equity stake	As long as financial assistance is outstanding	As long as financial assistance is outstanding
For which employees?	CEO, CFO, and next 3 most highly compensated executive officers	Top 25 executives[c]	Top 25 executives[c]
Limits unnecessary and excessive risk taking?	Yes, for top 5 senior executive officers (SEOs) (except for auction purchases of troubled assets)	Yes, for *all* employees	Yes
Bonus Recoupment Provision?	Yes, applies to top 5 SEOs (except for auction purchases of troubled assets)	Yes, applies to top 25 senior executives	Yes, applies to top 25 senior executives. Also mandates that firm must actually exercise the clawback[f]
Golden Parachute Payment Limit?	Yes, 3X average annual compensation	Yes, prohibits any parachute payments for top 10 executives	Yes, prohibits any parachute payments for top 10 executives. Also clarifies that golden parachute includes payments made in connection with a change-in-control
Annual Pay Limit?	No	No	No, but encourages firms to pay salary in the form of stock that cannot be converted to cash until government is paid back in full

(Continued)

265

Table 11.1 (*Continued*)

	Programs Under President Bush	Programs Under President Obama	
	TARP & Treasury Restrictions[a]	The Stimulus Bill[b]	Treasury Regulations[e]
Incentive Compensation Limit?	No	Yes, any incentive award must be in the form of restricted stock and limited to 1/3 of total annual compensation, vesting only when government is paid back in full[d]	Yes, reinforces the Stimulus Bill's limitation on bonuses
Were Tax Deduction Limits Under IRS Rule 162(m) reduced?	Yes, from $1,000,000 to $500,000 and elimination of performance compensation exemption	No change	No change
Annual Say on Pay Required?	No	Yes	Yes
Any Other Limitations?	No	Policies prohibiting "luxury" items	Yes, prohibits tax gross-up payments on perquisites, golden parachutes, or any other compensation

[a] Emergency Economic Stabilization Act of 2008
[b] American Recovery and Reinvestment Act of 2009
[c] Number is reduced along with the amount of aid received
[d] Does not apply if a valid, written contract was in place on or before February 11, 2009
[e] TARP Standards For Compensation and Corporate Governance, Department of the Treasury, June 15, 2009
[f] Unless the firm can demonstrate that it is unreasonable to do so

their compensation consultants.[9] At the same time, the Treasury appointed a Special Master to approve specific compensation arrangements for the 25 highest paid executives at seven institutions receiving exceptional financial assistance (e.g., AIG, Bank of America, and Citigroup).

After outlining the early history of legislative attempts to limit executive compensation, this chapter will analyze the three recent sets of executive compensation restrictions at financial institutions receiving federal assistance.[10] Although the excesses of the last decade cannot be justified, this chapter will argue that these broad-based restrictions are likely to have unintended or adverse consequences that are not in the best interests of federally assisted institutions or their shareholders. Instead, this chapter will argue for a customized compensation model, designed for each financial institution through a different process of corporate governance that I call "accountable capitalism."

Broad-Based Restrictions on Executive Compensation Have Usually Backfired

In 1984, Congress attempted to curb excessive executive compensation by changing the section of the tax code regarding severance payments that were remitted to senior executives in connection with a change-in-control of the company.[11] It prohibited the company from taking a tax deduction on any severance payment over three times the executive's average annual compensation. It also levied a 20 percent excise tax on the executive for such severance payments. In response, many companies ramped up potential severance payments to exactly three times the executive's average annual compensation. Further, if the potential severance payment exceeded that amount, many companies agreed to forego the favorable income tax deduction and sometimes even agreed to pay the excise tax on the executive's behalf.[12]

In another attempt to curb excessive executive compensation, Congress enacted a change to the tax code in 1993.[13] This change prohibited any company from deducting any annual compensation over $1 million for their senior executives, with an exception for performance-based pay, such as stock options. In response, many companies ratcheted up their CEO's base salary to at least $1 million per year. Some companies deferred payment of nonperformance-based bonuses over $1 million to the year after those senior executives retired. Other companies continued to pay their senior executives nonperformance-based bonuses in excess of $1 million and simply did not deduct the excess. Still other companies made mega stock-option grants to their senior executives because there was no limit on the tax deductions for this type of performance-based pay. This resulted in these executives receiving huge rewards when the whole U.S. stock market rose sharply during the late 1990s.

These two attempts to rein in executive compensation illustrate how broad-based legislative efforts tend to backfire and result in serious unintended consequences. It is likely that this same type of disconnect between well-meaning objectives and actual effects will also be the fate of the three successive sets of restrictions on executive compensation applied to TARP recipients. Let us consider these three federal restrictions in chronological order:

1. The restrictions established by Congress through the Bailout Act in October of 2008
2. The restrictions imposed by Congress through the Stimulus Act in mid-February of 2009
3. The restrictions issued by the Treasury in the rules it adopted in June of 2009

Compensation Restrictions 1: The Loopholes in TARP

When Treasury Secretary Paulson first proposed the 2008 Emergency Economic Stabilization Act (the "Bailout Act"), he stressed the need to buy troubled assets from financial institutions and suggested that any limits on executive pay would discourage companies from participating.[14] Disagreeing with Paulson, Congress inserted specific pay restrictions on financial institutions that sold assets to the federal government. These restrictions distinguish between assets purchased directly from financial institutions and assets purchased through auctions run by the federal government. As mentioned before, Paulson quickly changed his mind about buying troubled assets in favor of recapitalizing banks. But these distinctions are again relevant as the Obama Administration has released plans for purchasing troubled assets.[15] (See Chapter 10.)

The Bailout Act contains programs other than the troubled asset relief program (collectively known as TARP), such as programs where the federal government takes a meaningful equity or debt position in a financial institution. These other programs also have executive compensation restrictions that became important when the Bush Administration bought preferred stock in over 300 financial institutions.[16] (See Chapter 9.)

The initial restrictions on executive compensation under TARP contain many loopholes and inconsistencies. To begin with, all these restrictions apply only to the CEO, the Chief Financial Officer (CFO), and the other three most highly compensated senior executive officers (together, SEOs) who perform a general policy-making function for a financial institution receiving federal assistance. Accordingly, while Goldman Sachs received $10 billion in preferred stock from the U.S. Treasury, it would clearly be allowed to pay a $20 million bonus to a derivatives trader who had made large profits for the firm over the prior year. Although most Wall Street CEOs have foregone bonuses for 2008, other Wall Street employees reportedly received approximately $18.4 billion in bonuses for 2008.[17]

The compensation restrictions on executives at companies where the government has bought stock or purchased assets directly (though not through an auction) include a further prohibition on taking "unnecessary and excessive risks that threaten the value of the financial institution."[18] However, this prohibition applies only to the activities of the five SEOs and again would not apply to a derivatives trader at Goldman Sachs who takes billions of dollars of risk every day.

The restrictions that accompany federal purchases of stock and direct asset purchases (though not auction asset purchases) contain a clawback provision, requiring a financial institution to recoup any incentive compensation that is both paid during the relevant period and based on materially inaccurate financial statements or other performance metrics. Again, this provision applies only to the five SEOs at the financial institution, and not to the derivatives trader. On the other hand, this provision may be too broad because it does not require any participation by the relevant SEO in approving the inaccurate financial statement or designing a performance metric. By contrast, the

2002 Sarbanes–Oxley Act (SOX), which was passed after the failures of Enron and WorldCom, allows for the clawback of executive bonuses if there is a financial restatement on the part of the issuer "as a result of misconduct."[19]

In addition, the Bailout Act established certain prohibitions on severance payments upon termination (called golden parachutes). **Although these prohibitions are exceedingly complex and may differ slightly depending on the specific TARP program involved, they do share three troublesome limitations.** First, the prohibitions on golden parachutes apply only to the five SEOs. Second, they prohibit golden parachutes only if the payments exceed three times the SEO's average compensation over the last five years. For example, if a CEO received a salary and bonus of $4 million per year on average over the last five years, a $12 million golden parachute payment by a financial institution receiving federal stock would be acceptable under TARP's provisions, even if the CEO were terminated for poor performance. Third, TARP does not prohibit the payment of a golden parachute payment above three times annual compensation after the end of the company's participation in TARP.[20] However, this loophole was closed by the Treasury's rules in June of 2009.

Compensation Restrictions 2: The Stimulus Act of 2009 Goes Too Far

Given these ambiguities and inconsistencies in TARP's restrictions on executive compensation, the top officials in the new Obama Administration rightly believed that tighter restrictions were needed. In February of 2009, the Treasury proposed rules on executive compensation that would have applied only to financial institutions receiving federal assistance in the future. However, before the Treasury could formally adopt these rules, Congress added an even tighter set of restrictions on executive compensation in the American Recovery and Reinvestment Act of 2009 (the 2009 Stimulus Act), which apply to both current and future recipients of government aid. Most importantly, it limited bonuses or any other type of incentive award to grants of restricted shares not exceeding one-third of annual compensation. Nevertheless, this limit did not apply, if a valid employment agreement was in place as of February 11, 2009, as was the case for the $165 million in retention bonuses paid out by AIG during March of 2009.[21]

The number of senior executives subject to this legislative restriction on annual bonuses depends upon the amount of financial assistance received by the financial institution according to the following schedule. For institutions receiving:

- Less than $25 million in assistance, the highest compensated executive
- From $25 million up to $250 million in assistance, the five most highly compensated executives
- From $250 million up to $500 million in assistance, the five SEOs and the 10 next most highly compensated executives
- $500 million or more in assistance, the five SEOs and the next 20 most highly compensated executives.

Unfortunately, these legislative limits on bonuses are likely to lead to much larger annual salaries at TARP institutions, thereby weakening the link between executive pay and performance. For instance, Morgan Stanley increased the base salaries of its four top executives just below the CEO from $300,000–$323,000 in 2008 to $750,000–$800,000 in 2009.[22] Even a staunch critic of excessive compensation, Harvard Professor Lucian Bebchuck, lambasted the provisions in the 2009 Stimulus Act: "Mandating that at least two-thirds of an executive's total pay be decoupled from performance, as the stimulus bill does, is a step in the wrong direction."[23] Professor Bebchuck also pointed out that allowing only one form of incentive pay—restricted shares—could have perverse results. For example, if an executive ran a division of a large bank, he or she should be compensated mainly on that division's performance, rather than the stock price of the whole bank.

Because Congress applied its new restrictions on executive compensation to all institutions that have received, or will receive, federal assistance under TARP, it recognized that some banks would object to the retroactive application of these restrictions. Accordingly, the 2009 Stimulus Act specifically permitted any TARP recipient to repay any federal assistance, even if the institution did not raise capital from other sources or did not complete the initial three-year waiting period for repayment.[24] The legislative repeal of these two repayment conditions in the original terms of Treasury's preferred stock is troublesome, although the regulators retain administrative control over the repayment plan of any specific bank. Instead of raising new capital, banks could deplete their existing capital cushions in order to redeem the federal government's preferred shares.[25] To avoid the new restrictions on executive compensation, several small banks quickly redeemed their federal preferred stock, and 10 large banks followed suit later in 2009.

Beside these troublesome provisions on bonuses and stock repayment, Congress in 2009 imposed tougher measures on several other subjects than those in the Bailout Act of 2008. Some of these tougher measures were further elaborated in the June, 2009 rules adopted by the Treasury.

- The Stimulus Act expands the prohibition on golden parachutes in the Bailout Act to include not only the five SEOs but also the next five most highly compensated executives for all financial institutions that have received or will receive federal assistance.
- Whereas the Bailout Act required a clawback of bonuses paid to the five SEOs based on inaccurate performance metrics, the Stimulus Act extends this requirement to the next 20 most highly compensated executives. The Treasury's rules also force the TARP recipient to exercise these broader clawback rights unless it can justify why not.
- The Stimulus Act still requires that compensation plans for only the top five executive officers be designed to avoid incentives for unnecessary risk taking, but further prohibits compensation plans for any employee of a TARP recipient if they would encourage earnings manipulation. The Treasury rules also require the institution's compensation committee to publicly disclose its analysis of such risk-taking incentives.
- The Stimulus Act requires TARP recipients to provide an annual shareholder vote on a nonbinding resolution to approve executive compensation packages. The Bailout Act had no comparable requirement.
- The Stimulus Act of 2009 requires that financial institutions receiving federal assistance adopt policies against expenditures that could be viewed as excessive or luxury items, and that the institution's

CEO and CFO personally certify the need for any such expenditures. Although the adoption of such policies may be justifiable for TARP institutions, the personal certification by the CEO and CFO constitute a poor use of their time.

Compensation Restrictions 3: The Treasury Rules Go Further Than the Stimulus Act of 2009

The Treasury's June 2009 rules prohibit TARP firms from reimbursing taxes due on any compensations items. As mentioned earlier, some companies cover the excise taxes levied by the IRS on golden parachute payments if they exceed three times an executive's annual compensation.

- The Treasury rules expand the SEC's requirement to disclose perquisites received by the top five SEOs of public companies to include all executives of TARP institutions subject to the bonus limits and receiving perquisites over $25,000 per year. Such perquisites include company payments for personal expenses such as aircraft use.
- The Treasury rules require the compensation committee of TARP institutions to be composed entirely of independent directors. This requirement is already met by almost all institutions listed on the New York Stock Exchange and most listed on other markets.
- The Treasury rules require more detailed disclosures on services rendered by compensation consultants to financial institutions and their compensation committees. However, disclosure is too mild a medicine for a situation in which a potential conflict of interest is likely to become an actual conflict. If consultants earn significantly more fees for advising the company's executives on human resource issues, they are likely to be overly generous when evaluating pay proposals involving executives for the compensation committee of the same company's board.[26] Therefore, Congress should prohibit any compensation consultants from providing material services to both the company and its independent directors (or committee of independent directors). This prohibition would be similar to the one in SOX barring the same accounting firm from both auditing a company's financial statements and providing significant consulting services to the same company.

Finally, the Treasury rules establish the Office of the Special Master with broad powers over TARP firms receiving exceptional federal assistance, namely, AIG, Bank of America, and Citigroup, plus four auto-related firms. The Special Master also has narrower powers on executive compensation at other TARP firms. Both these powers are summarized in Table 11.2.

Table 11.2   Powers of the Special Master of TARP Compensation

For all TARP Recipients

- To interpret the application of the restrictions on executive compensation and corporate governance requirements of the Stimulus Bill, including the specific application of any terms or conditions in a contract between the Treasury and a TARP recipient.
- To oversee the review of bonuses, retention awards, and other compensation paid before February 17, 2009, and where appropriate, negotiate reimbursements to the Federal Government.

For "Exceptional" TARP Recipients

- To review and approve any compensation proposed to be paid to the top 5 senior executives and the next 20 most highly paid employees.
- To review and approve the compensation *structure* for the 100 most highly paid employees and any executive officers that are not among the 100 most highly paid employees.
- To issue these final and non-appealable approvals based on a clear set of principles to ensure that compensation is structured in such a way that gives those employees incentives to maximize long-term shareholder value and protect taxpayer interests.
- These six general principles are to ensure that executive compensation:
    i. encourages long-term value creation;
   ii. reflects the company's competitive constraints and its need to repay Treasury;
  iii. appropriately allocates among components of pay (e.g. salary, bonus, etc.);
   iv. is based on performance through metrics tailored to the executive;
    v. is consistent with pay for those in similar positions at similar entities; and
   vi. reflects the current and/or prospective contributions of the executive.
- Automatic approval if total compensation for one executive is not more than $500,000 (with any additional compensation paid only in the form of long-term restricted stock in the amount of 1/3 of total annual compensation).

More generally, Treasury Secretary Geithner announced five principles for executive compensation at all publicly traded companies. These principles sensibly articulate functional guidelines, rather than rigid standards for such companies:[27]

1. Compensation should properly measure and reward performance.
2. Compensation should be structured to account for the time horizon of risk.
3. Compensation practices should be aligned with sound risk management.
4. Golden parachutes and supplemental retirement plans should be re-examined to determine whether they align the interests of executives and shareholders.
5. The process of setting compensation should promote transparency and accountability.

Accountable Capitalism and Executive Compensation

Many commentators predict that the combination of legislative and Treasury curbs on executive compensation will drive talented employees out of banks receiving financial assistance. In combination, these restrictions imply that many top executives of the country's largest banks receiving federal aid are not likely to receive annual compensation more than $500,000 in cash, plus $250,000 in restricted shares that would fully vest if and when the bank repaid all its federal assistance. In addition, the top executives could not receive any severance payments if they lost their job because of a hostile takeover of the bank or a debate about bank strategy, despite strong performance. If you were a talented executive vice president of a large bank who earned an average of $1.5 million per year ($500,000 in base pay and $1 million in performance pay), would you accept these restrictions that would result in a 50 percent pay cut, or would you find a job in another financial institution not receiving federal assistance and, therefore, not subject to such pay restrictions? Alternatively, would you take your group from the bank and form a new company that would perform similar functions for the bank and other financial institutions without these restrictions on executive compensation?

These questions illustrate the inherent limitations of any broad-based prohibitions on executive compensation. As shown by the prior discussion on the impact of the two tax code revisions during the 1980s and 1990s, lawyers are ingenious in circumventing these restrictions, so the restrictions are rarely effective and sometimes are counterproductive. To avoid the statutory restrictions on executive bonuses, for example, Wells Fargo raised the base salary of its CEO from $900,000 to $5.6 million for the next year. Other banks are granting multimillion-dollar signing bonuses, because the bonus restrictions apply only to the highest paid bank executives in the prior year.[28]

Moreover, the multiple rounds of federal restrictions on executive compensation have undermined significant aspects of the government's efforts to clean up the banks. Because of these restrictions, some firms have decided not to participate in the private-public partnerships to buy toxic assets from banks (see Chapter 10). Although the Treasury Department announced that the executive compensation restrictions do not apply to these partnerships, potential participants fear that Congress will later pass retroactive legislation limiting or taxing their profits on these partnerships.[29]

In theory, a regulatory authority should articulate a set of compensation objectives that would be applied to a financial institution by a board of directors with extensive knowledge of that institution. In practice, the boards of directors of large mega banks have generally done a poor job of establishing a compensation system for senior executives. The Sarbanes-Oxley Act increased the percentage of independent directors on boards, who now follow much more elaborate procedures in running their board committees. But the procedural approach embedded in SOX was ineffective in many instances. Although the boards at Merrill Lynch and Lehman Brothers were composed of over 90 percent independent directors, they did not appear to have fully comprehended the excessive risk taking by the bank's senior executives, and they rewarded these executives with huge bonuses.

While I believe that executive compensation packages are best customized for each financial institution by its board of directors, from my experience I have developed a set of principles that would provide useful guidance on compensation for senior executives at large financial institutions. These principles are based on the realistic premise that top financial executives have job opportunities in many types of financial firms, which themselves can be located in various countries. These principles, designed to promote "accountable capitalism," fall into three main categories:

1. Base salary and bonus
2. Stock-related awards
3. Termination-deferral issues

Base Salary and Bonus

1. **Keep Base Salaries Low:** Financial institutions should always keep base salaries of senior executives as low as practical, with the bulk of the annual cash payment comprising a bonus based on performance. Specifically, try to keep the salaries of the highest-paid executives and investment experts no higher than $300,000–$400,000 per year. That salary is sufficient to support the monthly needs of any family, while allowing for a wide range of bonuses dependent upon performance. There is no need for most CEOs to receive base salaries of more than $1 million in addition to their normal pension and health benefits.

2. **Extend the Period for Measuring Performance:** Bonuses should be based on performance over a period of three years, rather than just on the past year (with appropriate exceptions for new employees and those on leave). If we want financial institutions to take a longer-term perspective, we need to expand the time horizon for determining bonuses. However, financial markets move quickly, so a horizon of five to ten years is an eternity. The best we can hope for is a three-year measurement period for cash bonuses. In addition, bonuses should not be guaranteed by an employment contract, with the exception of a first-year bonus for new hires who may have foregone compensation at their former employer in order to join their new company.

3. **Build in Downside Risk:** Bonus programs are usually aimed at rewarding good performance, but they need to be designed in such a way that top executives will lose most or all of their bonuses when their company or unit performs poorly. It cannot be a heads-I-win-a-lot, tails-I-win-a-little type of executive bonus program; there has

to be significant downside risk for the executive in order for the pay to be truly linked to performance. Although Wall Street bonuses fell from 2007 to 2008, nine banks receiving federal assistance distributed bonuses of almost $33 billion in 2008. Six of those nine banks actually paid out more in bonuses than their profits in 2008.[30]

4. **Rely Heavily on Quantitative Metrics:** In my experience, it is too hard to implement a bonus system with a truly wide range of results unless the board establishes quantitative metrics for at least two-thirds of the bonus payout. Of course, qualitative factors should be included in bonus determinations, but they tend to be mushy and produce high grades for most senior executives.

Stock Options and Restricted Stock

1. **Tie Exercise Price to Relevant Stock Index:** A substantial portion of a senior executive's compensation should be in some form of stock, preferably with a heavy dose of indexed stock options. If the stock subsequently does well, the executive does well with the options. If the stock subsequently declines in price, the options become virtually worthless. However, sometimes a company's share price rises mainly because of a general market boom, even if the institution is doing poorly. To prevent windfall profits in these situations, the exercise price of options should be annually adjusted upward if the institution's share price does not rise as high as the company's peers, as measured by the relevant stock index. Conversely, an institution's CEO could be doing an excellent job, while the general stock market tanks. In that case, the institution should decrease the exercise price each year consistent with the decrease in the relevant stock index. But the adjustments in the exercise prices of options must be symmetrical—the same methodology on the upside and the downside.

2. **Do Not Reprice Options with Fixed Exercise Price:** Unfortunately, most stock options have fixed exercise prices that do not move with market indexes. If the stock's price sinks lower after the grant of the stock option, the option is considered underwater and is, therefore, of little value to the option holder. In those situations, institutions sometimes reduce the exercise price of all outstanding options, although they never increase their exercise prices

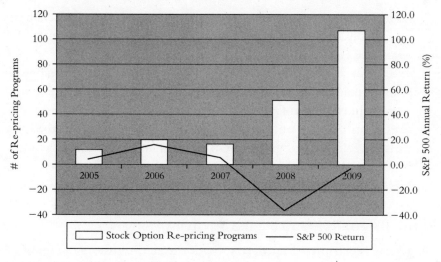

Figure 11.1 Re-pricing Stock Options
Source: Radford Consulting, a unit of Aon Corporation.

in booming stock markets. In this manner, an institution undermines the role stock options play in aligning the interests of its top executives with those of its shareholders. As you can see from Figure 11.1, many companies have or are seeking to re-price options in connection with the recent severe downturn in the market.[31] In order to keep the management and shareholders aligned, the exercise price of *nonindexed* stock options should remain the same during a significant market downturn.

3. **Put Performance Conditions on Restricted Shares:** Grants of restricted shares do not align executive performance as closely to shareholder value as stock options. Restricted shares that vest over a period of several years are essentially a form of deferred bonus, with a modest performance kicker. Suppose the executive receives 10,000 restricted shares when the company's stock price is $50 per share (a $500,000 value), and the share price declines to $40 at the end of a three-year vesting period. The senior executive still receives $400,000 at the end of the vesting period even though the stock declined 20 percent during this period. Therefore, restricted shares should vest over time only if appropriate targets are met—such as a 10 percent

increase in shareholder value (including market price and dividends) or a 10 percent increase in the institution's earnings per share.

4. **Mandate Holding of 50+ Percent of Shares:** When senior executives acquire shares through restricted stock or stock option grants, they should also be required to hold at least half of them until retirement or termination. That requirement would prevent executives from cashing out their whole stock position at the top of a market cycle, thereby giving them a longer-term interest in the institution's success. But they could sell half their shares to cover their taxes and generate a little cash for family needs.

Termination, Retirement, and Payment Deferrals

1. **Limit Severance Payments:** Senior executives should be entitled to reasonable severance pay if they are terminated when institutions are acquired or for other events beyond their control. But any severance payment should not exceed three times the average base pay and bonus of an executive over the last five years, and this calculation should exclude stock awards. The severance payment should be lower if the executive is also receiving other substantial benefits at the time of termination, such as any accelerated vesting of stock options or restricted stock. Institutions should not agree to make any severance payments to executives terminated for poor performance or other specified causes.

2. **Limit Base for Pension Calculations:** Retirement payments from pension and 401(k) plans are a legitimate and important benefit for senior executives. However, pension benefits can become huge if they are calculated on a formula that includes all cash bonuses and stock-related compensation. For example, McKesson Corp. CEO John Hammergren's estimated lump-sum pension payout was calculated at $84.6 million as a result of including 150 percent of his bonus payment as well as crediting him with years of service that he did not actually serve.[32] These pension formulas should be limited to base pay and actual cash bonuses up to a reasonable dollar ceiling for each senior executive, and should not include any other performance-based compensation.

3. **Avoid Lump Sum Payouts:** Financial institutions usually insist that departing executives agree not to reveal confidential

information, solicit existing clients, or work for a direct competitor for reasonable time periods. These agreements are much easier to enforce if the institution withholds some payments from already departed senior executives. A company should, therefore, design its retirement and severance arrangements for senior executives so they receive payments over a few years, rather than in a lump sum.

4. **Defer a Portion of Bonus Payment:** Institutions should have the right to recoup bonuses if senior executives knowingly participated in the falsification of financial reports or other performance metrics used in calculating their bonuses. Therefore, an institution should defer a certain percentage of the executive's bonus over two or three years, with payment subject to certain conditions. By retaining a portion of an executive's bonus, an institution can more easily recoup that portion if it turns out that the performance metrics were falsified or the lucrative deals soon fell apart.

Please see Table 11.3 for a detailed summary of these executive compensation principles.

Mega Banks Need a New Type of Board of Directors

Because executive compensation arrangements are so complex, every mega bank (i.e., a bank with over $100 billion in assets) needs a board of directors that designs and implements compensation packages that are customized for its senior executives. These compensation packages should align the interests of the institution's executives with those of its shareholders, while not encouraging excessive risk taking that would likely jeopardize the institution's solvency. More generally, the board of directors should monitor closely the activities of the institution's senior executives to ensure that they are earning long-term profits for its shareholders without threatening the interests of the FDIC as the bank's insurer.

Bring in the Watchdogs . . .

Unfortunately, the directors of many mega banks were not effective watchdogs over the last decade. Most directors of mega banks attend six in-person board meetings per year, each lasting one day. In addition,

Table 11.3   Executive Compensation Principles

Base Salary & Bonus	• Base salaries should not exceed $300,000–$400,000 per year. • Bonuses should be based on a three-year performance period (with exceptions for new employees and those on leave). • Bonuses should generally not be guaranteed in an employment contract. • Bonuses should be structured in a way that executives stand to lose as much money in bad times as they stand to gain in good times. • Bonuses should contain quantitative metrics for at least 2/3 of the bonus calculation.
Stock Grants	• The exercise price of a stock option should be adjusted upward or downward in line with the rise or fall of the relevant stock index. • The exercise price of fixed-price stock options should not be lowered during a significant market downturn. • Restricted stock grants should vest over time only if certain shareholder-related performance targets are met. • A significant portion of all stock grants should be required to be held either until retirement or termination.
Termination & Deferral Issues	• Severance payments should not exceed three times the average base pay and bonus of an executive over the last five years. Companies should not contractually agree to make any severance payments to executives terminated for poor performance or other specified causes. • Pension formulas should be limited to base pay and cash bonus up to a specified level, excluding other performance-based compensation. Retirement and severance arrangements should not be given in a lump sum and should be received over a period of a few years. • Companies should retain the right to recoup bonuses if current or departed executives knowingly participated in the falsification of any performance metric used in calculating their bonuses. Companies should use deferred bonus programs to help ensure performance goals were in fact based on the long-term performance.

directors of public companies spend time reviewing materials, traveling to meetings, and participating in conference calls between meetings. The total time spent on company business by a public company director is less than 200 hours per year, subtracting reasonable travel time.[33] This is simply not enough time to follow the activities of a global financial institution with many lines of business, and to hold senior management accountable for running these businesses. A recent report by Nestor Advisors concludes that large banks need independent directors with more financial experience and more time to spend on board matters.[34]

Most directors of mega banks are not experts on financial matters. I have personal experience in examining closely the board members of two large banks. I was surprised to find how few independent directors had been executives at financial institutions. This appears to be typical in the large U.S. banks. In the case of another bank, Citigroup, only one independent director had a financial services background;[35] and, until very recently, he was the CEO of a large, nonfinancial company, thereby limiting his time available to spend on the complex issues at Citigroup.

In my case, I ultimately decided not to serve as a director of either of the two large banks because of potential conflicts of interest with MFS Investment Management, my main employer. Perhaps other capable candidates with relevant industry experience do not qualify as independent because they work for service providers, customers, or competitors of the financial institution.

As a result of SOX and shareholder pressures, approximately 78 percent of all directors are now independent, including those at financial institutions.[36] In establishing standards for director independence, stock exchanges have set a relatively low limit on professional relationships that directors may have with the company and still be deemed independent. Independence certainly has merit in addressing concerns about potential conflicts, but it may come at the price of relevant experience. Recent amendments by the major U.S. stock markets have taken a step in the right direction by making it easier for a director to be deemed independent despite inconsequential relationships with the company.[37]

Some commentators believe that the key to more effective boards is the appointment of an independent chair of the board, who is not the CEO of that same institution. The separation of board chair from the CEO has been studied extensively in both Europe and the United States.[38] The conclusion of these studies is clear: There is no statistically significant difference, in terms of stock price or accounting income, between companies with independent chairs and those without one. Of course, it may make sense to appoint an independent chair because of the specific needs of an institution—for example, an institution that needs a high-ranking spokesperson to deal with foreign governments.

As a general matter, however, it suffices to have a lead director who organizes the executive sessions of the other independent board members and helps to set the agenda for board meetings.

... and an Accountable Board of Super-Directors

A Special Master is an emergency measure to supervise a few institutions needing exceptional federal assistance. A Special Master is not desirable or feasible as a permanent mechanism to approve compensation arrangements at all financial institutions. If we want to have effective boards of directors at large financial institutions, we need to follow a different model based loosely upon the boards of companies controlled by private equity funds. Although such private companies are different from public companies, we can learn from these situations. Private equity boards are much smaller than boards of publicly traded financial institutions; these smaller boards typically have 4 to 8 members. Boards of large public banks, by contrast, usually have 10 to 18 members. Furthermore, the private equity directors almost always have extensive experience in the relevant industry.

Most importantly, the experienced directors of private equity boards spend a lot more time on company business than directors of most public companies. The typical private equity director spends several days every month on company business. These directors are involved at an early stage in major strategic decisions, like starting new products and making acquisitions. They monitor closely the financial performance of these companies through detailed monthly reports. If these reports show the company is not meeting its operating plan, the directors will be on the telephone with tough questions for the CEO. **Furthermore, these directors on private equity boards actively participate in fashioning performance-based compensation packages for the company's top executives and implementing them each year.**

Not surprisingly, directors of private equity companies are paid differently than independent directors of public companies. The latter receive average compensation of about $200,000 per year at large public companies,[39] including a modest amount of stock-related compensation. Although directors of private equity companies typically receive less annual compensation, they are rewarded for their much greater time commitment and efforts by substantial equity awards. These awards pay off only if the private equity fund actually realizes a profit on its equity investment in the relevant company.

Of course, there are significant differences between public and private companies. According to several studies, however, we can improve boards of public companies by adopting several of the most useful features of boards of private companies controlled by private equity funds, such as smaller boards with larger time commitments to board work.[40] In addition, to increase the pool of directors with relevant industry experience, public boards should drop their requirements for mandatory retirement at age 70 or 72. These formalistic limits should be replaced by a periodic analysis by the board collectively of each member's ability to serve effectively as a director. A person at age 74 or 78 may be fully capable of performing the duties of a board member at a financial institution.

In short, a mega bank should have a board of super-directors—a small group of independent directors with extensive experience in financial institutions who spend several days per month on the financial institution's business, and serve on only one other board of a public company. They would be paid in cash a director's fee of $50,000 to $70,000 per year, together with a combination of stock options and restricted stock valued at $300,000 to $500,000 at the time of grant. Such super-directors could implement the concept of "accountable capitalism" in the U.S. financial sector, holding senior executives at every mega bank accountable for its performance. These super-directors would have the expertise, time, and incentive to understand the complexities of large financial institutions, monitor their performance closely, and implement customized systems for executive compensation.

Shareholders Need a Reasonable Way to Participate in the Nomination of Directors

If we have more powerful boards of directors at financial institutions, we should also make sure that shareholders have appropriate input into the selection of directors. Generally, the duties of company officers, directors, and shareholders are determined by the interplay among state law, the company's charter and bylaws, stock exchange requirements, and federal regulations. In short, directors represent the company's shareholders as well as the company and have a legal duty to act in their best interest. In my view, shareholders should have four enhanced rights as the owners of the financial institution. Specifically, they should have:

1. The right to have directors submit their resignations if they do not receive a majority of favorable votes cast at an annual meeting
2. The right to elect all directors every year, instead of staggered boards
3. The right to nominate their own directors through a low-cost process of soliciting proxies
4. The right to vote on an advisory resolution about the executive compensation packages of the institution's top five executives

A Director Should Be Elected by a Majority of the Votes Cast at an Election

Contrary to the popular view, shareholders generally do not have meaningful input into the election of directors at their company. Under the traditional plurality voting standard, shareholders can either cast their votes in favor of a director, or withhold their votes for a director. The number of withheld votes has no legal effect on the outcome of the election: As long as one share is voted in favor of a director, such director is legally elected to the board. Companies defend this practice because it avoids a failed election that could leave the company without enough directors to oversee the company. In fact, plurality voting is the default standard under the corporate laws of many states, including Delaware, the state where most large companies are incorporated.

Some companies have formally recognized that a large number of withheld votes should have some significance. These companies have instituted policies that require any director who receives less than a majority of the votes cast to submit his or her resignation to the board of directors. Although that director is still technically elected, the board can decide if there is a strong reason to override the will of the majority of its voting shareholders by either accepting or rejecting the director's resignation.[41] Approximately 68 percent of large public companies have adopted some form of majority voting in director elections over the past few years, but only 25 percent of smaller public companies have adopted this procedure.[42] **Every financial institution director should be required to submit his or her resignation if he or she does not receive majority support from shareholders who vote. This requirement would help insure that shareholders could potentially oust one or more directors if they are ineffective.**

The Entire Board of Directors Should Be Elected Every Year

About 50 percent of large companies still maintain staggered boards, which allow shareholders to elect only one-third of the board of directors each year.[43] For example, if an institution has 12 directors, four would be elected each year to serve three-year terms. **Staggered boards are an inappropriate constraint on shareholders' right to elect the full board annually.** In fact, shareholder proposals to "de-stagger" boards generally gain majority support from shareholders. Accordingly, many companies have agreed to drop their staggered boards and allow all directors to be elected and held accountable to shareholders each year. But a large percentage of smaller public companies still maintain a staggered board.

Staggered boards were justified historically as promoting continuity among board members. But continuity can be achieved by other measures, such as abolishing term limits for directors and making sure that multiple directors do not retire in the same year. The primary reason for a staggered board at the present time is to deter or slow down a hostile takeover of a company.[44] For instance, a hostile bidder may propose its own slate of directors as part of a plan to take control of a financial institution. With a staggered board, it would take the hostile bidder two years instead of one to elect a majority of the institution's directors.

Shareholders of every financial institution should have the right each year to choose all members of its board of directors to run the institution. Of course, supporters of staggered boards would argue that they are needed to prevent a hostile bidder from potentially exploiting the company, such as using its assets to back a loan to buy the company's shares. However, such tactics are usually prohibited by state, antitakeover laws. In any event, these arguments are inapplicable to the board of a financial institution because any new control person would have to win advance approval for its post-takeover plan from a regulator.

Shareholders Need a Low-Cost Effective Method to Nominate Directors

In 2009, the SEC proposed that shareholders continuously holding more than a specified amount of a company's shares for at least one year be allowed to nominate their own independent candidates for up to one-quarter of the company's directors. The SEC also proposed that these nominees would appear in the company's proxy statement—the materials sent to all shareholders by the company with its proposed slate of directors and any other matters to be put to a shareholder vote. The SEC stressed that it was "an extremely costly process" for shareholders to send out their own proxy solicitation materials for their own director candidates.[45]

Not surprisingly, this proposal, called proxy access, has been sharply criticized by corporate representatives who believe that having multiple candidates in the company's proxy statement would be confusing to investors. More fundamentally, the SEC's proposal is likely to be challenged under a prior court decision invalidating an SEC rule prohibiting exchanges from listing the shares of any publicly traded corporation that reduced the current voting rights of any of its shareholders.[46] That decision suggests that states should establish the ground rules for shareholder voting rights and the SEC should ensure full disclosure of all material information by all relevant parties utilizing those rules.

This debate could be resolved with an approach that addresses both the cost and legality of shareholder-nominated directors by building on existing procedures. Shareholders are already allowed to nominate their own director candidates if they draft and distribute their own proxy statement and proxy card. However, these shareholder proponents must pay for the cost of printing and delivering this proxy material to *all* the shareholders of the company. To help reduce this potential cost, a shareholder that continuously owns a specified percentage of the financial institution's shares (alone or together with others) and is not seeking control of the institution (a qualified shareholder), should not be required to mail proxy materials about its director nominees to all of the institution's shareholders.[47] **Instead, the qualified shareholder**

should be permitted to mail its proxy statement and proxy card for its director nominees only to a small group of shareholders with large stakes in the company.

In addition, the qualified shareholder should be required to post its proxy statement and card on the Internet so that these materials would be available for review by all company shareholders. However, some smaller shareholders might not be aware of the information about a director nominee if it were promulgated primarily through the qualified shareholder's web site. **To address this concern, the institution's proxy statement should be required to list in a prominent place the name of any director candidate nominated by a qualified shareholder as well as the web address where all shareholders can obtain more information about such nominee.**[48]

To further address the potential cost issue, shareholders of every public company should have the right to adopt or reject a binding bylaw requiring the institution to reimburse reasonable expenses of director candidates nominated by a qualified shareholder, who are successful in winning board seats. The institution already pays for all proxy expenses in connection with management director nominees put forward by the board. Therefore, shareholders should have the right to decide whether a similar benefit should be provided by the institution to successful director nominees put forth by a qualified shareholder (not seeking control of the company). Such a binding bylaw could be voted upon by shareholders under the newly adopted amendments to the state of Delaware's corporate laws.[49] Other states would have to adopt similar laws to Delaware in order for such a binding bylaw on reimbursement of proxy expenses to be voted upon by shareholders.

Companies Should Hold Advisory Votes on Executive Compensation

Well before the most recent market turmoil, shareholder groups put forth proposals at annual shareholder meetings that sought to limit excessive executive compensation. Typically, it is the board's compensation committee that determines executive compensation; shareholders have very little opportunity for meaningful input on this subject other than submitting and voting on shareholder proposals. Under current law, a publicly traded company must allow a shareholder proposal on executive compensation to be voted upon by all its shareholders as long as the vote on the proposal passes all procedural and content requirements, including that the proposal is advisory in nature. But even if a proposal is approved by a majority of shareholders, the company's board of directors does not have to act on the proposal.

During the last few years, shareholder groups have been pushing for a general say-on-pay policy, which would legally require every publicly traded company to hold an advisory shareholder vote each year about its executive compensation programs as described in the company's proxy statement. The UK has already adopted a say-on-pay policy requiring every UK publicly traded company to hold an annual shareholder advisory vote on its overall executive compensation practices. A majority of shareholders have voted against a UK CEO's pay package in only a very small number of situations involving egregious pay practices—for example, a large golden parachute guaranteed to a CEO without regard to his performance. Although these shareholder votes are not legally binding, boards of directors have been quite responsive to substantial negative votes by shareholders. These resolutions have also prompted fruitful discussions between directors and shareholder groups on the principles that should be followed in designing packages prior to shareholders voting on them. **In short, the United States should follow the UK approach because it has been successful in curbing the worst practices in executive compensation, especially at poor-performing companies,**[50] **and in promoting a constructive dialogue on the subject with shareholders.**

The United States could expect similar results to those of the UK if Congress adopted a say-on-pay policy for all publicly traded companies. On the other hand, some argue that compensation packages are too complex for a shareholder vote, and that the design of such packages should be left entirely to the compensation committee of the board. Although both arguments have some validity, the UK experience shows that most institutional shareholders will generally make the effort to understand complex pay packages and attempt to police only the outer limits of the compensation committee's decisions. With the increased compensation disclosure required by the SEC since 2007, as well as available research reports from proxy advisory firms on compensation issues, shareholders now have the adequate tools to make informed decisions on advisory votes about executive compensation.

A broader counterargument is that increased stockholder power through measures like say-on-pay would increase the fixation of institutional investors on quarterly results,[51] which was allegedly one of the contributing factors to the financial crisis. However, the focus on short-term profits was driven more by the short-term metrics used by directors to set executive bonuses than the pressures from institutional shareholders. Many CEOs intensified the focus on short-term results by publicly projecting earnings per share for the next quarter. Most institutional investors oppose such quarterly earnings guidance.

The most vocal supporters of say on pay are public pension plans, investing mainly through index funds that inherently have a long-term perspective. In casting advisory votes annually on the CEO's compensation package, these plans are not encouraging short-term performance. Rather, they are supporting incentives to promote long-term profitability, such as bonuses based on multiyear performance and restricted stock with long holding periods. In addition, active managers of institutional accounts have been willing to support public companies, such as those in the biotech industry, with no current profits but good prospects for long-term growth.

As a practical matter, say-on-pay is coming to the United States. In 2008, shareholders submitted advisory proposals to have a say on pay at 78 companies, garnering an average of about 41 percent of the shareholder votes.[52] As mentioned earlier, in February of 2009 Congress required all current and future recipients of TARP funds to hold advisory shareholder votes on say-on-pay until the federal government is paid back in full.[53] Later in 2009, Congress is likely to vote on bills requiring all publicly traded companies to hold advisory shareholder votes on say on pay, and requiring federal regulators to prohibit imprudently risky compensation practices at all financial institutions.[54]

Summary

Excesses in compensation of financial executives have been a major source of public outrage after the most recent market meltdown.

In response, Congress passed two sets of restrictions on executive compensation—one under TARP in October of 2008, and a second in the Stimulus Bill in February of 2009. In June 2009, the Treasury issued rules implementing these legislative restrictions on executive compensation, together with further restrictions on institutions receiving exceptional federal assistance.

The restrictions of TARP were filled with ambiguities and inconsistencies. The restrictions applied only to the CEO, the CFO, and the three other most highly compensated senior executives (collectively, the SEOs). TARP contains no specific limits on salaries, cash bonuses, or stock awards. Its prohibitions on golden parachute payments apply only if they exceed three times the SEO's average annual compensation over the last five years. Moreover, TARP contains tenuous distinctions among capital injections, direct federal purchases of assets, and asset purchases through auctions.

The Obama Treasury proposed rules on executive compensation that would have applied only to institutions receiving federal assistance in the future. However, before these rules could be finalized, Congress in the Stimulus Act of 2009 passed new restrictions on executive compensation, which applies to all financial institutions that have received, or will receive, federal assistance. Most importantly, the Stimulus Act limits annual bonuses to restricted shares equal to one third of total annual compensation for top executives at TARP firms. This bonus ceiling will lead many financial institutions to increase guaranteed base salaries, thus unlinking pay and performance.

In addition, the Stimulus Act of 2009 imposed further restrictions on executive compensation at TARP institutions. These include:

- Adoption of policies against expenditures viewed as excessive or luxury, with CEO and CFO certification of compliance with such policies.
- Expansion of the prohibition against golden parachutes from the five SEOs to include the next five most highly compensated executives.
- Extension of the requirement to clawback bonuses based on inaccurate performance metrics from five SEOs to include the next 20 most highly compensated executives.

In its June 2009 rules, the Treasury went further than the Stimulus Act of 2009 in certain areas. For example, TARP recipients may not make payments to cover taxes on any compensation items. TARP recipients must also make more detailed disclosures on services rendered by compensation consultants to TARP recipients. However, disclosure is mild medicine for a potential conflict of interest that is likely to become an actual conflict of interest. Therefore, Congress should prohibit the same compensation consultant from providing advice on human resource issues to the financial institution and also providing advice on executive compensation to the compensation committee of its board.

Most creatively, the Treasury established a Special Master to approve the specific compensation arrangements for the five SEOs and the other 20 most highly compensated executives, and the structure of compensation for the next 100 highest paid employees, at TARP firms receiving exceptional federal assistance. These firms include AIG, Bank of America, Citigroup, as well as four auto-related firms. To provide guidance for TARP firms and public companies more generally, Treasury Secretary Geithner announced a sensible set of normative principles instead of rigid or uniform standards.

In principle, restrictions on executive compensation packages for top executives at a financial institution should be set by a board of directors who know the institution well and spend enough time to design appropriate incentives. In practice, directors have not done a good job on setting executive compensation at many mega banks, despite compliance with the additional procedures mandated by SOX.

To implement "accountable capitalism" in the financial sector, the U.S. needs a different type of board of directors at large financial institutions. Although companies controlled by private equity funds are different from public companies, financial institutions can learn a lot from the boards in companies controlled by private equity funds. These are small boards composed of directors with extensive experience in financial institutions. These directors would spend several days a month at the institution, and limit themselves to one other publicly traded board. They would be paid lower base fees than the average director, plus much larger amounts of stock-related compensation. In short, these super-directors would have the expertise, time, and incentive to hold accountable the managers of financial institutions.

Because boards of directors would be more powerful under my proposal, shareholders should have more meaningful input into the election of these super-directors. Financial institutions should have all directors elected each year, rather than staggered boards of directors. Any director not receiving a majority of votes cast should be required to submit his or her resignation for consideration by the board.

Although qualified shareholders already have the right to nominate their own directors, this is a costly process under current SEC rules. Therefore, the SEC has proposed that shareholders be allowed to nominate up to 25 percent of a company's directors and that shareholder-nominated directors be included in the company's proxy solicitation materials. However, this SEC proposal is likely to be challenged under a prior federal court decision suggesting that the setting of voting rules for company elections is generally governed by state laws, whereas the SEC usually sets the disclosure rules for company elections.

Here is a compromise proposal that avoids these legal problems and addresses the cost issue. Any shareholder who owns a specified percentage of the outstanding stock and is not seeking control of the financial institution—that is, a qualified shareholder—should be permitted to deliver proxy materials only to large shareholders of the institution. In addition, the qualified shareholder should post its proxy statement and proxy card on a freely accessible web site. To ensure that all shareholders of the institution are aware of this web site, the institution should be required to list prominently in its proxy statement the name of any such director candidate and the relevant web site address. Shareholders should also be allowed, under Delaware and other state laws, to vote on a binding bylaw on whether a financial institution should reimburse reasonable proxy expenses to a successful director candidate nominated by a qualified shareholder.

Finally, all publicly traded financial institutions should be required each year to hold a shareholder advisory vote on the compensation practices of the company. Such say-on-pay votes have worked well in the UK. Shareholders have used these advisory votes to object to only a very small number of egregious CEO compensation packages and have engaged in constructive dialogue with management on appropriate executive compensation incentives.

Chapter 12

Were Accounting Rules an Important Factor Contributing to the Financial Crisis?

O ur financial crisis has vaulted into the public spotlight the previously arcane concept of fair-market-value accounting (FMV), popularly called mark-to-market. Fair-market-value is an accounting method that requires certain assets to be revalued each quarter at current market prices, based on recent trades or other indicators of current value. The alternate method is historical cost accounting, which requires assets to be carried on a company's books at their historic costs, unless their value has been permanently impaired.

Fair-market-value has been under attack because many claim that it amplified the speed and severity of our financial collapse. By the fall of 2008, the public debate about FMV had become so heated that Congress required the Securities and Exchange Commission (SEC) to conduct a study of FMV and gave the SEC the authority to suspend FMV accounting, if needed. What would it mean for banks if the SEC suspended FMV? Suppose a bank bought a mortgage-backed bond for $1 million, which could be sold at only $400,000 today, but which the bank management believes will be worth $750,000 in several years. Under FMV accounting, the bond would be valued at $400,000, the current market value of the bond. Under historic cost accounting, the bond would be valued at $750,000, the original cost of $1 million, as reduced by a permanent impairment of $250,000.

FMV's critics include the American Bankers Association, former House Speaker Newt Gingrich, and publisher Steve Forbes. As Forbes wrote in a March 2009 editorial: "Mark-to-market accounting is the principal reason why our financial system is in a meltdown. . . . When times are good, [mark-to-market] artificially boosts banks' capital, thereby encouraging more investing and lending. In a downturn, it sets off a devastating deflation."[1] In other words, Forbes argues that, during periods of financial distress, mark-to-market accounting can feed a vicious circle in which declining securities prices erode bank capital, thus forcing banks to sell additional assets on the open market in order to maintain their required leverage ratios (e.g., a minimum amount of capital required to support a certain amount of bank assets). These forced sales can produce additional downward pressure on asset prices, thus beginning the circle anew.

Supporters of FMV include the world's two largest accounting standard-setting organizations: the UK-based International Accounting Standards Board (IASB) and the U.S.-based Financial Accounting Standards Board (FASB). Both bodies maintain that no system is perfect and that FMV is the best option available. As FASB Chairman Robert Herz asserted in a December 2008 speech, "What are the alternatives? To use original cost or some other smoothed value that ignores current market conditions, or to rely solely on management estimates of value that may ignore current market conditions and that thus far have often proven highly overoptimistic? . . . The harsh reality is that we can't just willy nilly suspend or modify the financial reporting when there is bad news. Changing the accounting does not make the underlying problems go away."[2]

Chapter 12 will begin by exploring the differences between FMV and historical cost accounting, and then evaluating the arguments for and against FMV. It will agree with the conclusion of the SEC's study at the end of 2008 that FMV should *not* be suspended. Instead of such a temporary ban, it will suggest revisions to FMV and related policies, including specific proposals for additional disclosures and unlinking financial accounting from bank capital requirements.

Second, this chapter will address the current debate about whether the United States should switch from its current accounting system, known as Generally Accepted Accounting Principles (GAAP), to the international system known as International Financial Reporting Standards (IFRS). Some commentators believe that a switch would help prevent global financial crises in the future by harmonizing all accounting standards. Others support IFRS because it is principles-based, as opposed to U.S. GAAP, which is rules-based. They believe that a global regulatory system based on general principles will be more effective than one based on detailed rules in preventing another financial crisis.[3]

Chapter 12 will argue that the shift from U.S. GAAP to IFRS can be justified on a cost-benefit basis only for the largest 100–300 U.S. global companies. It will also show why a regulatory system needs detailed rules as well as general principles to be effective.

The Difference Between FMV and Historical Cost Accounting

A company's assets and liabilities are listed on its balance sheet, the part of the financial statement that portrays its financial position at a specific date in the past (usually the end of a quarter or year). The balance sheet is a two-column table, with assets (i.e., what a company owns) in the left column, and liabilities (i.e., what a company owes) plus equity (sometimes called capital) in the right column. The value of a company's assets on the left side of its balance sheet must always equal the sum of its liabilities and equity on the right side.

By contrast, the income statement is the part of the financial statement that portrays a company's profitability over a period of time, such as a quarter or a year. The main elements of the income statement are revenues, expenses, gains, and losses. Revenues are the cash and other income a company generates, and expenses are the costs incurred in order to generate those revenues. The difference between revenues and expenses is profit. Gains and losses, on the other hand, are one-time events such as sales of securities or real estate. An asset sold for more than its value on a company's balance sheet produces a gain, and an asset sold for less than its value on a company's balance sheet produces a loss. A gain or a loss on an asset listed on the balance sheet flows through the income statement as a profit or loss.

Historical cost accounting and FMV are the two main methods to account for assets and liabilities of financial institutions, as well as other companies. We will explain the differences between the two accounting methods, evaluate the arguments pro and con for FMV, and advocate a modified version of FMV.

How Does Historical Accounting Work?

Under historical cost accounting, assets on the balance sheet are carried at their purchase or original value, unless there is a permanent impairment (i.e., a permanent decline in the value of the asset).[4] The carrying value of an asset may also decline below its historical cost due to depreciation, as with a building.[5] If the asset is sold, the difference between historical cost and the selling price flows through the income statement as a gain or loss. For example, suppose hypothetical financial institution ABC originates an interest-only mortgage loan for $200,000. Under historical cost accounting and assuming no impairment, ABC's loan would remain on its balance sheet at this historical cost until repaid in full. Even if the market price of the loan declined to $180,000 two years later, it would remain on the balance sheet at $200,000. If ABC decided to sell the loan for $180,000, however, the $20,000 difference between this sale price and historical cost would run through ABC's income statement as a loss.

Historical cost accounting has advantages and disadvantages. Its main advantages are that it is simple to calculate and difficult to manipulate. The price a company paid to acquire an asset, after all, is relatively straightforward. Historical cost's main disadvantage is that it can significantly understate or overstate an asset's current value, thus understating or overstating a company's equity. The original purchase of the asset may have occurred decades ago, at a price completely unrelated to its current value; for example, a building purchased 20 years ago for $2 million that now could easily be sold for $8 million.

Even in historical cost accounting, current market values come into play through the concept of permanent impairments, which decrease the value of assets. Regulators require companies each quarter to scrutinize carefully their assets for permanent impairments. When a company and its auditor agree that assets are permanently impaired, they must be written down to current value, with the resulting losses flowing through the income statement. In 2008, U.S. banks recognized $25 billion in losses due to permanent impairments in goodwill alone, an intangible asset, in this situation representing the ongoing value of an acquired business.[6]

Due to permanent impairments, historical cost accounting and FMV are similar in that both should ultimately reflect the decline in value of impaired loans and securities. But there are differences. Notably, FMV reflects declines in loan and security prices more quickly and smoothly over time, whereas permanent impairments typically occur less frequently in larger lumps. To illustrate, suppose that the market price of ABC's $200,000 mortgage loan decreases $5,000 per quarter over four quarters due to credit-related reasons. Under FMV, the balance-sheet value of that loan at the end of each quarter would be current market value; at the end of the year, that loan would be valued at $180,000. Under historical cost accounting, however, the loan would remain on the balance sheet at its original $200,000 value for the entire year regardless of market prices. Only if ABC's managers were to judge the loan permanently impaired at the end of that year would the historic value of the loan on its balance sheet be reduced to the current market value of $180,000. At that time, the $20,000 loss would flow through the income statement to the balance sheet.

How Does FMV Accounting Work?

Under FMV, by contrast, assets are revalued at current market prices each quarter, based on recent trades or on other indicators of current value. But some assets are easier to price than others. For example, liquid and tradable assets, like debt and equity securities, are much easier to price than unique and illiquid assets, like real estate or art. This is why the majority of assets accounted for at fair value are debt and equity securities.

Imagine that our same institution, ABC, purchases one General Electric bond (a debt security) at par value of $100 and places it in its trading account. Under FMV, that bond would appear on ABC's balance sheet each reporting period at its current market value, and the bond's sequential change in value would flow through its balance sheet to ABC's income statement as a gain or loss. For example, if the price of the bond were to decline from $100 to $80, a $20 loss would flow through its income statement to its balance sheet. If the price of the bond then subsequently rose from $80 to $90, a $10 gain would flow through the income statement to the balance sheet.

This example demonstrates the accounting treatment for securities classified as Trading. The only other two classifications for securities under U.S. GAAP are Held-To-Maturity (HTM) and Available-For-Sale (AFS). Loans have two analogous classifications: Held-For-Investment (HFI) and Held-For-Sale (HFS). Company management teams decide how to classify their securities and loans. Table 12.1 and Table 12.2 summarize these classifications and their accounting treatments.

If a company's management team classifies a security as Trading, that security is subject to FMV accounting. Accordingly, unrealized gains and losses from that security would flow through the income statement, as in our General Electric bond example earlier. Because unrealized gains and losses on Trading securities flow through the income statement each quarter, they affect the equity account on the balance sheet and also affect bank regulatory capital. Bank regulatory capital, by way of background, is the adjusted calculation of equity that regulators use to determine whether a bank is well capitalized; if regulatory capital gets too low, a bank can fail. (See Chapter 6.)

Many debt securities are classified as HTM, our second classification for securities, and nearly all loans are classified as HFI, the analogous loan classification under U.S. GAAP. These classifications may be applied only when an institution has the intent and ability to hold a loan or security to maturity. Securities HTM and loans HFI are both accounted for at historical cost; in other words, they are *not* subject to mark-to-market accounting.

Table 12.1   U.S. GAAP Accounting by Security Classification

	1. Trading Securities	2. HTM Securities	3. AFS Securities
Balance Sheet	Carried on balance sheet at fair value. Changes in fair value affect equity.	Carried on balance sheet at historical cost. Can affect equity only in the event of a permanent impairment.	Carried on balance sheet at fair value. Changes in fair value are reflected in the Accumulated Other Comprehensive Income, a special equity account line-item.
Income Statement	Unrealized gains and losses flow through the income statement and are included in earnings.	Unrealized gains and losses flow through the income statement only in the event of a permanent impairment.	Unrealized gains and losses are reflected in Other Comprehensive Income, a special income statement line-item that is excluded from earnings.
Regulatory Capital	Unrealized gains and losses affect regulatory capital.	Unrealized gains and losses affect regulatory capital only in the event of a permanent impairment.	Unrealized gains and losses affect regulatory capital only in the event of a permanent impairment.

Table 12.2   U.S. GAAP Accounting by Loan Classification

	1. Trading Loans	2. HFI Loans	3. HFS Loans
Balance Sheet	N/A.	Carried at historical cost. Can affect equity only in the even of an OTTI.*	Carried at the lower of cost or market. Declines in fair value hit equity if fair value is less than cost.
Income Statement	N/A.	Can flow through the income statement only in the event of an OTTI.*	Declines in fair value flow through the income statement if fair value is less than cost.
Regulatory Capital	N/A.	Can affect regulatory capital only in the event of an OTTI.*	Declines in fair value affect regulatory capital if fair value is less than cost.

*OTTI = Other Than Temporary Impairment

The final classification for securities is AFS. As with Trading, the AFS classification requires mark–to–market accounting. However, unrealized gains and losses on AFS debt securities do *not* flow through the income statement and do *not* affect regulatory capital.[7] The analogous classification of AFS for securities is HFS for loans. Loans HFS are reported at their original cost or fair value, whichever is lower at the relevant time. If the fair value of a loan declines below its cost, such a decline is recognized in income. In practice, fewer than 5 percent of aggregate loans have typically been classified as HFS. This was the case even during the housing boom, which was the heyday of originate–to–sell financial institutions like Countrywide Financial, which tended to classify more of their loans as HFS.

In short, contrary to popular opinion, most loans and securities are not marked–to–market. In 2008, only 45 percent of the aggregate assets of financial institutions were marked–to–market, and almost half of that 45 percent were securities AFS where quarterly losses in market value did not impact the institution's regulatory capital or income statement.[8] With respect to banks specifically, only 31 percent of their assets were market–to–market and almost one–fourth of that 31 percent were securities AFS where quarterly market losses likewise did not impact the bank's regulatory capital or income statement.[9]

Arguments Pro and Con FMV

Fair-market-value has a big advantage: It produces accurate and timely valuations during functioning markets. As IASB Vice-Chairman Tom Jones opined in October 2008, "When there isn't an illiquid market I think fair value captures reality. I can't think of any other system that does."[10] For example, if the price of a widely traded General Electric bond declines from $100 to $95, Mr. Jones would rather see the balance sheet reflect fair value of $95 than cost of $100.

At certain times, however, markets are abnormal; extreme market conditions can sometimes produce unrealistic prices. During such times, some investors feel that FMV can do more harm than good by allowing unrealistic prices to be reflected on balance sheets. As illustrated by the example at the start of this chapter, if distressed market conditions cause trading securities to decline temporarily to a level below what bankers believe to be their long-term recoverable value, FMV may understate the value of the assets and result in unjustified decreases in equity.

Let us imagine that general economic distress causes the market price of our General Electric bond to decline to $75, even though we and other investors believe the sum of the bond's discounted future cash flows to be $95. In this case, FMV may understate the bond's "intrinsic" economic value on the balance sheet due to liquidity concerns unrelated to General Electric. Of course, the opposite can occur. Fair market value accounting may lead to overstated asset and equity values during ebullient times like the dot-com bubble. Not surprisingly, few bankers complained when FMV accounting increased their reported profits.

Regulators Gave Initial Guidance on Applying FMV in Illiquid Markets

Because the SEC and the FASB recognized that it is difficult to mark-to-market an asset without a trading market, they provided additional guidance with the release of the *Statement of Financial Accounting Standards No. 157* (FAS157)—the accounting standard that established guidelines for measuring fair value. FAS157 sets forth a hierarchy of valuation methods based on available inputs to measure FMV. Companies must value and classify their assets and liabilities at the highest hierarchy level applicable.

Level 1 is the highest hierarchy level. Level 1 assets, such as U.S. Treasury bonds, are valued at observable market prices, trade actively, and are highly liquid. Level 2 assets, such as some residential and commercial mortgage-related assets, lack direct market prices but can be valued using observable market inputs. Finally, Level 3 assets, such as private equity investments, lack observable market prices and have at least one unobservable valuation input. These assets are illiquid. Table 12.3 summarizes these classifications.

When assets are classified as Level 3, companies are allowed to mark them to model, rather than to market. Marking an asset to model means pricing it using a valuation model instead of a market quote. Level 3 assets are not priced using market quotes because quotes are not available for these assets; all assets classified as Level 3 lack liquid markets, and thus lack readily determinable market prices.

Table 12.3 FAS157 Valuation Hierarchy

	Level 1 Assets	Level 2 Assets	Level 3 Assets
Liquidity	Most liquidity.	Moderate liquidity.	Least liquidity.
Valuation Method	Valued at direct market prices from identical instruments trading.	Valued using observable market inputs.	Valued using a financial model, such as a discounted cash flow model.

Over time, assets can be transferred from Level 2 to Level 3 if their markets become inactive and distressed. For example, as 2008 progressed, investor demand for commercial mortgages and commercial mortgage-backed securities withered. This caused many banks to reclassify those assets as Level 3 and mark them to model. Goldman Sachs, for instance, transferred a net $3.2 billion of assets from Level 2 to Level 3 between November 2007 and November 2008. As the company's 2008 annual report explained, this increase "principally [reflected] transfers from Level 2 . . . of loans and securities backed by commercial real estate, reflecting reduced price transparency for these financial instruments."[11]

Although FAS157 has been helpful in providing financial institutions with a framework for judging the fair value of an asset, its implementation could be improved. The Level 3 classification was probably underutilized in 2008. Management teams at various financial institutions have stated privately that they were reluctant to reclassify too many assets as Level 3 because of uncertainty about the exact parameters of that classification and potential legal challenges to classifying certain assets as Level 3.

Congress Insists on More Clarification of FMV

In October 2008, there was an uproar in Congress and corporate America about FMV because of uncommonly illiquid markets after the failure of Lehman Brothers. In response, the FASB released a staff position paper clarifying the application of FMV in illiquid markets.[12] The staff highlighted the flexibility companies have to reclassify assets and liabilities as Level 3, and mark them to model when markets become inactive. The staff stressed that companies did not have to use prices from forced or distressed sales to value Level 3 assets.

However, this staff position paper did not explain how to identify when a market is sufficiently inactive to qualify a previously Level 2 asset as Level 3, and what exactly constitutes a distressed sale. In a testy March 12, 2009 hearing, various members of Congress implored FASB Chairman Robert Herz to make it easier for companies to mark assets to model. U.S. Representative Paul Kanjorski threatened that "if regulators and standard setters do not act to improve the standards, then Congress will have no other option than to act itself."[13]

Four days later, the FASB issued a proposal that gave companies a more concrete method of determining when to classify assets and liabilities as Level 3. This proposal included a test to be used in determining whether a market is inactive and distressed. This test will provide managements and auditors with additional cover to use Level 3 and reduce the stigma associated with marking to model. The final version of this rule was adopted by the FASB on April 2, 2009.[14] At the same time, the FASB adopted another rule allowing companies, when recognizing losses from permanent impairments of securities below their cost to fair-market-value, to report in their income statements only the credit portion of the losses (and to put the non-credit losses in Other Comprehensive Income).

As a result of these FASB rulings, banks will increase the amount of their trading assets marked-to-model and the portion of their securities impairments not due to credit losses. Without these rulings, the earnings of the banks in S&P's financial index would have been nearly cut in half for the first quarter of 2009.[15] Although bankers are cheering these steps by the FASB, the rulings will have adverse effects on the programs described in Chapter 10 to encourage private buying of toxic assets. Toxic assets marked-to-model are likely to be valued by banks at higher prices than toxic assets marked-to-market. To avoid taking real losses, banks will not want to sell toxic assets below the prices on their books. So it will be even more difficult for banks and private investors to reach agreement on a fair price for toxic assets.

At the same time, the increasing use of the mark-to-model method will raise questions among investors about the accuracy of bank valuations for toxic assets. As Warren Buffet has pointed out, mark-to-model can sometimes degenerate into "mark-to-myth."[16] **A model is as good as its assumptions. In order for investors to understand how the banks arrived at values for assets under mark-to-model, they should be**

required to disclose a supplemental schedule containing a list of Level 3 assets with a summary of their key characteristics and, most importantly, the material assumptions employed in their valuation. In its final rule, the FASB mandated additional disclosures in these areas so investors can better understand the valuation models used by banks for Level 3 assets.

Arguments for Further Changes to FMV Accounting

Although some complain that unrealized losses under FMV reduce regulatory capital, this claim applies only to the 45 percent of aggregate financial institution assets that are marked-to-market. As mentioned earlier, nearly half of those assets were accounted for as available-for-sale, where marks to market do not affect income or regulatory capital.

Others argue that FMV can cause healthy banks to become insolvent and fail because this accounting method can lead to large decreases in regulatory capital due to the markdown of illiquid securities. Although possible in theory, this rarely occurs in practice. If the price of an asset declines in an illiquid or distressed market, it should be classified as Level 3 and marked-to-model rather than marked-to-market. More concretely, the SEC report in December, 2008, concluded that FMV was "not a primary underlying cause of the 2008 bank failures studied."[17] The SEC report found that fair value was applied to a limited extent for most of the failed banks it examined. Moreover, for the few failed banks that recognized "sizable fair value losses,"[18] the SEC concluded that the reporting of these losses was not the reason they failed. Instead, the cause of these failures was credit-driven loan losses that eroded shareholder equity.

Three Suggestions for Revising FMV Accounting

Nevertheless, there are three changes that should be made to the current rules for FMV accounting. **Under current rules, there is an anomalous difference between the accounting treatments for loans HFS and securities HFS. Though assets in both categories are**

classified as for sale, they have different accounting treatments.
Loans held-for-sale are accounted for at the lower of cost or fair value,
with decreases in fair value below cost flowing through the income statement and affecting regulatory capital. In contrast, decreases in the fair
value of securities held-for-sale do not affect regulatory capital. **There
is no reason that loans held-for-sale should have a different
accounting treatment than securities held-for-sale, particularly
considering that securities held for sale are oftentimes securitized loans. Loans held-for-sale should be accounted for using
the same accounting treatment for securities held-for-sale.**

Another odd feature of FMV is that it allows distressed firms to
increase their earnings by reducing the value of their own debt to its
current trading price. For example, reducing the value of its own bonds
allowed Lehman Brothers to report $1.4 billion of gains during the quarter
of 2008 immediately prior to its failure in September 2008.[19] **Companies
should not be permitted to reduce the value of their own debt to
market prices except in special circumstances.[20] In the extreme
case, a bank could report a huge jump in its capital the day
before it went bankrupt because all of its bonds would be slashed
in value.**

Third, and more broadly, the International Accounting Standards
Board has proposed to eliminate the middle category of available-for-
sale (AFS) in fair value accounting, leaving only the categories of trading and held-to-maturity.[21] **This is a sensible change since AFS
is a murky category with a complex accounting treatment.**
As mentioned earlier, although AFS assets are marked-to-market, any
gains or losses on these assets do not affect regulatory capital or income;
instead they are warehoused in that unique account called other comprehensive income (OCI). However, the proposal has generated
opposition from financial firms claiming that it would shift many AFS
assets to the trading category—thereby increasing the volatility of their
quarterly income statements and capital accounts.

Transparent Accounting Is Necessary for a Financial Recovery

As mentioned earlier, Congress asked the SEC to study whether FMV
should be suspended. In its report released at the end of December of

2008, the SEC recommended that FMV not be suspended. The SEC concluded that FMV "[did] not appear to be a 'cause' of financial institution failures" and that suspending FMV would "erode investor confidence in financial statements."[22]

Like Congress, European politicians have called for the suspension of mark-to-market accounting during times of financial crisis. For example, French President Nicolas Sarkozy proposed suspending FMV, because it leaves bank balance sheets "at the whim of speculators."[23] Nevertheless, a poll conducted of the European membership of the Institute of Certified Financial Analysts indicated that 79 percent were opposed to the suspension of FMV, and 85 percent thought that a suspension would decrease confidence in the banking system.[24]

FMV accounting should not be suspended simply because there is a financial crisis. Without transparency on current losses, it is very difficult for a government to take the aggressive actions needed to resolve a financial crisis. Japan is a case directly on point. Japanese stocks declined about 60 percent between 1990 and 1992, and have been generally weak since, while Japanese commercial real estate prices declined about 50 percent between 1992 and 2002. However, despite a deteriorating economy, Japanese authorities discouraged Japanese banks from recognizing losses from bad loans for years, thus making it difficult for anyone to judge the solvency of banks. For their part, Japan's technically insolvent banks engaged in loan-portfolio evergreening, that is, they continuously rolled over problem loans made to failing Japanese companies in order to obscure losses and make their financial condition look healthier than they really were. This misallocation of capital hampered economic growth and helped to extend the Japanese recession for over a decade.[25]

Similarly, federal officials allowed S&Ls to mask their weak financial condition through accounting tricks during the 1980s. For example, regulatory accounting did not require S&Ls to write-off goodwill—the intangible value of an ongoing business over and above the value of its tangible assets—in so many situations that a troubled institution's goodwill would often exceed its capital. Because of these regulatory accounting devices that were not well disclosed, insolvent S&Ls continued to gather deposits and make loans for years. When they were finally forced into insolvency, they had grown so much that their failures were very costly to the federal government.

Although transparent accounting allows a country to better deal with financial crises, disclosure of losses from FMV does *not* automatically have to result in reductions of a bank's earnings or capital. As we have seen, the current losses for debt securities held in the category of available-for-sale do *not* reduce earnings or regulatory capital. In addition, regulators count, for Tier II capital, less than half of a bank's unrealized gains on stocks.[26] **Such partial recognition for capital purposes could be applied to other types of securities in the portfolios of banks as long as the accounting implications were fully disclosed to investors.**

In short, we can have the best of both worlds by unlinking the accounting rules for FMV from the regulatory rules for bank capital. We can have reasonable differences between financial accounting and regulatory capital as long as the bank fully discloses these differences. Indeed, the SEC Advisory Committee on Financial Reporting recommended that every company report for each quarter two different numbers for earnings per share— one for total earnings per share and the other for earnings per share without FMV losses or gains.[27] If banks would follow this recommendation, investors would better understand what portion of bank earnings came from actual cash flows and what portion came from unrealized losses or gains in trading accounts. At the same time, executives could better explain how their banks were continuing to earn stable profits from core operations, as distinct from quarterly fluctuations due to movements in the securities markets.

Should the United States Adopt International Financial Reporting Standards?

As the debate between fair-market-value and historical cost accounting impacts the current financial crisis, so the debate between IFRS and U.S. GAAP will influence financial crises in the future. United States GAAP sets the ground rules for accounting by U.S. companies; they are established by the FASB, subject to veto by the SEC. IFRS (International Financial Reporting Standards) have been adopted by over 100 countries, including the European Union (EU); they are set by the International Accounting Standards Board (IASB).

The advocates of IFRS believe that the adoption of one international accounting standard will reduce costs, increase financial transparency, and promote global harmonization. They also believe that IFRS, because it is based on general principles rather than detailed rules, would provide a more effective regulatory strategy than U.S. GAAP.[28]

The second part of this chapter will begin by outlining the "road-map" to shift U.S. companies rapidly from U.S. GAAP to IFRS.[29] **It will argue that the U.S. should not adopt IFRS until several significant issues are resolved, and then only for 100 to 300 of the largest global U.S. companies. It will also explain why the U.S. needs a regulatory system based on a combination of general principles and detailed rules.**

There Are Significant Differences Between International and U.S. Accounting Standards

In August of 2008, the SEC proposed a roadmap for the U.S. to move from U.S. GAAP to IFRS. The roadmap envisioned a final U.S. decision on adopting IFRS in 2011, with a target date for the actual transition in 2014. The roadmap also proposed an early option for certain U.S. global companies, which would allow them to choose to adopt IFRS in 2009 or 2010. **Although the adoption of IFRS may make sense in the long term, the early option for large U.S. companies is misguided. As outlined here, there are many issues that need to be resolved before the United States should adopt IFRS. This early option would weaken the negotiating power of the United States in resolving these issues.**

There are still significant differences between United States and international accounting systems, which will take several years to resolve through the joint efforts of the FASB and IASB. As Table 12.4 shows, these differences include important areas such as research and development costs, joint ventures, and revenue recognition.[30] Unlike

Table 12.4   Accounting Standards: GAAP vs. IFRS

	U.S. GAAP	IFRS
Inventory accounting	LIFO inventory accounting allowed	LIFO inventory accounting prohibited
R&D costs	Generally counted as an expense when they occur	Capitalized, if certain criteria are met
Residual value of property, plant, and equipment (PP&E)	Residual value of PP&E may not be revised upward	Residual value of PP&E may be revised upward or downward
Subsequent reversal of an impairment loss	Prohibited	Allowed for all assets with the exception of goodwill, if certain criteria are met
Oil, gas, insurance	Has industry-specific standards	Few industry-specific standards
Investments in joint ventures	Generally use the equity method, with a few exceptions	May use either the equity method or proportionate consolidation
Revenue recognition	Delivery is required to have occurred as evidence that the risks and rewards of ownership have been transferred	Delivery is not required as evidence that the risk and rewards of ownership have been transferred

SOURCE: Deloitte, PricewaterhouseCoopers.

U.S. GAAP, IFRS does not offer customized standards for industries like oil and gas or mutual funds. Most importantly, IFRS does not permit a firm to use a popular form of inventory accounting called LIFO (last in and first out) and instead forces firms to account for their inventories under FIFO (first in, first out). This difference in inventory accounting can substantially alter a firm's income for tax purposes.[31]

Given these significant differences in standards, it is not surprising that the two accounting systems produce different amounts of income for financial reporting purposes. According to a Citigroup survey, the median net income of foreign companies filing financial statements with the SEC under IFRS is six percent higher than they would have reported under U.S. GAAP.[32] Therefore, the United States should not allow company executives to choose between the two accounting standards because executives will obviously select the one with the highest reported income.

International accounting standards are set by the IASB, which was historically financed by voluntary contributions from companies and auditors. Although several large countries have committed to support the IASB through fee assessments, the IASB must obtain a guaranteed source of financing for its whole budget to retain its independence. If the U.S. wants to transfer fee assessments that now support the FASB this transfer would take an act of Congress.[33]

National Differences Undermine Benefits of IFRS

In providing permanent financing for the IASB, Congress should recognize that the United States would be relinquishing the SEC's veto over accounting standards applicable to U.S. companies. The threat of this veto is a powerful constraint on the FASB, although the veto has rarely been invoked by the SEC. The plan is for the IASB to be monitored by an international board of regulators, presumably including the SEC, but the powers of this board are unclear.

Some countries adopt international accounting standards only if they are each approved by the relevant government body. In the EU, for example, any new international accounting standard does not become effective until it is "endorsed" by the EU Parliament, the EU Commission, and the EU Council of Ministers. Likewise, Congress could condition its financial support of IASB on the SEC's retention of its veto over the application of each international accounting standard to U.S. public companies.

Yet national procedures for approving international accounting standards create the potential for significant country differences, which would undermine the benefits of global uniformity offered by IFRS. National approval procedures also create the potential for legislative battles that could undercut the independence of the IASB. In late 2008, for example, the EU Parliament publicly threatened to replace the IASB's standard for mark-to-market accounting unless it allowed banks to switch assets to categories that would be valued under historical cost accounting. The IASB promptly revised the relevant standard to allow the switching of assets to different categories, albeit with a disclosure requirement.[34] As a result of such switches, Deutsche Bank increased its reported income for the third quarter of 2008 by €845 million.[35]

Even if all countries adopted the same version of IFRS, its application in practice would vary significantly from country to country. There is no international agreement on auditing standards, which govern how accounting principles are applied in company audits. Charles Niemeier, a member of the Public Company Accounting Oversight Board, cited a French study on the application of IFRS within the EU to show that each EU country was practicing "nostalgic accounting." In other words, each country's application of IFRS followed the lines of its accounting principles before IFRS was adopted by the whole EU.[36]

Costs Are Too High for Smaller U.S. Companies to Adopt IFRS

As the benefits of one uniform accounting standard are being eroded by national differences, the costs of moving from U.S. GAAP to IFRS are becoming more definite. The SEC estimated that it would cost $32 million for one large U.S. company to switch to IFRS.[37] In addition, all accountants currently practicing would have to be retrained, and all accounting courses at colleges would have to be revised. Similarly, all investment analysts would need to be educated about the differences between U.S. GAAP and IFRS.

Considering the costs and benefits of adopting IFRS, I believe the switchover from U.S. GAAP makes sense only for 100 to 300 of the largest U.S. companies with extensive global operations. These companies are already submitting financial reports for their foreign subsidiaries under IFRS, so they already incur the costs to translate these statements back to U.S. GAAP. By contrast, the other 6,000 or 7,000 publicly traded companies in the United States have modest foreign operations and relatively small accounting departments. Consider Brooks Automation, a Massachusetts company serving the semiconductor industry. Although 36 percent of its $526 million in revenue came from foreign sales in 2008, the company's chief financial officer says that switching to IFRS would cost millions of dollars without providing any substantial benefits.[38]

In short, the FASB should work with the IASB to reconcile their accounting standards to the maximum extent feasible. Then Congress and the SEC should attempt to resolve the funding and governance issues for the IASB, as mentioned

earlier. If all these efforts are successful after several years, however, the SEC should then require only the largest global companies in the United States to adopt IFRS. Of course, maintaining a different accounting system for 100–300 large global U.S. companies would have its costs, but these would be much lower than the costs involved in switching from U.S. GAAP to IFRS for the 6,000 to 7,000 U.S. companies with modest global operations.

Should Regulatory Systems Be Based on General Principles or Detailed Rules?

The advocates of IFRS also emphasize that it is principles based rather than rules based. Many American executives say they would prefer the flexibility of financial regulations couched in terms of general principles instead of detailed rules. American executives offer the Financial Services Authority (FSA) in the UK as a model of an effective financial agency based on general principles, and conversely they criticize American accounting standards as being too filled with detailed rules.[39]

General Principles Have Pros and Cons

General principles have distinct advantages. They are flexible enough to accommodate new financial products without requiring a lengthy amendment process. They allow detailed rules to be avoided on certain subjects because they can be addressed by referring to general principles. General principles also cannot be easily avoided by finding technical loopholes.

However, general principles often provide so much flexibility that they allow financial institutions to circumvent normal accounting rules. For example, IFRS sets forth the general principle that financial statements should constitute a "true and fair" representation of a company's financial position. This general principle was utilized by Société Générale, with the approval of the French authorities, to move a $9.7 billion trading loss from January of 2008 to its 2007 financial statements.[40]

General principles may not provide enough certainty for executives trying to stay on the right side of the law. American executives often ask for more detailed guidance on how to apply accounting standards. General principles may also be too vague to allow regulators to bring enforcement cases. In fact, the current CEO of the FSA, Hector Sants, is now "eager to bury the notion of principles-based regulation in favor of a more muscular approach based on results."[41]

Detailed Rules Have Pros and Cons

Detailed rules have the opposite advantages and disadvantages. They provide concrete guidance to executives seeking certainty in planning transactions. Similarly, they allow regulators to bring enforcement cases based on violations of specific directives or conditions. Detailed rules also promote consistent treatment of similar transactions within and between countries.

However, detailed rules can be too dense and too confusing. They are usually too narrow to apply to new products. Moreover, financial firms are very skilled in circumventing detailed rules, even if the result undermines the intent of the regulator. This happened, for example, when banks circumvented the post-Enron rules delineating when transactions may be done off their balance sheets. (See Chapter 3.)

We Need a Mix of Principles and Rules

The obvious solution is a regulatory system that has a mix of general principles and detailed rules. In fact, the FSA has more than 8,000 pages of rules, which apply its general principles of less than 200 words. **The particular mix of general principles and detailed rules should depend on the regulatory function to be performed, the subject matter to be regulated, and the litigation risks associated with the regulation.**[42]

General principles are most useful when their application is transparent and readily understood. In the United States and the UK, tender offers are, for example, regulated through a few general principles, supplemented by a small set of procedural rules. This works well because the main players in a tender offer can easily see—and protest if needed—the application of the relevant regulatory principles, for example, that minority shareholders receive equivalent consideration to large shareholders.

By contrast, no regulator should rely on general principles in determining the unfunded liabilities of a defined benefit plan. That determination involves projected accruals for current workers, expected longevity of retired workers, and the choice of a discount rate. Given the complexity of these factors, the calculation should be governed by detailed rules to avoid inconsistent results among similar companies.

More generally, the United States should expressly establish what I call the "trumping axiom." If the application of detailed rules produces a result in conflict with the underlying general principles, the principles should trump the rules.

Summary

The financial crisis has brought to the public spotlight two previously technical debates: First, whether the SEC should suspend the application of accounting based on current market values (FMV) in favor of accounting based on historical costs; and second, whether U.S. companies should adopt international accounting standards (IFRS) or stay with the current U.S. standards (U.S. GAAP). The second debate also involves the question of whether the U.S. regulatory approach should rely more on general principles and less on detailed rules.

Historical cost accounting is not static; it incorporates current market values through the concept of permanent impairment. Every quarter a bank and its audit firm must decide whether the current market value of any of its assets is substantially lower than the historic value of such assets. If the value of a bank asset is permanently impaired, its historic cost must be written down to its current market value.

FMV accounting has much less impact on financial institutions than popularly thought. Only 45 percent of the aggregate assets held by financial institutions are marked-to-market. Roughly 55 percent of the assets of the average financial institution are held to maturity, which are valued under historical cost accounting. Of the 45 percent of assets marked-to-market, almost half are designated available-for-sale and thus do not usually affect the institution's earnings or its regulatory capital.

Nevertheless, there are legitimate concerns about FMV. Most importantly, it is very difficult for a bank to identify the fair value of an illiquid asset that has not traded actively in months. In response, the FASB has issued two interpretations. One allows a bank to disregard the price in a forced or distressed sale of an otherwise illiquid asset. The other delineates specific criteria for when an asset may be considered illiquid and, therefore, valued on cash flow assumptions.

Although these rulings were cheered by bankers, they will lead to higher valuations of toxic assets. This will make it even more difficult for bankers and investors to agree on a "fair price" for toxic assets. In addition, if bankers value more assets by marking-to-model, rather than marking-to-market, bank shareholders may become even more skeptical about whether toxic assets are being accurately valued. The solution: If bankers value assets using internal models, they should publicly disclose the material assumptions they are employing in these models.

In truth, there is no perfect accounting system for financial institutions. Historical cost accounting tends to mask adverse effects and, therefore, hinder efforts to deal with financial crises, as demonstrated by the financial crisis in Japan during the 1990s and the S&L crisis in the United States during the 1980s. Therefore, we should use FMV accounting, with the modifications for illiquid assets, to produce the most accurate picture of banks for investors. But FMW accounting should not push a bank into insolvency because of short-term market movements. Bank regulators can set capital requirements in a different manner than FMV accounting, as long as those differences are fully disclosed.

On the second set of issues addressed by this chapter, the SEC has announced a roadmap for the United States to move from U.S. GAAP to IFRS by 2014, with an early option to adopt IFRS for certain large global U.S. companies. This early option is a bad idea because it would undermine the bargaining power of the United States in resolving the major outstanding issues in moving from U.S. GAAP to IFRS.

The IASB and the FASB must address substantive differences between U.S. and international accounting standards, which will take years to reconcile. The IASB must obtain a permanent funding mechanism with an appropriate governance structure. Most importantly, the IASB must figure out how to prevent significant national differences in the adoption and application of IFRS, since these differences would undermine the benefits of one uniform accounting standard across the world.

The costs of adopting IFRS are estimated at $32 million for a large U.S. company. These costs are justified for the 100 to 300 large U.S. companies with global operations, because they are already preparing financial statements for their foreign subsidiaries under IFRS. But these costs are hard to justify for the 6,000 to 7,000 U.S. public companies that have modest overseas operations. Therefore, even if all relevant issues can be resolved, we should not force smaller and midsize companies to adopt IFRS.

Advocates of IFRS tout its reliance on general principles, rather than detailed rules. General principles articulate regulatory objectives that can avoid the writing of lengthy standards, and can be applied flexibly to new financial instruments. General principles also cannot be easily avoided by finding technical loopholes. However, general principles are too vague to supply concrete guidance to business executives, or to provide a definitive basis for enforcement cases. They can also be interpreted differently from country to country, leading to different national treatments of the same transaction.

Detailed rules have the opposite advantages and disadvantages. They provide specific guidance to executives planning transactions. Similarly, regulators can base enforcement actions on specific violations of detailed rules. They also promote comparable treatment of similar transactions. On the other hand, detailed rules are often dense and hard to understand. They are usually too narrowly drafted to apply to new products. Moreover, they may be circumvented by financial executives, who are skilled at finding technical loopholes.

The obvious solution is a regulatory system that would have an optimal mix of general principles and detailed rules. Moreover, the United States should expressly adopt the trumping axiom: If the application of detailed rules produces a result in conflict with the underlying general principles, the principles trump the rules.

Part Four

THE FUTURE OF
THE AMERICAN
FINANCIAL SYSTEM

The current financial crisis has evoked broad criticisms of the United States economy for both its emphasis on consumption over savings and its free-wheeling brand of capitalism. Without actually naming the United States, Chinese Premier Wen Jiabao explained at the 2009 Davos conference that the current financial crisis was attributable to an "unsustainable model of development characterized by prolonged low savings and high consumption; excessive expansion of financial institutions in blind pursuit of profit."[1] At the same conference, Prime Minister Vladimir Putin of Russia rebuked the United States for running huge trade deficits with China and financing them through the sale of Treasury bonds:

> The entire economic growth system, where one regional center prints money without respite and consumes material wealth, while the other regional center manufactures inexpensive goods has . . . suffered a major setback.[2]

President Nicolas Sarkozy of France was more succinct in pronouncing the end of free-market capitalism: "Le laisser-faire, c'est fini."[3] Similarly, German Chancellor Angela Merkel criticized the American system of "unfettered capitalism,"[4] with excessive risks and insufficient constraints. Other EU leaders spoke with pride about Europe's kinder and gentler form of capitalism. For example, European Commission president Jose Manuel Barroso said: "In Europe, we have a social market economy"[5] with a much stronger safety net than the United States to weather financial storms.

The final part of this book will respond to these critiques from two perspectives. Chapter 13 will address the two sets of international challenges most relevant to the United States: correcting imbalances in global capital flows and forging international agreements to strengthen financial regulation.[6] First, can American consumers reduce the huge U.S. current account deficit by spending less and saving more? And even if the U.S. current account deficit is gradually reduced, will foreign investors continue to finance the remaining shortfall by buying U.S. Treasuries? Second, is it likely that the United States and other major countries will bind themselves to tougher international standards for financial regulation since there is no built-in global enforcement mechanism? Or is it more realistic for the United States and other major countries to agree *not* to backtrack on existing commitments to open markets?

In the United States, Congress can decide to adopt whatever brand of capitalism it chooses in response to this financial crisis. To approach this decision systematically, Chapter 14 organizes the myriad proposals being made to fix the U.S. financial system into three main questions. First, what would be the optimal scope and structure for federal regulation of financial institutions? Second, what would be the most effective and equitable strategies for the federal government to pursue in resolving this financial crisis? Third, because market discipline alone has not been sufficient to constrain excessive risk-taking, what other mechanisms would be available to hold accountable the senior executives of financial institutions?

Chapter 13

The International Implications of the Financial Crisis for the United States

For the last decade, the global economy has been far out of balance. Americans have been voracious consumers of foreign goods and oil, importing far more than they have exported. This excess is represented in Figure 13.1 showing the current account deficit of the United States. This deficit went from zero in 1991 to more than $800 billion by the end of 2006,[7] although it declined to $673 billion in 2008, and further still in 2009.[8] During the same period, most of the Asian countries—led by China—have exported much more than they have imported. Similarly, the revenues of oil producing nations have increased much faster than their domestic expenditures as the price of oil rose.

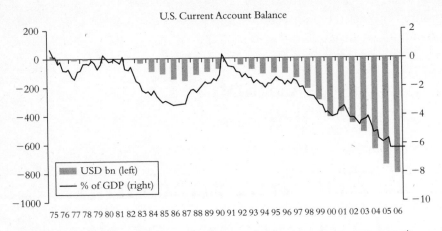

Figure 13.1　United States Current Account Deficit vs. GDP 1975–2006*

*This chart is in nominal dollars.

SOURCE: U.S. Department of Commerce and Bureau of Economic Analysis.

This imbalance in the real economy has been counterbalanced by a global recycling of financial capital from the Asian exporters and oil producers, who have invested heavily in U.S. Treasuries as well as American stocks and bonds. Historically, wealthy countries have exported capital to emerging markets. In a reversal of historical roles, however, the suppliers of capital to the United States—the world's wealthiest country—have been the Asian exporters and oil producers,[9] based mainly in emerging markets where capital has traditionally been scarce. Despite its Gross Domestic Product (GDP) of only $5,000 to $6,000 per person, for example, China is now the largest owner of Treasury securities issued by the United States, which has a GDP close to $47,000 per person.[10]

This circular arrangement was mutually beneficial to all the countries involved for almost a decade. American consumers shopped until they dropped and bought a lot of gas-guzzling vehicles. In turn, China and the other Asian exporters found strong demand for their consumer exports, as the Middle Eastern countries enjoyed rising oil prices. As a result, the United States ran large current account deficits and sold large amounts of Treasury and corporate bonds, which were snapped up by investors in Asia and the Middle East looking for safe investments.

However, this global circle was broken by the financial crisis. When American consumers experienced sharp declines in the value of their homes and retirement accounts, they cut back dramatically on their spending. In turn, this cutback in American demand for imports forced many Asian factories to shut down. This reduction in American consumption and Asian production contributed significantly to the plunge in oil prices from $140 to $40 during 2008. In addition, central banks and other foreign institutions incurred big losses on their U.S. holdings of blue-chip stocks and MBS.

Over the long term, global reliance on excessive American consumption is unsustainable, and U.S. dependence on foreign investors is downright dangerous. Therefore, how do we establish a more balanced allocation of global capital flows? One obvious answer would be to increase China's imports in order to reduce its trade surpluses, which generate such large reserves for China to invest. Another obvious answer would be to increase the U.S. savings rate in order to generate more potential American buyers of U.S. Treasury securities. This chapter will begin by making concrete suggestions about how China can encourage more import consumption at home, and how the United States can generate more household savings here in America. Yet, even if the U.S. personal savings rate rises to 8 percent per year, the United States is likely to remain dependent on foreign sources to finance the growing U.S. budget deficits over the next decade. This chapter will argue that, subject to certain conditions, U.S. Treasury bonds will continue to be relatively attractive to foreign investors.

The financial crisis has driven home the growing interdependence of the global financial system and its increasing susceptibility to cycles of boom and bust. Is this financial crisis a truly unique event, or just a particularly severe example of a reccurring trend? This chapter will argue that boom and bust cycles in finance are accelerating for several reasons, including the increasing globalization of capital markets and the closer correlations among all classes of financial assets. But the United States and other countries can reduce the local impact of the next financial bust if they adopt anticyclical measures for their own financial institutions, regardless of whether other countries follow suit.

In theory, a global problem should have a global solution. But is it feasible to persuade all major powers to adopt and implement uniform standards of financial regulation? This chapter will argue that it is very difficult to obtain agreement on new international standards, which are, in any event, virtually impossible to enforce. More realistically, the major industrialized and developing nations comprising the G20 should lead a campaign to preserve the existing benefits from global trading by *not* raising tariffs and *not* erecting other barriers to trade.

How Can We Correct the Global Imbalance in Savings and Spending?

The global financial system is particularly vulnerable to crises because of the vast amounts of capital being recycled each year. With so much Middle Eastern and Asian capital looking for better returns, a new investment product can quickly attract trillions of dollars—and just as quickly blow up due to changes in market conditions or more accurate assessments of the product's risks. To reduce this vulnerability of the global financial system, China and the United States must address its underlying causes, namely, the chronic trade surpluses in China and huge trade deficits in the United States. In order to correct these imbalances, Chinese families should consume more and save less, and U.S. households should consume less and save more. However, breaking these historical patterns is challenging because they have served important personal and societal needs.

Will Chinese Families Spend More?

If China is to become less dependent on exports, it must develop more demand for goods and services from its own population. The problem is that China has historically been a country of savers, not spenders, and it will be challenging to alter this long-standing mindset. The average savings rate for urban households in China has been amazingly high, estimated to have risen from 15.4 percent in 1995 to 22.4 percent in 2005.[11] As the number of middle-class families in China has grown rapidly over the last few years, they have generated more consumer demand for Western goods. Chinese imports from all countries rose 18.5 percent from 2007 to 2008.[12] Nevertheless, consumer spending constitutes only 36 percent of GDP in China, as compared to roughly 70 percent in the United States.[13]

To limit the impact of the global slowdown, China in late 2008 announced a $585 billion stimulus package of infrastructure spending and tax benefits for business.[14] Although this package is comprised, to some degree, of already planned measures, China is also revving up its state lending to bolster its economic growth.[15] More crucially for personal savings, China added over $120 billion in initiatives during 2009 to improve health care over the next three years.[16] This latest set of initiatives, though too small in size, focused on one of the two key factors driving the personal savings rate in China.

Chinese households save so much mainly because their wages are relatively low and their social safety net is generally weak. Despite its communist ideology, China has nothing close to universal health care.[17] When a medical crisis arises, most Chinese families must pay out of their pockets for most of their treatment and drugs. To persuade Chinese families to consume more and save less, China must fully address their legitimate concerns about the cost of health care.

Similarly, China must substantially improve its retirement system if it wants Chinese consumers to spend more and save less. The modern Chinese retirement system, which started in 1997, does not generally cover rural workers, who comprise a majority of the Chinese labor force. Retirement coverage of urban workers is spotty, and retirement plans are poorly funded because of the legacy pension commitments from the late twentieth century, when workers made no pension contributions to support their retirement benefits.[18] In addition, workers cannot now count on their children to support them in their old age.

Will U.S. Households Save More?

By contrast, Americans have been rabid consumers and reluctant savers for more than a decade. As Figure 13.2 shows, the U.S. personal savings rate relative to disposable income fell from 10 percent in the 1970s to *negative* 2.5 percent in 2005, as Americans increased their household debt to exceed their disposable personal income. Although the calculation of the U.S. personal savings rate does not include unrealized appreciation in retirement plans, the inclusion of this factor would still leave the personal savings rate close to zero in 2005.

Americans need to save more and spend less in order for the U.S. trade deficit to decline and the country to become less dependent on foreigners to buy U.S. Treasury bonds. To encourage these changes in behavior,

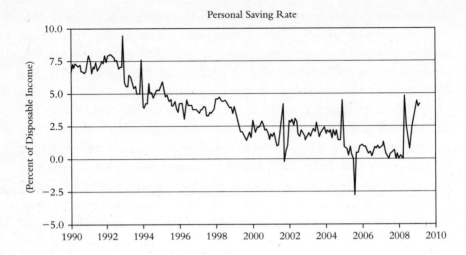

Figure 13.2   The Decline in U.S. Personal Savings Rate
SOURCE: Federal Reserve Bank of St. Louis, research.stlouisfed.org.

Congress should adopt various measures to promote saving. **If Congress wants to have the biggest impact on the American personal savings rate, it should enact the Automatic Individual Retirement Account (IRA) for the 75 million workers (one-half of the total U.S. labor force) who do not have any retirement plan at work.**[19] **Under the Automatic IRA, employers with more than 25 employees would be required to transmit payroll deductions for their employees to a retirement plan provider, but would not have to make any contribution to the plan.** Employees would be presumptively included in the retirement plan, unless they opt out. The Automatic IRA was strongly endorsed by the Obama Administration, which supported other measures to increase American savings.[20]

Even without new retirement legislation, the current financial crisis is spurring Americans to spend less and save more. According to the U.S. Bureau of Economic Analysis, the personal savings rate exceeded 5 percent in the second quarter of 2009.[21] Americans are likely to spend less as they lose their jobs and default on their mortgages. Banks have already seen a marked shift in consumer behavior from borrowing with credit cards to buying with debit cards.[22]

This shift from consumer spending to saving is very positive from the perspective of promoting a more balanced allocation of global capital flows. For example, an 8 percent decrease in consumer spending would add $800 billion in domestic savings to help finance U.S. deficits. But this shift would imply a steep drop in consumer demand at a time when the U.S. government is trying to stimulate economic growth. In fact, current government policy toward consumers is somewhat schizophrenic. Despite all the public rhetoric about the need for households to save more, the Stimulus Act of 2009 handed out tax rebates to many families, who were supposed to spend more to revive the economy. However, consumers cannot increase savings and spending at the same time.

If the United States wants to increase personal savings *and* stimulate the economy, the country needs to replace the decline in consumer spending with another component of domestic demand. One candidate is government spending, which accounts for approximately two-thirds of the $787 billion in the 2009 stimulus package. But this approach cannot be repeated annually because the United States already will have huge budget deficits, as detailed later. **The other main alternative is promoting business investments, especially to boost American exports, which are encouraged in the 2009 stimulus package through measures such as tax credits for alternative energy projects and accelerated tax deductions for equipment purchases.** Many economists have suggested other ways to increase business investment,[23] a subject beyond the scope of this book.

How Can We Finance the Rising U.S. Budget Deficits?

Even if personal savings in the United States rose to 8 percent per year ($800 billion in 2009), the U.S. budget deficit would still be rising faster. In August of 2009, the U.S. budget deficit for fiscal year 2008–2009 was projected by the Congressional Budget Office to reach $1.6 trillion, which is over 11 percent of GDP; this constitutes the largest budget deficit by a huge margin since World War II.[24] Over the next decade, the budget deficit is projected to average $1 trillion per year, staying in the 7 percent to 9 percent of GDP range, according to a study done for the Brookings Institution.[25]

These large budget deficits imply a significant increase in the external debt of the United States, which is likely to rise from $5.8 trillion at the end of fiscal 2007–2008 to more than $16 trillion by the end of the next decade. (This assumes a $1.6 trillion deficit in 2008–2009 and an annual deficit of $1 trillion for the next 9 years.) Such a projection is consistent with a study of severe financial crises in recent decades; that study points out that tax revenues drop sharply after countries experience a severe banking crisis, regardless of tax rates.[26] With this steep rise in U.S. external debt, our debt service payments could reach 4 percent of GDP, which is the current level of the entire military budget.[27]

Debt service will thus present a serious challenge to limiting future budget deficits, as will efforts to reach universal coverage in healthcare and avoid tax increases on the middle class. **To constrain the growth of U.S. budget deficits, Congress should adopt "paygo" legislation that would require (from 2011 forward) every dollar of federal spending increases or tax cuts to be matched by a dollar of federal spending cuts or tax increases.** However, the version of paygo proposed by the Obama Administration has too many exemptions. It would not apply to a few trillion dollars of budget items, such as Medicare payments to doctors, modifications to the alternative minimum tax, and continuation of the Bush tax cuts for the middle class.[28]

In sum, even if the United States has a personal savings rate of 8 percent ($800 billion), it will not be able to fund from internal savings a budget deficit of over $1 trillion per year (although its net trade deficit would decline gradually). This conclusion is explained in mathematical terms in the Appendix at the end of this chapter. Accordingly, foreign investors will be needed to buy U.S. Treasuries to finance a significant portion of the U.S. external debt.

China, Japan, and the Middle East Are the Big Potential Buyers of U.S. Treasuries

The three largest holders of U.S. dollar reserves and U.S. Treasuries in 2008 were, in order of size, China, Japan, and the Middle Eastern oil producers. By May, 2009, China had more than $2 trillion in foreign currency reserves; it was the largest holder of U.S. Treasuries—with almost $700 billion at the end of 2008 and $800 billion by May, 2009.

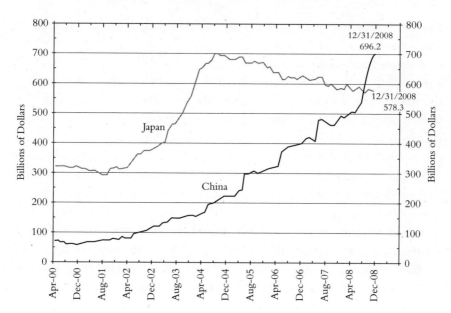

Figure 13.3   Chinese and Japanese Holdings of U.S. Treasuries
SOURCE: Bianco Research L.L.C.

Over the last five years, China's foreign currency reserves have been rising rapidly. (See Figure 13.3.) Although the rate of growth will slow, China will continue increasing its reserves. Japan has foreign currency reserves close to $1 trillion; it was the second largest holder of U.S. Treasuries, with $578 billion at the end of 2008 and $677 billion in May 2009. Although Japan's economy is in recession, it will continue to maintain large foreign currency reserves available for investment. The oil producing countries held U.S. Treasuries of $193 billion in May 2009, with the Middle Eastern nations holding the vast majority of this amount.[29] Although the foreign currency reserves of the oil producing countries will rise or fall with the price of oil, they are likely to have substantial currency reserves to invest over the next 10 years.

Will China, Japan, and the Middle Eastern oil producers continue to be significant buyers of U.S. Treasuries? My answer is a conditional yes. All of these countries have their own reasons for favoring a strong U.S. dollar. To begin with, they all want to preserve the value of their vast current holdings of U.S. Treasuries. If a firm owes you $100,000 and may not pay, that is its problem. But if a firm owes you $100 billion and may not pay, that becomes your problem! In addition, the exports of China and

Japan are quite important to their economies; these exports will become less attractive to U.S. consumers if the U.S. dollar drops in value relative to the Japanese yen or Chinese yuan. For many Middle Eastern countries, a large drop in the value of the U.S. dollar would require a large jump in the price of oil (priced in U.S. dollars) to maintain their same purchasing power. But a high price of oil leads to global political pressures to increase oil production, which these countries would prefer to avoid.

Yet both the Asian exporters and Middle Eastern oil producers are likely to demand higher interest rates on U.S. Treasuries, and will probably look to diversify their portfolios by holding some government securities in currencies other than the U.S. dollar. The rate on short-term Treasuries was close to zero at the start of 2009 because investors across the globe were seeking safety over yield. However, as the economies of the world strengthen, bond investors will again seek higher yields. The percentage of central bank reserves in U.S. dollar investments gradually declined from 71 percent in 2000 to 64 percent by the end of 2008.[30] This decline represents a rational decision by central banks to hedge against the risk that the U.S. dollar will depreciate relative to other currencies.

The U.S. Dollar vs. the Yen and Euro

As Einstein said, everything is relative. Although the U.S. dollar may be vulnerable due to the large trade and budget deficits of the United States, the long-term outlook for the Yen, and probably the Euro, is worse. At the end of 2008, Japan's net sovereign debt was 115 percent of its GDP, as compared to only 41 percent for the United States.[31] By 2014, the IMF projects that Japan's gross sovereign debt will exceed 200 percent of its GDP, more than twice the comparable statistic for the U.S.[32] Over the next few decades, Japan has a much tougher demographic challenge than the United States: the ratio of workers to retirees is projected to be 2:1 in Japan by 2025; the United States will not reach that ratio until after 2040.[33] Although the Yen appreciated in 2008 as hedge funds under pressure were forced to pay back their Yen-denominated loans, the future of the Japanese currency is dim.

The prospects for the Euro, meanwhile, are less certain. When the Euro first went into circulation, the interest rates on all Euro nations converged. Since the financial crisis, however, the interest rates on sovereign bonds in five Euro nations facing deep recessions (Portugal, Ireland, Italy, Greece, and Spain) have diverged significantly from the interest rate on sovereign bonds of Germany—the strongest economy in the EU.[34] This divergence suggests that investors believe that some Euro nations may default on their sovereign debt or be forced to drop the Euro, since the basic rules for the Euro-currency zone generally prohibit bailouts of a weak member by strong members.[35] In addition, many of the newer EU members from Eastern Europe are pressing to adopt the Euro as a currency. Yet the financial crisis has driven home the dangers of allowing these weaker economies to become part of the Eurozone.[36]

More fundamentally, the long-term status of an international currency depends on factors such as population expansion, economic growth and quality of trading markets. In my view, these factors favor the U.S. dollar, although some economists predict that the Euro will become the primary global currency.[37] The population of the U.S. is rising, as the population of the EU is stagnating or even declining.[38] Over the last decade, economic and productivity growth has been substantially higher in the United States than in Europe.[39] And the trading market for U.S. dollars is deeper and more liquid than the trading market for Euros.

Addressing the Concerns of Foreign Investors

Despite these fundamental weaknesses in the Yen and Euro, the U.S. must address the legitimate concerns of foreign investors about a potential depreciation of the U.S. dollar. In fact, the U.S. dollar went from parity with the Euro near the end of 2002 to $1.60 = €1 in mid-2008. Although the U.S. dollar became much stronger in the second half of 2008 as investors sought a safe haven in U.S. Treasuries, this flight to safety will slow down when the global economy revives. For example, if the U.S. dollar were to fall in value by 20 percent relative to other currencies over the next five years, this would mean a 20 percent loss in principal for a foreign investor buying 5-year Treasuries. Suppose a foreign investor bought $1 billion in 5-year U.S. Treasuries with the equivalent of $1 billion in Yen or Euro. But when these Treasuries were redeemed, they were worth in U.S. dollars only $800 million in Yen or Euros.

Recognizing this risk, the Governor of the People's Bank of China, Zhou Xiaochuan, suggested that a new currency reserve system, based on Special Drawing Rights (SDRs) of the International Monetary Fund (IMF), could prove more stable and economically viable than one based on the U.S. dollar.[40] SDRs represent a basket of four currencies—dollars, euros, yen, and pounds—so in theory they could help central banks diversify their currency reserves. In practice, the total outstanding amount of SDRs at the end of 2009 will constitute less than 5 percent of total global reserves.[41] China has also allowed more international transactions to be denominated in renminbi (yuan),[42] but it still is not a freely convertible currency. Thus, while the SDR and the renminbi are not likely to supplant the U.S. dollar during the next decade, these Chinese efforts demonstrate the depth of foreign concerns about the U.S. dollar.

In order to meet these concerns, the United States must first address the question of interest rates and inflation. Although interest rates and inflation are now very low, foreign investors worry that the Federal Reserve will not be quick enough to raise interest rates to head off inflation when the economy begins to rebound. They are asking the question: Can the Fed nimbly switch directions just at the right time? **In response, the Federal Reserve should publicly set an inflation target, which would commit it to raise interest rates if core inflation (i.e., inflation excluding food, energy, and seasonal items) exceeds a specified percentage for a specified time period.**

The merits of inflation targets have been debated extensively by economists.[43] Those opposed have emphasized that an inflation target may unduly reduce the flexibility of the Fed in achieving its dual goals of maximizing employment and maintaining price stability. For example, the Fed might raise rates to prevent inflation, even if that would not be the best monetary policy to promote job growth at that time. On the other hand, Canada, Sweden, and the UK have already adopted inflation targets, which have successfully anchored inflation expectations. Supporters of inflation targets would also argue that price stability should be a higher priority goal for the Fed than maximizing employment, and the central bank is the agency with the most tools to promote price stability.

I support the Fed's formal adoption of an inflation target, expressed as a range to allow the Fed a degree of flexibility. An inflation target would be a significant symbol, which would help defuse the concerns of many foreign investors about the erosion of the U.S. dollar's value. An inflation target would also help the Federal Reserve explain its interest rate moves to Congress and the American public. In the current environment, the Fed could say it is keeping its target interest rate close to zero because it is fighting a recession in which core price inflation is minimal. When prices start to rise, as they inevitably will, the Fed could explain why it is raising interest rates in light of its inflation target. **Moreover, the Fed should move quickly because it is politically easier to adopt an inflation target when interest rates are low than when they are high.**

Second, the Federal Reserve must take greater care to preserve its political independence so it can freely decide to fight inflation by raising interest rates, even if that decision is unpopular. The Fed is an independent central bank that normally generates annual profits; it is not a political arm of the executive branch like the Treasury. However, due to its involvement in the bailout program, the Federal Reserve has increased the size of its balance sheet from $850 billion in mid-2007 to over $2 trillion in mid-2009, and has decreased its holdings of U.S. Treasuries from 90 percent to 30 percent of its portfolio.[44] Most problematically, it has guaranteed almost $400 billion in toxic assets against losses for Citigroup, Bank of America, and AIG. (See Chapter 7.)

This radical shift in the size and quality of the Fed's holdings raises concerns about large losses in its portfolio, although so far the Fed has generally reaped gains from its higher risk assets. In response to these concerns, the U.S. Treasury has agreed "in the long term and as authorities permit [to] seek to remove from the Fed's balance sheet or to liquidate" the toxic assets the Fed has acquired.[45] **However, this is too vague an agreement without any definite time commitment. As Jeffrey Lacker, President of the Federal Reserve of Richmond, Virginia, has suggested, the Treasury should go further "to stipulate that the emergency lending [of the Fed be] transferred to the books of the Treasury after a brief period of time has elapsed."**[46]

Third, to increase the funds available for the bank bailout, the Treasury has been leaning on the Fed to make large loans to risky ventures. At the request of the Treasury, for example, the Fed agreed to provide low-interest, nonrecourse financing to public-private partnerships to purchase toxic assets. (See Chapter 10.) The Treasury has been approving the Fed's exercise of its emergency lending powers, and will continue to do so in the future.[47] As a result of asset guarantees, loan commitments and support for troubled institutions, the total potential exposure of the Fed to the financial bailout was approximately $7.3 trillion at the end of March of 2009—over 10 times the $700 billion Congress has appropriated for this purpose. (See Table 7.3 in Chapter 7.)

The Treasury is exploiting the Fed's lending capacity to avoid returning to Congress to seek an additional appropriation for the bailout. Although Congress has implicitly acquiesced to this avoidance strategy, some politicians have begun to press for extensive government audits of the Fed's programs, including its implementation of monetary policy.[48] Such audits would be unwise; they would undermine the independence of the Fed necessary to carry out monetary policy. **To avoid a confrontation with Congress, as well as the courts under the Freedom of Information Act,[49] the Fed should adopt a more forthcoming policy on disclosing information about its role in the financial bailout.** Although the Fed has legitimate concerns about provoking runs on financial institutions that receive certain types of emergency funding, it could safely publish a lot more information about its programs, including the names of institutions receiving nonemergency loans and financial guarantees.

The Frequency of Financial Crises Is Rising

Even if the Asian exporters and Middle Eastern oil producers continue to finance the U.S. budget deficits, the global recycling of capital makes the financial system vulnerable to more frequent financial crises. During the last decade, the world has experienced two major financial crises in addition to the current one. In 1997–1998, the Asian financial crisis caused the collapse of the local currency in several Asian countries and led to the Russian default on its ruble debt in 1998. The second financial crisis was associated with the burst of the dot-com bubble in 2000–2001.

The Asian financial crisis had one immediate impact on the U.S. financial system. The Russian default on its ruble debt almost brought down Long-Term Capital, a large hedge fund that was bailed out by Wall Street at the behest of the Federal Reserve Bank of New York. (See Chapter 5.) Senior officials at the New York Fed believed this bailout was necessary to prevent the failure of Long-Term Capital, which they felt could have caused a systemic failure in the U.S. debt markets.

The Asian financial crisis also led indirectly to the current financial crisis in the United States. After seeing Asian countries without significant reserves struggle to defend their currencies, government officials throughout the emerging markets began to hoard U.S. dollars as insurance against future currency attacks. In 2002, when Fed Chairman Greenspan sharply lowered U.S. interest rates on U.S. Treasuries, these same officials sought higher yields from their U.S. dollar reserves by buying MBS. To produce these higher yields, Wall Street encouraged loan originators to write higher-yielding subprime mortgages. The steep jump in default rates on these subprime mortgages in 2007 precipitated the current financial crisis.

The second financial crisis during the last decade was associated with the bursting of the dot-com bubble. This not only bankrupted many Internet companies but also led to a sharp decline in the overall U.S. stock market from 2000 to 2002. Further, the dot-com bust undercut the overly optimistic projections of many U.S. companies, such as WorldCom and Enron, two high fliers that engaged in fraudulent tactics to hide their deteriorating financial conditions. The discovery of these frauds led to the 2002 passage of the Sarbanes-Oxley Act, which substantially increased the governance procedures of U.S. public companies.

Although many Americans view this financial crisis and the Great Depression as the two main financial crises during the last century, this is a very narrow view of global history. The increasing frequency of financial crises across the world has been well documented by Professors Barry Eichengreen and Michael Bordo,[50] who found 38 financial crises between 1945 and 1971 as compared to 139 financial crises between 1973 and 1997. Of these latter 139 crises, 44 took place in high-income countries. An IMF survey of 113 episodes of financial stress over the past three decades found that countries with financial sectors more oriented to capital markets, like the U.S., suffer larger financial shocks than countries more dependent on traditional banks.[51] The explanation: In countries with a high degree of financial sophistication and innovation, financial firms greatly increase their leverage in good times, which intensifies their problems in bad times.

So we should ask two questions: Why are financial markets increasingly prone to bubbles that burst? And what measures can the United States and other countries realistically adopt to dampen the boom-bust cycles? These questions are especially important to the United States because its financial sector is the most oriented to the capital markets. Therefore, the United States is likely to suffer the most severe shocks in any global financial crisis.

Contrary to popular opinion, the true cost of this financial crisis to the United States vastly exceeds the $700 billion appropriated by Congress for the bank bailout. In 2009, the Obama Administration inserted and withdrew a placeholder in its proposed budget for up to $250 billion more. Moreover, the IMF has estimated that the United States will spend $1.8 trillion over the next five years to stabilize its financial system,[52] and that most countries recover only half their direct cash outlays for financial rescues.[53] Nevertheless, direct cash outlays represent a narrow slice of total bailout spending. As shown by Table 13.1 the maximum potential federal exposure to the financial crisis—including the Fed, FDIC, Treasury and HUD—exceeded $14.4 trillion at the end of March of 2009,[54] as compared to the U.S. GDP estimated at $14 trillion for 2009.

The Psychological and Economic Causes of Financial Bubbles

Investor responses to financial asset prices seem to defy the normal laws of supply and demand. If the price of diamonds goes up, for instance, we buy fewer diamonds. If the price of diamonds goes down, we buy more. By contrast, investors tend to buy more and more stocks as prices rise, even though they have become more expensive relative to their earnings. This clearly happened during the dot-com bubble. After the bubble burst and stock prices declined sharply, most investors shied away from stocks for several years, even though the prices of some stocks had become very attractive relative to the earnings of their respective companies. This also happened after the stock market crash in October of 1987. In this current financial crisis, many investors became so fearful of stocks that they bought massive amounts of U.S. Treasury bills with a zero rate of interest.

It seems that people are more vulnerable to what psychologists call the herd effect in securities versus other assets. That is, people tend to follow the opinion leaders, instead of themselves evaluating the merits of the investments. Perhaps people lack the quantitative tools and know-how to analyze stock prices relative to company earnings

Table 13.1 Maximum and Actual Exposure of U.S. Government to the Financial Bailout ($Bn)

As of March 25, 2009	Maximum Exposure[a]	Actual Exposure[b]
U.S. Treasury		
TARP	700.00	599.50[c]
GSE conservatory	400.00	200.00
Line of credit to FDIC	500.00[d]	0.00
Guarantee of money market funds	3,200.00[e]	2,500.00[f]
Citigroup guarantee of troubled assets	5.00	5.00[g]
Bank of America guarantee of troubled assets	7.50	0.00[h]
Tax breaks for banks	29.00	29.00[i]
Treasury Total ($Bn)	*4,841.50*	*3,333.50*
FDIC		
FDIC liquidity guarantees	1,400.00[j]	316.50[j]
Public-private partnerships	500.00	0.00[k]
Citigroup guarantee of troubled assets	10.00	10.00[g]
Bank of America guarantee of troubled assets	2.50	0.00[h]
FDIC Total ($Bn)	*1,912.50*	*326.50*
HUD		
Hope 4 Homeowners	300.00[l]	12 300.00
Loan modification	75.00[m]	75.00
HUD Total ($Bn)	*375.00*	*375.00*
Fed		
Fed Total ($Bn) (see Table 7.3)	*7,353.80*	*1,786.70*
Total Potential Exposure of US Government		
Treasury Total	4,841.50	3,333.50
FDIC Total	1,912.50	326.50
HUD Total	375.00	375.00
Fed Total	7,353.80	1,786.70
U.S. Government Total ($Bn)	**14,482.80**	**5,821.70**

[a] Unless denoted otherwise, all figures in this column are based upon FDIC "Supervisory Insights" (Summer 2009). These figures represent the maximum potential exposure that could be taken on by the relevant government entity, but do not represent the actual or probable exposures taken on by those entities.
[b] These figures represent the actual potential exposures taken on by the relevant government entities as of March 25, 2009, but do not represent the actual or probable losses that might be incurred by those entities.
[c] Source: Pittman and Ivry, Bloomberg.com (March 31, 2009)
[d] Of the $500 billion, $400 billion must be approved by Treasury and Federal Reserve.
[e] MM fund assets insured by Treasury at end of 2008.
[f] MM fund assets insured by Treasury as of March 31, 2009.
[g] Actual guaranteed amount
[h] Unclear if guarantee issued
[i] Source: Robert Willens
[j] Source: Pittman and Ivry, Bloomberg.com (March 31, 2009)
[k] FDIC temporarily suspended its part of the PPIP program.
[l] Amount of new home insurance
[m] See Chapter 10

SOURCE: Federal Reserve Statistical Release H.4.1 (March 26, 2009); Treasury, FDIC, HUD, and Federal Reserve press and other releases; "Financial Rescue Nears GDP as Pledges Top 12.8 Trillion." *Bloomberg*, (March 31, 2009).

and other relevant factors. Perhaps people have less of an intuitive feel for intangibles as opposed to hard assets, so they more readily look to others for direction. Perhaps the herd effect on the upside can more easily be fed by new financial instruments, as opposed to physical items like iPods where supply may be limited by manufacturing constraints.

The herd effect is reinforced by the fact that no one can predict when or how a financial bubble will end. At some point in a financial bubble it is no longer supportable by rational analysis. But a bubble can go on for one, two, or even three years after that point, because human greed and jealousy of your neighbor's profits can overcome rational analysis. If you sell too early, you can miss out on a lot of gain. For example, Yale Professor Robert Shiller correctly pointed out in 2003 that U.S. housing prices were grossly inflated,[55] but they continued to rise for three years.

The frequency of boom and bust cycles in financial assets has increased due to several factors. One key factor is globalization. Investors from around the world can easily bring huge amounts of money to bear on a hot opportunity in one country, but can also leave just as quickly as they came. Between 2000 and 2008, England and Ireland received foreign investments equal to 20 percent of their GDP, and Spain received foreign investments equal to an amazing 50 percent of its GDP.[56] All three countries experienced huge run-ups in housing prices, which then fell sharply in 2008. More generally, three-quarters of all credit booms financed with foreign monies end up in crashes.[57]

Globalization leads to much closer correlation among markets in different countries and different asset categories. For instance, many investors have tried to diversify the risks of their portfolios by buying a blend of high-grade bonds and stocks across the world. However, in the last quarter of 2008, the prices of investment grade bonds (other than U.S. Treasuries) plummeted as the S&P 500 declined sharply. Similarly, the correlations between the S&P 500 and stock indexes of smaller companies and foreign companies rose dramatically between 2004 and 2008, as illustrated in the Table 13.2. When a financial crisis hits, it rapidly spreads to all securities markets, including those of emerging markets. There are no safe havens!

The fast pace of financial innovation is another factor behind the higher frequency of booms and busts. A good illustration is credit default swaps. Like many financial innovations, these swaps offer significant benefits to investors, as well as substantial opportunities for mischief. Credit default

Table 13.2   Rolling 12-Month Correlations to the S&P 500

Year Ending	S&P Small-cap (U.S.), %	S&P Mid-cap (U.S.), %	MSCI EAFE Developed Non-U.S. Markets, %	MSCI Emerging Markets, %
12/31/2004	83.3	93.8	72.1	61.9
12/31/2008	95.7	97.9	92.8	83.9

SOURCE: Bianco Research L.L.C.

swaps allow investors to hedge against the credit risk of a bond, as distinct from its interest rate risk. However, as explained in Chapter 4, they can bankrupt an insurer if the risks of these swaps are not fully understood.

Both the globalization of financial markets and the fast pace of financial innovation are facilitated by the high speed and low costs of financial trading. For example, hedge funds are capable of doing business from any tax haven, since executing trades between small island and money centers is so cheap. For the same reason, the sponsor of a new product can easily find some jurisdiction that will allow that product to grow rapidly with little or no consideration of its downside risk.

Each Country Has an Interest in Its Own Anticyclical Measures

The United States and other countries with well-developed capital markets each have their own interest in adopting anticyclical measures. If another global financial crisis occurs, a country with overcapitalized banks will do better than a country whose banks have the standard levels of capital. In other words, the adoption of anticyclical measures in every country with an advanced economy makes sense without an international agreement on such measures.

The current capital requirements for banks in most countries are procyclical. In good times, as the earnings of banks and the value of bank assets rise, so does their capital. With more capital, they can make more loans and buy more securities. For example, if a bank has a 15 to 1 leverage limit on its assets relative to its capital, it can use $1 million in capital to acquire $15 million in assets. If its capital increases to $2 million due to profits, it can double its assets to $30 million in order to seek even higher profits.

On the other hand, a high leverage ratio creates a downward spiral in bad times. If the bank goes from $2 million to $400,000 in capital because of current losses, it usually cannot raise new capital from this weakened position. Instead, the bank must reduce its $30 million in assets quickly to $6 million to maintain its 15 to 1 leverage ratio ($6 million to $400,000 = 15 to 1). When many banks dump assets at the same time, the value of most loans and securities plummet, leading to more losses at banks and more dumping of assets.

To dampen the effects of business cycles on the financial system, bank regulators should require banks and other financial institutions to build up excess capital in good times so they have bigger capital cushions in bad times. These capital cushions should be especially large for financial institutions that seem likely to be deemed too big to fail, because they will be supported by the national government if they run short of capital.

Similarly, bank regulators should require financial institutions to build up excess reserves for loan losses in good times, so these reserves can be drawn upon in bad times. However, securities regulators have traditionally been concerned about excess loan loss reserves at financial institutions. They are concerned that banks would cover up their losses by quietly drawing down these reserves to absorb losses in bad times. **The solution: Require banks to report excess reserves separately from normal reserves on their financial statements. Then investors could see clearly whether and when banks were depleting their excess reserves to cover current losses.**

Anticyclical measures like these have been implemented in Spain with some degree of success. They also have been supported by the Financial Stability Forum, an international group of bank regulators,[58] as well as by the Obama Administration.[59] Although the Forum has no enforcement powers, it is working with the Basel committee of banking experts from across the world. By the end of 2009, the Basel committee plans to make anticyclical proposals, which are likely to be adopted by the many countries now following Basel II. (See Chapter 6.)

Unfortunately, the Financial Stability Forum supported the new accounting rule allowing European banks to shift their assets from the trading category subject to fair value accounting (FMV) to the held-to-maturity category subject to historical cost accounting. But this was mainly a political decision, designed to mask losses of European banks in their trading portfolios. As a result of such accounting shifts, European banks increased their profits by \$29 billion in 2008.[60]

The Forum's position is consistent with the stance of many bankers and politicians, who want FMV accounting suspended in favor of historical cost accounting in this financial crisis. However, FMV has already been modified to allow bankers to value illiquid assets on the basis of internal models rather than market prices. (See Chapter 12.) **No country should go further and suspend FMV accounting because that would obscure the financial position of banks and thereby delay remedial responses.** Such delayed responses happened in Japan during the lost decade of the 1990s, and in the United States during the savings and loan crisis in the 1980s. Suspension of FMV accounting would also undermine the confidence of investors in the financial statements of banks.

A better approach would be to provide disclosures that are as accurate as possible, but unlink financial accounting methods from bank capital requirements, as explained in Chapter 12. Such unlinking already occurs in the category of securities held for sale, where market losses or gains do not alter a bank's regulatory capital. Such unlinking could be extended to other asset categories as long as these extensions were fully disclosed. Under this approach, banks could provide investors with up-to-date financial statements, without depleting their regulatory capital.

The Potential for International Financial Regulation Is Limited

Besides adopting these anticyclical measures, regulators face formidable challenges in trying to prevent financial booms and busts. The low cost and high speed of executing transactions allow market participants to ramp up quickly the volume of a new financial product. The globalization of the markets allows financial transactions to be carried out in almost any country. Most regulators are a few steps behind the fast-moving changes in the capital markets. Furthermore if new products or financial transactions fall outside the existing jurisdiction of the regulatory agencies, it may take a year or more to pass legislation broadening their jurisdiction.

For these reasons, the current financial crisis has spawned many efforts to increase coordination and harmonize standards among international regulators. Academics have made thoughtful proposals to start a new international organization, loosely modeled on the World Trade Organization (WTO), that would have the power to prescribe international standards for regulating financial institutions.[61] Politicians have been more radical and grander, with French President Sarkozy calling on global leaders to adopt wide-ranging reforms for "re-founding capitalism,"[62] while British Prime Minister Gordon Brown has advocated "a new Bretton Woods—a new financial architecture of the years ahead."[63]

In my view, these far-reaching proposals are politically unviable to the extent that they require all major countries to agree on uniform standards and bind themselves to an enforcement mechanism (such as the WTO procedures for binding resolutions of disputes). Every country jealously protects its sovereignty. As Barney Frank, Chairman of the House Financial Services Committee, declared, "no one is going to give up their sovereignty," especially in important areas like financial services.[64] No country will cede control of its financial regulation to any global organization because, at the end of the day, the costs of bank failures must be absorbed by each national government. As the saying goes, banks are international in life, but national in death. Moreover, no country easily embraces a global uniform standard because each country wants to make its own trade-offs between financial stability and financial innovation in setting its standards.[65]

Most of these proposals implicitly assume that the current financial crisis would have been prevented if the major countries had agreed on global standards for regulating financial institutions. In fact, there was one harmonized global standard for financial regulation—the Basel accords on bank capital requirements, developed painstakingly through years of international negotiations. However, the Basel accords were an important factor causing the excesses in the securitization of mortgages—the heart of the financial crisis. Basel I, which was effective in the United States until the start of 2008, treated all residential mortgages and all securities backed by residential mortgages as low-risk assets that could be supported by very small amounts of bank capital. (See Chapter 6.)

Build Up Existing International Organizations

Given the challenges of creating uniform financial standards and international enforcement mechanisms, the major countries should address the global aspects of the financial crisis through existing international organizations like the IMF. The United States should continue to strongly support the IMF, which offers conditional loans to struggling countries in the emerging markets. More recently, the IMF began to offer loans to healthy developing countries, like Mexico, without the usual IMF demands to raise interest rates and reduce public expenditures.[66] **The availability of nonconditional IMF loans should help rebalance global capital flows by allowing these developing countries to stop hoarding U.S. dollars. In the event of any future attack on their local currency, these countries would automatically have the financial support of the IMF.**

In 2009, the countries in the Group of 20 (G20)—the largest developed and developing economies—agreed in principle to increase the IMF's lending capacity from $250 billion to $750 billion.[67] The EU and Japan are each supplying $100 billion in loans to the IMF, plus $10 billion from Canada and $4.5 billion from Norway.[68]Although the Obama Administration also came through with a $108 billion line of credit to the IMF, it was a hard sell in Congress. To gain 50 swing votes from antiwar Democrats, the Administration had to delete an unrelated amendment to prohibit the release of photos showing U.S. soldiers abusing Iraq war prisoners.[69]

The willingness of China and other large emerging economies to contribute more to the IMF depends on whether it will revise its voting allocation to give them more recognition.[70] At the start of 2009, for example, Belgium had more votes in the IMF than India and Brazil, and only 1.57 percent fewer votes than China. Although the IMF has set up a committee to study a realignment of voting rights, smaller industrialized countries are reluctant to lose much voting power.[71] As shown in Table 13.3, the current proposals would increase the voting rights of China, India, and Brazil each by less than 0.50 percent. **Thus, the United States should push for a larger reallocation of voting rights at the IMF to better reflect the economic power of the advanced emerging markets.**

Table 13.3 IMF Existing vs. Proposed Voting Share by Country

	IMF Voting Share	
	Existing (%)	Proposed (%)
United States	16.77	16.73
Japan	6.02	6.23
Britain	4.86	4.29
France	4.86	4.29
China	3.66	3.81
Russia	2.69	2.39
Belgium	2.09	1.86
India	1.89	2.34
Brazil	1.38	1.72

SOURCE: IMF.

The G20 has also asked the newly renamed Financial Stability Board (formerly the Financial Stability Forum)[72] to collaborate with the IMF in order to achieve the objectives of harmonizing financial policies and monitoring systemic risk. But the actual results of this collaboration remain to be seen, since neither the IMF nor the Board has enforcement powers in either area. For instance, when the IMF in 2002 floated a thoughtful proposal for restructuring the debts of troubled sovereign nations,[73] it provoked considerable debate but little action. In 2008, the IMF was summarily rebuffed when it tried to bring about financial reform in industrialized countries:

> This past spring the IMF worked up a plan for the U.S. to recapitalize its banks and presented it to the Treasury, where it was ignored . . . The British and French are no different, said Simon Johnson, former IMF Chief Economist.[74]

At most, large industrial powers are sometimes able to force smaller countries to amend their laws with threats of international repercussions. Diplomatic pressure has been effective in loosening Switzerland's secrecy laws that allow the Madoffs of the world to hide ill-gotten gains. Other small countries have announced concessions on tax secrecy, including the Cayman Islands, Liechtenstein and Monaco. The G20 has formally noted that the Organization for Economic Co-operation and Development (OECD) will publish a list naming countries that fall short of the new financial transparency standards, in an attempt to "name and shame" governments that have not moved forward with this commitment.[75]

In terms of positive collective action among large industrialized countries, the most fruitful approach in the finance area seems to be voluntary coalitions of the willing. For example, various countries have joined a "college of regulators" to coordinate supervision of each global financial institution.[76] This is a useful way for regulators in multiple countries to obtain an overall perspective on an institution doing business in many countries. But those joining such a college would have no enforcement mechanism if one country were too lenient on the institution.

Other forms of voluntary cooperation can be based on best practices or codes of conduct, promulgated by a respected international organization. A good illustration is the Code of Conduct for credit-rating agencies formulated by the International Organization of Securities Commissioners (IOSCO) published originally in 2003 and amended in 2008.[77] This Code of Conduct has already served as a model for several jurisdictions, including the European Union, in setting their standards for credit-rating agencies. Yet each country is free to adopt its own variant of IOSCO's Code of Conduct and enforce that variant within its own boundaries as it sees fit.

All Countries Should Resist the Pressures to Adopt Protectionist Measures

If the financial crisis lingers, all national governments will face rising internal pressures to become protectionist. Protectionism can take many forms—not only raising tariffs on imported goods but also limiting banks to local loans, imposing restrictions on foreign labor, and keeping foreigners from bidding on government contracts. Given the public frustration with a long recession, one protectionist measure adopted by one country is likely to lead to many protectionist measures by other countries. This is a self-defeating exercise. **In addressing the financial crisis, the international community would probably be most effective by persuading individual countries *not* to adopt new protectionist measures.**

It is much easier to maintain existing world trade compacts than to overcome inertia by winning global agreement on new uniform standards.

Let's start with an obvious example. When the United States bailed out General Motors and Chrysler, it was inevitable that other countries would follow suit. Since then, France, Germany, and the UK have given large subsidies to their auto companies. In the end, these four national governments contributed billions of dollars in subsidies to more than six car companies, which will compete for a shrinking volume of car sales at low margins or actual losses. As German Chancellor Merkel has recognized, these subsidies to local car companies constitute protectionism and should be temporary.[78] Yet, she also noted, "the German economy is very reliant on exports, and this is not something you can change in two years; it is not something we even want to change."[79] The only European country to reject aid to its car companies was Sweden, where the Minister of Enterprise, Maud Olofsson, declared: "We are very disappointed in G.M., but we are not prepared to risk taxpayers' money. This is not a game of Monopoly."[80]

In the financial field, each EU country has been racing to rescue its banks without regard to the impact on other countries within or affiliated with the EU. By unilaterally jumping to guarantee all bank borrowings, Ireland effectively forced other EU countries to follow suit. British Prime Minister Brown complained that British firms were being hurt because foreign banks were retreating to their home markets.[81] Yet the UK, like other EU countries, has pushed banks with scarce government capital to lend more to local businesses.[82] Moreover, the UK invoked its antiterrorist laws to freeze the UK assets of two of Iceland's largest banks—an affiliated member of the EU for trading purposes—despite no apparent connection to terrorist groups. This freeze, which accelerated Iceland's economic breakdown, was designed to ensure that British depositors in Icelandic banks were repaid.[83] Although the EU's antitrust authorities usually object to national subsidies limited to local companies, they approved the packages for rescuing banks under the EU's exception to its open competition laws for preventing "a serious disturbance."[84] As explained by John Hele, an executive of ING, a large Dutch bank that promised to lend to Dutch firms in return for government capital: "You expect a nationalistic element when private actors have been replaced by national ones."[85]

When Congress passed the Stimulus Act of 2009, it included buy-American provisions requiring American iron, steel, and manufactured goods to be used in all stimulus-funded projects unless they drive up the total project costs by 25 percent or more, or if a federal official publicly finds that application of this section would not be "in the public interest."[86] The Obama Administration claimed that this requirement was neutered by adding a consistency condition—that the buy-American provisions "shall be applied in a manner consistent with U.S. obligations under international agreements." But this claim is disingenuous for several reasons.[87]

First, WTO rules do not clearly address the obligations of member countries to prevent national stimulus packages from favoring local bidders. Although this subject is covered by a separate international procurement agreement, many of the largest countries in the world (such as China and India) are not signatories to the procurement agreement. Second, the procurement agreement is filled with loopholes. For example, the procurement agreement has a general exclusion for governmental funds designated for mass transit and highway projects—the core of much stimulus spending. Third, the procurement agreement does not normally apply to contracts of local governments. Although 37 U.S. states signed on to the procurement agreement, many added further exceptions relevant to stimulus spending, such as construction services and construction-grade steel.

In short, states and cities have considerable leeway in keeping foreign materials out of state stimulus projects. The result: "Lobbied by congressman, their procurement officials have made it difficult or impossible for foreign components to be part of a bid."[88] In response, "a string of Canadian municipalities launched boycotts of U.S.-made products in reaction to America's stimulus package, which Canadian companies say is shutting them out of contracts."[89] **Therefore, the Obama Administration should establish one federal office to handle all requests for application of the consistency condition to stimulus projects at all governmental levels.**

Protectionism is also evident on labor issues. A poll by the German Marshall Fund found British and Americans to be particularly hostile to foreign workers because they "steal jobs."[90] In the UK, for instance, workers at oil refineries and power plants staged a walk-out in early 2009 to protest the use of foreign labor.[91] Section 1611 of the Stimulus

Act of 2009 increases the hurdles for hiring foreign skilled workers that must be jumped by U.S. financial institutions receiving federal assistance.[92] These institutions must now prove that they have tried to recruit American workers at the same wages and are not replacing U.S. citizens with foreigners. Lloyd Blankfein, CEO of Goldman Sachs, has warned that Section 1611 invites retaliatory measures from other countries.[93] **The United States and other industrialized countries should not impose these types of restrictions on the entry of foreign workers. If they do, the result will be a rise in personal discrimination and a fall in economic efficiency as jobs are not filled by the most qualified people.**

The G20 Should Take the Lead in Completing a Trade Agreement

To create counter-pressures against protectionism, the Group of 20 promised collectively after its November 2008 meeting in Washington, DC, to avoid taking actions with "potentially adverse impacts on other countries."[94] Within two days, however, India raised its tariffs on steel, and Russia raised its tariffs on cars. A World Bank report found that "since the Washington meeting, 17 members of the Group of 20 had adopted 47 measures aimed at restricting trade."[95] Currently, "the WTO is hoping to shame its 153 members into keeping trade open by cataloguing protectionist excesses and publishing a bimonthly list."[96]

As Pascal Lamy, director-general of the WTO, remarked: "The G20 declaration [against protectionism] is a political commitment. I cannot transform a political commitment into a legal commitment. That is what the Doha Round is for."[97] Lamy is right. The Doha Round is the current series of global trade negotiations, which was started in 2001, and is dying a slow death. **The G20 should push for the completion of the Doha Round as the most effective international strategy for reviving the global economy.**

The Doha Round was stalemated in 2008. Europe needed to reduce its tariffs more on agricultural imports and the United States needed to reduce its government subsidies more for agricultural exports. These reductions would be very important for many emerging markets with large farm sectors, such as Argentina, Indonesia, and Malaysia. Simultaneously, the advanced emerging economies—most importantly,

China, India, and Brazil—needed to drop their tariff and nontariff barriers to foreign imports, such as special licensing requirements and limits on foreign ownership. Dropping these nontariff barriers would provide benefits particularly to the less developed countries, which view China, India, and Brazil as high-priority markets for their exports.

In exchange for significant reductions in their tariffs and subsidies on agricultural products, the United States and EU should insist on substantial decreases in trade barriers on imports of foreign goods and services into the larger and more advanced emerging markets. A global trade agreement along these lines would not only help the emerging markets increase their agricultural exports but would also provide many benefits to American firms because the United States is the biggest exporter in the world. Specifically, the United States would be able to export more industrial goods (e.g., computers and telecom equipment), professional services (e.g., legal and financial) and agricultural products where the United States is a leading producer (e.g., beef, pork, corn, and wheat). Furthermore, breaking down the barriers to foreign imports into the top tier of the emerging markets helps the lower tier of emerging markets, such as parts of Africa and Asia, achieve economic growth. As these lower-tier emerging markets develop, they will become more interested in importing U.S. technology and meat as well as more likely to invest in U.S. Treasuries.

Nevertheless, it may not be feasible to reach such a broad global agreement, given the political opposition to free trade in many countries. In 2008, India led the emerging markets in militating against the completion of the Doha Round. In 2009, by contrast, senior Chinese officials have publicly endorsed the global fight against protectionism and the advancement of the Doha Round.[98] Despite Obama's antitrade rhetoric in his presidential campaign, his Special Trade Representative has been trying to persuade Congress to approve trade agreements with Colombia and Panama, which Democrats had opposed in 2007 and 2008.[99] **If China took the lead along with the United States, perhaps both could move the Doha Round to a successful conclusion. This would be the biggest international contribution to overcoming the global economic recession.**

A more modest goal would be for all countries in the G20 to legally bind themselves to their current tariff levels. At

present, most countries have actual tariffs at much lower levels than their legal commitments under the WTO. Therefore, countries like India and Russia can raise their tariffs significantly without violating their WTO commitments. If the G20 countries took the lead in legally binding their actual tariff levels, this would put some real clout behind their eloquent statements against protectionism. **Similarly, most countries have higher actual levels of market access and national treatment for foreigners than their WTO commitments. These actual levels should be made into binding commitments so they can be enforced under WTO rules.**

Summary

The global imbalance in capital flows was a significant contributing factor to the current financial crisis. The United States consistently ran very large trade deficits, which were financed largely by the recycling of capital into U.S. Treasury bonds by Asian exporters and oil-producing countries with the largest trade surpluses. To rectify this global imbalance, China should ramp up domestic consumption and reduce personal savings. This shift would require China to develop much better health care and retirement systems, whose deficiencies are currently the main reasons for the very high savings rate of Chinese families. Conversely, the United States should encourage more savings and less consumption by American families. For instance, Congress could enact new automatic savings programs for workers without retirement plans sponsored by their employer, and replace substantial drops in consumer spending with other elements of aggregate demand.

Even if the personal saving rate in the United States rises to 8 percent per year, the country would still have to finance a substantial portion of its external debt budget from foreign sources because of rising U.S. budget deficits. Asian exporters and oil producers can reasonably be expected to help finance these deficits by buying substantial amounts of Treasury bonds, but these two groups are likely to demand higher interest rates and increase the diversification of their portfolios. Moreover, these foreign inflows of capital depend on confidence that the Federal Reserve will raise interest rates to head off inflation, even when politically unpopular. The confidence of foreign investors in the Fed would be enhanced if it adopts specific inflation targets, avoids long-term guarantees of troubled assets, and generally maintains its institutional independence. Investor concerns could also be assuaged if Congress imposed an effective paygo restriction on it annual budgets.

The recycling of global capital flows makes the world more vulnerable to financial crises. In trading stocks, investors often exhibit the herd effect, blindly following the opinion leaders. Instead of behaving according to the normal laws of supply and demand, they tend to buy more stocks as their market prices rise and fewer stocks when their market prices fall sharply. These characteristics of investor behavior will lead to more frequent booms and busts as the pace of financial innovation increases, the cost of trade executions decreases and the spread of globalization allows financial firms to locate almost anywhere.

In order to reduce the frequency and impact of future financial crises, banking regulators should adopt anticyclical measures. Such measures are in the interest of each country, regardless of whether they are adopted by other countries. If a national regulator requires its banks to build up higher capital levels and excess loan reserves in good times, these banks will have larger cushions to absorb losses in bad times. To ensure transparency for investors, banks should specifically disclose the build-up and depletion of any extra capital or reserves.

Because it so difficult to reach international agreement on new collective actions, the international community should expand the scope of existing organizations like the IMF, and reallocate its voting rights to reflect the rise of large emerging economies. The international community can also put together new coalitions of the willing, like the college of supervisors to coordinate the various national regulators for a global financial institution. Furthermore, a respected international group can promulgate a code of conduct in a particular area, such as regulation of credit rating agencies. These codes serve as models of best practice for any country choosing to strengthen its regulations in the relevant are. But each country is free to adopt its own version of the code, and enforce this version within its boundaries as it sees fit.

Most importantly, nations should agree *not* to adopt protectionist measures because they give other countries incentives to retaliate with their own parochial measures. Despite the eloquent tirade against protectionism by the G20 in the fall of 2008, 17 of its members promptly adopted new trade restrictions. In order to kick start the global economy, the G20 should revive the Doha Round of trade negotiations. Europe should substantially reduce its barriers to agricultural imports, and the United States should substantially reduce its subsidies for agricultural exports. In exchange, the United States and Europe should obtain significant decreases in the current tariff and nontariff barriers to the import of foreign goods and services into the largest emerging markets—China, India, and Brazil. If such a broad agreement is not politically feasible, all countries should legally bind their current levels of tariffs, market access, and national treatment of foreigners, so these levels could not be raised without violating WTO rules.

Appendix to Chapter 13

The following equation illustrates the relationship between how much the United States needs to borrow from foreigners on the one hand, and the level of U.S. savings, investment, and government spending on the other hand.

Exports − Imports (Net trade surplus or deficit)	=	Savings (Business and Personal)	−	Investment (Direct Investment in Fixed Assets)	+	Net Government (Tax Revenue − Spending)

On the right-hand side of the equation, the first item is the total of internal U.S. savings from businesses and individuals. The question is whether this private savings total, minus the direct investment in U.S. fixed assets, exceeds the net government surplus or deficit. If the answer is no, the United States will fill the gap by generating dollar reserves from foreign governments through a trade deficit, that is, when exports are lower than imports on the left side of the equation. In that event, foreign governments need to invest a significant portion of their dollar reserves in U.S. Treasuries.

Let's consider the situation of the United States in 2006, 2009, and 2011.

(% = % of GDP)

2006 (Known)	−6%	=	+14% (personal = 0; business = +14)	−	(+17%) (investment)	+	(−3%) (budget deficit)
2009 (Estimated)	−4%	=	+19% (personal = +8; business = +11)	−	(+12%) (investment)	+	(−11%) (budget deficit)
2011 (Projected)	−4%	=	+17% (personal = +8; business = +9)	−	(+14%) (investment)	+	(−7%) (budget deficit)

This comparison shows why the United States is not likely to generate sufficient internal savings, even with a personal savings rate at 8 percent of GDP, to finance its large budget deficits and estimated levels of direct investment. In 2009, for example, even if total savings were as high as 19 percent (personal savings of 8 percent + business savings at 11 percent), and fixed investment fell as low as 12 percent, the 7 percent net of these two items (19 percent − 12 percent = 7 percent) would still be insufficient to fund the U.S. budget deficit of 11 percent.

As a result, the United States will continue to run substantial trade deficits. This means that United States dollars will continue to pile up at the central banks of our major trading partners that have trade surpluses. (The amount of the U.S. trade deficit each year must be offset by the same amount of surplus U.S. dollars sent abroad.) The central banks with large reserves of U.S. dollars are the main potential buyers of the U.S. Treasuries issued to finance our budget deficits.

Chapter 14

The New Structure of U.S. Financial Regulation

lthough the potential for international harmonization of financial rules is limited, the U.S. Congress is actively considering many proposals to increase regulation of U.S. financial institutions in response to the financial crisis. But these proposals do *not* involve an ideological choice between "unfettered capitalism" and a "social market economy," as suggested by European leaders in the introduction to this Part IV. Rather, these proposals involve practical decisions about the extent and manner of government participation in the U.S. financial sector. This chapter will organize the proposals into three groups: the structure of the U.S. regulatory system for financial institutions; the best strategies for the federal government to resolve this financial crisis; and the available mechanisms for limiting excessive risk taking without stifling financial innovation.

First, a regulatory structure for financial institutions should perform several key functions: reduce the frequency and severity of macroeconomic crises, supervise the safety and soundness of financial institutions, and protect investors as well as other consumers of financial services. In evaluating reform proposals, the United States should seek a regulatory structure that would respond quickly to financial crises, bring to bear expertise on relevant issues, and perform in an efficient manner. This chapter will apply these criteria to proposals to establish a systemic risk regulator, fill certain regulatory gaps, and reorganize the current array of financial agencies.

Second, in trying to resolve the financial crisis, the federal government has so far focused mainly on banks, investing almost $200 billion in 600 banks and subsidizing the purchase of toxic assets from banks. In evaluating these strategies, this chapter will ask whether they were effective and fair. In this context, effectiveness means being targeted at the critical problems and implemented in ways that are most likely to correct these problems. Fairness means that those who bear the costs of any strategy also are likely to enjoy its benefits.

Third, the wide breadth of federal guarantees of debt issued by financial institutions has severely undermined the market discipline normally imposed on them by large debt holders. Similarly, the federal bailouts of institutions deemed too big to fail have reduced private incentives to monitor mega banks (over $100 billion in assets) and weakened competitive constraints in the financial sector. This chapter will explore the other mechanisms available for ensuring that financial executives run profitable institutions without engaging in excessive risk taking. These mechanisms include more oversight by federal examiners and boards of directors.

This chapter will set forth an integrated set of recommendations that would fix the U.S. financial system. Some of these recommendations appear in prior chapters; others are new. To help readers make their way through the regulatory maze, Figure 14.1 outlines the current regulatory structure for financial institutions in the United States, and Figure 14.2 summarizes the regulatory structure proposed by this chapter, with proposed changes appearing shaded and with bold text.

How to Redesign the Overall Regulatory System

The financial crisis resulted partly from deficiencies in the formulation and execution of U.S. regulatory policies. In particular, according to the

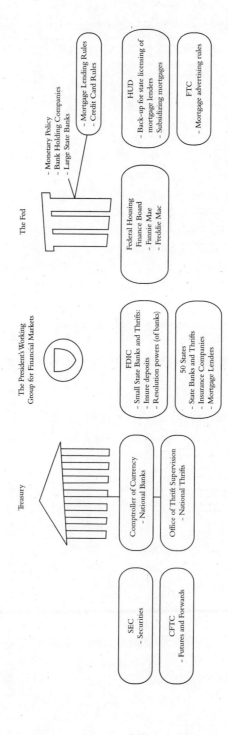

Figure 14.1 Current U.S. Regulatory Framework for Financial Institutions

357

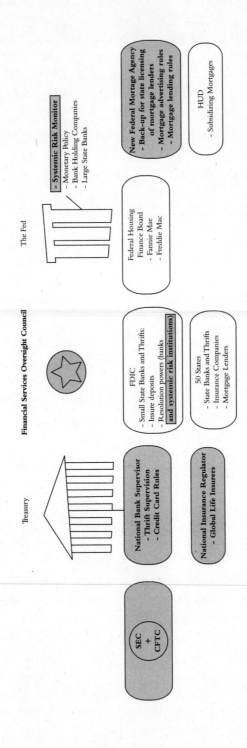

Figure 14.2 Proposed U.S. Regulatory Framework for Financial Institutions

U.S. Treasury, "regulators did not take into account the harm that large, interconnected, and highly leveraged institutions could inflict on the financial system and on the economy if they failed."[1]

So what measures should the United States adopt to monitor and regulate systemic risks? And how should these measures be integrated within the overall organizational framework for regulating financial institutions?

Congress Should Designate a Systemic Risk Monitor

Though hard to define, systemic risk generally means the threat that the collapse of one financial institution or product would likely wreak havoc on the rest of the financial system. **As explained later, Congress should designate a federal agency to focus on the key predictors of systemic failures. The logical choice for the role of risk monitor is the Federal Reserve, though it should not become the primary regulatory of all financial institutions posing systemic risks.**

The Risk Monitor Should Concentrate on Four Key Factors Although the designated agency should look broadly at the entire financial system, it should concentrate on the four key factors historically associated with financial crises in advanced economies: **inflated prices of real estate, institutions with very high leverage, asset-liability mismatches, and fast-growing products or institutions.**

- In Europe, Japan, and the United States, financial crises have often started with sky-high prices of commercial and residential real estate financed by credit booms.[2] When those prices become unsustainable and lenders tighten their standards, the real estate market crashes. Such crashes will increasingly reverberate throughout the financial system because so many mortgages are now securitized and sold to investors around the world.
- Institutions with very high leverage ratios have the greatest potential to make ripples throughout the financial system. Suppose an institution has a leverage ratio of 25 to 1, with $100 billion in assets supported by $4 billion in capital (with $96 billion in debt). Its capital can be reduced to $1 billion if only a few of its large investments

sour. In order to maintain a 25 to 1 ratio of assets to capital, the bank will be forced to sell tens of billions of dollars of its assets and pay down its debt obligations. These forced sales are likely to drive down prices for assets held by other financial firms, which may in turn incur losses and start to sell their assets.

- A mismatch between assets and liabilities presents a fundamental threat to a financial system. In the 1980s, the assets of S&Ls were mainly long-term mortgages with fixed rates, but their liabilities were mainly short-term deposits with volatile interest rates. This mismatch brought down the S&L industry. In the current financial crisis, the most vulnerable point in a financial institution's armor was its heavy reliance on short-term loans to finance relatively illiquid forms of mortgages and real estate. Lehman's inability to replace these short-term loans as they became due was a significant factor pushing the firm into bankruptcy.

- As new financial products and institutions grow quickly, they can sometimes introduce material risks that fall in the crevices of the regulatory system. A good example is the special purpose entity, a shell company that did not fully disclose its assets or liabilities because the sponsoring bank figured out how to circumvent the accounting rules governing when related companies must be put on a bank's balance sheet. These accounting orphans grew rapidly as vehicles for pooling and securitizing mortgages until they fell apart in late 2007, forcing their bank sponsors to recognize billions of dollars of previously undisclosed liabilities.

Who Should Be the Systemic Risk Monitor?

The U.S. Treasury has proposed that systemic risk be monitored by a newly formed Financial Services Oversight Council (FSO Council), which would replace and expand the existing President's Working Group for Financial Markets.[3] Headed by the Secretary of Treasury, the FSO Council would have seven other members: the Chairman of the Federal Reserve Board, the National Bank Supervisor (a new office), the Director of the Consumer Financial Protection Agency (a new agency), the Chairman of the Securities and Exchange Commission (SEC), the Chairman of the Commodities Futures Trading Commission (CFTC) and the Director of the Federal Housing Finance Agency (the current regulator of Fannie Mae and Freddie Mac).

In my view, Congress should designate one agency as the systemic risk monitor to ensure that someone has the clear responsibility for this important function. Having one risk monitor will also provide one U.S. contact point for coordination of risk monitoring activities with other countries. By contrast, having the FSO Council in charge of risk monitoring is an invitation to avoid responsibility—what is everybody's job becomes no one's job. Of course, the risk monitor should receive input from all the other members of the FSO Council, but there needs to be one agency that integrates all these inputs to reach a conclusion.

For several reasons, the Fed makes sense to perform the role of risk monitor.[4] The Fed already stays in close touch with market developments as part of its job of setting interest rates. It has a long-term perspective on the economy, which is necessary to monitor systemic risks. It also has the ability to make emergency loans to troubled financial institutions. Most importantly, because the Fed is going to be asked to bail out all types of large financial institutions, it has a strong incentive to prevent them from reaching the brink of failure.

However, the Fed is already overloaded with important responsibilities, such as maintaining price stability, regulating bank holding companies, as well as setting rules for mortgage lending and credit cards. The Fed is more oriented toward macroeconomics than consumer protection, so Congress should transfer to another agency the functions of setting rules for mortgage lending and credit cards (as discussed later). **Instead, the Fed should develop more in-house expertise on nonbanking areas critical to systemic risk monitoring, such as hedge funds and capital markets.**

As the risk monitor, the Fed should follow closely the activities of any financial institution, as well as any financial product, that poses material risks to the entire financial system. The institutions would include not only banks but also a relatively small number of insurance companies, broker-dealers, pension plans, money market and hedge funds. The Fed should receive from the primary regulators of these institutions whatever information it deems appropriate. To allow effective risk monitoring Congress should remove the restrictions it imposed in 1999 on the Fed's ability to require reports from subsidiaries of financial service holding companies that are supervised by other regulators.[5]

If the Fed as the risk monitor concludes that a large bank holding company or its affiliates pose a material systemic risk, the Fed already has the power to curtail the risky activities of those entities. If the Fed decides that a nonbanking institution poses a material systemic risk, it should develop a remedial plan by working together with the relevant regulatory agency or agencies having the necessary powers. If there is a dispute between the risk monitor and a primary regulator on a remedial plan, this dispute should be resolved by the new FSO Council. In some cases, the Fed may determine that the needed actions are beyond the existing powers of any regulatory agency—for instance, when an unregulated financial product starts to grow quickly. **In those situations, the Fed would propose legislation to Congress about how the new product should be regulated.**

The Fed Should Not Be the Primary Regulator of All Systemic Institutions The Treasury has also suggested that the Fed become the exclusive regulator of all institutions whose failures would pose material risks to the entire financial system (systemic institutions), including any nonbanking institution.[6] This suggestion is misguided for several reasons. First, it is unclear how anyone would know in advance all the financial institutions that might be systemically risky. Although some institutions like Citigroup might be obvious choices, the list of other institutions would likely depend on the particular market situation and would probably change from time to time. Second, if the Fed became the primary regulator of a nonbank financial firm, that action would send an implicit signal to investors that the firm is probably too big to fail. Such a signal would undermine the incentives of investors to monitor the activities of that firm. Third, systemic risk is sometimes created by a new product offered by many institutions of different sizes. In those situations, the problem can be solved only by collective action by regulators of various financial institutions. Finally, the Fed could not possibly have sufficient in-house expertise to be the primary regulator of so many different types of financial institutions, including life insurers, securities underwriters, hedge funds, money market funds, and pension plans. With the support of the other regulatory agencies, the Fed could develop enough expertise in these areas to monitor systemic risks. However, it would take much more expertise for the Fed to become the primary regulator of so many types of financial institutions on a day-to-day basis.

Instead, large institutions and risky products should continue to be supervised on a daily basis by their existing functional regulator organized by type of financial service—for example, the SEC as the regulator of money market funds and the Labor Department for pension plans. These functional regulators have the expertise needed to be effective supervisors in an era when each segment of the financial industry is rapidly evolving. This combination of the Fed as risk monitor, with each functional regulator supervising one or more potential systemic institutions, would also assuage the Congressional concerns that the Fed would have too much power under the Treasury's proposal.

The one exception should be when a very large or risky financial institution becomes insolvent. The FDIC currently has flexible powers to appoint a conservator or establish a bridge bank in addition to putting a bank into receivership. By contrast, if a holding company of a financial institution reaches the brink of failure, "there are only two untenable options: obtain emergency funding from the U.S. government as in the case of AIG, or file for bankruptcy as in the case of Lehman Brothers."[7] Yet the insolvency of a leveraged financial institution has adverse repercussions not only for its debt holders but also for its trading counterparties and firms with similar portfolio holdings. According to the Squam Lake Group, a nonpartisan group of 15 distinguished economists, "the FDIC's resolution mechanism avoids many of the costs associated with a standard bankruptcy. By quickly changing bondholders into stockholders and, when necessary, quickly transferring assets to healthy firms, the FDIC minimizes the economic disruption of a failed bank."[8]

Therefore, I support the Treasury's proposal for a resolution procedure applicable to a systemically significant institution to avoid its disorderly liquidation.[9] Specifically, the proposal would extend the FDIC's flexible resolution powers to holding companies for banks and thrifts, as well as holding companies controlling broker-dealers, insurance companies and futures

commission merchants. This new resolution regime should also cover a very large hedge fund, like Long-Term Capital, whose near failure threatened the whole bond market. However, this resolution regime would not automatically apply to any entity designated in advance as a systemic institution. To invoke this new resolution authority for any financial institution, the Secretary of the Treasury would have to reach three conclusions in light of the then current circumstances:

- The financial institution is likely in danger of becoming insolvent.
- Its insolvency would likely have serious adverse effects on U.S. economic conditions or financial stability.
- Taking emergency action would avoid or substantially mitigate those effects.

Functional Regulation Needs Several Modifications Functional regulation has several advantages. It provides an agency with specialized expertise to oversee the relevant financial function. It establishes a level playing field for all firms performing the same financial function; they are all subject to the same set of regulations. In addition, a functional regulator is smaller and more nimble than a division of a large umbrella bureaucracy. Congress and the public have a better chance to evaluate the effectiveness of a government regulator as a stand-alone agency, than as part of a large organization. However, Congress needs to expand functional regulation in five areas.

First, Congress should create one federal regulator for the function of mortgage origination. As the Treasury has explained,[10] the regulation of mortgage origination is presently scattered across federal and state agencies. At the federal level, the Federal Reserve sets the rules on mortgage lending, the Federal Trade Commission issues rules on mortgage advertising and the Department of Housing and Urban Development (HUD) acts as a back-up licensing agency for mortgage lenders if they are not licensed by one of the 50 states. **Congress should combine these rulemaking functions into one new federal agency with a consumer protection orientation. Congress should also give that agency sufficient resources to enforce the rules on mortgage origination in conjunction with the states.**

Second, Congress should allow a small number of global U.S. life insurers to apply for a national charter,[11] **just as banks may obtain a national charter.** At present, all U.S. insurance companies are chartered and regulated by the 50 states. This arrangement imposes a substantial administrative burden on large life insurers without much benefit, as they utilize the same actuarial tables for people in all states. With a national charter, a life insurer could simply obtain approval for its policies from the federal insurance regulator—probably a new agency—and file a notice of such policy approval with all relevant states. Of course, the states would object to a national charter for any insurance company. Under this proposal, however, states would retain jurisdiction over all property and casualty insurers since they tend to be more oriented to local conditions. States would also retain jurisdiction over the vast majority of life insurers—those that do not reach the high size requirement for a national charter.

Third, Congress should bolster regulatory coverage in the area of financial derivatives, as discussed in Chapter 4. **Specifically, Congress should grant to the Securities and Exchange Commission (SEC) or Commodities Future Trading Commission (CFTC) broad authority to regulate all financial derivatives, including those negotiated in private markets as well as traded on public exchanges.** Whoever has this authority should move quickly to establish a centralized clearing mechanism for CDS contracts, which are currently negotiated in private markets with little information available about who owns which contracts. If most CDS contracts were standardized and settled through a centralized clearing corporation, it could identify the parties to these contracts and require them to make cash deposits at the start of each CDS contract. As market prices moved, the parties would be required to increase or decrease their cash deposits in order to limit the disruption that might be caused by the demise of any party to a CDS contract.

Several groups within and outside the United States have been approved by regulators as a clearing house for CDS. However, no clearing house for CDS has been successfully launched because of infighting among various groups who hope to have the dominant facility. **It would be most operationally efficient to have only one global clearing house for all CDS, or perhaps one for the United**

States and another for Europe. One centralized clearance and settlement system has dramatically lowered costs and risks for stock trading in the United States. On the other hand, certain CDS contracts will be so customized that they cannot easily be processed through a centralized clearinghouse. To encourage financial institutions to use standardized CDS contracts, regulators should set substantially higher capital requirements for parties to customized instead of standardized CDS contracts.[12]

Fourth, Congress should strengthen functional regulation in the area of hedge funds, which are active traders and short sellers. The assets of hedge funds have grown dramatically, from less than $250 billion in 1995 to almost $1.8 trillion at the end of 2007. During that period, the near collapse of one highly leveraged hedge fund, Long-Term Capital, almost wreaked havoc in the bond markets. Other hedge funds have been involved more recently in major scandals such as the hedge fund run by Bernie Madoff. Yet, neither hedge funds nor their managers are required to register with any federal agency.

Congress should require the managers of hedge funds over a certain size to register with the SEC under the Investment Advisers Act of 1940. Such registration would not limit their investment strategies, although they would be subject to SEC inspections. **In addition, as explained in Chapter 5, Congress should require a handful of very large hedge funds to submit nonpublic reports with information relevant to systemic risks, such as leverage ratios and liquidity measures.** However, the same registration and reporting requirements should not apply to managers of venture capital or private equity funds, as the Treasury has proposed.[13] These two types of funds are not traders or short sellers; they acquire controlling interests through negotiated agreements in a wide range of operating companies.

Fifth and finally, **Congress should enhance functional regulation by providing a consolidated regulator for any diversified financial conglomerate offering multiple financial services through regulated and unregulated subsidiaries.** The Fed already plays the role of consolidated regulator for all the parts of a diversified financial conglomerate organized under a bank holding company. However, a broad array of companies may own exempt banks—such as trust companies, credit card banks, or industrial loan companies—without becoming a bank holding company. An even broader array of industrial companies may own one savings and loan association with few regulatory restrictions. As the Treasury has suggested, Congress should generally close these loopholes to keep industrial companies like John Deere or Target from owning a bank, unless the exempt bank does not take insured deposits or it is broadly prohibited from extending any credit to the industrial company as well as the company's affiliates.[14]

In contrast to the Fed, the SEC and CFTC have limited jurisdiction over holding companies of registered firms. For example, the SEC had jurisdiction over only 7 of the 200 affiliates of Lehman Brothers.[15] Therefore, **Congress should broaden the jurisdiction of the SEC and the CFTC to include the parent and all affiliates of any broker-dealer or commodity futures merchant if that parent or affiliate is not already supervised by a competent agency.** This legislative change would ensure that transfers within the consolidated group are not manipulated to hide problems, and that risky activities are not shifted to an unsupervised affiliate, without duplicating coverage of an already supervised affiliate. For example, the SEC would not have supervisory authority over any part of a bank holding company other than its broker-dealer or mutual fund adviser already registered with the SEC. On the other hand, the SEC's supervisory powers would extend to an affiliate of a SEC-registered broker if that affiliate were not regulated by the Fed or other financial agency.

Limited Mergers of Financial Agencies Are Needed In response to the financial crisis, many commentators have called for streamlining the current system of functional regulation. Some have suggested mergers of regulatory agencies in a particular area; others have recommended one umbrella agency for all financial services. Although I support a limited number of mergers of regulatory agencies, I strongly oppose an umbrella financial regulator because it would be cumbersome and unnecessary.

The United States has four prudential regulators of banks at the federal level: the Comptroller of the Currency for national banks; the Office of Thrift Supervision (OTS) for national S&Ls; the Federal Reserve for bank holding companies and the larger state-chartered banks that are members of the Federal Reserve System; and the FDIC for the smaller state-chartered banks that are not members of the Federal Reserve System.

This multiplicity of federal regulators creates duplicative bureaucracies and allows banks to choose the regulator that treats them best. On the other hand, many of these redundancies and inconsistencies have already been eliminated through a federal banking council, which adopts uniform rules for all four agencies on any topic of significance.[16] Furthermore, as a practical matter, the time to complete any regulatory merger is long, and the dislocation costs are substantial. It took over a decade to merge the insurance funds for banks and thrifts, although that merger was a clear winner.

The strongest case for a merger is the one between the OTS and the Comptroller of the Currency; the merged agency would then have regulatory authority over all nationally chartered banks and thrifts.[17] Although the powers of thrifts are still somewhat different from the powers of national banks, they have become much closer during the last decade. In addition, since this merger involves two types of national charters, it would not be opposed by the states.

The FDIC works with state regulators to supervise smaller banks chartered by the states. FDIC officials argue that they need to be involved in bank regulation as part of their role as the insurer of bank deposits. This is a credible argument, though some would say that a bank insurer should have an arms-length relation with the banks. In any event, the elimination of the FDIC as a bank regulator in favor of the Comptroller of the Currency would be politically opposed by most state regulators and small state-chartered banks. Similarly, Fed officials argue that they need to be involved in bank regulation as part of their role in setting interest rates and overseeing the money supply. Again, this is a credible argument. Though some would like to see the Fed as a pure monetary authority, it is the sole regulator of bank holding companies, which include many of the large institutions considered to pose systemic risk to the financial system.

The case for merging the SEC and the CFTC is more compelling from a policy perspective. When the CFTC was created, the trading of futures on boards of trades was concentrated in agricultural products like soybeans. Now most trading volume on boards of trade involves financial futures on stock indices, interest rates, and bonds. In many cases, the financial futures markets now set the prices for the cash market in stocks or bonds, that is, trading markets regulated by the SEC.

To increase regulatory coordination of related financial products, both Republican and Democratic former SEC chairs have supported the merger of the SEC with the CTFC.[18] But the hitch has always been the Senate Agriculture Committee, which has jurisdiction over the CFTC, while the Senate Banking Committee has jurisdiction over the SEC. **A possible solution might be joint oversight of a merged CFTC-SEC by both Senate Committees, perhaps through a select subcommittee with members from both Senate Committees.**[19]

Overlapping and Omnibus Agencies Are Not Needed

The Treasury has proposed to create a Consumer Financial Protection Agency (CFPA), originally suggested by Harvard Professor Elizabeth Warren. Under the original version of this proposal, one agency would regulate all financial products offered to retail investors, including mortgage loans, credit cards, bank deposits, and mutual funds.[20] As mentioned earlier, Congress should combine into one agency all federal regulators of various aspects of mortgage origination. But this organizational coherence would then be lost by combining mortgage loans with so many different products. For instance, combining mutual funds and mortgage loans is like mixing apples and grapefruits. Mutual funds are registered as securities offerings at the SEC and sold to investors across the country. Mortgage loans are offered by real estate brokers or banks to their local customers; at that stage, mortgages are not securities. Thus, it does not make sense to develop a second group of federal employees with deep securities expertise outside of the SEC, as the Treasury recognized in its final proposal.

As explained in Chapter 1, mortgage loans are offered by many non-bank lenders as well as banks. In 2008, Congress gave the states a leading role in registering mortgage lenders. By contrast, most credit cards will be offered by national banks across the country, because the Treasury allowed American Express and Discover Financial Services to convert into bank holding companies. (See Chapter 9.) In 2009, Congress enacted much tougher federal rules for consumer protection on credit cards,[21] which should supplant the myriad state laws on this subject. It would be disruptive and inefficient for the CFPA to inspect and enforce its own rules on particular products offered by national banks, like credit cards, if all their other assets and liabilities were supervised by a different agency. **For all these reasons, the regulator of credit cards should be an agency with a national approach to depository institutions. This could be the National Bank Supervisor, the result of a merger of the Office of Thrift Supervision into the Comptroller of the Currency, as suggested by the Treasury.**[22]

The Treasury justified the creation of the CFPA partly because American consumers deserve simpler and clearer disclosures, as well as "vanilla" financial products that are easy to understand. Indeed, these should be goals for all agencies dealing with consumers. However, the proposed new agency would go much further "to protect consumers of credit, savings, payment, and other consumer financial products and services, and to regulate providers of such products and services."[23] This could include most deposits, loans, leases, and fixed annuities[24] offered by financial firms to consumers. Despite the Treasury's stated objective "to prevent mission overlap,"[25] the CFPA's scope of authority would be so broad that it would overlap with the jurisdiction of every federal and state regulator of financial firms in the country. Although the Treasury urged coordination among agencies, a more likely result would be conflict, confusion, and delay. **To minimize agency overlap and maximize consumer benefits, the CFPA's jurisdiction should be limited to mortgage loans plus other financial services provided primarily by nonbank lenders to low-income borrowers, such as payday loans and debt collection services.**

Others advocate a much broader consolidation of financial regulation than all retail financial products; they suggest a merger of all financial regulators into one umbrella agency.[26] This is the model adopted by the UK in its Financial Services Authority (FSA). The model would have the advantage of built-in coordination among the regulators of the providers of various financial services (banking, securities, and insurance) for diversified financial conglomerates.

On the other hand, most of the benefits of a coordinated regulatory approach to diversified financial conglomerates can be achieved by existing arrangements or less drastic proposals. The risk monitor, whatever its organizational form, will look at the relationships among the subsidiaries of financial conglomerates. The Fed already has a broad-based jurisdiction over the relationship between a bank holding company and its nonbanking affiliates. As mentioned before, Congress should grant a similar authority to the SEC and the CFTC with regard to the otherwise unsupervised affiliates of securities brokers and commodities futures merchants, respectively.

In any event, the coordination gains for an umbrella financial agency would be outweighed by the extra layer of bureaucracy imposed by such a structure. During a financial crisis, the United States needs a quick response. But an umbrella agency may slow down decision-making because of the need to obtain several levels of approval. Did the coordinated model of the FSA prevent a financial meltdown in the United Kingdom? Several Congressional leaders have also expressed concerns about putting all our financial regulatory eggs in one basket.[27] If the one umbrella agency misses a serious new problem in financial services, there would be no other agency likely to find the problem.

More fundamentally, the gaps in the U.S. regulatory system did *not* result from the absence of an umbrella financial regulator; key issues did *not* inadvertently fall into the crevices between functional regulators. For instance, Congress made a conscious decision in 2000—on the recommendation of the Treasury, the Fed and the SEC—not to regulate credit default swaps (see Chapter 4). Because of effective judicial challenges and heavy legislative lobbying by hedge funds, they have not been subjected to any federal registration or reporting requirements. These were issues of political power, not organizational structure.

Strategies for Resolving This Financial Crisis

In the current financial crisis, the federal government bailed out many banks and other types of financial institutions at a huge cost to tax payers. The direct cash outlays are likely to go as high as $1.8 trillion,[28] of which the U.S. government is likely to recoup approximately half according to studies of financial crises in other countries.[29] However, direct cash outlays constitute a small portion of the U.S. government's total potential exposure to this financial crisis. As shown earlier by Table 13.1, the maximum potential exposure of the Fed, the FDIC, the Treasury and HUD to this financial crisis exceeded $14.4 trillion in March of 2009, if we included all loans, guarantees, asset purchases, and stock investments, as well as direct cash outlays.[30]

In light of these enormous potential costs, we should ask several questions: Which financial institutions are really too big to fail? If institutions are bailed out, what are the most effective and fairest ownership structures? Are purchases of troubled assets the best way to increase loan volumes in the United States?

Bailing Out Financial Institutions That Really Are Too Big to Fail

When the federal government bailed out Fannie Mae and Freddie Mac, they were too big to fail. They owned or guaranteed roughly half the mortgage debt in the United States, and their bonds were widely viewed by investors as the moral obligations of the U.S. government. However, why was Bear Stearns too big to fail, and Lehman Brothers was not?

What Should Be the Criteria for Too Big to Fail? In my view, there are only two valid reasons for bailing out a financial institution. The first reason is to protect the system for processing payments, like checks or wire, because that system is critical to the operation of the U.S. economy. Under this criterion, a handful of the biggest money center banks are probably too big to fail. The second reason is more difficult to apply; it involves situations in which the failure of one large interconnected financial institution is likely to lead to the failure of many large institutions. In trying to predict the systemic impact of one institution's failure, the regulator should ascertain how substantial that institution's liabilities are to other large firms and how easily that institution's functions can be replaced by healthy financial providers.

Most of the 300 banks recapitalized by the Bush Administration do not satisfy these criteria. Because they were solvent, banks like J.P. Morgan tried to reject the Treasury's initial offer to purchase their preferred stock in October, 2008. Other banks must be solvent because they quickly redeemed Treasury's preferred stock after the restrictions on executive compensation were adopted in February of 2009. Moreover, both the Bush and Obama Administrations bought preferred stock from many small banks that were obviously not too big to fail.

With respect to nonbank lenders, the Bush Administration recapitalized two credit card companies, American Express and Discover Financial. Although they were big in terms of assets, their failure would probably not have caused the insolvency of many large firms. These credit card companies do business with millions of customers and merchants, who could readily find other credit card providers.

What should be done to instill some discipline into the bailout process? The Obama Administration's proposal is too limited. Before exercising its emergency lending powers to help beleaguered financial institutions, the Federal Reserve would have to obtain approval from the U.S. Treasury.[31] In fact, the Fed has worked closely with the Treasury in designing the central bank's special lending programs during the financial crisis. Indeed, because of limited Congressional appropriations for the financial rescue, the Treasury has compromised the Fed's independence by pushing it to guarantee troubled assets and make nonrecourse loans to bail out nonbanks as well as banks.[32]

In 1991, Congress was concerned that it was too easy for federal regulators to bail out large banks under the vague rubric of too big to fail. Therefore, Congress established specific procedures to be followed before a bank may be bailed out, namely, a supermajority vote of the FDIC and Fed boards, an express rationale by the Treasury Secretary, and an after-the-fact audit by the Comptroller General.[33] Congress also directed the federal officials to apply a cost-benefit test, or explain why the tests were not appropriate for an emergency bailout. However, when the Fed bailed out Bear Stearns and AIG during 2008, these procedures did not apply because the firms were not banks. **To hold senior government officials accountable for all bailouts, Congress should extend the 1991 statute to federal bailouts of any type of financial institution.**

Bailing Out Should Not Be an All-or-Nothing Decision The Bush Administration generally protected all the creditors of the financial institutions it bailed out, while letting their shareholders fend for themselves. In fact, the federal government has a range of available tools at its disposal, which should be applied flexibly in light of the specific circumstances of each institution.

Let's consider the AIG subsidiary that wrote protection against defaults of billions of dollars of troubled mortgage-backed securities. The U.S. government bailed out all creditors of AIG, including payment of over $60 billion to very sophisticated counterparties that had

CDS contracts with AIG. On the other hand, if the federal government had allowed that AIG subsidiary to file for bankruptcy, that subsidiary could then have reneged on all of its CDS contracts.[34] A possible compromise: threaten to file for bankruptcy and propose a settlement at 70 to 80 cents on a dollar of default protection to AIG's large counterparties. They probably would have accepted such a compromise, instead of taking the risk of a much lower recovery after a lengthy bankruptcy proceeding.

Another instructive example is the Treasury's offer to buy over $20 billion in preferred stock in at least seven life insurers.[35] None of those life insurers processed payments for the economy and most did not write large amounts of CDS protection. Why were they bailed out? The main concern seems to have been a fear of large-scale withdrawals by policy holders, potentially causing a run on the insurer. But this concern could have been addressed directly if the Fed provided the life insurers with enough short-term loans to cover potential withdrawals by their policy holders. Another concern may have been the reduction in bond-buying capacity if several life insurers became insolvent. But most of these bonds would then be bought by healthy life insurers or other healthy financial institutions, which would acquire the business of the insolvent companies or attract the former customers of such companies.

The Treasury Should Have Majority Ownership of Troubled Mega Banks In bailing out troubled mega banks, the U.S. Treasury has purchased preferred stock in all cases except Citigroup.[36] **The Treasury's preferred stock usually pays a dividend of only 5 percent per share. By contrast, Warren Buffett receives a preferred dividend of 10 percent per share from Goldman Sachs, one of the best capitalized American banks.**

Similarly, the Treasury's preferred shares carry warrants to purchase common shares of the mega bank equal to only 15 percent of the face value of the preferred stock. The 15 percent is much too low; such preferreds usually carry warrants to purchase common shares equal to 100 percent of the face value of the preferreds. Suppose a bank has common shares with a total market capitalization of $100 million, and the Treasury buys $40 million of preferred stock, along with warrants to buy common shares equal to 15 percent of the face value of the preferred stock. This would mean $6 million in common shares (15 percent of $40 million), or only 6 percent of the bank's common shares.

If the dividend and warrant levels of Treasury's preferred stock are based on market indicators, it would be an appropriate way for the federal government to recapitalize a relatively healthy bank. The Treasury would be earning a reasonable annual dividend as a passive investor in a healthy bank with the right to participate in the bank's upside through the warrants. However, the Treasury should *not* recapitalize relatively healthy banks. This is a drastic remedy that should be utilized only if a mega bank is so troubled that it is in danger of failing. In that event, the Treasury should buy common shares of the troubled mega bank.

Treasury officials are reluctant to purchase common shares of a troubled mega bank because they favor private ownership over nationalization. This reluctance is unwarranted. (See Chapter 9.) No one is proposing long-term government ownership of mega banks in a socialist mode. Instead, the proposal is for temporary government control of troubled mega banks until they can be rehabilitated. Similarly, when the FDIC declares a bank insolvent and takes it over, the government owns 100 percent of the bank until it can be sold. No one complains that such FDIC action constitutes nationalization because it is temporary.

If a mega bank gets into serious trouble, the Treasury should purchase its common shares, rather than its preferred stock. This approach would ensure that the U.S. Treasury owns a significant portion of the upside as well as the downside of banks in serious trouble. The percentage of common shares held by existing bank shareholders would be reduced through dilution, but they should not be wiped out. **In my opinion, government ownership of troubled banks should not exceed 80 percent, with at least 20 percent remaining with private shareholders. This 20 percent would provide the potential stock awards for talented executives to return the bank to profitability.** This 20 percent would also make it easier for the federal government to sell its shares at a later date when they would have a recognized market price.

The Treasury Should Use Bad Banks Instead of Subsidizing Purchases of Toxic Assets

If the federal government takes majority ownership of seriously troubled banks, it opens the door to isolating their toxic assets in a "bad bank"—a much better approach than the current private-public partnerships to purchase toxic assets from banks.

Private–Public Partnerships Do Not Make Sense

The Treasury is establishing partnerships to purchase toxic assets, with equity from the Treasury and a private investor, together with non-recourse, low-interest loans provided by the Fed or the FDIC.[37] For example, the Treasury and a hedge fund would both contribute $50 million to a partnership, which would then receive a nonrecourse $600 million loan at very low interest rates from the Fed or FDIC to purchase $700 million in toxic assets. The key attraction for the private investor is the nonrecourse loan, in which borrowers cannot be liable for repayment even if they default on the loan.

Treasury officials believe that such generous financing will set market prices for toxic assets. However, if these partnerships agree on a price for toxic assets with the banks, the price will not represent a market price because no other type of private investors will have access to such generous financing. Moreover, these partnerships represent one-way capitalism. If the partnership later sells the toxic assets for a large gain, the private investor will receive 50 percent of the profits. On the other hand, if the partnership sells the toxic assets at a large loss, most of the loss will be borne by the federal government because the loan is nonrecourse.

Separate the Toxic Assets in Bad Banks

The federal government should not subsidize private investors to make artificially high bids for toxic assets. This is the government swapping "cash for trash," in the words of Nobel Laureate Economist Joseph Stiglitz.[38] **Since the right price for toxic assets will probably not be known for several years, the federal government should divide any troubled mega bank into a bad bank with the toxic assets and a good bank with the other assets. The government can sidestep the pricing problem by giving shareholders and bondholders of the troubled**

bank the same proportionate interest in both the bad and good banks.[39] In particular, if Treasury owns the same majority of both the bad bank and the good bank, taxpayers would have most of the upside as well as most of the downside of the troubled bank.

The bad bank would be run by workout specialists, who might take several years to sell the toxic assets at a reasonable price. Since the price of toxic mortgage assets ultimately depends on the default rate of the underlying mortgages, the government should attempt to lower this default rate. The Obama program of financial support for loan modifications is a step in the right direction, but the program should be more focused on reducing the outstanding balances on underwater mortgages below the current market value of the homes subject to these mortgages. Unless such principal reductions occur, as explained in Chapter 10, many holders of modified mortgages will have no equity in their homes and will be likely to default again.

Freed of the managerial demands of toxic assets, the officers of the good bank could concentrate on gathering deposits and making loans. However, the volume of new loans made by the good bank will be heavily dependent on whether it can sell these loans to be packaged into asset-based securities in order to have the sale proceeds available to make more loans.

Fundamental Reforms of the Loan Securitization Process Should Be a High Priority

The volume of lending in the United States has nosedived due to the collapse of loan securitization. Financial institutions are no longer able to sell their loans to investors and use the cash proceeds to make new loans. The monthly issuance of asset-backed securities in the United States peaked at over $100 billion at the of 2006, dropped to $40 billion in September of 2007, and was close to zero in September of 2008.[40] Most investors will not buy a securitized loan because they have no confidence in the process. Despite its historic defects, securitization should not be discarded; it is the key mechanism to increase lending, which is needed to revive the U.S. economy. **Therefore, the United States should create a transparent vehicle for loan securitization in which all parties involved have skin in the game.**

Reforms for Borrowers, Lenders, and Credit-Rating Agencies Let's start with the borrowers. **The United States needs to improve the quality of loans by requiring significant down payments for all mortgages, together with proper documentation of the financial resources of all borrowers.** Standard provisions for most loans would be helpful, especially on the subject of modifications, so there would be specified procedures for changing loans sold into the secondary market.[41]

Mortgage lenders have little incentive to originate sound loans if they can sell 100 percent of these loans into the secondary market with no liability for defaults. **Lenders should retain at least 5 percent of a mortgage so they have the incentive to do careful due diligence on the borrower and generate proper documents for the mortgage.**[42]

Many investors in asset-backed securities relied on credit ratings, which turned out to be grossly inflated. These inflated ratings were driven by bond issuers who shopped around for the highest possible rating. Unfortunately, it is not feasible to have rating agencies paid for by investors. Since large institutional investors do their own in-depth analysis of bonds, they refuse to pay for the work of the credit-rating agencies. **As explained in Chapter 3, the SEC should establish a pool of independent experts, who would select a rating agency for each significant bond offering and negotiate the fee for obtaining the rating.** The fees of the rating agency would continue to be paid by the bond issuer.[43]

We Need Transparent SPEs Backed by Capital Critics also complained that the securitization process took place in special purpose entities (SPEs), which were kept off the balance sheets of the sponsoring banks. The banks took no capital charge for these SPEs and made limited disclosures about them. In 2009, the Financial Accounting Standards Board (FASB) effectively required that all securitizations be done on the balance sheet of the sponsoring banks. However, the FDIC will allow only 4 percent of a bank's assets on its balance sheet to be securitized and sold as asset-backed bonds to investors. The FDIC has a legitimate concern that the holders of these bonds would have higher priority claims than the agency to the assets of the bank in the event of its insolvency.[44]

The FASB is overreacting; this should not be an all-or-nothing decision. In fact, after securitizing mortgages or other loans through an SPE, a bank divests itself of most, but not all, of the risks associated with these loans. For instance, the investors in the SPE's securities usually assume most of the risks that the underlying loans may default or interest rates may rise. But the bank may retain some of these risks, for instance, by absorbing credit losses above a specified level. Investors want to see the precise amount of risk retained by the sponsoring bank relative to the financial condition of the assets held by the SPE. But the sponsor's risk and the SPE's financial condition would be obscured if the assets and liabilities of the SPE were commingled with all those on the bank's balance sheet.

Here is an intermediate solution that would resuscitate the securitization process with full public disclosure and capital charges that would accurately reflect the risks retained by the bank sponsor of SPEs. **To promote full transparency about each SPE's assets and liabilities, each SPE would remain off the balance sheet of the sponsoring bank. But the SPE would have to make detailed disclosures about the loans it holds and the bonds it sold. In addition, the financial statements of the sponsoring bank would have to include detailed disclosures about every SPE the bank sponsored, in particular, all of the bank's continuing and contingent obligations to support each SPE and its investors. Then the bank regulators would impose appropriate capital charges on the bank sponsor for all these obligations, depending on the magnitude of these obligations and their probability of being called upon.**

The Normal Constraints on Financial Institutions Are Eroding

In trying to resolve the financial crisis, the federal government has extended guarantees to a broad range of banks and other financial institutions. These guarantees, together with the bailouts discussed earlier, have undermined the market discipline normally exercised by bond holders on financial institutions. These guarantees and bailouts have also increased concentration in the financial sector and decreased price competition for financial services. With little market discipline and weak competitive constraints, what other mechanisms are available to ensure that financial institutions do not take excessive risk in their efforts to maximize profits?

Federal Guarantees Are Too Broad and Too Cheap

The federal government has provided an overly broad safety net for financial institutions and their debt holders. The FDIC's program for guaranteeing bank debt is too broad and too cheap. Congress should have not extended to 2013 the increase in the bank deposit insurance maximum from $100,000 to $250,000. In addition, the federal government has been too willing to guarantee troubled assets against losses at very low premiums.

FDIC Guarantees of Debt Are Too Broad In response to the financial crisis, the FDIC has guaranteed over $300 billion in debt issued by banks, thrifts, or their holding companies for up to three years. This guarantee covers 100 percent of the debt issued.[45] As a result, sophisticated investors in these debt offerings will not look at the financial statements or managerial quality of the debt issuer; they will look only to the FDIC for repayment of the debt.

The FDIC should limit its guarantees to 90 percent of bank debt. Its blanket guarantees deprive bank regulators of an important source of market discipline for banks, namely, sophisticated investors in bank debt. One economist explained why we need the input of bank creditors:

> That's because even smart and honest regulators can monitor a financial firm only so well. A firm's balance sheet doesn't always reflect its true health . . .
>
> What the banking system needs is creditors who monitor risk and cut their exposure when that risk is too high. Unlike regulators, creditors and counterparties know the details of a deal and have their own money on the line.[46]

Similarly, the FDIC guarantee of debt is too broad. It covers not only banks and thrifts but also their holding companies, though with higher guarantee fees. Bank holding companies engage in a broad range of securities, insurance and real estate activities as well as banking. Thrift holding companies include industrial companies like John Deere and General Electric.[47] **The scope of the FDIC guarantee should be narrowed to avoid creating unfair competition between these holding companies and other similar businesses that happen not to own a bank or thrift.**

The FDIC Should Not Extend Its Guarantee Programs After one extension, the FDIC program for guaranteeing bank debt is scheduled to end on October 31, 2009. It should come to a halt then, despite likely pressure from bankers to extend the program further. **In any event, when financial institutions redeem their preferred stock from the U.S. Treasury, they should no longer be permitted to issue bonds with FDIC guarantees and should refinance their outstanding FDIC-guaranteed bonds as soon as practical.** However, the Treasury did not impose either requirement on the 10 mega banks that redeemed their Treasury's preferred stock in June of 2009.

The FDIC guarantee is a valuable public subsidy that should not be available to healthy banks. Consider the following comparison between 3-year bonds insured by the FDIC and substantially similar non-insured bonds issued by Bank of America and J.P. Morgan as of May 27, 2009.[48] As the comparison demonstrates, the FDIC's guarantee is worth 408 bps or 4.08 percent $(450 - 42 = 408)$, to the Bank of America, and 227 bp or 2.27 percent $(266 - 39 = 227)$ to J.P. Morgan. But the FDIC's guarantee fees range from 75 bps (0.75 percent) to 125 bps (1.25 percent). **Therefore, the FDIC should raise its fees to better reflect the actual value of its guarantee to the particular institution. Note that a 1 percent increase in the FDIC's guarantee fee for $10 billion of bonds for 3 years is worth $300 million to the government ($100 million per year for three years).**

Name of Issuer	Maturity Date (Month / Year)	Basis points (bps) over U.S. Treasuries	FDIC insurance
Bank of America	6/12	+42 bps	Yes
Bank of America	9/12	+450 bps	No
J.P. Morgan	6/12	+39 bp	Yes
J.P. Morgan	10/12	+266	No

The other FDIC guarantees involve insurance for bank deposits. In 2008, Congress raised the maximum deposit insurance from $100,000 to $250,000 per account. This higher maximum was scheduled to end on December 31, 2009, but was extended to 2013. In 2013, there will be tremendous pressure to make permanent the $250,000 maximum for FDIC insurance.

In 2013, Congress should revert to the $100,000 maximum for FDIC insured deposit accounts. The average deposit account balance at FDIC-insured banks is under $6,000, and 98 percent of bank deposit accounts are under $100,000.[49] Thus, increasing the deposit insurance maximum to $250,000 produces almost no benefits to small depositors, who are the intended beneficiaries of such insurance. However, increasing the insured maximum to $250,000 will impose significant costs on the FDIC. The historical pattern is well established: Weak banks will try to grow out of their problems by attracting lots of deposits through high deposit rates and national advertising. When these weak banks become insolvent, as many do, the clean-up costs to the FDIC will be much higher with a $250,000 maximum for insured deposits than with a $100,000 maximum.

In addition, the FDIC now offers to guarantee *without any limit* business transaction accounts at banks.[50] These are generally noninterest-paying transaction accounts that are used by firms to handle receipts and disbursements on a daily basis. The FDIC was concerned that small business would not utilize bank accounts unless they were fully insured. However, the FDIC should encourage firms to conduct due diligence in choosing a bank to handle their receipts and disbursements. With unlimited FDIC-insurance on their deposit accounts, firms will have no incentive to conduct such due diligence. **Therefore, the FDIC should cap the insurance limit for business transaction accounts at $250,000 or allow unlimited deposit insurance only for truly small businesses.**

The Federal Government Should Charge a Much Higher Fee for Guaranteeing Troubled Assets The federal government has issued a few direct guarantees of troubled assets, in addition to many implicit guarantees. Most notably, the federal government guaranteed $301 billion in troubled assets of Citigroup, with a deductible of $29 billion. The price: $7 billion of Citigroup's preferred stock. But the premium for these asset guarantees was much too low—2.6 percent of assets after the deductible for Citigroup ($7 billion divided by $272 billion, the difference between $301 billion and $29 billion). These troubled assets had been marked down by only 11 percent[51]—much less than writedowns of troubled assets at other mega banks. Moreover, the Treasury should not accept payment in preferred stock because that will be worthless in the event the bank becomes insolvent which is the same event likely to trigger the Treasury's obligation to cover the losses on these troubled assets. **In the future, the Treasury should charge a guarantee fee for troubled assets, payable only in cash, much closer to a market rate.**

Federal Actions Have Increased Concentration in the Financial Sector

The collective impact of these government guarantees, together with federal bailouts, has been to push the financial services industry into a wave of mergers and acquisitions. If the federal agencies rescue any financial institution that is too big to fail without defining the phrase, then smart executives will make sure that they become part of very large complexes. Smart executives also will see that the federal government is prepared to support mergers as a way to bail out troubled institutions.

The Justice Department Should Discourage Acquisitions by Mega Banks The result of these federal policies will be a financial services industry dominated by a handful of mega banks, which will have the advantages of federally guaranteed borrowings and federally insured deposits as well as the implicit federal backing in the too big to fail doctrine. Small and middle-size banks will be at a tremendous competitive disadvantage to these mega banks, and so will mutual funds. Dominated by an oligopoly of the mega banks, some have already begun to charge higher interest rates and credit card fees.[52]

Goldman Sachs is an important case on point. After receiving almost $13 billion from AIG in full payment of a credit default swap, (see Chapter 4), Goldman Sachs repaid its $10 billion in preferred stock in

June 2009. A month later, the firm reported record-breaking net income of $3.4 billion for the second quarter; the firm also set aside compensation for employees at an annual run rate of $700,000 per employee. These record profits were reportedly the result of very large profit margins in the bond markets, where Goldman no longer faced competitors such as Bear Stearns or Lehman Brothers.[53] In addition, Goldman Sachs and the reduced group of primary dealers made "luxurious" profits by selling mortgage-backed securities to the Federal Reserve, which announced in advance its intention to buy these securities.[54]

Given the growing concentration in the market for Wall Street services, the federal government should resist the understandable urge to allow mega banks to acquire weak or failing financial institutions. More generally, the Justice Department should reject any merger or acquisition of a financial institution if the resulting institution is likely to pose a serious risk to the financial system or is likely to be subsequently considered too big to fail. These criteria are more relevant than the traditional antitrust analysis about what percentage of national or local deposits would be controlled by the resulting banking institution.[55] Deposits are no longer the best measure of risk to the financial system

Some have suggested that the Justice Department should go further by breaking up existing mega banks because they are likely to be deemed too big to fail. However, this is impractical in most cases. There are significant efficiencies in having a large bank processing payments and making loans. A nationwide bank also is less risky than a regional bank due to the diversification of its customer base. Moreover, U.S. banks must compete against the mega banks of other countries, both inside and outside the United States. Because foreign mega banks will not be broken up, they will have a tremendous competitive advantage over U.S. banks if they are disassembled.

Reinstatement of Glass Steagall Is Not a Viable Response Another possible response to the increasing concentration in the financial section would be to reinstate the Glass–Steagall Act. This would mean that commercial banks would be forced to divest some of their securities units, including any unit underwriting stocks or corporate bonds. **The reinstatement of Glass Steagall would create more systemic risk:**

A freestanding investment bank is more likely to fail than a universal bank combining traditional banking functions with securities activities. In addition, the Act's reinstatement would be impractical in today's globalized capital markets.

If U.S. commercial banks were prohibited from engaging in any securities activities, those activities would be performed by broker-dealers. Some of those broker-dealers would become quite large and present systemic risks to the financial system. Yet they would have limited sources of short-term financing: commercial paper and repurchase agreements. As we observed in 2008, these are fickle sources of short-term financing that pose serious risks of inadequate cash to run an investment bank. Faced with a potential liquidity crisis, Goldman Sachs and Morgan Stanley converted quickly to commercial banks in order to obtain two additional financing sources: gathering insured deposits from retail investors and borrowing from the Federal Reserve. These two sources are more stable and less costly than selling commercial paper or making repurchase agreements.

Nor would the reinstatement of the Glass Steagall Act substantially reduce insolvencies of banks. As explained in Chapter 6, the main reason for banks becoming insolvent in 2008 was losses on their loans, the traditional function of banks. The mega banks were not stuck with the dregs of their securities underwritings; they suffered the largest losses on their portfolio holdings of triple-A tranches of mortgage-backed bonds, which they had been allowed to buy under the Glass Steagall Act.

Moreover, even when Glass Steagall applied to American banks, it did *not* prohibit them from engaging in any securities activities outside the United States. In Europe, Asia, and the rest of the Americas, U.S. banks must compete with universal banks that offer their customers a full range of financial services. **Given the globalization of financial services, it would be impractical to prevent American banks from engaging in securities activities at foreign locations. A better approach, as suggested by President Obama, would be to follow the example of Canada where universal banks have done well during the financial crisis because of effective regulatory constraints on the combination of commercial banking with full securities powers.**[56]

The United States Needs New Methods for Holding Financial Executives Accountable

Because federal bailouts of large banks have become widespread, and government guarantees of bank liabilities have expanded, there is little market discipline left in the U.S. financial sector. Instead, the job of monitoring the ongoing financial condition of mega banks is falling heavily on the shoulders of federal regulators. However, given the complexity of banking transactions and the rapid pace of financial innovation, federal regulators are not likely to design effective compensation structures appropriate for the different situations of mega banks. As explained by Gretchen Morgenson, a financial columnist at the *New York Times*:

> It's hard to believe that regulators are savvy enough about both pay packages and risky compensation incentives at financial companies to recognize when either or both have become dysfunctional. Remember, these are the same regulators who allowed brokerage firms to increase their leverage to wildly high levels, who helped break down investor protections put in place during the Great Depression, who let big banks balloon their balance sheets with poisonous assets and who were unable to spot the decades-long fraud of Bernie Madoff.
>
> That's some track record. How do you think they will do when it comes to pay? A much better fix would be to hold compensation committees and directors themselves accountable for pay policies and responsible for discouraging reckless managerial practices.[57]

So, can the independent directors of mega banks hold accountable the senior executives of these banks? Since 2002, when the Sarbanes-Oxley Act (SOX) was passed, all mega banks have elected boards composed primarily of independent directors, who are the only directors allowed to serve on the bank's audit, compensation, and nominating committees. These boards seem to have complied with the detailed procedures mandated by SOX, such as annual reviews of internal controls and CEO certifications of financial statements. Nevertheless, the boards of many mega banks approved huge bonuses for short-term profits and failed to stop excessive risk taking.

Here Is a New Model for the Boards of Mega Banks In most mega banks, few directors had extensive experience with financial institutions. On average, these mega banks had 10–18 directors with an average of six in-person board meetings per year, plus occasional conference calls in between. But that time commitment is inadequate to truly understand the complex activities of a mega bank. Even if a director diligently read the board materials and attended all board meetings, he or she would just be scratching the surface of the activities of these banks.

By contrast, consider the model of a board of a company controlled by a private equity fund.[58] The board of such a company is composed of five or six directors, each with extensive expertise in the relevant industry. These directors spend several days each month at the company, so they are quite familiar with its activities. Moreover, directors of companies controlled by a private equity fund are paid much differently than the directors of most bank holding companies. The directors of the large bank holding companies on average receive annual compensation around $200,000, of which a portion may be invested in the shares of the parent bank holding company. Directors of companies controlled by private equity receive lower annual bases and much larger stock grants. They also insist on a much stronger link between executive pay and company performance.

The New Boards as Effective Watchdogs If the United States wants directors of mega banks to be effective watchdogs, it should move to the private equity model of boards. There are enough retired executives from financial institutions to fill the slots on small boards. These directors can be paid enough to limit their other commitments so they can spend two or three days each month at the mega bank. **In short, they will be super-directors, with the experience, the time, and the financial incentive to be effective watchdogs of complex financial institutions.**[59]

A board of super-directors will be in a good position to hold the mega bank's executives accountable in meeting their goals. The top executives of a publicly traded bank have a fiduciary duty to obtain good profits for the bank's shareholders over the long term. They also have a responsibility to protect the solvency of the bank as an FDIC-insured institution. Super-directors can hold accountable the top executives of a mega bank to fulfill their dual goals of optimizing long-term profits without taking excessive risks that jeopardize the bank's solvency. Given the rise of moral hazard and the decline of competition in the financial sector, super-directors are critical to fixing the U.S. financial system and moving to accountable capitalism.

Summary

Congress should pass legislation giving one federal agency the role of monitoring systemic risk. This agency should focus on four factors historically associated with financial crises: inflated prices of real estate, institutions with high leverage, mismatches between assets and liabilities, and fast-growing products or institutions. In addition, Congress should adopt special procedures for dealing with insolvencies of large nonbanking institutions posing material risks to the financial system.

The Fed should be the designated agency for risk monitoring. This function is consistent with the Fed's review of economic and market conditions as part of its role in setting monetary policy. Because the Fed is now called upon to rescue all types of financial institutions, it would have a strong incentive to help them avoid getting to the brink of failure.

However, the Fed should not be the primary regulator of all large financial institutions posing material systemic risks, that is, of all systemic institutions. The inclusion of an institution in that category would create moral hazard. More fundamentally, the Fed does not have the expertise to become the primary regulator of hedge funds, money market funds, pension plans, and life insurers as well as banks. These institutions should continue to be supervised by their functional regulator such as the SEC for broker-dealers. If the Fed believes that actions should be taken to prevent failure of a particular institution outside its normal jurisdiction, the Fed should work with the relevant primary regulator to take such actions. Any disputes between the Fed and the primary regulator should be resolved by the new Financial Services Oversight Council, headed by the Secretary of Treasury.

Congress should improve the current system of regulation by financial function, with a different agency for each of banking, securities, and insurance. Congress should establish the SEC as the primary regulator of managers of hedge funds, who should register under the

Investment Advisers Act. Congress should repeal the exemptions and exclusions for credit derivatives from the federal commodities and securities laws. Congress should establish a federal insurance charter and federal insurance regulator for a handful of large and truly global life insurers, headquartered in the United States.

Congress should also create a new federal agency with an investor-protection orientation to serve as the rule maker and enforcer for the function of mortgage origination. However, Congress should not create a consumer finance agency with broad jurisdiction over credit cards, savings accounts, and all retail financial products. The jurisdiction of such an agency would overlap with the functions of every federal and state regulator of financial firms, thus leading to conflict, confusion, and delay.

Congress should merge a few of the financial regulatory agencies, such as the SEC with the CFTC and the Comptroller of the Currency with the OTS. But Congress should resist calls for consolidating all financial regulators into one umbrella federal agency. The huge transition costs would outweigh the potential benefits of coordination. More fundamentally, the addition of another layer of bureaucracy is likely to impede quick action when needed to deal with financial innovation or to respond to a financial crisis.

The Treasury now distinguishes between banks receiving redeemable preferred stocks and those receiving exceptional assistance. If the Treasury is going to contribute capital to relatively healthy banks, it should employ the model for redeemable preferred stock with dividend and warrant levels based on market practices. But it is unclear why recapitalizing healthy banks is needed. Instead, the federal government should articulate its criteria for too-big-to-fail, and explain their application to every federal bailout of a financial institution.

To provide taxpayers with an equitable stake in a mega bank that needs exceptional assistance, the Treasury should contribute capital by purchasing common shares. As a result, the Treasury is likely to hold a majority ownership of the bank's common shares, while the ownership interests of other shareholders will be reduced. This is not permanent nationalization in the socialism sense; this is temporary majority ownership by the government until it can dispose of the mega bank. By owning a majority of the troubled mega bank's shares, the Treasury can enjoy most of the bank's upside gains as well as absorbing most of its downside losses.

With majority ownership of seriously troubled banks by the federal government, it can divide them into good banks and bad banks. The good banks would return to the normal business of taking deposits and making loans; the bad banks would work out and sell toxic assets over several years. If the U.S. Treasury and other existing securities holders were given equal ownership in interest in both banks, taxpayers would participate in the potential upside as well as shoulder losses. Moreover, splitting a troubled institution in this manner would avoid the intractable problem of setting a fair price now for the sale of its toxic assets.

This splitting of a troubled institution into two banks is a much better approach than the creation of heavily subsidized public–private partnerships to try to buy toxic assets. These partnerships are another example of one-way capitalism: Private investors receive 50 percent of the upside but little of the downside on toxic assets that are actually purchased. Moreover, the partnerships are likely not to set a market price on many toxic assets, because the government will not provide generous subsidies to buy them on a regular basis.

The government's focus on recapitalizing banks and buying their toxic assets seems to be based on the assumption that banks are the primary originator of new loans. In fact, banks accounted for only 22 percent of the credit extended in the United States. The main cause of reduced lending has been the collapse of the loan securitization process, which allows banks and nonbanks to sell loans and re-lend the cash proceeds multiple times. The volume of new issues of securitized loans has fallen off a cliff, from $100 billion a month in 2006 to almost zero at the end of 2008.

To revive the process of securitizing loans, the United States needs to establish proper incentives at each stage of the process. We need to ensure that mortgages are appropriate for the resources of borrowers, and that mortgage brokers have skin in the game when they sell loans. We need to control the conflicts of interest of credit-rating agencies and reformulate the capital requirements for bank sponsors of special purpose entities (SPEs) that issue asset-backed securities. But all asset securitization should not be forced back on to the balance sheets of banks. Instead, bank sponsors should publicly disclose and back with capital their continuing or contingent obligations to any SPE they sponsor.

In response to the financial crisis, the federal government has substantially increased its intervention into the financial markets. Although such intervention is justified in certain cases, federal guarantees of debt offering are too extensive. To avoid moral hazard, the FDIC should guarantee 90 percent, rather than 100 percent, of debt offerings by banks and thrifts. Further, Congress should not extend beyond 2013 the higher limits on FDIC deposit insurance. The previous limits covered 98 percent of all depositors. The United States should move away from a financial sector with broad-based government guarantees to one with market discipline exerted by sophisticated and at-risk investors in bank debt.

The federal government should not be encouraging mergers among large institutions in the financial sector, which is now dominated by a handful of mega banks. The Justice Department should reject mergers that are likely to create more mega banks that are too big to fail. However, we should not attempt to increase competition in the financial sector by reinstating the barriers of the Glass Steagall Act to the securities activities of banks. Freestanding investment banks present systemic risks because they have limited sources of short-term liquidity: commercial paper and repurchase agreements. Banks with securities powers can also obtain short-term financing through Fed loans and retail deposits.

Given the decline in investor discipline and market competition, the monitoring of financial institutions has been left mainly to federal regulators. But there are limits to the effectiveness of any federal regulator in light of the fast pace of financial innovation and complexity of financial transactions. On a regular basis, the outside directors of a mega bank should be responsible for monitoring its activities. However, most outside directors of mega banks are not financial experts, do not spend enough time on board matters, and do not have a large equity stake in these institutions. If the United States wants effective board oversight of complex financial institutions, we should move to the private equity model for their boards. Under that model, a small group of super-directors with extensive financial expertise would spend several days every month at the bank; they would also have substantial holdings of the bank's stock.

A board of super-directors would be well-placed to monitor the financial condition of a mega bank and set the compensation of its senior executives in order to attain its dual goals of maximizing long-term profits for its shareholders without taking risks that would materially jeopardize the bank's solvency. Thus, super-directors are critical to fixing the U.S. financial system and moving it to accountable capitalism.

Notes

The Financial Crisis: A Parable

1. All the characters in this parable are fictitious.
2. Federal Reserve Statistical Release: Z1 Flow of Funds Accounts of the United States. www.federalreserve.gov/releases/z1/
3. Ethan Cohen-Cole, Burcu Duygan-Bump, Jose Fillat, and Judit Montoriol-Garriga, "Looking behind the aggregates: A reply to "Facts and Myths about the Financial Crisis of 2008." *Federal Reserve Bank of Boston Quantitative Analysis Unit*, November 12, 2008, Fig. 1A.
4. Federal Deposit Insurance Corporation, "Monthly Reports on Debt Issuance under the Temporary Liquidity Guarantee Program." March 31, 2009. Online at www.fdic.gov/regulations/resources/TLGP/reports.html.
5. Congressional Oversight Panel, "February Oversight Report: Valuing Treasury's Acquisitions." February 6, 2009, p. 5.
6. David Enrich and Dan Fitzpatrick, "Loans Shrink as Fear Lingers." *Wall Street Journal*, July 27, 2009, A1.

Part I: The U.S. Housing Slump and the Global Financial Crisis and Chapter 1: The Rise and Fall of U.S. Housing Prices

1. www.irrationalexuberance.com.
2. Board of Governors of the Federal Reserve System, "Federal Reserve Statistical Release z.1: Flow of Funds of the United States." December 9, 2003, and December 11, 2008 releases.
3. www.irrationalexuberance.com.

4. International Monetary Fund, "Currency Composition of Official Foreign Exchange Reserves (COFER)," March 31, 2009. Available online at www.imf.org/external/np/sta/cofer/eng/index.htm.

5. U.S. Treasury data: Major Foreign Holders of Treasury Securities. www.treas.gov/tic/mfhhis01.txt.

6. Francis E. Warnock and Veronica Cacdac Warnock, "International Capital Flows and Interest Rates." National Bureau of Economic Research Working Paper No. 12650, October 2006. A digest of this paper can be found online at www.nber.org/digest/nov06/w12560.html.

7. Federal Reserve Board, "Intended Federal Funds Rate: Change and Level, 1990 to Present." Available online at www.federalreserve.gov/fomc/fundsrate.htm.

8. John Taylor, "Housing and Monetary Policy." Presentation at the Policy Panel at the Symposium on Housing, Housing Finance, and Monetary Policy sponsored by the Federal Reserve Bank of Kansas City in Jackson Hole, Wyoming, September 2007, Figure 1.

9. Office of Federal Housing Enterprise Oversight, "Mortgage Markets and the Enterprise." February 19, 2009, p. 21. This report can be found online at www.ofheo.gov/media/research/MME2007revised.pdf.

10. Gretchen Morgenson, "Thundering Herd Faltered and Fell." New York Times, November 9, 2008, p. BU1.

11. Inside Mortgage Finance data appears in Major Coleman IV, Michael LaCour-Little, Kerry D. Vandell, "Subprime Lending and the Housing Bubble: Tail Wags Dog." April, 2008, The Paul Merage School of Business, p. 39, Table 7.

12. Edward Gramlich, "Booms and Busts, the Case of Subprime Mortgages." Paper presented at the Federal Reserve of Kansas City's Economic Symposium, Jackson Hole, Wyoming, August 31, 2007.

13. Ibid.

14. Edmund Andrews, "Fed Shrugged as the Subprime Crisis Spread." New York Times, December 18, 2007, Business section,

15. Historical data of The Department of Housing and Urban Development can be found at www.huduser.org/datasets/pdrdatas.html.

16. Office of Federal Housing Enterprise Oversight, 2008 Report to Congress. p. 6. This report is available online at www.ofheo.gov/AnnualReports.aspx.

17. Federal Reserve Board, "Board Issues Final Rule Amending Home Mortgage Provisions of Regulation Z (Truth in Lending)." Federal Reserve Press Release, July 14, 2008. Available on Fed's web site, www.federalreserve.gov/newsevents/default.htm.

18. Jonathan Peterson, "Bonuses to Loan Brokers Scrutinized." Los Angeles Times, March 27, 2006, p. C1.

19. On July 23, 2009, the Fed proposed a ban on steering fees. Federal Reserve Board Press Release, July 23, 2009.

20. Alex J. Pollock, "Bank Consolidation, Subprime Mortgage Issues, and the One-Page Mortgage Disclosure." Testimony before the U.S. House Committee on Oversight and Government Reform Subcommittee on Domestic Policy, May 21, 2007. On July 23, 2009, the Fed proposed a similar one-page disclosure document for borrowers, Press Release supra note 19.

21. HR 1728, Mortgage Reform and Anti-Predatory Lending Act (Passed the House on May 7, 2009).

22. John Gittelsohn and Ronald Campbell, "Street of Broken Dreams." *Orange County Register*, August 12, 2007, Money section.

23. Peter Henderson, Tim McLaughlin, Andy Sullivan, and Al Yoon, "Frenzy of Risky Mortgages Leaves Path of Destruction." *Reuters*, May 8, 2007.

24. Carol Lloyd, "Impossible Loan Turns Dream Home into Nightmare." *San Francisco Chronicle*, April 15, 2007, p. D-2.

25. Steve Westley of the United States Government Accountability Office, "Financial Markets and Community Investment: Overview of the Subprime Mortgage Crisis." Presented at the Hudson Institute, October 24, 2007, pp. 21–22.

26. Alan Hummel on behalf of the Appraisal Institute American Society of Appraisers American Society of Farm Managers and Rural Appraisers National Association of Independent Fee Appraisers, "Ending Mortgage Abuse: Safeguarding Homebuyers." Presented Before the Senate Committee on Banking Subcommittee on Housing, Transportation and Community Development, June 26, 2007, pp. 3–4.

27. Department of Housing and Urban Development, "SAFE Mortgage Licensing Act: About the Act." Available online at www.hud.gov/offices/hsg/sfh/mps/smlicact.cfm.

28. James Hagerty, "HUD Unveils New Rules for Mortgages." *Wall Street Journal*, November 13, 2008, p. D3.

29. James Rowley, "FTC to Draft New Curbs on Mortgage-Lending Abuse, Chairman Says." Bloomberg.com, March 20, 2009.

30. Fraud Enforcement and Recovery Act of 2009 (enacted on May 21, 2009).

31. The June 2009 Treasury White Paper, *Financial Regulatory Reform: A New Foundation: Rebuilding Financial Supervision and Regulation*, proposes to create a Consumer Financial Protection Agency to consolidate federal oversight of mortgage origination as well as other financial products like credit cards and bank deposits. The Treasury's proposal is too broad, however, as discussed in Chapter 14. But the Treasury would retain the role of the FTC in policing lending practices.

32. Benjamin Keys, Tanmoy K. Mukherjee, Amit Seru, and Vikrant Vig, "Did Securitization Lead to Lax Screening? Evidence from Sub Prime Loans." EFA 2008 Athens Meetings Paper, December 25, 2008.

33. House of Representatives, H.R. 1728 (passed by House on May 7, 2009). It is unclear whether the 5 percent refers to first losses up to 5 percent, or a 5 percent prorated proportion of all losses. While Section 213(1)(2)(B) of the proposed Bill prohibits mortgage creditors from directly or indirectly hedging against the risk of the 5 percent loss, it is unclear whether such an antihedging ban would be practically enforceable.

34. Proposed Changes to Capital Requirements Directive (CRD), New Article 122a, CRD Potential Changes, available at www.europa.en.

35. Mara Der Hovanesian, "Bonfire of the Builders." *Business Week*, August 13, 2007. This article is available online at www.businessweek.com/.

36. Carolyn Said, "Mortgage Meltdown: Plenty of Blame for Lending Mess." *San Francisco Chronicle*, February 3, 2008, p. C-1.

37. Financial Crimes Enforcement Network, "Mortgage Loan Fraud: An Update of Trends Based Upon an Analysis of Suspicious Activity Reports." April, 2008, p.9.

38. Office of Inspector General Department of Housing and Urban Development, "Follow Up of Down Payment Assistance Programs Operated by Private Nonprofit Entities." September 25, 2002, p. iii.

39. Dina El Boghdady, "No Money Down Disappearing as Mortgage Option." *Washington Post*, August 5, 2007, p. A01.

40. U.S. Treasury Internal Revenue Service, "IRS Targets Down-Payment-Assistance Scams; Seller-Funded Programs Do Not Qualify As Tax Exempt." IR-2006-74, May 4, 2006.

41. Quoted in "FHA's No Money Down Loan Program." PBS Nightly Business Report, April 25, 2008.

42. General Accounting Office: "Rural Housing Services, Overview of Program Issues 05-382T." page 7, Testimony before the Subcommittee on Housing and Community Opportunity, Committee on Financial Services, House of Representatives, March 10, 2005.

43. The American Recovery and Reinvestment Act will retroactively benefit homebuyers who purchased homes in the second half of 2008 with a repayable $7,500, which will have to be paid in annual installments over a 15-year period. U.S. Treasury Internal Revenue Service, "First-Time Homebuyer Credit." Updated April 21, 2009. Available online at www.irs.gov/newsroom/article/0,,id=204671,00.html.

44. Ibid.

45. NRS 115.010. Online at www.leg.state.nv.us/nrs/NRS-115.html. Florida Constitution: Article X SECTION 4. Online at www.leg.state.fl.us/.

46. Alan Zibel, "Other Woes Makes Foreclosure Crises Hard to Break." *Associated Press*, October 26, 2008.

47. Louise Story, "Home Equity Frenzy Was a Bank Ad Come True." *New York Times*, August 15, 2008, p. A1.

48. Harvard University Joint Center for Housing Studies, "The State of the Nation's Housing 2008." p. 37. Available online at www.jchs.harvard.edu/publications/markets/son2008/son2008.pdf.

49. Christine Dugas, "Home-Equity Loans Dry Up." *USA Today*, September 5, 2007. Available online at www.usatoday.com/money/perfi/credit/2007-09-05-credit-cards_N.htm.

50. Federal Reserve Bank of San Francisco Economic Letter, "U.S. Household Deleveraging and Future Consumption Growth 2009-16." May 15, 2009. http://frbsf.org/publications/economics/letter/2009/el2009-16.html.

Chapter 2: Fannie and Freddie

1. Fannie Mae's reported losses in 2008 totaled $58.7 billion, which exceeded Fannie Mae's net income for the last 17 years. James Hagerty, Damian Paletta, "Red Ink Clouds Role of Fannie, Freddie." *Wall Street Journal*, February 27, 2009, p. A2. Freddie Mac's reported a loss of $50.1 billion for all of 2008, exceeding Freddie Mac's net income from 1971 to 2006. James Hagerty and Aparajita Saha-Bubna, "Freddie Loss: $23.9 Billion; Help Sought." *Wall Street Journal*, March 12, 2009, A3.

2. The Housing and Economic Recovery Act of 2008 permanently increased this limit to a maximum of $625,500 for FHA-insured loans in high-cost areas of the country like New York and California. *Housing and Economic Recovery Act of 2008 FAQ* www.hud.gov/news/recoveryactfaq.cfm.

3. The Federal Deposit Insurance Corporation (FDIC) is an independent federal agency, established in 1933, that insures deposits in member commercial banks. The Securities

and Exchanges Commission (SEC) is a federal agency which regulates the offering and trading in securities.

4. Department of Housing and Urban Development, "Overview of the GSEs' Housing Goal Performance, 1993-2003." and "Overview of the GSEs' Housing Goal Performance, 2000-2007." Available online at www.huduser.org/Datasets/GSE/gse2007.pdf.

5. "Briefing: Home Ownership." *Economist*, April 18, 2009, p. 78. Tiffany Chaney and Paul Emrath, "US vs. European Housing Markets: In-Depth Analysis." *National Association of Homebuilders*, May 5, 2006, Table 1. Available online at www.nahb.org/generic .aspx?genericContentID=57411.

6. Federal Register Vol. 65, No. 47, March 9, 2000, p. 12692.

7. Quoted in Carol D. Leonning, "How the HUD Mortgage Policy Fed the Crisis." *Washington Post*, June 10, 2008, p. A01.

8. Ibid.

9. Ibid.

10. Quoted in Daryl Strickland, "Fannie Mae Moves to Loosen Home Loan Credit Rules." *Los Angeles Times*, October 1, 1999, p. C1.

11. James Hagerty, "Fannie, Freddie Executives Knew of Risks." *Wall Street Journal*, December 10, 2008, p. A2.

12. Quoted in Charles Duhigg, "Pressured to Take More Risk, Fannie Reached Tipping Point." *New York Times*, October 5, 2008, p. A1, New York edition.

13. Office of Federal Housing Enterprise Oversight, *2008 Report to Congress*, April 15, 2008.

14. Dwight M. Jaffe, "On Limiting the Retained Mortgage Portfolios of Fannie Mae and Freddie Mac." University of California Berkeley, June 30, 2005, Figure 2, p. 6.

15. Office of Federal Housing Enterprise Oversight News Release, "Consent Order Issued in Action Against Former Freddie Mac Chairman and CEO Leland C. Brendsel." November 6, 2007.

16. Office of Federal Housing Enterprise Oversight News Release, "OFHEO Issues Consent Orders Regarding Former Fannie Mae Executives." April 18, 2008.

17. Warren Buffett, Letter to Shareholders, 2008, p. 16.

18. Bethany Mclean, "The Fall of Fannie Mae." *Fortune*, January 24, 2005.

19. "Dems Rip New Fannie Mae Regulatory Measure." *United Press International*, August 1, 2005.

20. Alan Greenspan, "Monetary Policy and the State of the Economy." Hearing Before the U.S. House of Representatives Committee on Financial Services, February 17, 2005, p. 19 of transcript. Available online at www.house.gov/financialservices/media/pdf/109-4.pdf.

21. Congressional Budget Office, "Updated Estimates of the Subsidies to the Housing GSEs." April 8, 2004, Tables 4 and 5. The $20 billion total did not include the value of the state and local tax exemptions of Freddie Mac.

22. Wayne Passmore, "The GSE Subsidy and Value of Government Ambiguity." *Federal Reserve Finance & Economic Discussion Series*, December, 2003, pp. 2-3 and 27. Papers in this series can be found online at www.federalreserve.gov/Pubs/feds.

23. Quoted in "Paulson's 'bazooka' backfires." found at money.cnn/galleries/2008/fortune/0812/gallery.dumbest_moments_2009.fortune/7.html.

24. U.S. Treasury White Paper, *Financial Regulatory Reform: A New Foundation: Rebuilding Financial Supervision and Regulation.* June 2009, pp. 40–44.

25. Alfred E. Kahn, *The Economics of Regulation: Principles and Institutions.* Cambridge, MA: MIT Press, 1998.

26. James Hagerty, "New Task Seen for Fannie, Freddie." *Wall Street Journal*, March 30, 2009, p. A7.

27. Mortgage industry consultant Andrew Davidson has compiled a series of policy options calling for Fannie's and Freddie's transformation into cooperatives. James Hagerty, "U.S. Rethinks Roles of Fannie, Freddie." *Wall Street Journal*, December 1, 2008, p. A5.

Chapter 3: Mortgage Securitization in the Private Sector

1. New York University Stern School of Business, *Restoring Financial Stability: How to Repair a Failed System.* Edited by Viral V. Acharya and Matthew Richardson. Hoboken, NJ: John Wiley & Sons, 2009, p. 63.

2. Ethan Cohen-Cole, Burcu Duygan-Bump, Jose Fillat, and Judit Montoriol-Garriga, "Looking Behind the Aggregates: A Reply to 'Facts and Myths about the Financial Crisis of 2008.'" *Federal Reserve Bank of Boston Quantitative Analysis Unit*, November 12, 2008, Fig. 1B.

3. Jalal Soroosh and Jack. T Ciesielski, "Accounting for Special Purpose Entities Revised: FASB Interpretation 46(R)." *The CPA Journal Online*, July 2004. At www.nysscpa.org/cpajournal/2004/704/essentials/p30.htm.

4. Bradley Keoun, "Citigroup's $1.1 Trillion of Mysterious Assets Shadows Earnings." *Bloomberg*, July 14, 2008. Online at www.bloomberg.com/apps/news?pid=20601109 & refer=home&sid=a1liVM3tG3aI.

5. Ibid.

6. Carol Loomis, "Robert Rubin On the Job He Never Wanted." *Fortune Magazine Online*, November 28, 2007. Available through CNNmoney.com at http://money.cnn.com/2007/11/09/news/newsmakers/merrill_rubin.fortune/index.htm.

7. FASB Interpretation 46 (R), revised in December, 2003.

8. FASB Statements 166 and 167 (Adopted on June 12, 2009).

9. If these revised FASB rules had been in place at the end of 2008, for example, the leverage ratio (Tier 1 capital relative to average adjusted assets) would have dropped from 6.08 percent to 3.87percent for Citigroup, and from 6.44 percent to 3.38 percent for Bank of America. Committee on Capital Markets Regulation, *The Global Financial Crisis: A Plan for Regulatory Reform.* May 2009, p. 188 (I am a member of that Committee).

10. Krishna Guha, Tom Braithwaite, Francesco Guerra, and Aline Van Duyn, "Treasury plans strict rules for securitization." *Financial Times*, June 16, 2009, p. 1. See Treasury White Paper, *Financial Regulatory Reform: A New Foundation: Rebuilding Financial Supervision and Regulation.* June 2009, p. 42.

11. Treasury White Paper, ibid, suggests that Fannie Mae and Freddie Mac might become, among other things, the insurers of covered bonds.

12. Henry J. Paulson, "United States Department of the Treasury: Best Practices for Residential Covered Bonds." July, 2008. www.treas.gov/press/releases/reports/USCoveredBondBestPractices.pdf.

13. Federal Deposit Insurance Corporation, "Covered Bond Policy Statement." July, 2008, at Section (b), Federal Register, vol. 73, April 23, 2008, p.21952.

14. American Securitization Forum, *Restoring Confidence in the Securitization Markets*. 2008, pp. 39–40.

15. Under the FASB's revised rules, the footnotes of the bank's financial statements would aggregate the assets and liabilities from all of its SPEs, rather than for an individual SPE.

16. Committee on Capital Markets Regulation, *The Global Financial Crisis: A Plan for Regulatory Reform*. May, 2009, p. 132.

17. Ibid.

18. This summary is based on IMF, "The Danish Mortgage Market—A Comparative Analysis." IMF Country Report No. 071123, March 2007.

19. George Soros, "Denmark Offers a Model Mortgage Market." *Wall Street Journal*, October 10, 2008, p. A15.

20. Frank Partnoy, "How and Why Credit Rating Agencies Are Not Like Other Gatekeepers." *University of San Diego Legal Studies Research Paper Series*, Research Paper No. 07-46, May 2006, p. 69.

21. House Committee on Oversight and Government Reform, "Credit Ratings and the Financial Crisis." October 28, 2008. Available online at http://oversight.house.gov/documents/20081022112135.pdf.

22. Partnoy, supra note 20, p. 65.

23. Testimony of Jerome S. Fons Before the United States House of Representatives Committee on Oversight and Government Reform, October 22, 2008, p. 4 of transcript. Available online at http://oversight.house.gov/documents/20081022102726.pdf.

24. SEC Release No. 34-57967 "Proposed Rules for Nationally Recognized Statistical Rating Organizations." June 16, 2008, p. 22.

25. "Credit Rating Agencies and the Financial Crisis." Congressional Hearings by Committee on Oversight and Government Reform, Henry A. Waxman, Chairman, October 22, 2008, opening statement.

26. Nick Baumann, "Credit Rating Exec, 'We Sold Our Souls to the Devil'." *Mother Jones*, October 22, 2008. Available online at www.motherjones.com/politics/2008/10/credit-rating-exec-we-sold-our-souls-devil.

27. Pursuant to Credit Rating Agency Reform Act of 2006. The number of recognized credit rating agencies as of June 2008 is referenced in SEC Release No. 34-57967 "Proposed Rules for Nationally Recognized Statistical Rating Organizations." June 16, 2008, p. 5.

28. Bo Becker and Todd Milbourn, "Reputation and Competition: Evidence from the Credit Rating Industry." Harvard Business School Finance Working Paper 09-051, October 2, 2008.

29. SEC Release No. 34-59342, "Amendments to Rules for Nationally Recognized Statistical Rating Organizations." Effective date April 10, 2009. The SEC has also asked for public comment on whether it should delete any reliance on credit ratings in its rules. The proposal appears to be stalemated.

30. SEC Release No. 34-58070 www.sec.gov/rules/proposed/2008/34-58070.pdf.

31. "Bond Basics: Characteristics" Investopedia, a Forbes Digital Company www.investopedia .com/university/bonds/bonds2.asp.

32. Richard Cantor, Owain ap Gwilym, and Stephen Thomas, "The Use of Credit Ratings in Investment Management in the US and Europe." *Social Science Research Network Working Paper Series*, February 2007.

33. Treasury White Paper, supra note 10, p. 46.

34. Partnoy, supra note 20, pp. 91–92.

35. Ibid, pp. 86–87.

36. The Municipal Bond Fairness Act, HR 6308, 110th Congress, August 2, 2008 Session. This bill did not pass the House in 2008, and has not been introduced again in 2009 as of May.

37. Egan-Jones is the one credit-rating agency paid by investors, but it is small.

Chapter 4: Credit Default Swaps and Mathematical Models

1. This figure is a significant modification of one that can be found in Janet M. Tavakoli, *Credit Derivatives and Synthetic Structures*. Hoboken, NJ: John Wiley & Sons, 2001.

2. Warren E. Buffett, "Berkshire Hathaway Letter to Shareholders 2008." February 27, 2009.

3. These values are notional amounts. The notional amount of a swap or other derivative product is the value used to calculate payments on it. International Swaps and Derivatives Association, "The ISDA Market Survey: What the Results Show and What They Don't Show." *ISDA Research Notes*, Fall, 2008, www.isda.org.

4. Quoted in Michael Lewis, "The End." Portfolio.com, November 11, 2008. www.portfolio .com/news-markets/national-news/portfolio/2008/11/11/The-End-of-Wall-Streets-Boom.

5. State of New York Insurance Department, "Re: Credit Insurance Policy Issued to Financial Institution" June 16, 2000. Available online at www.ins.state.ny.us/gco2000/rg006161 .htm.

6. State of New York Insurance Department, "Circular Letter No. 19: Best Practices for Financial Guaranty Insurers." September 22, 2008. www.ins.state.ny.us/circltr/2008/ c108_19.htm Withdrawn by the New York Insurance Department in First Supplement to Circular Letter No. 19 (November 20, 2008).

7. "Everything You Ever Wanted to Know about Monoline Insurers." *Finance Week*, June 18, 2008. www.financeweek.co.uk/item/6196.

8. Ibid.

9. Lavonne Kuykendall, and Kerry E. Grace, "Ambac Slides 9.9% as its Net Worth Turns Negative." *Wall Street Journal*, February 26, 2009, p. C5.

10. Mary Williams Walsh, "MBIA Plans to Spin Off Municipal Bond Unit." *New York Times*, February 19, 2009, p. B3.

11. Radi Khasawneh, "Monolines face 'grim' future following ratings downgrade." *Financial News Online*, October 31, 2008.

12. Michael Aneiro, "Cities and States Feel the Squeeze—With Muni Market Frozen, Fallbacks Are Raising Taxes, Cutting Services." *Wall Street Journal*, November 28, 2008, p. C1.

13. Jack Herman, "N.Y. Official Eyes TARP for Insurers." *Bond Buyer*, October 21, 2008. www .bondbuyer.com/article.html?id=20081020CHNJB04G.

14. Business Wire "Fitch Downgrades SCA, XLCA & XLFA; Place on Rating Watch Evolving." *Reuters*, July 29, 2008. www.reuters.com/article/pressRelease/idUS173648 +29-Jul-2008+BW20080729.

15. Jack Herman, "The Bond Buyer; Ambac to Settle a CDO Exposure." *Bond Buyer*, August 4, 2008. www.bondbuyer.com/article.html?id=2008080146D32WSN.

16. Jonathan Laing, "Defusing the Credit-Default Swap Bomb." *Barron's*, November 17, 2008. p. 45.

17. Federal Reserve Board Press Release, September 16, 2008. www.federalreserve.gov/newsevents/press/other/20080916a.htm.

18. U.S. Treasury and Federal Reserve Board Joint Press Release, March 2, 2008. www.federalreserve.gov/newsevents/press/other/20090302a.htm.

19. Bhattiprolu Murti, "AIG, Maiden Lane Will Pay $62 Billion to Settle Derivatives." *Wall Street Journal*, March 17, 2009.

20. Sudeep Reddy and Michael R. Crittenden, "Fed's Kohn Concedes Risk in AIG Rescue." *Wall Street Journal*, March 6, 2009, p. A3.

21. Lucian Bebchuk, "AIG Still Isn't Too Big to Fail." *Wall Street* Journal, March 20, 2009, p. A13.

22. Ibid.

23. "Title 17: Commodity and Securities Exchanges, Part 35.2 Exemption of Swap Agreement (d)." 58 FR 5594, January 22, 1993. Available online at www.gpoaccess.gov/.

24. Quoted in Peter S. Goodman, "Taking a Hard New Look at a Greenspan Legacy." *New York Times*, October 9, 2008, p. A1.

25. Robert E. Rubin, Alan Greenspan, and Arthur Levitt, "On Legislative Proposal on CFTC Concept Release." Letter to Congress, June 5, 1998. Available on Treasury web site at www.treas.gov/press/releases/docs/cftcltr.htm.

26. Alan Greenspan, "The Commodity Exchange Act and OTC Derivatives." Testimony Before U.S. Senate Committee on Agriculture, Nutrition, and Forestry, July 30, 1998. Available online at https://federalreserve.gov/boarddocs/testimony/1998/19980730.htm.

27. Dean Kloner, "The Commodity Future Modernization Act of 2000." *29 Securities Regulation Law Journal 286*, July 17, 2001, p. 60.

28. Anthony Faiola, Ellen Nakashima, and Jill Drew, "What Went Wrong." *Washington Post*, October 15 2008, p. A01.

29. Serena Ng, "Nasdaq Opens Derivatives Clearinghouse." *Wall Street Journal*, January 6, 2009, p. C2.

30. www.crmpolicygroup.org.

31. The three approved sponsors of CDS clearinghouses are ICE, an affiliate of USTrust; DERI/SERVE, a subsidiary of Depository Trust Company; and the Chicago Mercantile Exchange.

32. ISDA, Credit Derivatives Physical Settlement Matrix 20090408 (released April 8, 2009). Letter from Treasury Secretary to Senator Harry Reid, May 13, 2009.

33. Treasury White Paper *Financial Regulatory Reform: A New Foundation: Rebuilding Financial Supervision and Regulation*. June 2009, pp. 46-48.

34. Serena Ng, "Banks Seek Role in Bid to Overhaul Derivatives." *Wall Street Journal*, May 29, 2009, p. C1.

35. SEC, Litigation Release 21023, May 5, 2009.

36. Treasury White Paper, supra note 33, p. 4.

37. Buffett, supra note 2.

38. Quoted in Lewis, supra note 4.

39. Kristopher Gerardi, Andreas Lehnert, Shane Sherlund, and Paul Willen, "Making Sense of the Subprime Crisis." Federal Reserve Bank of Atlanta Working Paper 2009-2, February 2009. Available at www.frbatlanta.org.

40. Eric Dash, and Julie Creswell, "Citigroup Saw No Red Flags Even as It Made Bolder Bets." *New York Times*, November 23, 2008, p. A1. Nomi Prins, "The Risk Fallacy." *Fortune*, October 28, 2008. http://money.cnn.com/2008/10/27/magazines/fortune/riskfallacy_prins.fortune/index3.htm.

41. "In Plato's Cave." *Economist*, January 24, 2009, p. 14.

42. Joe Nocera, "Risk Mismanagement." *NY Times Sunday Magazine*, January 4, 2009, p. 24.

43. Steve Lohr, "In Modeling Risk, the Human Factor Was Left Out." *New York Times*, November 5, 2008, p. B1, New York edition.

44. Uday Rajan, Amit Seru, and Kikrant Vig, "The Failure of Models That Predict Failure: Distance, Incentives and Defaults." *Chicago GSB Research Paper No. 08-19, Ross School of Business Paper No. 1122*, October 2008 (quote from abstract).

45. Prins, supra note 40.

46. Carrick Mollenkamp, Serena Ng, Liam Pleven, and Randall Smith, "Behind AIG's Fall, Risk Models Failed to Pass Real-World Test." *Wall Street Journal*, November 3, 2008, p. A16.

47. Prins, supra note 40.

48. Dash and Creswell, supra note 40.

49. Ibid.

50. Mollenkamp, Ng, Pleven, and Smith, supra note 46.

51. Associated Press, "AIG CEO takes pay cut in 2007." *Forbes.com*, April 4, 2008.

52. Federal Reserve Board, Remarks by Chairman Alan Greenspan at the American Bankers Association Annual Convention, New York, October 5, 2004. (Italics in original).

Part II: Impact on Stock and Bond Markets and Chapter 5: Short Selling, Hedge Funds, and Leverage

1. Chairman Ben S. Bernanke, *The Economic Outlook*. Testimony Before the Joint Economic Committee, U.S. Congress, March 28, 2007, www.federalreserve.gov/newsevents/testimony/bernanke20070328a.htm.

2. The ABX is a synthetic tradeable index referencing a basket of triple-A MBS; this particular index is based on pools of subprime mortgages, which were issued in the first half of 2007.

3. *Profile of Mutual Fund Shareholders, 2008*. Investment Company Institute Research Series, Winter 2009.

4. E.S. Browning, "After the Collapse, Guarded Hope for '09." *Wall Street Journal*, March 2008. p. R1.

5. Eleanor Laise, "Five Ways to Fix Up Your 401(k)." *Wall Street Journal*. January 31, 2008.

6. SEC Administrative Proceeding Release No. 34-55931. June 20, 2007.

7. James Chanos, "Hedge Fund Strategies and Market Participation." Prepared Statement for SEC Roundtable on Hedge Funds, May 15, 2003.

8. "Lay Blames Enron Failure on Attack of Short Sellers." *International Herald Tribune.* April 28, 2005.

9. SEC Release No. 34-55970, June 28, 2008, p. 11, Footnote 33.

10. Andrew Sorkin, "Saving Wall St. (for Now)." *New York Times.* March 18, 2008. Short-sale data referenced in this section were provided by Dr. Yaneer Bar-Yam, New England Complex Systems Institute.

11. Bill Saporito, "Are Short Sellers to Blame for the Financial Crisis?." *TIME*, September 18, 2008.

12. Statement of Richard S. Fuld, Jr. Before the U.S. House of Representatives Committee on Oversight and Government Reform October 6, 2008, p. 10. http://oversight.house.gov/documents/20081006125839.pdf.

13. Jed Horowitz, "Thain Blasts Ratings Agencies, Short-Sellers for Leveling Wall Street." *Investment News*, September 22, 2008.

14. The SEC announced in July of 2009 that self-regulatory organizations (SROs) would soon publish every day the aggregate short-selling volume in each equity security for that day, as well as information regarding individual short sale transactions in exchange-listed equity securities on a one-month delayed basis. SEC Press Release 2009-172, "SEC Takes Steps to Curtail Abusive Short Sales and Increase Market Transparency." July 27, 2009.

15. Ana Avramovic, "Examining the Wake of the Short Sale Restriction." Credit Suisse AES Analysis, 13 October 2008.

16. Arturo Bris,, "Shorting Financial Stocks Should Resume." *Wall Street Journal*, September 29, 2008, p. A25.

17. Federal Register Vol. 72, No. 127, July 3, 2007, p. 36350.

18. Min Zhao, "The Tick-Test Rule, Investors' Opinions Dispersion, and Stock Returns: The Daily Evidence." Working Paper Draft, Finance Department, University of Tennessee, October 2007.

19. Federal Register supra note 17, p. 36350.

20. SEC Release No. 59748, April 10, 2009. www.sec.gov/rules/proposed/2009/34-59748.pdf.

21. SEC, Press Release 2009-185 (August 17, 2009).

22. NASDAQ OMX, "NASDAQ OMX, in Cooperation With Other U.S. Markets, Proposes a Modified Rule to Further Reduce Abusive Short Selling." March 24, 2009.

23. Randall Dodd, "Public Interest Demands Hedge Fund Rules." Global Policy Forum, January 12, 2007.

24. "The Incredible Shrinking Funds." *Economist*, October 25, 2008, p. 84.

25. Edward Chancellor, "So Much Money, So Little Talent." *Wall Street Journal*, August 24, 2005, p. A10.

26. Geraldine Fabrikant, "Watch out for layers of fees for hedge funds." SFGate.com, November 2003.

27. Quoted in Alan Abelson, "Up and Down Wall Street." *Barron's*. September 26, 2005, p. 5.

28. Deborah Brewster, "Record Run on Hedge Funds." *Financial Times*, January 15, 2009. p. 13.

29. Anuj Gangahar, "Funds of Hedge Funds Shrink by 30% in Year." *Financial Times*, March 11, 2009, p. 14.

30. Goldstein vs. SEC, 451 F. 3d 873 (DC Cir. 2006).

31. SEC Release No. IA-2628. Final Rule: Prohibition of Fraud by Advisors to Certain Pooled Investment Vehicles. August 3, 2008.

32. Section 3(c)(1) and Section 3(c)(7) of Investment Company Act of 1940. In addition, if a hedge fund does not make a public filing and has fewer than 500 investors, it will not be required to register as a reporting company under the Securities Exchange Act of 1934.

33. SEC Release No. 33-8766; IA-2576. Proposed Rule: Prohibition of Fraud by Advisors to Certain Pooled Investment Vehicles; Accredited Investors in Certain Private Investment Vehicles.

34. Rule 205-3 of the Investment Advisers Act of 1940.

35. Fact Sheet: Legislation for the Registration of Hedge Funds Delivered to Capitol Hill, TG-214, July 15, 2009.

36. Treasury White Paper, *Financial Regulatory Reform: A New Foundation: Rebuilding Financial Supervision and Regulation*, June 2009, p. 37.

37. Stephen J. Brown, William N. Goetzmann, Bing Liang, "Fees on Fees in Funds of Funds." June 14, 2004. pp. 24–25.

38. Quoted in Craig Karmin, "Mr. Swenson Plays It by the Book." *Wall Street Journal*. January 13, 2009, p. C3.

39. This high percentage reflects, among other factors, the average "backfill bias" in hedge fund returns from 1994 to 2003 as presented in, Burton G. Malkiel and Atanu Saha, "Hedge Funds: Risk and Return." *Financial Analysts Journal*, December 2005, p.16, Exhibit 2. Malkiel and Saha explain that backfill bias occurs when a hedge fund manager selectively includes the best returns from previous data (either yet unreported or reported to another data base) into their fund's current results report.

40. "When markets turn." *Economist*, January 22, 2009, online edition. www.economist.com.

41. *Hedge Funds, Leverage, and the Lessons of Long-Term Capital Management.* Report of The President's Working Group on Financial Markets, April 1999.

42. Timothy Geithner, "Liquidity and Financial Markets." Keynote address at the 8th Annual Risk Convention and Exhibition, Global Association of Risk Professionals, New York City, February 28, 2007. www.ny.frb.org/newsevents/speeches/2007/gei070228 .html.

43. Patrick McGuire and Kostas Tsatsaronis, "Estimating Hedge Fund Leverage." *BIS Working Paper No. 260*, Bank for International Settlements, September, 2008, p. 11.

44. "Committee Holds Hearing on Hedge Funds and the Financial Market." Committee on Oversight and Government reform, November 13, 2008. Transcripts available online at http://oversight.house.gov/story.asp?ID=2271.

45. Statement by Timothy Geithner U.S. Treasury Secretary before the U.S. House of Representatives Committee on Financial Services, March 26, 2009.

46. Mark Jickling and Donald J. Marples, "Taxation of Hedge Fund and Private Equity Managers." *Congressional Research Service*, July 5, 2007, p. 6.

47. *Emergency Economic Stabilization Act of 2008*, HR 1424, Title VII, Sec. 457A, (a). Available online at http://frwebgate.access.gpo.gov.

48. *A New Era of Resposibility: Renewing America's Promise*. U.S. Office of Management and Budget, February 26, 2009, p. 122.

49. Securities and Exchange Commission, Office of Inspector General's (OIG) report on Audit of SEC's Oversight of Bear Stearns and Related Entities: The Consolidated Supervised Entity Program, Report No. 446 A, Sec.gov, September 25, 2008. www .sec-oig.gov/Reports/AuditsInspections/2008/446-a.pdf.

50. Andrew Lo, "Hedge Funds, Systematic Risk, and the Finanicial Crisis of 2007-2008." *U.S. House of Representatives Committee on Oversight and Government Reform*. November 13, 2008, pp. 9-10, Figure 3.

51. "BIS Quarterly Review." Bank for International Settlements, June, 2009, Table 19. www.bis.org/statistics/otcder/dt1920a.pdf. Market values are usually much higher than notional values of derivatives.

52. Fortune, Peter, "Margin Requirements, Margin Loans, and Margin Rates: Practice and Principles." *Federal Reserve Bank of Boston New England Economic Review*, September 1, 2000, p. 27.

53. "Wild-animal spirits." *Economist*, January 22, 2009, online edition. www.economist.com.

54. "Credit Markets Get Ugly as Tarp Turns its Back on Toxic Assets." *Financial Times*, November 20, 2008, p. 43.

55. Lo 2008, supra note 50, pp. 8–9.

Chapter 6: Leverage At Brokers and Banks

1. FDIC, "Final Rule on Advanced Capital Adequacy Framework—Basel II." *Financial Institution Letters* 107, December 7, 2007.

2. Securities and Exchange Commission, "Final Rule: Alternative Net Capital Requirements for Broker-Dealers That Are Part of Consolidated Supervised Entities." June 9, 2004. www .sec.gov//rules/final/34-49830.htm.

3. Securities and Exchange Commission, Office of Inspector General's (OIG) report on Audit of SEC's Oversight of Bear Stearns and Related Entities: The Consolidated Supervised Entity Program, Report No. 446 A, Sec.gov, September 25, 2008, p. 19. www.sec-oig .gov/Reports/AuditsInspections/2008/446-a.pdf.

4. Stephen Labaton, "Agency's '04 Rule Let Banks Pile Up New Debt." *New York Times*, October 3, 2008, p. A1.

5. Recording of SEC open meeting on April 28, 2004, remarks of Annette Nazareth, Director of SEC Division of Market Regulation. Recording available online at: www .connectlive.com/events/secopenmeetings/2004index.html.

6. Ibid, remarks of Commissioner Harvey Goldschmid.

7. OIG Report, supra note 3, p. 19.

8. Recording, supra note 5, Remarks of Commissioner Goldschmid and Director Nazareth.

9. SEC Adopting Release for Final Rule, supra note 2, Summary.

10. OIG Report, supra note 3, p viii.

11. The Treasury has suggested that the SEC cease to provide consolidated regulation to investment banks, which should seek consolidated regulation under the Federal

Reserve. Treasury White Paper, *Financial Regulatory Reform: A New Foundation: Rebuilding Financial Supervision and Regulation.* June 2009, pp. 36–37. However, smaller investment banks and smaller broker-dealers should not be subject to the Fed's jurisdiction unless they are part of a bank holding company.

12. "Growing Insecurities." *Economist,* January 17, 2009, p. 73.

13. The Treasury would create an Office of National Insurance with the responsibility to monitor all aspects of the U.S. insurance industry and to coordinate with international insurance regulators. Treasury White Paper, supra note 11, pp. 39–40.

14. Beth Healy, "Markopolos: SEC's regional turf tiffs hampered case." *Boston Globe,* February 5, 2009. www.boston.com/business/articles/2009/02/05/markopolos_secs_regional_turf_ tiffs_hampered_case/.

15. Marcy Gordon Associated Press, "Schapiro Pledges Toughness at SEC." *Washington Times,* January 16, 2009, www.washingtontimes.com/news/2009/jan/16/crisis-of-onfidence/.

16. Neil A. Simon, "Finra had authority to examine Madoff's firm." *InvestmentNews.com,* January 18, 2009. online edition at investmentnews.com.

17. David Scheer and Jesse Westbrook, "Madoff 'Tragedy' Said to Have Escaped Scrutiny by the SEC." Bloomberg.com, December 15, 2008.

18. Ibid.

19. Joanna Chung, "SEC to enlist help on fraud." *Financial Times,* April 1, 2009, p. 15.

20. SEC Press Release 2009-109, May 14, 2009.

21. Financial Planning Association vs. SEC, 482 F.2d 481 (DC Circuit 2007).

22. Rand Institute for Civil Justice, "Investor and Industry Perspectives on Investment Advisers and Broker-Dealers." Sponsored by the U.S. Securities and Exchange Commission (SEC), January 3, 2008. www.sec.gov/news/press/2008/2008-1_randiabdreport.pdf.

23. See Treasury White Paper, supra note 11, pp. 71–72.

24. See, for example, Testimony of Robert Kuttner before the Committee on Financial Services U.S. House of Representatives, Washington D.C. October 2, 2007, http:// financialservices.house.gov/hearing110/testimony_-_kuttner.pdf.

25. 12 U.S.C. § 24 (seventh).

26. Federal Reserve Notice, Docket No. R-0841, "Revenue Limit on Bank Ineligibile Activities of Subsidiaries of Bank Holding Companies Engaged in Underwriting and Dealing in Securities." December 20, 1996, www.federalreserve.gov/boarddocs/press/ boardacts/1996/19961220/R-0841.pdf. The increased amount of underwriting permitted over time arose from changing interpretations of the phrase *engaged principally* in securities business.

27. Alex Tabarrok, "Glass Steagall: The Real History." *Marginal Revolutions,* September 19, 2008, www.marginalrevolution.com/marginalrevolution/2008/09/glass-steagall.html.

28. Eugene White, 1986, "Before the Glass-Steagall Act: An Analysis of the Investment Activities of National Banks." *Explorations in Economic History* 23, January, 1986, pp. 33–55.

29. Randall S. Kroszner and Raghuram G. Rajan, "Is the Glass-Steagall Act Justified?: Evidence from the U.S. Experience with Universal Banking 1921-1933." *American Economic Review,* 1994, vol 84, pp. 810–832. Available on professor Rajan's web site http://faculty.chicagobooth .edu/raghuram.rajan/research/papers/randy1.pdf.

30. This one significant player in the market for mortgage-backed securities was Washington Mutual. "Failed Bank List." FDIC.gov, www.fdic.gov/bank/individual/failed/banklist.html.

31. *Report and Recommendations Pursuant to Section 133 of the Emergency Economic Stabilization Act of 2008: Study on Mark-To-Market Accounting.* Office of the Chief Account Division of Corporation Finance, U.S. SEC. December 30, 2008, pp. 4, 118–120.

32. "Shareholder Report on UBS Write-Downs." UBS, April 18, 2008, p. 14.

33. Louis Story and Ben White, "The Road to Lehman's Failure Was Littered With Lost Chances." *New York Times*, October 6, 2008, p. B1.

34. *Federal Deposit Insurance Corporation Improvement Act of 1991, 12 U.S.C. 1811.*

35. John Gapper, "The Case for a Glass-Steagall 'Lite.'" *Financial Times*, March 15, 2009, p. 15.

36. Ibid.

37. See also Section 23A of the Federal Reserve Act.

38. Treasury White Paper, supra note 11, p. 31.

39. Compare Office of the Comptroller of the Currency, "Today's Credit Markets, Relationship Banking and Tying." September, 2003, pp. 30–31; with Steven Drucker and Maju Puri, "Tying Knots: Lending to Win Equity Underwriting Business." *Proceedings* by Federal Reserve Bank of Chicago, May 2004, p. 2. www.chicagofed.org/news_and_conferences/conferences_and_events/files/2004_bank_structure_the_tying_of_lending_and_equity.pdf.

40. Drucker and Puri, ibid, p. 2.

41. 12 USC 1972.

42. GAO, "Bank Tying: Additional Steps Needed to Ensure Effective Enforcement of Tying Prohibitions." GAO Report 04–3, October 10, 2003.

43. "The Wall Street Fix" web site, under Worldcom/Player, for PBS's *Frontline*, May 8, 2003. quoting Jack Grubman "What used to be a conflict has now become a synergy."

44. Joseph Kahn, "A New Financial Era: The Impact; Financial Services Industry Faces a New World." *New York Times*, October 23, 1999, p. C1.

45. Andy Kessler, "The End of Citi's Financial Supermarket." *Wall Street Journal*, January 16, 2009, p. A11.

46. Information and comprehensive documents about the Basel Committee and Accords can be found at the Bank for International Settlements web site under 'Basel Committee.' www.bis.org/bcbs/index.htm. For information about the U.S. implementation of Basel Accords, Initiatives, and other Basel related matters, see Basel II section of Federal Reserve Boards web site. www.federalreserve.gov/GeneralInfo/basel2/.

47. Federal Reserve Board Governor Randall S. Kroszner, "Basel II Implementation in the United States." Remarks at the New York Bankers Association Annual Washington Visit, Washington, D.C., July 12, 2007.

48. Rules and Regulations, Federal Register, Vol. 72, No. 235, sec II, December 7, 2007, p. 69297.

49. Charles W. Calomiris, "Most Pundits Are Wrong About the Bubble." *Wall Street Journal*, October 18–19, 2008, p. A13.

50. FDIC chair Sheila Bair Remarks to the Institute of International Bankers Annual Washington Conference, Washington, DC, March 2, 2009. www.fdic.gov/news/news/speeches/chairman/spmar0209.html.

51. Quoted in Bob Moon and Amy Scott, "Banks Brace for Basel II." *Marketplace*, July 2, 2008.

52. "Proposed Enhancements to the Basel II Framework." Bank for International Settlements web site, January 2009, pp. 22–24. See also Treasury White Paper, supra note 11, pp. 24–25.

53. Federal Register, supra note 48, p. 69297-69298.

54. To be capable of absorbing the bank's losses, the terms of the subordinated debt would have to provide that the bank's failure to pay dividends on its stock or interest on its subordinated debt would not constitute an event of default.

55. "The Feasibility and Desirability of Mandatory Subordinated Debt." Report to Congress by Board of Governors of the Federal Reserve System and the United States Department of the Treasury, December 2008, p. 56. See also, Douglas D. Evanoff and Larry D. Wall, "Subordinated Debt and Bank Capital Reform." Federal Reserve Bank of Atlanta Working Paper 2000-24, November 2000, pp. 49–50.

56. Luc Laeven and Giovanni Majnon, "Loan Loss Provisions and Slowdowns." Federal Reserve Bank of Boston, web site, March 14, 2002, Abstract. www.bos.frb.org/bankinfo/conevent/slowdown/laeven_majnoni.pdf.

57. Adair Turner, *The Turner Review: A Regulatory Response to the Global Banking Crisis*. March 2009, p. 63.

58. Thomas Catan and Jonathan House, "Spain's Bank Capital Cushions Offer a Model to Policy Makers." *Wall Street Journal*, November 10, 2008, p. A12.

59. Victor Mallet, "Spain's lenders see salvation in mergers." *Financial Times*, March 30, 2009, p. 16.

60. "Inadequate." *Economist*, March 12, 2009, online edition.

61. Larry D. Wall and Timothy W. Koch, "Bank Loan-Loss Accounting: A Review of Theoretical and Empirical Evidence." *Federal Reserve Bank of Atlanta Economic Review*, Second Quarter 2000, p. 1.

62. Michael H. Sutton, "Current Developments in Financial Reporting." Speech presented to the 1997 Conference of Banks and Savings Institutions of American Institute of Certified Public Accountants, Washington, D.C. November 7, 1997. www.sec.gov/news/speech/speecharchive/1997/spch195.txt.

63. Basel II counts banks large loan loss reserves as Tier 2 capital. This applies to up to 1.25 percent of risk weighted assets for small banks using the standardized approach, and up to 0.6 percent of risk weighted assets for large banks using the advanced approach. *Basel II: International Convergence of Capital Measurement and Capital Standards: A Revised Framework—Comprehensive Version*. Bank for International Settlements, June 2006, pp. 15–16.

64. Statement by Timothy Geithner U.S. Treasury Secretary before the U.S. House of Representatives Committee on Financial Services, March 26, 2009. See Treasury White Paper, supra note 11, p. 31.

65. The contingency reserve would be reported below the line on the bank's income statement and would be kept in a separate account on its balance sheet similar to the account currently used for OIC (other included income).

66. Roddy Boyd, "The last days of Bear Stearns." *Fortune*, March 31, 2008, online at CNNmoney.com

67. "Financial Reform: A Framework for Financial Stability." Group of 30, January 2009, p. 13. See Treasury White Paper, supra note 11, p. 28.

68. Treasury White Paper, supra note 11, p. 24.

69. Several academics have suggested that banks sell "reverse convertible debentures," which would automatically convert into common shares when a bank's market value falls. Mark J. Flannery, "No Pain, No Gain?" in Chapter 5, *Capital Adequacy Beyond Basel: Banking Securities and Insurance*. Hal S. Scott (Ed.) Oxford, UK: Oxford University Press, 2005. In practice, it is unclear if private investors would buy such a security since it would lose any of its priority in insolvency just as the bank experiences a serious decline.

Chapter 7: Impact on Short-Term Lending

1. The Reserve Fund, "A Statement Regarding the Primary Fund." Press Release, September 16, 2008. Online at www.ther.com/pdfs/Press%20Release%202008_0916.pdf.

2. Quoted in Nick Paumgarten, "The Death of Kings." *New Yorker*, May 18, 2009, p. 45.

3. Federal Deposit Insurance Corporation, "FDIC Announces Plan to Free Up Bank Liquidity." Press Release, October 14, 2008. www.fdic.gov/news/news/press/2008/pr08100.html.

4. Federal Reserve, Press Release, March 18, 2009 www.federalreserve.gov/newsevents/press/monetary/20090318a.htm.

5. Ibid.

6. Ben Bernanke, "Deflation: Making Sure 'It' Doesn't Happen Here." Remarks before the National Economists Club, Washington D.C., November 21, 2002. (emphasis in original).

7. Congressional Budget Office, "The Budget and Economic Outlook: An Update." August 2009.

8. Alan J. Auerbach and William G. Gale, "The Economic and Fiscal Crisis: 2009 and Beyond." Working Paper. Available online at www.econ.berkeley.edu/~auerbach/fiscal_future.pdf.

9. "The 2% Illusion." *Wall Street Journal*, February 27, 2009, p. A12.

10. Geoff Dyer and Alan Beattie, "Wen calls on US to offer fiscal guarantees." *Financial Times*, March 14, 2009, p. 1.

11. Glen Somerville, "Geithner tells China its dollar assets are safe." *Reuters*, June 1, 2009.

12. Weekend Interview With Richard Fisher, "Don't Monetize the Debt." *Wall Street Journal*, May 23–24, 2009, p. A9.

13. Fredric S. Mishkin, "The Fed Still has Plenty of Ammunition." *Wall Street Journal*, December 15, 2008, p. A19.

14. Compare Benjamin Friedman, "Why the Federal Reserve Should Not Adopt Inflation Targeting." *International Finance* 7:1, 2004, pp. 129–136; with F. S. Miskin, "Why the Federal Reserve Should Adopt Inflation Targeting." *International Finance* 7:1, 2004, pp. 117–127; and Andrew T. Levin, Fabio M. Natalucci, and Jeremy M. Piger, "The Macroeconomic effects of Inflation Targeting." Federal Reserve Bank of St. Louis, 2003.

15. "Term Auction Facility." Board of Governors of the Federal Reserve System web site, www.federalreserve.gov/monetarypolicy/taf.htm.

16. "Term Securities Lending Facility." Board of Governors of the Federal Reserve System web site www.federalreserve.gov/monetarypolicy/tslf.htm.

17. "Primary Dealer Credit Facility." Board of Governors of the Federal Reserve System web site, www.federalreserve.gov/monetarypolicy/pdcf.htm.

18. Quoted in William D. Cohan, *House of Cards*. New York, NY: Doubleday, 2009, p. 115.

19. "Asset-Backed Commercial Paper Money Market Mutual Fund Liquidity Facility." Board of Governors of the Federal Reserve System web site, www.federalreserve.gov/monetarypolicy/abcpmmmf.htm.

20. "Money Market Investor Funding Facility." Board of Governors of the Federal Reserve System web site, www.federalreserve.gov/monetarypolicy/mmiff.htm. This facility has not yet gone into operation as of June 1, 2009.

21. "Commercial Paper Funding Facility." Board of Governors of the Federal Reserve System web site www.federalreserve.gov/monetarypolicy/cpff.htm The highest rated commercial paper is designated as one of the following: A-1 / P-1 / F-1.

22. "Term Asset-Backed Securities Loan Facility." Board of Governors of the Federal Reserve System web site, www.federalreserve.gov/monetarypolicy/talf.htm. Also, Federal Reserve Press Release, February 10, 2009.

23. After the FDIC and the Treasury take $15 billion in losses, the Fed would absorb further losses through a non-recourse loan, subject to fees and loss sharing by Citigroup. Joint Statement by Treasury, Federal Reserve and the FDIC on Citigroup (Nov. 23, 2008).

24. As of May 7, 2009, LIBOR was below 1 percent. www.bloomberg.com/markets/rates/keyrates.html (Accessed on May 7, 2009).

25. Speech by Mervyn King, Governor of the Bank of England to the CBI, Institute of Directors, Leeds Chamber of Commerce and Yorkshire Forward at the Royal Armouries, Leeds, October 21, 2008, p.5 of transcript. Bank of England web site www.bankofengland.co.uk/publications/speeches/2008/speech362.pdf

26. Federal Reserve H.4.1 Statistical Releases October 25, 2007 and June 11, 2009.

27. Kenneth N. Kuttner, "The Federal Reserve as Lender of Last Resort during the Panic of 2008." Department of Economics, Williams College, December 14, 2008, pp. 10–11.

28. Charles I. Plosser, President and Chief Executive Officer, Federal Reserve Bank of Philadelphia, "A Perspective on the Outlook, Output Gaps, and Price Stability." Presented at Money Marketeers, The Down Town Association, New York, May 21, 2009. www.phil.frb.org/publications/speeches/plosser/2009/05-21-09_money-marketeers.cfm.

29. Federal Reserve and Treasury Joint Press Release, March 23, 2009.

30. Treasury White Paper, *Financial Regulatory Reform: A New Foundation: Rebuilding Financial Supervision and Regulation.* June 2009, pp. 78–79.

31. Federal Reserve Statistical Release H.4.1 March 26, 2009, in addition to publically available information on Federal Reserve purchases and guarantees; also, Bob Ivry and Mark Pittman, "Financial Rescue Nears GDP as Pledges Top $12.8 Trillion." Bloomberg.com, March 31, 2009.

32. Craig Torres, "Fed Considers More Disclosure on Emergency Programs." Bloomberg.com, April 15, 2009; see also Pittman, "Court Orders Federal Reserve to Disclose Emergency Loan Details," Bloomberg.com, August 25, 2009.

33. Rich Miller and Craig Torres, "Bernanke Success May Come at Cost of Congress Curbing Fed Power." Bloomberg.com, June 12, 2009.

34. Federal Deposit Insurance Corporation Press Release, "FDIC Announces Plan to Free Up Bank Liquidity." October 14, 2008. www.fdic.gov/news/news/press/2008/pr08100.html.

35. Federal Deposit Insurance Corporation Press Release, "Treasury, Federal Reserve and the FDIC Provide Assistance to Bank of America." January 16, 2009. www.fdic.gov/news/news/press/2009/pr09004.html.

36. Federal Deposit Insurance Corporation FIL-14-2009, "Extension of Temporary Liquidity Guarantee Program," March 18, 2009. www.fdic.gov/news/news/financial/2009/fil09014.html.

37. Richard A. Posner, "The Economy: Blowing Bubbles" Hoover Institution Stanford University www.hoover.org/publications/digest/22730444.html citing Becker-Posner Blog on December 23, 2007.

38. Damian Paletta, "FDIC Chief Raps Rescue for Helping Banks Over Homeowners." *Wall Street Journal*, October 16, 2008.

39. "President Obama and Secretary Geithner Announce Plans to Unlock Credit for Small Businesses" White House Press Release, March 16, 2009, www.whitehouse .gov/the_press_office/President-Obama-and-Secretary-Geithner-Announce-Plans-to-Unlock-Credit-for-Small/.

40. Federal Reserve Board, "Source-of-Strength" Policy, Statement No. 17, May 18, 1987.

41. Kellie Geressy, "Investors Buy $17.25 Billion in Banks' Bonds." *Wall Street Journal*, November 28, 2008, p. C2.

42. Any industrial company could become a thrift holding company before 1999 by acquiring only one thrift; all these thrift holding companies were grandfathered by the Gramm-Leach-Bliley Act of 1999. Since 1999, a company acquiring a thrift or a bank would generally have to limit its activities to financial services to qualify as a financial services holding company.

43. General Electric, "FDIC approves GE for debt-guarantee program." *GE Reports*, November 14, 2008. Available online at www.gereports.com/fdic-approves-ge-for-debt-guarantee-program/.

44. Scott Patterson, "Life Insurers Are Finding Their Fates Tied to Stocks." *Wall Street Journal*, March 31, 2009, p. C1.

45. Evan G. Greenberg, "The Insurance Industry Doesn't Need Subsidies." *Wall Street Journal*, October 31, 2008, p. A15.

46. Peter Eavis, "Life After Debt for Wall Street." *Wall Street Journal*, December 3, 2008, p. C14.

47. "Resurrection on Wall Street." *Barron's*, March 16, 2009, p. 21.

48. Trevor A. Schauenberg, "GE Capital Letter to Investors." www.ge.com/pdf/investors/GE_Capital%20Letter_11122008.pdf.

49. Marcus Walker, Sara Schaefer Munoz, and David Gauthier-Villars, "Next Move in European Bailouts: Paying for Them" *Wall Street Journal*, October 14, 2008, p. A3.

50. Charles Forelle and Joellen Perry "Drawing on Experience of Past Rescue, Sweden Outlines Bank-Bailout Plan." *Wall Street Journal*, October 21, 2008, p. A5.

51. Ian Austen, "Wary of Finding its Banks at a Disadvantage, Canada Decides to Guarantee Loans." *New York Times*, October 24, 2008, p. B4.

52. New York University Stern School of Business, *Restoring Financial Stability: How to Repair a Failed System*. Viral v. Acharya and Matthew Richardson (Eds.). Hoboken, NJ: John Wiley & Sons, 2009, pp. 331–333. The five money center banks are: Bank of America, Citigroup, Goldman Sachs, JPMorgan Chase, and Morgan Stanley.

53. To facilitate comparison, the price of this bond has been recalculated relative to the three-year Treasury bond.

54. Robin Sidel and Deborah Solomon, "Treasury Lets 10 Banks Repay $68 Billion in Bailout Cash." *Wall Street Journal*, June 10, 2009, p. A1.

55. Mark Gongloff, "Banks Profit from US Guarantee." *Wall Street Journal*, July 27, p. C1.

Chapter 8: Insuring Deposits and Money Market Funds

1. Federal Deposit Insurance Corporation Press Release, October 7, 2008. www.fdic .gov/news/news/press/2008/pr08093.html.

2. U.S. Department of the Treasury Press Release hp-1161, "Treasury Announces Temporary Guaranty Program for Money Market Funds." September 29, 2008. www .treasury.gov/press/releases/hp1161.htm.

3. FDIC Consumer News Winter 2007/2008 Update www.fdic.gov/consumers/consumer/ news/cnwin0708/limits.html.

4. "Financial Institution Letters—FDIC Deposit Insurance Coverage" FDIC.gov, October 3, 2008. www.fdic.gov/news/news/financial/2008/fil08102a.html.

5. James B. Thomson, "Raising the Deposit-Insurance Limits: A Bad Idea Whose Time Has Come?" Federal Reserve Bank of Cleveland Economic Commentary, April 15, 2000. www .clevelandfed.org/research/commentary/2000/0415.htm.

6. Federal Deposit Insurance Corporation, "75th Anniversary Confidence and Stability Statement." www.fdic.gov/anniversary/about.html.

7. U.S. Department of Labor CPI Inflation Calculator www.bls.gov/data/inflation_ calculator.htm.

8. Thomson, supra note 5. Thompson notes that "mean deposit levels are a high-biased esti-mate of the balances held by the typical small depositor, being skewed by a small number of high-balance accounts."

9. Including accounts over the FDIC's $100,000 threshold, the average account balance of nonbusiness, nonretirement accounts in the United States was $12,756 in June of 2008. Not including accounts above the FDIC's insurance limit, the average nonbusiness, nonretirement account, was $5,837 in June of 2008. Federal Deposit Insurance Corporation, "Statistics on Depository Institutions Report." www2.fdic.gov/sdi/main4.asp

10. Office of the Press Secretary, The White House, "Reforms for American Homeowners and Consumers." May 20, 2009, pp. 2–3.

11. The FDIC guarantee program also covers NOW accounts paying .5 percent or less in interest. FDIC, Temporary Guarantee Program: Frequently asked questions (January 12, 2009).

12. Alan S. Blinder and R. Glenn Hubbard, "Blanket Deposit Insurance is a Bad Idea." *Wall Street Journal*, October 15, 2008, p. A17.

13. Eric Lipton, "F.D.I.C. Increases Fees to Insure Bank Deposits." *New York Times*, February 28, 2009, p. B4.

14. Federal Deposit Insurance Corporation Press Release, "FDIC Extends Restoration Plan; Imposes Special Assessment." February 27, 2009. www.fdic.gov/news/news/press/2009/ pr09030.html.

15. Michael Crittenden, "FDIC Sets Fee Increase to Refill Its Coffers." *Wall Street Journal*, February 28–March 1, 2009, p. B2.

16. Damian Paletta, "Congress Raises FDIC Limits." *Wall Street Journal*, May 20, 2009, p. 16.

17. FDIC Press Release, "FDIC Adopts Final Rule Imposing a Special Assessment on Insured Depository Institutions." May 22, 2009.

18. James B. Thompson and Walker F. Todd. "Rethinking and Living with the Limits of Bank Regulation." *Cato Journal*, Vol. 9, No. 3, Winter 1990, 584; Eric Lipton and Martin Andrew, "For Banks, Wads of Cash and Loads of Trouble." *New York Times*, July 4, 2009, p. A1.

19. Damian Paletta,, "Banks are Failing Too Fast for Regulators." *Wall Street Journal*, January 23, 2009, p. C1.

20. Federal Deposit Insurance Corporation Press Release, "FDIC Announces Plan to Free Up Bank Liquidity: Creates New Program to Guarantee Bank Debt and Fully Insure Non-Interest Bearing Deposit Transaction Accounts." October 14, 2008. www.fdic.gov/news/news/press/2008/pr08100.html.

21. "The European Union's Week From Hell." *Economist*, October 11, 2008, p. 69.

22. Blinder and Hubbard, supra note 12, p. A17.

23. *Economist*, supra note 21 p. 69.

24. "Rescuing the Banks—But Will It Work?" *Economist*, October 18, 2008, p. 83.

25. "Asia and the Crisis—Here We Go Again" *Economist*, October 18, 2008, p. 51.

26. Keith Bradsher and Bettina Wassener, "HSBC Executive Calls Deposit Backing Unfair." *New York Times*, December 6, 2008, p. B3.

27. The highest quality money market instruments are rated A-1, P-1, or the equivalent, and the second highest rated money market instruments are rated A-2, P-2, or the equivalent.

28. 17 C.F.R. 270.2a-7 under the Investment Company Act of 1940 [15 USC 80a-1, et seq.].

29. Investment Company Institute, *2009 Investment Company Fact Book*, 49th edition, p. 146, Table 37.

30. Investment Company Institute, "Frequently Asked Questions about Money Market Mutual Funds." www.ici.org/my_ici/mmf_developments/faqs_money_funds

31. "In a recent survey of nearly two dozen fund companies, only three pledged to defend a $1 share price in their money market funds," reported Carole Gould for the *New York Times*. Gould, Carol, "Mutual Funds: Funds Watch; Three Funds That Won't 'Break Buck.'" *New York Times*, March 26, 1995, section 3 p. 7.

32. Securities and Exchange Commission, "Money Market Funds." www.sec.gov/answers/mfmmkt.htm.

33. Barbara Kiviat, "Feds Back Money Markets: Is Your Fund Safe?" *TIME*, September 19, 2008. Available online at www.time.com/time/business/article/0,8599,1842685,00.html.

34. Shefali Anand, "More Money-Market Funds Hit Trouble." *Wall Street Journal*, November 16, 2007, p. C2.

35. Henry Dubroff, "Mutual Fund's Failure Teaches a Lesson." *Denver Business Journal*, January 15, 1999, Online at http://denver.bizjournals.com/denver/stories/1999/01/18/newscolumn1.html?jst=cn_cn_lk.

36. Chuck Jaffe, "Cloud over money-market funds." MarketWatch.com, September 16, 2008. www.marketwatch.com/news/story/money-fund-breaks-buck-snaps/story.aspx?guid=%7b1AB6980B-6902-490C-A384-1D7B2C2479A1%7d&dist=msr_1.

37. Diya Gullapalli and Shefali Anand, "Bailout of Money Funds Seems to Stanch Outflow." WSJ.com, September 20, 2008. http://online.wsj.com/article/SB1221866 83086958875 .html?mod=article-outset-box.

38. Putnam, Press Release, September 18, 2008. https://content.putnam.com/shared/pdf/ prime_money_mkt_inst.pdf.

39. Ron Hauruni, "Putnam Liquidates $12 Billion Prime Money Market Fund." SeekingAlpha.com, September 19, 2008, http://seekingalpha.com/article/96301 -putnam-liquidates-12-billion-prime-money-market-fund.

40. John Brinsley and Rebecca Christie, "Treasury's Money Fund Insurance May End in 3 Months." Bloomberg.com, September 29, 2008. www.bloomberg.com/apps/news?pid=20 601213&refer=home&sid=a1Zwn.IvAPGg.

41. U. S. Department of the Treasury, Press Release, "Treasury Announces Extension of Temporary Guarantee Program for Money Market Funds." March 31,2009.

42. See, for example, Edward Yingling, "ABA Statement on Changes to Treasury Money Market Program." aba.com, September 21, 2008. www.aba.com/Press+Room/092108 MoneyMarketProgram.htm.

43. However, if a shareholder with an account of $50,000 at an insured money market fund on September 19, 2008, withdrew $10,000 on October 1, 2008 and then reinvested that same amount on October 10, 2008 in the same fund, the $50,000 would again be insured. United States Treasury Department, "Frequently Asked Questions about Treasury's Temporary Guaranty Program for Money Market Funds." Press Release HP-1163, September 29, 2008. www.treasury.gov/press/releases/hp1163.htm.

44. U.S. Treasury Department, "Treasury Announces Temporary Guarantee Program for Money Market Funds." September 19, 2008. www.treas.gov/press/releases/hp1161.htm.

45. "Virtually All Money Fund Families Now Covered by Treasury Guaranty." Crane Data, October 9, 2008 www.cranedata.com/archives/all-articles/1895/.

46. Daisy Maxey, "Low Treasury Yields Buffet Money Funds." *Wall Street Journal*, December 11, 2008, C11.

47. Jack Willoughby, "Money Funds Slowly Get Back on Their Feet." *Barron's*, December 8, 2008, p. 44.

48. ICI, supra note 29, p. 147, Table 38.

49. Investment Company Institute. "Trends in Mutual Fund Investing January 2009." ICI.org, February 26, 2009. (showing stock fund assets at $3.71 trillion).

50. Daisy Moxey, "Money Funds Begin to Cut U.S. Backing." *Wall Street Journal*, May 14, 2009, p. C9.

51. Investment Company Act Release 28807, June 30, 2009.

52. Sue Asci, Sue, "Treasury Money Funds are Turning Down New Cash from Investors." *Investmentnews*.com, January 11, 2009, www.investmentnews.com/apps/pbcs.dll/ article?AID=/20090111/REG/301119971/1030/MUTUALF

53. Ibid.

54. Quoted in Sam Mamudi, "Money market fund proposals cause a stir." *MarketWatch*, February 2, 2009. The Group of 30 is a private, nonprofit, international consulting body comprised of very senior representatives from the public and private sectors, as well as academia. www.group30.org/.

55. Group of 30, *Financial Reform: A Framework for Financial Stability*, January 15, 2009, p. 9.

56. "2008 Investment Company Fact Book." Investment Company Institute, 2008, pp. 11–12. www.icifactbook.org/.

57. My proposals to reduce the maturity of individual securities and the portfolio average go beyond those recommended by the Investment Company Institute.

58. I5 U.S.C.§ 80a Section 18 F (1) of the Investment Company Act.

59. Every fund in a mutual fund complex has cash on hand, but some will receive net inflows and others will face net outflows. If a prime fund faces net outflows, it may borrow cash from other funds in the complex under an interfund lending exemption. Such an exemption requires the independent directors to set a borrowing rate from the prime fund that is at least as high as the lending fund could have obtained from unrelated third parties for its short-term cash. Fidelity Investments was granted such an exemption. Investment Company Act of 1940 Release No. 28287.

60. "Success of Money Market Funds." Investment Company Institute Executive Summary. MFS is a member of the Institute, and I am a member of the Institute's board and executive committee.

61. Treasury White Paper, *Financial Regulatory Reform: A New Foundation: Rebuilding Financial Supervision and Regulation*. June 2009, pp. 38–39.

62. Report of the Money Market Working Group to Board of Governors of the Investment Company Institute, March 17, 2009, pp. 104–106. I am the Chairman of MFS Investment Management, which manages approximately $150 billion in assets, of which roughly 2 percent are in money market funds.

63. SEC No-Action Letter dated October 10, 2008. www.sec.gov//divisions/investment/noaction/2008/ici101008.htm.

64. To give a simple illustration, suppose a money market fund purchased commercial paper with a face value of $10 million 30 days before it matured at a price of $9,970,000. Under amortized accounting, the $30,000 discount would be gradually added to its purchase price at a rate of $1,000 per day for 30 days. This would be true under amortized accounting, even if the market quotation for this commercial paper was $9,965,000 three days after it was purchased by the money market fund.

65. For example, the issuer of the commercial paper with 30 days or fewer to maturity should be rated A-1, P-1 without being on credit watch.

Part III: Evaluating the Bailout Act of 2008 and Chapter 9: Why and How Treasury Recapitalized So Many Banks

1. Remarks by Secretary Henry M. Paulson, Jr. on the U.S. Economy, Housing and Capital Markets before the Washington Post 200 Lunch. May 16, 2008. www.treas.gov/press/releases/hp981.htm.

2. Quoted in Joe Nocera and Edmund L. Andrews, "Struggling to Keep Up as the Crisis Raced On." *New York Times*, October 23, 2008, p. A20.

3. Quoted in Brian Wingfield and Josh Zumbrun, "The Paulson Plan, Bad News for the Bailout." Forbes.com, September 23, 2008. www.forbes.com/2008/09/23/bailout-paulson-congress-biz-beltway-cx_jz_bw_0923bailout.html.

4. "Legislative Proposal for Treasury Authority to Purchase Mortgage-Related Assets." Available through the web site of Idaho Senator Mike Crapo. http://crapo.senate

.gov/issues/banking/documents/LEGISLATIVEPROPOSALFORTREASURY
AUTHORITY.doc.

5. Aaron Task, "Bailout on Trial: What Does Taxpayer Get Other than a $700B Bill?" *Yahoo Finance*, September 23, 2008, www.finance.yahoo.com.

6. Luke Mullins, "The Bailout Is Un-American." *The Home Front, US News and World Report*, September 23, 2008. www.usnews.com/blogs/the-home-front.

7. Information on the Emergency Economic Stabilization Act of 2008 can be found on the House Financial Services web site at http://financialservices.house.gov/eesa.html House495 and Senate roll call votes can be accessed through their respective web sites. www.clerk.house.gov and www.senate.gov/legislation.

8. Quoted in Nocera and Andrews, supra note 2, p. A20.

9. Federal Register Vol. 74, No. 113, "31 CFR Part 30. TARP Standards for Compensation and Corporate Governance; Interim Final Rule." June 15, 2009, pp. 28394–28423.

10. Congressional Oversight Panel, "February Oversight Report: Valuing Treasury's Acquisitions." February 6, 2009, p. 5.

11. U.S. Department of Treasury, "Treasury Announces Participation in Citigroup's Exchange Offering." February 27, 2009. http://treasury.gov/press/releases/tg41.htm.

12. Alan Roth and Robin Sidel, "YRC to Apply For Bailout Funds." *Wall Street Journal*, May 15, 2009, p. B3.

13. David Enrich, Robin Sidel, and Deborah Solomon, "Fed Sees Up to $599 Billion in Bank Losses." *Wall Street Journal*, May 8, 2009, A1.

14. John B. Taylor, "The Financial Crisis and the Policy Response." Working Paper 14631, National Bureau of Economic Research, Cambridge, MA, January 2009, p. 16.

15. Charlie Gasparino, "JPM's Dimon Ready to Give Back TARP Money?" *CNBC*.com, February 18, 2009. www.cnbc.com/id/29264721.

16. Treasury Press Release, "Treasury Announces $68 Billion in Expected CPP Repayments." June 9, 2009.

17. United States Treasury Troubled Asset Relief Program Report to the Congress, January 2009, sec. VI. www.treas.gov/press/releases/reports/0010508105_a_report.pdf.

18. Remarks by U.S. Treasury Secretary Geithner Before the Independent Community Bankers of America Annual Washington Policy Summit, Washington D.C., May 13, 2009.

19. Deborah Solomon, "Nine Banks to Repay TARP Money." *Wall Street Journal*, June 9, 2009, p. C3.

20. Quoted in Deborah Solomon, "More Banks to TARP: Thanks, But No Thanks." *Wall Street Journal*, January 31, 2009, p. B3.

21. Louise Story, "Some Bank's Want to Return Government Money." *New York Times*, February 11, 2009, p. B3.

22. U.S. Department of the Treasury, "Treasury Announces TARP Investment in GMAC." December 29, 2008, www.treas.gov/press/releases/hp1335.htm.

23. Michael J. de la Merced, "CIT Is Said To Approve Deal To Avert Bankruptcy." *New York Times*, July 20, 2009, p. B1.

24. Scott Patterson, Deborah Solomon, and Leslie Scism, "U.S. to Offer Aid to Life Insurers." *Wall Street Journal*, April 8, 2009, p. A1.

25. Leslie Scism, Michael R Crittenden, Matthew Karnitschnig, and Matthias Rieker, "Insurers Buy Banks in Effort to Get Aid." *Wall Street Journal*, November 18, 2008, p. A18; Edmund L. Andrews and Eric Dash, "Insurers Are Getting in Line for Piece of Federal Bailout." *New York Times*, October 25, 2008, p. B1.

26. Andrew Dowell and Jamie Heller, "U.S. Slates $22 Billion for Insurers From TARP." *Wall Street Journal*, May 15, 2009, p. A1.

27. Evan G. Greenberg, "The Insurance Industry Doesn't Need Subsidies." *Wall Street Journal*, October 31, 2008, p. A15.

28. Patterson, Solomon, and Scism, supra note 24, p. A4.

29. Liam Plevan, and Damian Paletta, "Insurers Back Away from TARP." *Wall Street Journal*, May 16–17, 2009, p. B1.

30. Merrill Lynch was also there, but was not directly recapitalized because it was acquired by Bank of America.

31. Former U.S. Treasury Secretary Hank Paulson, "CEO Talking Points." Prepared for the October 13, 2008 meeting and obtained by Judicial Watch under the Freedom of Information Act and released on May 13, 2009. Available through Judicial Watch web site at www .judicialwatch.org/news/2009/may/judicial-watch-forces-release-bank-bailout-documents.

32. U.S. Department of Treasury, "TARP Capital Purchase Program Senior Preferred Stock and Warrants: Summary of Senior Preferred Terms." www.treas.gov/press/releases/reports/document5hp1207.pdf.

33. David S. Scharfstein and Jeremy C. Stein, "This Bailout Doesn't Pay Dividends." *New York Times*, October 21, 2008, p. A29.

34. David Barstow and Mike McIntire, "Calls for Clarity in New Bailout for U.S. Banks." *New York Times*, February 10, 2009, p. B1.

35. David Enrich, Michael R. Crittenden, and Marice Tamman, "Bank Lending Continues to Decline." *Wall Street Journal*, April 20, 2009, p. A-1.

36. Quoted in Eric Lipton and Ron Nixon, "A Bank With Its Own Woes Lends Only a Trickle of Bailout." *New York Times*, January 14, 2009, p. A1.

37. John Coates and David Scharfstein, "The Bailout Is Robbing Banks." *New York Times*, February 18, 2009, p. A27.

38. Ibid.

39. Congressional Oversight Panel, supra note 10, p. 7.

40. Ben White, "Deal Seen as a Sign of Confidence." *New York Times*, September 24, 2008, p. A1. For details of Treasury's preferred stock purchases see, Congressional Oversight Panel, supra note10.

41. Andrew Barry, "Scoring Bargains With Preferred Shares." *Barron's*, June 15, 2009, p. 22.

42. Marina V.N. Whitman, "Economic Policy Will Have to Be Very Agile." *Wall Street Journal*, January 27, 2009, p. A13.

43. Quoted in Deborah Solomon and David Enrich, "U.S. Rescue Fund Is Likely to Foster Bank Takeovers." *Wall Street Journal*. October 21, 2008, p. A3.

44. Joe Nocera, "So When Will Banks Give Loans?" *New York Times*, October 25, 2008, p. B1.

45. Robin Sidel and Carolyn Cui, "J.P. Morgan Pursues Other Firms' Castoffs." *Wall Street Journal*, December 24, 2008, p. C2.

46. Internal Revenue Service Note 2008-78, September 30, 2008; see also Internal Revenue Service Note 2008-83, October 20, 2008.

47. Jesse Drucker, "Obscure Tax Breaks Increase Cost of Financial Rescue." *Wall Street Journal*, October 18, 2008, p. A3.

48. Jesse Drucker, "PNC Stands to Gain From Tax Ruling." *Wall Street Journal*, October 30, 2008, p. C1.

49. Drucker, supra note 47.

50. U.S. Department of the Treasury, "Secretary Geithner Introduces Financial Stability Plan." February 10, 2009, www.treas.gov/press/releases/tg18.htm.

51. For more details on the Financial Stability Plan see "Financial Stability Plan Fact Sheet." Available at www.financialstability.gov/docs/fact-sheet.pdf.

52. Eric Dash, "10 Large Banks Allowed to Exit U.S. Aid Programs." *New York Times*, June 10, 2009, p. A3.

53. Quoted in Andrew Clark, "Bank of America seals $50bn deal for Merrill Lynch." *Guardian.co.uk*, September 15, 2008.

54. E-mails presented at U.S. House of Representatives Committee on Oversight and Government Reform, Hearing on, "Bank of America and Merrill Lynch: How Did a Private Deal Turn into a Federal Bailout?" June 11, 2009. Available online at http://groc.edgeboss.net/download/groc/transfer/fed.e-mails.pdf.

55. Ibid.

56. Ibid.

57. Liz Rappaport and Dan Fitzpatrick, "Cuomo Urges Probe of B of A Deal Pressure." *Wall Street Journal*, April 29, 2009, p. C1.

58. Liz Rappaport, "Testimony Sheds More Light on Lewis's Perspective." *Wall Street Journal*, April 29, 2009, p. C3.

59. Quoted in Liz Rappaport, "Lewis Testifies US Urged Silence on the Deal." *Wall Street Journal*, April 23, 2009, p. A1.

60. Heidi Moore, "The Street Smarts of Bank of America's Ken Lewis." *WSJ Deal Journal*, January 16, 2009. It is now unclear whether this guarantee was actually issued. Dwight Cass, Anthony Currie, and John Foley, "An Unsigned Deal Could be Costly." *New York Times*, July 14, 2009, B2.

61. Michael J. de la Merced and Louise Story, "Nearly 700 at Merrill in Million-Dollar Club." *New York Times*, February 12, 2009, p. B1.

62. Asked to approve the settlement, Judge Rakoff questioned the adequacy of the $33 million fine paid by the Bank of America. Jess Bravin, "Judge Rips SEC on BofA Pact" *Wall Street Journal*, August 26, 2009, p. C3.

63. U.S. Department of the Treasury, "Joint Statement by Treasury, Federal Reserve and the FDIC on Citigroup." November 23, 2008, www.treas.gov/press/releases/hp1287.htm. For more details, see Treasury's "Summary of Terms: Eligible Asset Guarantee." November 23, 2008. www.treas.gov/press/releases/reports/cititermsheet_112308.pdf.

64. Congressional Oversight Panel, supra note 10, pp. 7–10.

65. David E. Sanger, "Nationalization Gets a New, Serious Look." *New York Times*, January 26, 2009, p. A1.

66. Facts Sheet, supra note 51, p. 2.

67. Andrew Bary, "Fixing the Banks." *Barron's*, March 2, 2009, p. 23.

68. David Enrich, Damian Paletta, and Randall Smith, "Citi Deal Clears Way for Greater U.S. Sway." *Wall Street Journal*, June 9, 2009, p. C1.

69. Federal Reserve, "The Supervisory Capital Assessment Program: Overview of Results." May 7, 2009, p. 3.

70. Krishna Guha, Tom Braithwate, and Peter Thal Larsen, "US wants hands-off role after stress tests." *Financial Times*, May 8, 2009, p. 1.

71. The White House Briefing Room, "Briefing by White House Press Secretary Robert Gibbs, 2/20/2009." February 20, 2009, www.whitehouse.gov/the_press_office/Briefing-by-White-House-Press-Secretary-Robert-Gibbs-2-20-2009/.

72. Deborah Solomon, "New Preferred Shares to Bolster Balance Sheets." *Wall Street Journal*, May 7, 2009, p. A2.

73. William M. Isaac, "Bank Nationalization Isn't the Answer." *Wall Street Journal*, February 24, 2009, p. A13.

74. David Enrich and Damian Paletta, "U.S. Ratchets Up Citi Oversight." *Wall Street Journal*, December 17, 2008, p. C1.

75. Dan Fitzpatrick, "After Uproar, Wells Fargo Calls Off Trip to Las Vegas." *Wall Street Journal*, February 4, 2009, p. C1.

76. Bank Holding Company Act § 225.144 Policy statement on equity investments in banks and bank holding companies. www.federalreserve.gov/newsevents/press/bcreg/bcreg20080922b1.pdf.

77. Ibid.

78. Henry Sender and Francesco Guerrera, "US Moves to Spur Bank Buyouts." *Financial Times*, June 13–14, 2009, p. 1.

79. FDIC, Final Statement of Policy on Qualifications for Failed Bank Acquisitions, attachment to FDIC Press Release 152-2009 (August 26, 2009).

80. Bettina Wassener, "Singapore's Sovereign Fund Loses 31% of Its Portfolio." *New York Times*, February 11, 2009, p. B2.

81. U.S. Department of the Treasury Committee on Foreign Investment in the United States (CFIUS), www.ustreas.gov/offices/international-affairs/cfius/.

Chapter 10: Increasing Lending Volumes and Removing Toxic Assets

1. "Financial Stability Plan Fact Sheet." Available at www.financialstability.gov/docs/fact-sheet.pdf.

2. Federal Reserve Statistical Release: Z1 Flow of Funds Accounts of the United States, March 12, 2009; G19 Consumer Credit, March 6, 2009.

3. See Chapter 3.

4. Deborah Solomon, "Geithner Banks on Private Cash." *Wall Street Journal*, March 23, 2009, p. A1.

5. U.S. Treasury Department Press Release, "Treasury Department Releases Details on Public Private Partnership Investment Program." March 23, 2009. www.ustreas.gov/press/releases/tg65.htm.

6. Victoria Ivashina and David Scharfstein, "Bank Lending During the Financial Crisis of 2008." July 30, 2009, EFA 2009 Bergen Meetings Paper, Abstract.

7. V.V. Chari, Lawrence Christiano, and Patrick J. Kehoe, "Facts and Myths about the Financial Crisis of 2008." *Federal Reserve Bank of Minneapolis Research Department*, October 2008, Fig. 2A.

8. David Enrich and Dan Fitzpatrick, "Loans Shrink as Fear Lingers." *Wall Street Journal*, July 27, 2009, p. A1.

9. Ethan Cohen-Cole, Ethan, Burcu Duygan-Bump, Jose Fillat, and Judit Montoriol-Garriga, "Looking behind the aggregates: A reply to "Facts and Myths about the Financial Crisis of 2008." *Federal Reserve Bank of Boston Quantitative Analysis Unit*, November 12, 2008, p. 3.

10. Ibid, Figure 1A.

11. Sudeep Reddy, "Homeowner Refinance in Droves Unseen Since '03." April 23, 2009, p. A4.

12. Saskia Scholtes and Chrystia Freeland, "Refinancing Offers Prospects of $18bn Savings for Homeowners." *Financial Times*, May 4, 2009, p. 1.

13. Federal Reserve Press Release, "Treasury and Federal Reserve announce launch of Term Asset-Backed Securities Loan Facility (TALF)." March 3, 2009.

14. Liz Rappaport, "TALF is Reworked After Investors Balk." *Wall Street Journal*, March 14–15, 2009, p. B4.

15. Federal Reserve Bank of New York, "Term Asset-Backed Loan Facility: Frequently Asked Questions." www.newyorkfed.org/markets/talf_faq.html.

16. The Fed now permits legacy CMBS, issued before January 1, 2009, to be legible collateral under the TALF program. CMBS stands for Commercial Mortgage-backed Securities. Federal Reserve Press Release, May 19, 2009.

17. Edmund Andrews, "Lender's Role for Fed Makes Some Uneasy." *New York Times*, June 13, 2009, p. A1.

18. Anusha Shrivastava, "Investors Back Away From Fed's TALF" *Wall Street Journal*, April, 2009, p. C8.

19. "Big Government Fights Back." *Economist*, January 31, 2009, p. 80.

20. U.S. Department of the Treasury, "Legacy Loans Program: Summary of Terms." March 23, 2009. www.treas.gov/press/releases/reports/legacy_loans_terms.pdf U.S. Treasury Department Press Release, "Treasury Provides Updated Guidance on Legacy Securities Public-Private Investment Program." April 6, 2009.

21. James Keller, "How Not to Price Toxic Bonds." *Barron's*, April 6, 2009, p. 41.

22. Scott Lanman and Craig Torres, "Fed Struggling to Win Over Investors Wary of 'Sharks' in TALF." Bloomberg.com April 3, 2009.

23. "FASB Issues Final Staff Positions to Improve Guidance and Disclosures on Fair Value Measurements and Impairments." April 9, 2009. at www.fasb.org/news/nr040909.shtml). In fact, the FDIC put on hold its legacy loan program during June of 2009.

24. For the purpose of illustration, 70 percent is used as a hypothetical percentage. In practice, this percentage could also be 80 percent or 60 percent.

25. Eugene A. Ludwig, "Thumbs Up for the Citigroup Bailout." *Wall Street Journal*, November 25, 2008, p. A13.

26. Glenn Hubbard, Hal Scott, and Luis Zingales, "From Awful to Merely Bad." *Wall Street Journal*, February 7, 2009, p. A11.

27. First American Core Logic, Summary of Second Quarter Negative Equity Data (August 13, 2009).

28. Peter Coy, "Project Lifeline: A Few Feet Shy." *BusinessWeek Online*, February 15, 2008.

29. Board of Governors of the Federal Reserve System, "Governor Randall S. Kroszner Testimony: Federal Housing Administration Housing Stabilization and Homeownership Act." April 9, 2008. www.federalreserve.gov/newsevents/testimony/kroszner20080409a.htm.

30. Tami Luhby, "Investors to Buy IndyMac—$13.9B." *CNNmoney.com*, January 2, 2009. http://money.cnn.com/2009/01/02/news/companies/indymac/index.htm.

31. Alan Zibel, "Gov't launches sweeping new loan aid effort." *Associated Press*, November 11, 2008.

32. Damian Paletta, Jessica Holzer, and Ruth Simon, "U.S. Steps Up Help for Homeowners." *Wall Street Journal*, November 12, 2008, p. A3.

33. Edmund L. Andrews, "White House Scales Back a Mortgage Relief Plan." *New York Times*, November 12, 2008, p. B1.

34. Ibid.

35. Carolyn Said, "HUD says lenders working to aid homeowners." SFGate.com, October 21, 2008.

36. House Financial Services Committee, Summary of S. 896, The Helping Families Save Their Homes Act of 2009, May 19, 2009.

37. Greenwich Financial Services v. Countrywide Financial Corp., 08 Civ. 11343 (S.D.N.Y., 2009).

38. U.S. Department of the Treasury, "Homeowner Affordability and Stability Plan: Fact Sheet." www.treasury.gov/initiatives/eesa/homeowner-affordability-plan/FactSheet.pdf.

39. Ibid.

40. Ibid.

41. Ibid. The first and second mortgages on the same home are often owned by different parties and may be handled by different mortgage servicers. This conflict is likely to lead to resistance in getting all parties to agree on equitable loan modifications to both first and second lien loan providers. To overcome that resistance, the Treasury's plan was revised to require mortgage servicers to modify the second mortgage when the first is modified. The government will share the costs of reducing the interest on the second mortgage and pay an additional fee to the mortgage servicer.

42. Ibid.

43. John Geanakoplos and Susan Koniak, "Matters of Principal." *New York Times*, March 5, 2009, p. A27; Stan Liebowitz, "New Evidence on the Foreclosure Crisis." *Wall Street Journal*, July 3–5, 2009, p. A13.

44. Ruth Simon, "Study Buoys Mortgage Modification." *Wall Street Journal*, April 4–5, 2009, p. B2.

45. "Up and Down Wall Street." *Barron's*, July 13, 2009, p. 9.

46. Congressional Oversight Panel, "Foreclosure Crisis: Working Towards a Solution." March 6, 2009, Chart 10, pp. 28-29.

47. Carrick Mollenkamp, "Mortgage Modifying Fails to Halt Defaults." *Wall Street Journal*, May 26, 2009, p. C3.

48. Glenn A. Hubbard and Chris Mayer, "First, Let's Stabilize Home Prices." *Wall Street Journal*, October 2, 2008, p. A19. See also Feldstein, Martin, "How to Stop the Mortgage Crisis." *Wall Street Journal*, March 7, 2009, p. A15.

49. Elizabeth Williamson and Ruth Simon, "Plan to Cut Foreclosure Rate Clears Key Hurdle." *Wall Street Journal*, January 9, 2009, p. A1.

50. Todd J. Zywicki, "Don't Let Judges Tear Up Mortgage Contracts." *Wall Street Journal*, February 13, 2009, p. A13.

51. U.S. Courts, The Federal Judiciary Press Release "Bankruptcy Filings Up in March." June 3, 2008. www.uscourts.gov/Press_Releases/2008/BankruptcyFilingsMar2008.cfm.

52. Adam J. Levitin and Joshua Goodman, "The Effect of Bankruptcy Strip-Down on Mortgage Markets." *Georgetown University Law Center*. February 6, 2008, quote in abstract.

53. Williamson and Simon, supra note 49.

Chapter 11: Limiting Executive Compensation and Improving Boards of Directors

1. Leo Hindery Jr., "Why We Need to Limit Executive Compensation." www.businessweek.com, November 4, 2008.

2. Mercer Consulting, "Study on US CEO Compensation Trend." May 15, 2008.

3. Eric Dash, "Has the Exit Sign Ever Looked So Good?" *New York Times*, April 8, 2007, p. 6.

4. Gretchen Morgenson, "Gimme Back Your Paycheck." *New York Times*, February 22, 2009, p. 1.

5. Martha Graybow, "Lehman's Fund Suffers Wealth Hit As Shares Fall." *Reuters*, September 12, 2008.

6. 110th Congress of the United States of America, *Emergency Economic Stabilization Act of 2008*. October 3, 2008.

7. Elizabeth Williamson and Heidi Moore, "Rescue Was Sold Softly to the Street." *Wall Street Journal*, October 10, 2008, p. A4.

8. 111th Congress of the United States of America, *American Recovery and Reinvestment Act of 2009*.

9. Department of the Treasury, TARP Standards for Compensation and Corporate Governance, June, 15, 2009.

10. Another bill pending in Congress, the Grayson-Himes Pay for Performance Act of 2009, would further restrict executive compensation at financial institutions receiving federal capital.

11. Deficit Reductions Act of 1984, Sections 280G and 4999 of the Internal Revenue Code.

12. This resulted in an additional average severance payment to top executives almost $14 million just to cover the imposed excise tax. RiskMetrics Group, "Gilding Golden Parachutes." November 2008, p. 3.

13. Section 162(m) of the Internal Revenue Code.

14. Greg Hitt, Deborah Solomon, and Michael M. Phillips, "Treasury Relents on Key Points." *Wall Street Journal*, September 23, 2008. p. A3.

15. These compensation limits do not apply to sponsors, underwriters or borrowers under the Term Asset-Backed Securities Loan Facility, which lends government money to finance the purchase of top-rated domestic asset-backed securities.

16. Congressional Oversight Panel February Oversight Report. February 6, 2009, p. 5.

17. Ben White, "What Red Ink? Wall Street Paid Hefty Bonuses." *New York Times*, January 29, 2009. p. A1.

18. 110th Congress of the United States of America, *Emergency Economic Stabilization Act of 2008*. October 3, 2008. (H.R. 1424 §111(b)(2)(A)).

19. Sarbanes-Oxley Act of 2002, Section 304, July 20, 2002.

20. Either December 31, 2009, or when the financial institution redeems the preferred stock from the federal government for direct purchases or stock positions. In addition, TARP prohibits the making of a new agreement on golden parachute payments for auction purchases exceeding $300 million before the end of 2009, though not for direct asset purchases or meaningful stock positions by the federal government.

21. Jackie Calmes and Louise Story, "Outcry Builds in Washington for Recovery of AIG Bonuses." *New York Times*, March 18, 2009 page A1.

22. Aaron Luccheti, "Morgan Stanley Boosts Salaries As Its Bonuses Are Limited." *Wall Street Journal*, May 23–24, 2009, p. B1.

23. Lucian Bebchuck, "Congress Gets Punitive on Executive Pay." *Wall Street Journal*, February 17, 2009, page A15.

24. 111th Congress of the United States of America, *American Recovery and Reinvestment Act of 2009*. February 17, 2009, p. 406. H.R. 1–406(2)(g).

25. Deborah Solomon and Mark Maremont, "Stimulus Bill Puts Retroactive Pay Curb on Bailout Recipients." *Wall Street Journal*, February 14-15, 2009, p. A10.

26. The median CEO salary for Fortune 250 companies in 2006 was 67% higher at companies with the largest conflict of interest with the pay consultant—the highest ratio of nonexecutive compensation work to executive compensation work. U.S. House of Representatives Committee on Oversight and Government Reform, "Executive Pay: Conflicts of Interest Among Compensation Consultants." December, 2007. The Treasury Department has proposed legislation for all public companies that would require any compensation consultant used by the compensation committee to meet independence standards set by the SEC. Department of Treasury, Investor Protection Act of 2009, July 16, 2009, subtitle D, p. 4.

27. Statement by Treasury Secretary Geithner on compensation, June 10, 2009. On July 1, 2009, the SEC announced that the agency is proposing to increase disclosures for all publicly traded companies on compensation consultants, risk management and director qualifications. SEC Press Release 2009-147, July 1, 2009.

28. Marshall Eckblad, "Wells Fargo Skirts TARP To Raise Pay." *Wall Street Journal*, August 7, 2009, p. C3; Kate Kelly and Sara Schaefer Muñoz, "Banks Ramp Up Pay Packages to Top Talent." *Wall Street Journal*, July 16, 2009, p. C1.

29. For example, the House of Representatives (but not the Senate) has passed a bill imposing a 90 percent excise tax on executive bonuses paid by companies receiving more than $5 billion in federal aid. Greg Hitt and Aaron Luchhetti, "House Passes Bonus Tax Bill." *Wall Street Journal*, March 20, 2009, p. A1.

30. New York Attorney General Andrew Cuomo, "No Rhyme or Reason: The 'Heads I Win, Tails You Lose' Bank Bonus Culture." July 2009.

31. Jonathan D. Glater, "Stock Options Are Adjusted After Many Share Prices Fall." *New York Times*, March 21, 2009, p. B1.

32. Mark Maremont, "Firms Use Generous Formulas To Boost Bosses' Pensions." *Wall Street Journal*, January 23, 2009, p. A11.

33. 34th Annual Board of Directors Study, Korn/Ferry Institute, 2008, p. 5.

34. Peter Larsen, "Spain shows the way in better handling of risk management." *Financial Times*, May 4, 2009.

35. David Enrich, Robin Sidel, and Joann S. Lublin, "Grundhofer, O'Neill, Thompson Are Likely Nominees for Citi Board." *Wall Street Journal*, March 13, 2009 p. C3.

36. RiskMetrics Group, "Board Practices: Trends In Board Structure at S&P 1,500 Companies." December 17, 2008, p.1.

37. SEC Release No. 34-58367, August 15, 2008.

38. Robert C. Pozen, "Before You Split That CEO/Chair . . . " *Harvard Business Review*, April 2006. The SEC has recently proposed increased disclosure by all companies on leadership structure, rather than mandating a separation between the Chair and CEO. SEC Press Release, supra note 27.

39. Roy Harris, "Board Compensation Jumps to Over $2 Million." www.cfo.com, November 19, 2008. www.cfo.com/article.cfm/12636126?f=related.

40. Viral Acharya, Conor Kehoe, and Michael Reyner, "Private Equity vs. PLC Boards in the UK: A Comparison of Practices and Effectiveness." *Journal of Applied Corporate Finance*, vol. 21, No. 1, p. 55, Winter 2009. See also, Robert C. Pozen, "If Private Equity Sized Up Your Business." *Harvard Business Review*, November 2007.

41. Some companies have replaced the plurality voting standard altogether with a majority voting standard where a director must receive a majority of the votes cast in order to be validly elected.

42. Annalisa Barrett and Beth Young, "Majority Voting for Director Elections." *The Corporate Library*, December 2008, pp. 1.

43. RiskMetrics Group, supra note 36, p. 2.

44. The combination of a staggered board and poison pill is an almost impenetrable takeover defense. Lucian Bebchuk, John C. Coates IV, and Guhan Subramanian, "The Powerful Antitakeover Force of Staggered Boards." *Stanford Law Review*, 54, 887 (2002).

45. SEC Press Release, "SEC Votes to Propose Rule Amendments to Facilitate Rights of Shareholders to Nominate Directors." May 20, 2009. The SEC also proposed to allow shareholders to propose a bylaw establishing a procedure for shareholder nominees to be included in the company's proxy materials. SEC Release No. 33-9046; 34-60089; IC-28765, June 10, 2009.

46. The Business Roundtable vs. SEC, 905 F.2d 406 (D.C. Cir 1990).

47. The SEC already allows proxy solicitations to be made by posting proxy materials on the Internet and mailing a one-page notice to all shareholders. However, the mailing costs for that notice can easily exceed a few million dollars.

48. For shareholders who might not have Internet access, the company's proxy statement should include a toll-free number for them to obtain a free copy of the proxy materials of the shareholder nominee.

49. Kara Scannell, "Policy Makers Work to Give Shareholders More Boardroom Clout." *Wall Street Journal*, March 26, 2009, p. B4.

50. Fabrizio Ferri and David Maber, "Say on Pay Vote and CEO Compensation: Evidence from the UK." *Harvard Business School*, June, 2008.

51. Martin Lipton, Jay W. Lorsch and Theodore N. Mirvis, "Schumer's Shareholder Bill Misses the Mark." *Wall Street Jou,rnal*, May 12, 2009, p. A15.

52. RiskMetrics Group, "Scorecard of Key Shareholder Proposals." December 31, 2008.

53. Securities and Exchange Commission, "Division of Interpretations of Section 7001 of the American Recovery and Reinvestment Act of 2009." February 26, 2009. (Division of Corp. Fin Interpretations).

54. See, e.g., H.R. 3269 (passed the House on July 31, 2009).

Chapter 12: Were Accounting Rules an Important Factor Contributing to the Financial Crisis?

1. Steve Forbes, "Obama Repeats Bush's Worst Market Mistakes." *Wall Street Journal*, March 6, 2009, p. A13. http://online.wsj.com/article/SB123630304198047321.html.

2. Bob Herz, "Lessons Learned, Relearned, and Relearned Again from the Global Financial Crisis—Accounting and Beyond." December 8, 2008, pp. 17, 21. www.fasb.org/articles&reports/12-08-08_herz_speech.pdf .

3. Blackstone Group CEO Stephen Schwarzman supported global accounting harmony and principles-based accounting in a November 2008 WSJ op-ed: "First, we need to finalize a common set of accounting principles across borders. In global markets, you cannot have global institutions abiding by differing standards of accounting and disclosure simple because they are headquartered in different countries. . . . Finally, we have to move to a principles-based regulatory system rather than a rules-based system. A system of rules and regulations is utterly incapable of dealing with the speed and complexity of the modern financial system." Stephen Schwarzman, "Some Lessons of the Financial Crisis." *Wall Street Journal*, November 4, 2008, p. A19 http://online.wsj.com/article/SB122576100620095567.html.

4. The technical term for "permanent impairment" under U.S. GAAP is "other-than-temporary impairment" (OTTI).

5. The carrying value of an asset may also decline due to amortization over its limited life, as with a patent.

6. Jack Healy, "Losses in Good-Will Values Compound Bank Troubles." *New York Times*, April 27, 2009, p. B1.

7. Instead, unrealized AFS gains and losses are reflected on the income statement in Other Comprehensive Income, a special line-item that is excluded from net income, and subsequently on the balance sheet in Accumulated Other Comprehensive Income, a special line-item within the equity account.

8. SEC Office of the Chief Accountant Division of Corporate Finance, "Report and Recommendations Pursuant to Section 133 of the Emergency Economic Stabilization Act of 2008: Study on Mark-To-Market Accounting." p. 49. www.sec.gov/news/studies/2008/marktomarket123008.pdf.

9. Ibid, p. 50.

10. Emily Chasan, "Mark-to-Market is Worth the Trouble, Rulemakers Say." *Reuters*, October 22, 2008. www.reuters.com/article/bondsNews/idUSN2240502120081023.

11. Goldman Sachs. 2008 10-K. January 27, 2009, p. 156, footnote (2). www.sec.gov/Archives/edgar/data/886982/000095012309001278/y74032e10vk.htm.

12. FASB. FASB Staff Position FAS 157-3. October 10, 2008. www.fasb.org/pdf/fsp_fas157-3.pdf.

13. U.S. House of Representatives Subcommittee on Capital Markets, Insurance, and Government Sponsored Enterprises, "Opening Statement of Congressman Paul E. Kanjorski." Hearing on Mark-to-Marketing Accounting: Practices and Implications, March 12, 2009. www.house.gov/apps/list/hearing/financialsvcs_dem/kanjorski031209.pdf.

14. Criteria for Level III, see FAS 107-1 and APB 28-1 (April 9, 2008); distinction between credit and non-credit losses, see FASB 115-2 and FASB 124-2 (April 9, 2008).

15. Jack Ciesielski, *The Analyst's Accounting Observer*, June 18, 2009.

16. Warren Buffett, *2002 Berkshire Hathaway Annual Report*. February 21, 2003, p. 13. www.berkshirehathaway.com/letters/2002pdf.pdf.

17. SEC Report, supra note 8, p. 97 www.sec.gov/news/studies/2008/marktomarket123008.pdf.

18. Ibid.

19. Lehman Brothers. "2008 Third Quarter Earnings Release." September 10, 2008, p. 5. www.lehman.com/press/qe/docs/091008_3q08_expected.pdf.

20. The market price of an issuer's outstanding debt should be reduced only to the extent the issuer is about to repurchase its own debt in the open market. The IASB has proposed more disclosures under IFRS 7 when a company recognizes significant gains by reducing the fair market value of its own debt. The FASB is making similar disclosure proposals. IASB Press Release "IASB Proposed Additional Disclosures for Investments in Debt Instruments." December 23, 2008.

21. International Standards Accounting Board, Exposure Draft ED/2009/7, Financial Instruments: Classification and Measurement, July 2009.

22. SEC Report, supra 8, p. 7. www.sec.gov/news/studies/2008/marktomarket123008.pdf.

23. "Fair Cop." *Economist*. October 2, 2008. www.economist.com/finance/displaystory.cfm?story_id=12342697.

24. CFA Institute. "CFA Members in Europe Vote Against Suspension of the Fair Value Standards." October 2, 2008. www.cfainstitute.org/aboutus/press/release/08releases/20081002_01.html.

25. See Richard J. Caballero, Takeo Hoshi, and Anil K. Kashyap. "Zombie Lending and Depressed Restructuring in Japan." January 2008. http://faculty.chicagobooth.edu/anil.kashyap/research/Zombiejan2008fulldocument.pdf.

26. For Tier II capital purposes, regulators count only 45 percent of a bank's pretax unrealized gains on equity securities. FDIC, Appendix A to Part 325 - Statement of Policy on Risk-Based Capital.

27. Final Report of the Advisory Committee on Improvements to Financial Reporting to the United States Securities and Exchange Commission. www.sec.gov/about/offices/oca/acifr/acifr-finalreport.pdf, pp. 32-33 (I chaired this Committee).

28. Gordon Crovitz, "Closing the Information GAAP." *Wall Street Journal*, September 8, 2008, p. A17.

29. SEC Press Release 2008-184, "SEC Proposes Roadmap Toward Global Accounting Standards to Help Investors Compare Financial Information More Easily." August 27, 2008. www.sec.gov/news/press/2008/2008-184.htm.

30. PricewaterhouseCoopers, "IFRS and US GAAP: Similarities and differences." IFRS Readiness Service, September, 2008. And Deloitte, "IRFSs and GAAP: A pocket comparison." IAS Plus Guide, March, 2007.

31. When a business buys an input to a product with increasing input prices over time, the LIFO method will reduce reported profits because it will use the costs of the last shipment, which is higher than earlier shipments. If the business used the FIFO method, it would report higher profits because the input cost in the earliest shipment was lower than the last shipment.

32. Citigroup, "Moving between US GAAP and IFRS changes key metrics." Valuation and Accounting Industry In-Depth, August 15, 2007, p. 1.

33. Sarbanes-Oxley Act §109(h).

34. Jack Ciesielski, "It's time to put the brakes on convergence." *FT.com*, Oct. 30, 2008.

35. Carrick Mallenkamp, "Accounting Change Lifts Deutsch Bank." *Wall Street Journal*, October 31, 2008, p. C2.

36. Marie Leone, "Regulator Rips Into Global Accounting Plan." CFO.com September 10, 2008. www.cfo.com/article.cfm/12202211.

37. Federal Register Vol. 73, No. 226, p. 70848, November 21, 2008.

38. Edward Iwata, "U.S. considers costly switch to international accounting rules." *USAToday.com*, January 6, 2009. www.usatoday.com/money/companies/regulation/2009-01-05-international-accounting-rule-switch_N.htm.

39. The critics of detailed rules often point to the 540 pages of the *Statement of Financial Accounting Standards No. 133: Accounting for Derivative Instruments And Hedging Activities*. June, 1998, can be found online at www.fasb.org/pdf/fas133.pdf

40. Floyd Norris, "Loophole Lets Bank Rewrite the Calendar." NYTimes.com, March 7, 2008. www.nytimes.com/2008/03/07/business/07norris.html?_r=1&scp=1&sq = norris+and+SocGen&st=nyt.

41. Peter Thal Larsen and Jennifer Hughes, "Sants Takes a Fresh View of Regulator's Principles." *Financial Times*, March 13, 2008, p. C17.

42. Robert C. Pozen, "Bernanke's False Dichotomy." *Wall Street Journal*, May 19, 2007, p. A8.

Part IV: The Future of the American Financial System and Chapter 13: The International Implications of the Financial Crisis for the United States

1. Marc Champion and Andrew Batson, "Russia, China Blame Woes on Capitalism." *Wall Street Journal*, January 29, 2009, p. A6.

2. Ibid.

3. Quoted in Roger C. Altman, "The Great Crash of 2008." *Foreign Affairs*, January/February 2009, p. 11.

4. Carrick Mallenkamp, Joellen Perry, and Alessandra Galloni, "Signs of the Future of Banking and Finance Emerge." *Wall Street Journal*, January 31– February 1, 2009, p. A7.

5. Quoted in Joellen Perry, "Europe Basks as U.S.-Style Capitalism Draws Fines." *Wall Street Journal*, January 30, 2009, p. A6.

6. This book does not attempt to address many other international aspects of the financial crisis.

7. U.S. Department of Commerce/Bureau of Economic Analysis, December 31, 2008. Available through the Economics Statistics Bureau at http://economicindicators.gov The United States has usually been a net exporter of services, as opposed to goods.

8. The U.S. current account deficit for 2009 is likely to be 3 to 4 percent of GDP.

9. The key oil producers include Saudi Arabia, United Arab Emirates, Nigeria, Russia, Venezuela, and Brasil. Norway is the only major producer of oil in the industrialized world.

10. International Monetary Fund, World Economic Outlook Database, April 2009.

11. Marcos Chamon and Eswar Prasad, "Why are Savings Rates of Urban Households in China Rising?" IMF Working Paper, June 2008, Table 1, p. 29.

12. Chen Deming, Chen, "Protectionism Doesn't Pay." *Wall Street Journal*, February 20, 2009, p. A17.

13. "Troubled Tigers." *Economist*, January 31, 2009, p. 77. Also, Hoover Institution at Stanford University, "Facts on Policy: Consumer Spending." December 19, 2006, www.hoover.org/research/factsonpolicy/facts/4931661.html.

14. Paul Maidment, "China Announces Massive Stimulus Package." Forbes.com, November 9, 2008.

15. China's fiscal stimulus, focused heavily on public infrastructure financed by state banks, equaled 5 percent of GDP. "Couching Tigers, Stirring Dragons." *Economist*, May 16, 2009, p. 79.

16. "Strong as an Ox." *Economist*, January 24, 2009, pp. 45–46.

17. Vincent Kolo, "China's Health Service—Not For the Poor!" *China Worker*, April 20, 2007.

18. Robert C. Pozen, "Insuring China's Future." *Wall Street Journal*, August 6, 2009, p. A12.

19. Testimony by Mark Iwry, "Making Savings for Retirement Easier through Automatic IRA's." Testimony Before House Committee on Ways and Means, June 26, 2008.

20. Treasury White Paper, *Financial Regulatory Reform: A New Foundation: Rebuilding Financial Supervision and Regulation*. June 2009, pp. 74–75.

21. United States Bureau of Economic Analysis, "Personal Savings Rate." At www.bea.gov/briefrm/saving.htm.

22. Robin Sidel, "Debit-Card Use Overtakes Credit." *Wall Street Journal*, May 1, 2009, p. M11.

23. See for example, Hal Varian, "Boost Private Investment to Boost the Economy." *Wall Street Journal*, January 7, 2009, p. A13 .

24. U.S. Congressional Budget Office, "The Budget and Economic Outlook: An Update," August, 2009.

25. Ibid, Table 1-1; William Gale and Alan Auerbach, "The Economic Crisis and the Fiscal Crisis 2009 and Beyond." *Brookings Institution Report*. February 19, 2009.

26. Kenneth S. Rogoff and Carmen M. Reinhart, "What Other Financial Crises Tell Us." *Wall Street Journal*, February 3, 2009, p. A15.

27. Mark Whitehouse, "Inflation is Tempting to Indebted Nations." *Wall Street Journal*, March 30, 2009, p. A19.

28. Gerald Seib, "White House Sends Signals on Deficit." *Wall Street Journal*, June 12, 2009, p. A2.

29. U.S. Department of Treasury, "Major Foreign Holders of Treasury Securities." www.ustreas.gov/tic/mfh.txt. IMF, "International Reserves and Foreign Currency Liquidity." June 2009, www.imf.org/external/np/sta/ir/hkg/eng/curhkg.htm#I

30. International Monetary Fund "Currency Composition of Official Foreign Exchange Reserves (COFER)." Online at www.imf.org/external/np/sta/cofer/eng/cofer.pdf.

31. Japanese sovereign debt from Merrill Lynch, "Growth Trends in the World Bond Markets." January 9, 2009; 2008 GDP from *CIA World Fact Book* U.S. figures from Congressional Budget Office, "The Budget and Economic Outlook: Fiscal Years 2009 to 2019." January 2009, p. 15, Table 4.

32. International Monetary Fund Staff Position Note, "Fiscal Implications of the Global Economic and Financial Crisis." June 9, 2009, p. 26.

33. Jeremy Siegel, "Impact of an aging population on global economy." *CFA Institute.* September 2007, Figures 1 and 2.

34. Landon Thomas, Jr., "Once a Boon, the Euro Is Now a Burden for Some." *New York Times*, January 24, 2009, p. A8.

35. "High Tensions." *Economist*, February 7, 2009, p. 10.

36. "Seeking Shelter." *Economist*, November 1, 2008, p. 61.

37. Menzie Chinn and Jeffrey Alexander Frankel, "The Euro May Over the Next 15 years Surpass the Dollar as Leading International Currency." *International Finance*, 2008.

38. Compare the 2009 estimated fertility rate of 2.05 in the United States with: Spain 1.31, Italy 1.31, Germany 1.41, and France 1.98. United States Central Intelligence Agency, *The World Factbook 2009*, Country Comparisons: Total Fertility Rate. www.cia.gov/library/publications/the-world-factbook/rankorder/2127rank.html.

39. Robert Atkinson, "Boosting European Prosperity Through The Widespread Use of ICT." The Information Technology & Innovation Foundation, November, 2007, p.1.

40. David Barboza, "China Urges New Reserve to Replace the Dollar." *New York Times*, March 24, 2009, p. A5.

41. On the limits of SDRs, see Robert C. Pozen, "Chatter about a new global currency is overblown." *Financial Times*, July 29, 2009.

42. Richard McGregor, "China moves to cut reliance on dollar." *Financial Times*, July 3, 2009, p. 4.

43. Compare Benjamin Friedman, "Why the Federal Reserve Should Not Adopt Inflation Targeting." *International Finance* 7:1, 2004, pp. 129–136; with F.S. Mishkin, "Why the Federal Reserve Should Adopt Inflation Targeting." *International Finance* 7:1, 2004, pp. 117-27; and Andrew T. Levin, Fabio M. Natalucci, and Jeremy M. Piger, "The Macro-economic Effects of Inflation Targeting." Federal Reserve Bank of St. Louis (2003).

44. Federal Reserve Statistical Release, H.4.1. June 14, 2007 and June 11, 2009.

45. Federal Reserve and U.S. Department of Treasury Joint Press Release, "The Role of the Federal Reserve in Preserving Financial and Monetary Stability Joint Statement by the Department of the Treasury and the Federal Reserve." March 23, 2009, www.federalreserve.gov/newsevents/press/monetary/20090323b.htm.

46. Remarks by Jeffrey Lacker, President, Federal Reserve Bank of Richmond at the National Association for Business Economics Washington Economic Policy ConferenceAlexandria, VA, March 2, 2009. www.richmondfed.org/press_room/speeches/president_jeff_lacker/2009/lacker_speech_20090302.cfm.

47. Treasury White Paper, supra note 20, pp. 78–79.

48. Sudeep Reddy, "No Longer Alone, Ron Paul Fights the Fed."WSJ.com, July 20, 2009. http://blogs.wsj.com/economics/2009/07/20/no-longer-alone-ron-paul-fights-the-fed/.

49. Bloomberg L.P. v. Board of Governors of the Federal Reserve System, 08-CV-9595 (S.D.N.Y.) August 24, 2009.

50. Michael Bordo and Barry Eichegreen, "Crisis Now and Then: What Lessons from the Last Era of Financial Globalization?" Nation Bureau of Economic Research Working Paper no. 8716, Table 6. Available online at http://michael.bordo.googlepages.com/w8716.pdf.

51. IMF, *World Economic Outlook,*, "Financial Stress and Economic Downturns." October, 2008, Chapter 4.

52. International Monetary Fund, *Global Financial Stability Report.* April, 2009, p. 48, Table 1.8.

53. IMF estimates from "Big Government Fights Back." *Economist*, January 31, 2009, pp. 79–80.

54. Federal Reserve Statistic Release H.4.1 March 26, 2009; and other releases from Federal Reserve, FDIC, Treasury and HUD; Bob Ivry and Mark Pittman, "Financial Rescue Nears GDP as Pledges Top $12.8 Trillion." Bloomberg.com, March 31, 2009.

55. Robert Shiller and Karl E. Case, "Is There a Bubble in the Housing Market?" Cowles Foundation Paper No. 1089. Available online at www.econ.yale.edu/~shiller/pubs/p1089.pdf.

56. "Greed—and fear." *Economist*, January 24, 2009, p. 4.

57. Ibid.

58. Financial Stability Forum, "Press Release: Financial Stability Forum Issues Recommendations and Principles to Strengthen Financial Systems." April 2, 2009.

59. Treasury White Paper, supra note 20, pp. 24, 28 and 31.

60. "Divine Intervention." *Economist*, July 18, 2009, p.14.

61. Carmen Reinhart and Kenneth Rogoff, "We need an international regulator." *Financial Times*, November 19, 2008, p. 11.

62. Norman Laurence and Alistair MacDonald, "G20 On Track for Changes in Financial Regulation." *Wall Street Journal*, January 29, 2009, p. A10.

63. Carrick Mollenkamp, Alistair MacDonald and Stephen Fidler, "For G20, Lofty Goals Have Fallen to Earth." *Wall Street Journal*, March 30, 2009, p. A1.

64. Quoted in Bob Davis, "IMF Urges Global Financial Rules." *Wall Street Journal*, March 6, 2009, p. A9.

65. Dani Rodrick, "A Plan B for global finance." *Economist*, March 14, 2009, p. 80.

66. Alan Beattie, "IMF is clear victor in policy melee." *Financial Times*, April 2, 2009, p. 4.

67. G20 Communiqué, April 2, 2009.

68. "Mission: Possible." *Economist*, April 11, 2009, p. 69.

69. Sarah O'Connor, "Obama's IMF boost exacts heavy toll." *Financial Times*, June 15, 2009, p. 4.

70. Bob Davis, "An Empowered IMF Faces Pivotal Test as Nations' Needs Grow." *Wall Street Journal*, March 31, 2009, p. A10.

71. "Supersizing the fund." *Economist*, February 7, 2009, p. 67.

72. While the Financial Stability Forum's members included members of the Group of 7— the seven largest and most developed economies—the Financial Stability Board includes members from the Group of 20. Gillian Tett, "Forum Emerges from the Shadows to Take a Wider Role." *Financial Times*, April 3, 2009, p. 4.

73. Anne Krueger, "A New Approach to Sovereign Debt Restructuring." International Monetary Fund, April, 2002.

74. Bob Davis, "Nations Strive for a Single Voice on Financial Crisis, But Rival Agendas Make It Tough to Act in Unison." *Wall Street Journal*, November 10, 2008, p. A2.

75. Vanessa Houlder, Alex Barker, and Jamil Anderlini. "Secrecy Era Over, Say Leaders." *Financial Times*, April 3, 2009, p. 4.

76. G20 Communiqué, "Declaration on Strengthening the Financial System." London, April 2, 2009. See also, Treasury White Paper, supra note 20, p. 81.

77. International Organization of Securities Commissioners, "The Role of the Credit Rating Agencies in Structured Finance Markets." May, 2008, available at www.iosco .org. See also Treasury White Paper, supra note 20, p. 88.

78. Neil King Jr., Alistair MacDonald, and Marcus Walker, "Buy American Drive, Other Global Trade Barriers, Stoke Fear." *Wall Street Journal*, January 31–February 1, 2009, p. A6.

79. Quoted in Martin Wolf, "Why G20 leaders will fail to deal with the big challenge." *Financial Times*. April 1, 2009, p. 11.

80. Quoted in Sarah Lyall, "Sweden's Government Says No to State Ownership of Saab, a National Icon." *New York Times*, March 23, 2009, p. A7 (International edition).

81. Bob Davis and Carrick Mollenkamp, "Financial Protectionism is Latest Threat to Global Recovery." *Wall Street Journal*, February 2, 2009, p. A2.

82. Phillip Webster and Christine Buckley, "Gordon Brown Gets Tough with Banks over Lending Freeze." *Times Online*, October 31, 2008.

83. Hannes H. Gissurarson, "Iceland Abandoned." *Wall Street Journal* (European edition), November 18, 2008, p. 12.

84. "The Enforcer." *Economist*, January 10, 2009, p. 59.

85. Quoted in "Briefing: Globalization under Strain." *Economist*, February 7, 2009, p. 70. The EU has established a European Risk Board to monitor systemic risks, but the Board has no power to implement remedial actions. Implementation is left entirely to each national regulator, which will not receive any financial assistance from other EU countries. "Divided by a Common Market." *Economist*, July 4, 2009, p. 73.

86. American Recovery and Reinvestment Act of 2009, Section 1605. This discussion is based on: Gary Hufbauer and Jeffrey Schott, "Buy American: Bad for Jobs, Worse for Reputation." Peterson Institute, PB09-2, February, 2009. They also analyze the application of North American Free Trade Agreement (NAFTA) to section 1605.

87. Gary Hufbauer and Jeffrey Schott, "America's free trade promises must be honoured." *Financial Times*, May 20, 2009, p. 9.

88. Ibid.

89. Sarah O'Connor, "US Companies Suffer Repercussions from Buy American Initiative." *Financial Times*, May 26, 2009, p. 2.

90. "The People Crunch." *Economist*, January 17, 2009, p. 59.

91. Neil King Jr., Alistair MacDonald, and Marcus Walker, "Crisis Fuels Backlash on Trade." *Wall Street Journal*, January 31–February 1, 2009, p. A1.

92. Stimulus Act of 2009 §1611(b)(1).

93. Francesco Guerrera, "Blankfein attacks US job rules." *Financial Times*, April 8, 2009, p. 15.

94. G20 communiqué, November 15, 2008.

95. Mark Landler, "Trade Barriers Rise as Slump Tightens Grip." *New York Times*, March 23, 2009, p. A1.

96. John W. Miller, "WTO Predicts Global Trade Will Slide 9% This Year." *Wall Street Journal*, March 24, 2009, p. A8.

97. Quoted in Chris Giles and Alan Beattie, "Pledges Fail to Turn Back Creeping Anti-trade Tide." *Financial Times*, April 1, 2009, p. 5.

98. For example, see editorial by China's Minister of Commerce, Chen Deming, "Strengthen US-China Trade Ties." *Wall Street Journal*, April 27, 2009, A15.

99. Greg Hitt, "Obama Pursues Trade Pacts Set Up by Bush." *Wall Street Journal*, May 19, 2009, p. A6.

Chapter 14: The New Structure of U.S. Financial Regulation

1. Treasury White Paper, *Financial Regulatory Reform: A New Foundation: Rebuilding Financial Supervision and Regulation*. June 2009, p. 5.

2. "Greed—and fear." *Economist*, January 24, 2009, p. 3; Michael Bordo and Barry Eichengreen, "Crisis Now and Then: What Lessons from the Last Era of Financial Globalization?" NBER Working Paper no. 8716, January 2002.

3. Treasury White Paper, supra note 1, p. 21. The FSO has more members than the President's Working Group for Financial Markets, which includes the Treasury, the Fed, the SEC and the CFTC.

4. Squam Lake Working Group on Financial Regulation, "A Systemic Regulator for Financial Markets." Council on Foreign Relations, Center for Geoeconomic Studies, May, 2009, p. 4.

5. Treasury White Paper, supra note 1, p. 11.

6. Ibid, pp. 22–23.

7. Ibid, p. 8.

8. Squam Lake Working Group on Financial Regulation, "An Expedited Resolution Mechanism for Distressed Financial Firms." Council on Foreign Relations, Center for Geoeconomic Studies, April, 2009, p. 3.

9. Statement by Timothy Geithner U.S. Treasury Secretary before the U.S. House of Representatives Committee on Financial Services, March 26, 2009, p. 6.

10. This proposal is narrower than the consumer protection agency proposed by the Treasury. In addition, it would be unwise, as suggested by the Treasury, to create a new agency for mortgage origination and leave the FTC with its current powers in that area. Treasury White Paper, supra note 1, p. 63.

11. Treasury, *Blueprint for a Modernized Financial Regulatory Structure*, March 2008, pp. 126–133.

12. Secretary Geithner has further suggested that all financial derivatives be traded on established exchanges. Letter from Treasury Secretary Geithner to Senator Harry Reid, May 13, 2009. This suggestion is discussed in Chapter 4.

13. Treasury White Paper, supra note 1, pp. 37–38.

14. Ibid, pp. 32–36. Many trust companies do not take deposits; they manage money through custodial or trust accounts, or serve as a trustee or custodian for certain retirement plans. Sections 23A and 23B of the Federal Reserve Act already prevent many transactions between an insured bank and the affiliates of its parent.

15. "Growing insecurities." *Economist*, January 17, 2009, p. 73.

16. For example, *Federal Register*, Vol. 73, No. 146, July 29, 2008, p. 43982 .

17. Treasury White Paper, supra note 1, pp. 32–33.

18. Arthur Levitt, "How to Restore Confidence in Our Markets." *Wall Street Journal*, October 22, 2008, p. A15. Kara Scannell, "SEC's Cox Backs Merger of Agency with CFTC." *Wall Street Journal*, October 24, 2008, p. A3.

19. To avoid a political battle, the Treasury has proposed better coordination between the SEC and CFTC, rather than a merger. Treasury White Paper, supra note 1, p. 49–50.

20. Zachary Goldfarb, Binyamin Appelbaum, and David Cho, "Administration Weighs Creating New Regulator for Financial Products." *Washington Post*, May 19, 2009.

21. "Credit CARD Act of 2009." Public Law No: 111–24.

22. Treasury White Paper, supra note 1, p. 32.

23. Ibid, p. 57.

24. Fixed annuities are regulated by state insurance agencies, and not by the SEC.

25. Treasury White Paper, supra note 1, p. 21.

26. Howell Jackson, "A Pragmatic Approach to the Phased Consolidation of Financial Regulation in the United States." November 12, 2008, p. 3. Available online at www .capmktsreg.org.

27. Remarks of Senator Christopher J. Dodd and Representative Barney Frank, reported in: "One Watchdog, or a Whole Pack." *New York Times*, June 3, 2009, p. B2.

28. International Monetary Fund, Global Financial Stability Report, April 2009, p. 48, Table 1.8.

29. "Big Government Fights Back." *Economist*, January 31, 2009, pp. 79–80.

30. The actual potential exposure was $5.8 trillion at the end of March, 2009. See Table 13.1.

31. Treasury White Paper, supra note 1, pp. 78–79.

32. Glenn Hubbard, Hal Scott and John Thornton, "The Fed's independence is at risk," *Financial Times*, August 21, 2009, p. 11.

33. Federal Deposit Insurance Corporation Improvement Act of 1991, 12 U.S.C. 1811.

34. Although the CDS subsidiary's obligations were guaranteed by the parent AIG, its insurance subsidiaries could have been protected in the bankruptcy of the CDS subsidiary.

35. See Chapter 9.

36. Ibid.

37. U.S. Department of Treasury Fact Sheet Public-Private Investment Program. p. 4.

38. Quoted in Benjamin Matthew, "Stiglitz Enabled Obama with Nobel Ideas to Scorn Them." Bloomberg.com, March 13, 2009.

39. R. Glenn Hubbard, Hal Scott, and Luigi Zingales, "From Awful to Merely Bad: Reviewing the Bank Rescue." *Wall Street Journal*, February 8, 2009, A11.

40. Ethan Cohen-Cole, Burcu Duygan-Bump, Jose Fillat, and Judit Montoriol-Garriga, "Looking Behind the Aggregates." Federal Reserve Bank of Boston Working Paper QAU08-5, November 2008, Figure 1A.

41. Oliver Hart and Luigi Zingales, "Economists Have Abandoned Principle." *Wall Street Journal*, December 3, 2008, p. A17.

42. See Chapter 1. The 5 percent retention level is proposed by the U.S. Congress and the European Commission.

43. See Chapter 3.

44. See Chapter 3.

45. See Chapter 7.

46. Tyler Cowen, "Why Creditors Should Suffer, Too." *New York Times*, April 5, 3009, p. C1, C2.

47. John Deere was one of many industrial companies that owned one thrift before May 4, 1999, and, therefore, was grandfathered as a unitary holding company by Title IV of the Gramm Leach Bliley Act of 1999. Many life insurance companies qualified under the same grandfather clause. After May 4, 1999, life insurance companies may still acquire a thrift if the insurance company qualifies as a financial services holding company, which generally excludes nonfinancial activities such as those carried out by John Deere.

48. Spreads on non-FDIC insured bonds recalculated relative to three-year Treasuries to allow better comparison.

49. See Chapter 8.

50. Ibid.

51. Hugo Dixon and Robert Cyran, "Vikram Pandit's Great Deal for Citi." *New York Times*, December 3, 2008, p. B2.

52. David Enrich, Marshall Eckbald, and Maurice Tamman, "Bailed-Out Banks Face Probe Over Fee Hikes." *Wall Street Journal*, April 13, 2009, p. A1.

53. "Keeping up with the Goldmans." *Economist*, July 18, 2009, p. 71.

54. Henny Sender, "Wall Street Profits from Fed Role." *Financial Times*, August 3, 2009, p. 1. The number of primary dealers decreased from 31 a decade ago to 18 in July 2009.

55. The Riegle Neal Act of 1994 prohibits the approval of any merger where the resulting bank controls more than 10 percent of the total amount of insured deposits in the United States or more than 30 percent in any state.

56. David Leonhardt, "After the Great Recession." *New York Times Sunday Magazine*, May 3, 2009, p. 28.

57. Gretchen Morgenson, "Imperfect Politics of Pay." *New York Times Sunday Edition*, August 9, 2009, p BU1.

58. See Robert C. Pozen, "If Private Equity Sized Up Your Business." *Harvard Business Review*, November 2007.

59. Ronald Gilson and Renier Kraakman, "The Directors Guild." *New York Times*, June 8, 2009, p. A19.

Glossary

General Terms

adjustable rate mortgage (ARM) – A mortgage whose interest rate adjusts periodically (e.g., yearly) to a new rate based on prevailing market rates at the time of adjustment.

alt-A mortgage – A loan to a home buyer who may be creditworthy but does not meet the standards for a conforming mortgage (e.g., the borrower cannot provide the normally required documentation).

American Recovery and Reinvestment Act of 2009 (The Stimulus Plan) – A statute providing for an economic stimulus package of $787 billion.

antideficiency statutes – State laws that limit or eliminate the right of a foreclosing lender from holding the borrower personally liable for any unpaid debt remaining after the sale of the foreclosed home.

arbitrage – An investment strategy to buy and sell related assets in order to profit from relatively small price differences between these assets, such as a call option for shares and the relevant shares.

asset-backed security (ABS) – A debt security collateralized by a specific group or pool of assets, such as home mortgages, credit-card receivables, or car loans.

bad bank – A bank specifically chartered by a federally insured bank to hold and sell nonperforming assets previously held by that federally insured bank.

bank holding company – A company that controls one or more banks.

base fee – The form of annual compensation, usually calculated as a percentage of the fund's assets, provided to a fund manager.

Basel Accords – A set of international agreements adopted by the Basel Committee on Bank Supervision, providing guidelines on capital and other matters.

basis point – 1/100th of one percentage point.

bear raid – The practice of attempting to push the price of a stock lower by selling it short and spreading unfavorable rumors about the issuer of that stock.

bond rating – A grade given to a bond by a credit-rating agency based on an evaluation of the bond issuer's ability to pay the bond's principal and interest in a timely fashion.

breaking the buck – When a money market fund's net asset value (NAV) declines below $1 per share.

call option – A contract giving the owner the right, but not the obligation, to buy a specified amount of a security at a specified price within a specified time.

capital – The stock of a financial institution plus specific forms of debt (e.g., subordinated debt) that count as capital for regulatory purposes.

capital requirements – The amount of capital a bank is required to hold (relative to its average assets) to meet its ongoing obligations and absorb unexpected losses.

central bank – The entity responsible for overseeing the monetary system of a nation (or group of nations). Central banks generally influence the money supply, function as the bank of the government, manage exchange reserves, and act as a lender of last resort.

clawback – The taking back of compensation paid to an employee or other person under specified conditions, such as finding wrongdoing by that person.

clearinghouse – An entity responsible for settling and clearing trades, collecting and maintaining margin, and reporting trading data.

collateral debt obligation (CDO) – A type of asset-backed security that is based on the cash flow from other securities, rather than a pool of whole assets such as mortgages.

commercial paper – An unsecured debt instrument issued by a corporation to finance its short-term needs, with a maturity of 270 days or less.

common stock – A security with ownership, and usually voting rights, in a company

conforming loan – A mortgage that does not exceed the amount of the maximum loan limits and meets the other requirements set by Fannie Mae and Freddie Mac.

conservatorship – An arrangement whereby one entity or person is appointed by a court to make legal decisions for a company or bank.

consumer price index (CPI) – An indicator of the level of prices paid by urban consumers for a representative basket of goods and services.

contingent obligation – An obligation that a bank may have to fulfill depending on future events, such as a guarantee in the event of credit losses.

counterparty risk – The risk to each party of a contract that the other party (i.e. the counterparty) will not honor its contractual obligations.

covered bonds – Bonds backed by mortgages or cash flows from other assets in a segregated account on the balance sheet of a financial institution.

credit default swaps (CDS) – Contracts that entitle the buyer to a payment on the default of a bond or other type of debt obligation in exchange for that bond or obligation.

credit guarantee – A promise to reimburse specified losses on the default of a mortgage or other debt obligation.

credit-rating agency – An entity that analyzes and rates the creditworthiness of companies issuing debt as well as structured financial products.

current account deficit – The amount by which a country's total imports of goods and services plus income payments exceeds its total exports of goods and services plus income receipts.

debt security – A tradable security, such as a bond or note, representing an obligation of the security's issuer to make payments as specified in the debt contract.

default – The failure to make timely payments (e.g., principal and interest) or meet other obligations as specified in the debt contract.

deflation – A general decline in prices, usually caused by a drastic reduction in government, personal, and/or investment spending.

deleveraging – The sale of assets or repayment of debts with the proceeds used to decrease or restore an institution's ratio of average assets to capital.

derivatives – Financial instruments, such as options to buy or sell stock, whose price is dependent upon or derived from the price of one or more other assets.

dividend – A distribution of a portion of a company's earnings, determined by the company's board of directors, to a class of its shareholders.

Emergency Economic Stabilization Act of 2008 (The Bailout Act) – An October 2008 law authorizing the U.S. Treasury to spend $700 billion dollars on buying troubled assets and recapitalizing financial institutions.

equity – Ownership interest in an asset after debts related to that asset are subtracted (e.g., $50,000 of equity in a house worth $200,000 with a mortgage of $150,000).

escrow account – In a mortgage arrangement, a separate account held in the borrower's name to pay obligations such as property taxes and insurance premiums.

exceptional assistance – When the U.S. Treasury purchases more than the standard amount of preferred stock (associated with a bailout) in a financial institution, such as multiple purchases of stock and guarantees of troubled assets; that institution is said to receive exceptional assistance.

face value – The dollar value of a security as stated by the issuer. For bonds, it is usually the amount paid to the holder at maturity.

fair market value (FMV) – FMV is an estimate of the price an entity would receive if it were to sell an asset, or pay if it were to relieve a liability.

fat tail distribution – A distribution curve wherein improbable events (the tails) are much more likely to occur than those of a normal distribution curve.

federal deficit – The federal government's expenditures in excess of its revenues.

federal funds rate – The daily interest rate charged by one bank when lending its balances at the Federal Reserve to another bank.

Federal Reserve discount window – The Fed's facility to allow banks and other eligible institutions to obtain short-term loans, usually to meet liquidity needs.

financial bubble – When there is a sharp and prolonged increase in prices of stocks, real estate, or other assets, which is unsustainable because it is not attributable to fundamental factors.

fiscal policy – Government spending and taxing policies.

fiscal quarter – A three-month period of a financial year (not always a calendar year) that serves as a basis for reporting earnings and paying dividends.

fixed-rate mortgage – A mortgage whose interest rate does not change between its origination and maturity dates.

fixed-income security – An investment that provides a return in the form payments as specified in the debt contract. A fixed-income security often makes principal and interest payments.

functional regulation – The system by which a different agency regulates each type of financial service (e.g., a securities broker by the Securities and Exchange Commission, and a national bank by the Comptroller of the Currency).

fund of hedge funds (FOFs) – A fund that invests all its assets in multiple other hedge funds.

future – A financial contract requiring the purchaser to buy an asset (and the seller to sell an asset), such as a bond or commodity, at a predetermined future date and price.

generally accepted accounting principles (GAAP) – The current set of accounting standards for the financial statements of U.S.-based companies.

Glass-Steagall Act – A statute, enacted in 1933 and repealed in 1999, that prohibited commercial banks from engaging in certain types of securities activities.

golden parachutes – Generous severance and benefit packages awarded by companies to exiting senior executives.

good bank – The federally insured bank remaining after its predecessor creates a bad bank and transfers its nonperforming assets to that bad bank.

goodwill – The intangible value of an ongoing business over and above the value of its tangible assets such as cash and real estate.

government sponsored enterprises (GSEs) – Shareholder-owned corporations like Fannie Mae and Freddie Mac, or government agencies like Ginnie Mae, chartered by Congress to promote stability, liquidity, and affordability in the housing sector.

gross domestic product (GDP) – The market value of all final goods and services created or provided within a country for a certain period of time (often annually).

hedging – An investment strategy to reduce specific risks of an investment, such as buying a put option on a stock to protect against a decline in the stock's price.

historical cost accounting – The method of accounting by which assets are valued at their purchase price or original value, absent a permanent impairment.

home equity loan – A loan secured by the equity in the borrower's home. Such loans are often used to finance home improvements, medical bills, or consumer purchases.

homestead exemptions – State laws designed to protect the homes of borrowers from their creditors in the event of bankruptcy of these borrowers.

illiquid market – A market in which assets are not actively traded and thus have no reliable market prices.

incentive fee – The portion of a fund manager's compensation based on a specified percentage of a fund's annual gains (or possibly losses).

index – A hypothetical basket of goods or portfolio of securities used to show changes in an economy, commodity, or securities market over time.

inflation – A general increase in the prices of goods and services in an economy leading to a general decrease in the purchasing power of consumers in that economy.

inflation target – An express policy by a central bank to raise interest rates if core inflation exceeds a specified percentage over a specified period of time.

insurable interest – A person paying insurance premiums has an insurable interest if he or she would suffer a loss if the event that is being insured against occurs.

interest rate risk – The risk that the value of a fixed-income asset will fall due to a rise in interest rates.

internal risk models – In-house mathematical models utilized by financial institutions to determine the riskiness of their investments.

international financial reporting standards (IFRS) – A set of accounting standards for financial statements that has been adopted by over 100 countries.

investment bank – An institution that acts as an underwriter for corporations and other entities issuing securities. Most offer advisory services and act as broker-dealers.

legacy loans – Existing loans owned by financial institutions.

legacy securities – Existing securities owned by financial institutions.

leverage ratio – The ratio of average assets to capital.

liquidity put – A promise to purchase some asset if the market for such assets becomes so illiquid that the holder cannot readily sell that asset at a reasonable price.

liquidity risk – The risk that a security or other asset cannot be sold quickly enough at a reasonable price in order to raise cash.

loan loss reserve – Monies specifically set aside by a financial institution to cover projected losses on loans or other assets.

loan-to-value ratio – The ratio of the amount of a mortgage or other loan to the value of an asset such as a home secured by that mortgage or loan.

London interbank offered rate (LIBOR) – The standard measure of the interest rate charged for an unsecured loan from one bank to another in the London wholesale market.

long position – The ownership of an asset, such as a stock, commodity or currency, generally with the expectation that the asset will rise in value.

market capitalization – The total dollar market value of a company's outstanding shares. The number of its outstanding shares times its price per share.

mark-to-market – A subset of fair market value accounting whereby assets are valued on the basis of their current fair market price or other market indicators.

mark-to-model – The pricing of an asset based on internal assumptions or financial estimates rather than current market prices.

maturity – The date at which the principal of a bond must be repaid.

mega banks – Banks with over $100 billion in assets.

monetary policy – The actions of a central bank or other authority to influence the money supply and interest rates to attain objectives such as price stability.

money market funds – A type of mutual fund that invests in relatively low-risk, short-term debt instruments and generally maintains a net asset value of $1 per share.

moral hazard – The situation that occurs when a person is totally insulated from risk and, therefore, has no incentive to prevent or mitigate such risk.

moral obligation – A perceived strong obligation, though not legally binding, such as the moral obligation of the federal government to rescue Fannie Mae and Freddie Mac.

mortgage-backed securities (MBS) – Securities which are supported by the cash flows from pools of mortgages.

mortgage modification – Amending the terms of a mortgage to change the interest payments, principal amounts, and /or due dates.

mortgage prepayment – Making payments on a mortgage before they are due to reduce or eliminate the principal amount of the mortgage.

mutual fund – A pooled vehicle, run by professional managers, that invests monies collected from savers in securities such as stocks, bonds, or money market instruments.

nationalization – When a national government eliminates all shareholders of a company and assumes 100 percent ownership of the company's shares.

negative amortization loan – A loan whose monthly payments do not cover the interest due on the loan; the uncovered interest is added to the loan's principal, to be paid later.

nonagency mortgage-backed securities – Mortgage-backed securities underwritten or guaranteed by financial institutions other than government sponsored enterprises.

nonbank lenders – Providers of credit that are not banks, such as some credit card companies, some mortgage lenders, money market funds, and auto lenders.

nonrecourse loan – Loan for which borrowers have no personal liability for unpaid amounts; if the loan defaults, borrowers can lose only their equity in the relevant asset.

normal distribution curve – A bell curve in which the first standard deviation encompasses 68.2 percent of its area, and the first two standard deviations encompass 95.4 percent.

notional amount – The predetermined dollar amount on a swap or other derivative instrument that is used to calculate payments made on that swap or instrument.

off-balance sheet – Assets and liabilities controlled by a firm through a separate legal vehicle whose assets and liabilities do not appear on the firm's balance sheet.

originate – To issue or make a mortgage or other type of loan.

originate-to-sell – Issuing or making a mortgage or loan with the explicit intent of selling it to another party.

over-the-counter (OTC) derivatives – Derivatives whose terms are privately negotiated, rather than standardized, and that do not trade on established exchanges.

permanent impairment – A permanent reduction in the fair market value of an asset accounted for at historical cost, other than temporary impairment.

policy rate – The target for short-term interest rates set by a country's central bank.

preferred stock – A form of capital that pays a fixed dividend each year, as opposed to common shares for which the directors use discretion about whether, and how much, to pay dividends.

price discovery – The method of determining the price for a specific commodity, security, or other asset through the interaction of buyers and sellers in a normal market.

primary dealers – The small group of large banks and big brokers that help the Federal Reserve implement monetary policy.

prime mortgage – A high-quality mortgage that meets the credit, documentation, and other standards set by Fannie Mae and Freddie Mac.

private equity fund – A pooled investment vehicle that buys control, or substantial amounts, of companies in an effort to increase their value and sell them at a later date for a higher price.

procyclicality – Anything that reinforces the prevailing economic trends, such as banks borrowing to purchase assets during good times and selling assets during bad times.

proxy access – When shareholders are allowed to nominate their own candidates for the company's directors, and those candidates appear in the company's proxy materials.

proxy statement – The materials sent to all shareholders, by the company or shareholders, with a proposed slate of directors and any other matters to be voted on.

public-private investment program (PPIP) – A program heavily subsidized by the government to help private investors buy troubled assets from banks.

put option – A contract giving the owner the right, but not the obligation, to sell a specified amount of an underlying asset at a specified price within a specified time.

recapitalization – A change in the mixture of a company's debt and/or equity, usually to make the company stronger and more stable.

receivership – A type of corporate bankruptcy in which a third party, a receiver, is appointed by a bankruptcy court or creditors to run the company and reorganize it for the benefit of creditors, subject to the court's approval.

repurchase agreements (repos) – A form of short-term borrowing in which institutions sell securities to investors, and buy them back (often the following day), at predetermined prices calculated to be the equivalent of interest.

reverse auction – An auction in which a cash buyer announces it will purchase a certain dollar amount of a particular security, holders of that security submit offers to sell, and the buyer accepts the offer with the lowest price up to the announced dollar limit.

risk-weighted assets – A bank's assets weighted according to perceived credit risk; for example, corporate loans usually have a higher risk rating than home mortgages.

run on the bank – When a large number of bank depositors withdraw their funds simultaneously and the bank's resources are insufficient to cover the withdrawals.

Sarbanes-Oxley Act of 2002 (SOX) – A statute passed after the Enron and Worldcom failures, which increases procedures for corporate governance, such as assessments of internal controls and certification of financial statements.

savings and loan associations (S&Ls) – A depository institution, also called a thrift, which specializes in taking deposits and making mortgages and other real estate loans.

say-on-pay – An annual shareholder vote on the company's executive compensation practices, which is advisory and not legally binding on the company's board.

securitization – The process by which cash flows from assets are packaged into securities and sold to investors.

senior executive officers (SEOs) – The most senior officers (generally the top five) who perform policy making functions of a company.

short position – Selling shares, borrowed rather than owned, or otherwise owning instruments (e.g., put options), to benefit from an anticipated decline in their value.

short selling – Betting that a stock's price will decline in the future, by borrowing and selling shares now, and purchasing and returning the shares later.

sovereign wealth fund (SWF) – A pool of money invested by a quasi-governmental entity for the benefit of a country's economy and citizens.

special drawing rights (SDRs) – A form of international currency reserves issued by the IMF to member countries and based on a basket of four currencies.

special purpose entity (SPE) – A separate legal and accounting entity from the bank or company sponsoring the entity, created for a particular investment purpose.

spread – The difference between two prices or rates, such as the bid and offer prices of a security (i.e., bid-ask spread), or the respective yields of two bonds differing in credit quality (i.e., the credit spread).

Standard and Poor's 500 Index (S&P 500) – An index of 500 stocks chosen to represent the general level of stock prices of large publicly traded U.S. companies.

stock warrants – Rights to purchase a specified number of shares at a specific priced within a specified time frame.

structured finance – A sector of finance created to help transfer risk through the use of complex techniques and separate entities (e.g., the securitization of mortgages and credit cards).

subordinated debt – Corporate debt that ranks below all other debt with regard to claims on ongoing company earnings and claims on company assets in bankruptcy.

subprime mortgage – A mortgage made to a borrower who does not qualify as credit-worthy enough for a prime mortgage and who, therefore, pays a higher interest rate.

super-directors – Directors of a financial institution who, like directors of private equity funds, have deep financial experience, substantial time to commit, and significant incentives to monitor closely the condition of the institution.

systemic risk – Material risk posed to the entire financial system by the potential collapse of a large, interconnected financial institution, or a high-volume risky product.

tariffs – A schedule of taxes imposed by a country on the foreign goods imported into it.

tax haven – A country or state that imposes little or no taxes on companies or individuals living or doing business there.

thrift – A depository institution, also called a savings and loan association, which specializes in taking deposits, originating home mortgages or other real-estate loans.

toxic assets – Mortgage-backed securities, related derivatives, and other assets that are not easily traded because no one can accurately price them.

tranche – One of several securities with specific risk/reward characteristics based on a particular claim to the cash flows from an underlying pool of assets, such as mortgages.

Troubled Asset Relief Program (TARP) – A government program to purchase assets and equity from financial institutions to strengthen the financial sector.

tying arrangements – In banking, the granting of loans to a customer on the condition that the customer will purchase other services from the bank.

umbrella regulator – A regulator in charge of an entire sector of the economy, or comprising all regulators of that sector, such as the UK's Financial Service Authority.

underwater mortgage – A mortgage in which the outstanding mortgage balance exceeds the current market value of the property securing the mortgage.

universal banks – Banks that engage in a broad range of securities and other financial activities as well as traditional banking functions such as making loans.

uptick rule – A former SEC rule that prohibited any short sale from being made unless the most recent sale price for a stock was higher than its immediately prior price.

Public and Quasi-Public Entities

Commodity Futures Trading Commission (CFTC) – CFTC is an independent agency with the mandate to regulate commodity futures, forwards, and option markets in the United States.

Department of Housing and Urban Development (HUD) – HUD is a cabinet-level agency whose mission is to increase homeownership, support community development, and increase access to affordable housing.

Federal Deposit Insurance Corporation (FDIC) – FDIC is the independent agency that insures all U.S. banks and thrifts; it also is the federal regulator of all state-chartered banks that are not members of the Federal Reserve system.

Federal Home Loan Mortgage Corporation (Freddie Mac) – Freddie Mac is a publicly chartered corporation with a mission to provide liquidity, stability, and affordability in the housing market.

Federal National Mortgage Association (Fannie Mae) – Fannie Mae is a publicly chartered corporation with the same mission as Freddie Mac.

Federal Reserve Board of Governors (Fed) – As the central bank of the United States, the Fed conducts the nation's monetary policy, supervises both state-chartered banks that are Fed members and all bank holding companies, maintains the stability of the financial system, and provides financial services such as payment processing.

Federal Trade Commission (FTC) – The FTC enforces certain consumer protection laws and tries to prevent anticompetitive business practices.

Financial Accounting Standards Board (FASB) – The FASB has been designated by the SEC as the organization responsible for setting accounting standards for financial statements of companies in the United States.

Financial Industry Regulatory Authority (FINRA) – FINRA is the self-regulatory organization for all securities firms doing business in the United States. It was created by the merger of the National Association of Securities Dealers and the regulatory unit of the New York Stock Exchange.

Group of Twenty (G20) – The G20 is an informal group of 20 important industrialized and developing economies that discusses key issues in the global economy.

General Accounting Office (GAO) – The GAO is an arm of Congress, headed by the Comptroller General, which conducts reviews and issues reports.

Government National Mortgage Association (Ginnie Mae) – Ginnie Mae is a government-owned corporation that guarantees to investors the timely payment of principal and interest on securities backed by federally insured or guaranteed loans.

International Accounting Standards Board (IASB) – The IASB is an independent standard-setting board whose mission is to develop a single set of high quality and understandable financial reporting standards for companies in all countries.

International Monetary Fund (IMF) – The IMF is an organization of over 180 countries, working to foster monetary cooperation, secure financial stability, facilitate international trade, promote economic growth, and reduce poverty around the world.

Office of the Comptroller of the Currency (OCC) – The OCC charters, regulates, and examines all national banks.

Office of Federal Housing Enterprise (OFHEO) – OFHEO is the former regulator of Fannie Mae and Freddie Mac; it has now become the Federal Housing Finance Agency.

Office of Thrift Supervision (OTS) – The OTS charters, regulates, and examines thrifts (savings and loans) with federal charters.

President's Working Group on Financial Markets (PWG) – Headed by the Treasury Secretary, the PWG coordinates U.S. policies in the financial area; its members include the Chairman of the Fed, Chairman of the SEC, and the Chairman of the CFTC.

Resolution Trust Corporation (RTC) – The RTC was a U.S. government-owned asset management company charged with liquidating assets of insolvent savings and loan associations (S&Ls) during the 1980s and 1990s.

Securities and Exchange Commission (SEC) – The SEC is an independent agency primarily responsible for enforcing the federal securities laws, regulating the securities industry and protecting investors.

World Trade Organization (WTO) – The WTO is an international organization that sets and enforces rules designed to facilitate the free trade of goods and services.

About the Author

Bob Pozen is currently the Chairman of MFS Investment Management, which manages over $150 billion for mutual funds and pension plans, and previously he was Vice-Chairman of Fidelity Investments. He also is a senior lecturer at Harvard Business School. Bob has written two textbooks as well as numerous articles on financial and regulatory issues in leading publications. He was recently Chairman of the SEC Advisory Committee on Improving Financial Reporting and a member of the President's Commission to Strengthen Social Security. Earlier in his career, he served as a senior staff member of the SEC, and Secretary of Economic Affairs for Massachusetts. Bob is an honors graduate of Harvard College and Yale Law School.

Index

ABS. *See* Asset-backed security
ABX index, during 2007–2008, 102
   definition, 402n2
Accounting
   domestic versus international standards, 310–312
   goodwill write-offs, 308–309
   historical, 298–299, 317
   off-balance sheet, 53–54
   principles, 425n3
   rules, 295–318
   transparent, 307–309
   violations, 34–36
Adjustable rate mortgage (ARM), 10–12
Advisers, distinction between brokers and, 136–138
AFS. *See* Available-For-Sale
AIG, xv, 93, 140, 213, 267, 271
   bail outs and, 77–79, 98
   credit default swaps and, 75–77
   potential and actual exposure of Federal Reserve
     and, 168
Allied Capital, 105
Alt-A mortgage, 14
   originators, 16
AMBAC, 75–77
American Bankers Association, 296
American Express, 213
American Recovery and Reinvestment Act of 2009
    (Stimulus Plan or Act), 252, 265–266,
    270–273, 292–293, 347–348, 395n33, 431n86
American Society of Appraisers, 395n26

American Society of Farm Managers and Rural
    Appraisers, 395n26
AMLF. *See* Asset-backed commercial paper money
    market mutual fund liquid facility
Andersen, Arthur, 35
Antideficiency statutes, 22
Antonov, Peter, xii, xiv, xv
Appraisal Institute, 395n26
Arbitrage, 111
Argentina, 348
ARM. *See* Adjustable rate mortgage
Asset-backed commercial paper (ABCP) money market
    mutual fund (MMMF) liquid facility (AMLF),
    162, 168
Asset-backed security (ABS)
   Fed support, 160–161, 166, 167, 236–241
   investing in, 92
   ratings, 144
   volume, 238, 377
AT&T, 173
Australia, 186
Available-For-Sale (AFS), 300, 307
   classification, 302

Bad bank, 249–250, 376–377
Bailout Act (or Bill) of 2008, 201–204, 268–269,
    270–272
   banks and, 205–233
   increasing lending volumes and removing toxic assets,
    235–262

Bailouts. *See* Financial bail outs
Bair, Sheila, 145, 252
Balance sheets, off-balance sheet financing, 49–58
Banco Santander, 221
Bank holding company, 213
   activities of, 130, 138
   conversion into, 212–214
   FDIC guarantee of borrowing, 169–175
Bank Holding Company Act, 141–142
Bank of America, 32, 98, 222, 267
   acquisition of Merrill Lynch, 98, 107, 130, 222,
     224–225
   investments in, xviii
   leveraging and, 133
Bankruptcy, 258–259
   Mortgage modification in, 261–262
Banks. *See also* Boards of directors; Executive
     compensation
   anticyclical measures, 147–150
   Bailout Act of 2008 and, 205–233
   capital for small banks, 211–212
   capital requirements to cope with excess leverage,
     149–150
   contingent reserves in good times, 147–149, 408n65
   credit ratings and internal risk ratings, 144–145
   FDIC guarantee of borrowings, 169–175
   Justice Department and, 207–208
   leverage ratio effects, 134
   leveraging at, 129–152
   models of federal ownership of, 223
   moving toxic assets to, 249–250
   need for a consolidated regulator, 134–136
   practical approaches to bank capital, 146–147
   reform of capital requirements, 143–147
   Spanish, 147–148
   statistics of depository institutions, 182
Barclays, 78
Barron's, 247
Barroso, Jose Manuel, 320
Base fee
   for hedge funds, 112–113, 117
Basel Accords, 130–131, 143–146, 342
Basis point
   example 192–193
Bear raid, 106
Bear Stearns, 118, 131, 149–150
   equity price and S&P ratings actions, 63
   failure of, 106–107
   leveraging and, 129–133
Belgium, 344
Bernanke, Ben (Fed chairman), 12–13, 97, 157, 161,
    201, 202, 224
Boards of directors, 263–294
   chair/CEO separation, 283–284, 424n38
   election of, 286–288, 424n41
   proxy access, 288–289
   shareholders and, 285–291
   voting standard, 424n41

Bond rating, 62–63
Bonuses, 90, 268–273, 277–278, 280–282
Bordo, Michael, 335
Born, Brooksly, 80, 81
Boston Private Bank & Trust Company, 212
Boston Private Financial Holdings, 212
Brazil, 8, 165, 343, 344, 349, 428n9
Breaking the buck, 187–188
Brendsel, Leo, 35
Brokers
   distinction between advisers and, 136–138
   leveraging, 129–152
Brookings Institution, 158, 327
Bubble. *See* Financial bubble
Buffett, Warren, 35–36, 77, 83, 218, 305–306
   preferred stock terms, 219
Bush, George W. (President), 98, 202, 210, 235, 251, 264
BusinessWeek, 251

Calomiris, Charles, 145
Canada, 159, 220, 332, 343
Capital
   mortgage, 41–43
   requirements for banks, 129–132, 143–147
Capitalism, one-way, xviii, 202, 210, 226, 235, 251
Capital One, 213
Capital requirements, 129–134, 143–150, 309
Cayman Islands, 344
Cayne, Jimmy, 164
CDO. *See* Collateral debt obligation
CDS. *See* Credit default swaps
Central bank
   independence, 166–168, 333
CEO. *See* Chief Executive Officer
CFO. *See* Chief Financial Officer
CFTC. *See* Commodity Futures Trading Commission
Chanos, Jim, 105
Chief Executive Officer (CEO), 263, 423n26
Chief Financial Officer (CFO), 269
China, 8, 319, 323, 324–325, 328–330, 332, 344, 349
Chrysler Corporation, 210, 346
CIFG, 76
Cisco, 183
CIT, 214
Citigroup, 53, 84, 88–90, 142, 222, 225–226, 267
   federal assistance and, 226–229
Clawback, 270, 281
Clearinghouse, 81–82
Coates, Professor, 217
Code of Conduct, 345
Collateral debt obligation (CDO), 73–75, 243, 248–249
Colombia, 349
Commercial paper, 153–154, 164–166
   short-term, 52, 153
Commercial paper funding facility (CPFF), 163, 168
Commodity Futures Modernization Act, 81
Commodity Futures Trading Commission (CFTC), 79–80
   definition, 443

Conforming loan, 253
Congress, 243, 395n33
  bail out laws and, 140, 167
  establishment of insurance on bank deposits, 181
  executive compensation and, 264–275, 422n10
  fair market value and, 304–305
  financial conglomerates and, 136
  regulation of Fannie Mae and Freddie Mac, 36–38
  tax deductions for mortgage interest and, 23–24
Congressional Budget Office, 37, 327–334
Conservatorship, 206
Consolidated regulator, 134–136
Consolidated Supervised Entities (CSE) program, 134–136
Consumer Federation of America, 31
Consumer Financial Protection Agency, 369–370, 395n31
Consumer Price Index (CPI), 181–182
Continental Illinois Bank, 227
Contingent obligation, 53–55
Counterparty risk, 78
Countrywide Financial, 32, 98
Covered bonds, 54–55
CPFF. See Commercial paper funding facility
CPI. See Consumer Price Index
Credit default swaps (CDS), 174, 214
  AIG and, 77–79
  bond investors and, 70–82
  clearinghouse for, 81–82
  collateralized debt obligation, 74
  common transaction, 70
  errors, 94
  federal regulations and, 79–81
  versus insurance contracts, 72–73
  mathematical models and, 69–96
  models, 83–92
  monoline insurers and, 75–77
  notional amounts outstanding, 71
  payouts, 79
  risks, 73–75
  trends, 91–92
Credit guarantees, 52
Credit-rating agency
  conflicted position of, 58–65
  rating downgrades, 60
  ratings users, 62–63
  reforms, 63–65
  regulatory responses, 60–61
  revenues, 58–59
Credit ratings, 60–62, 144–145
CSE. See Consolidated Supervised Entities program
Current account deficit, 321–322

Danish model, 56–58, 66
Davos conference (2009), 319
Debt security
  amortized cost, 197
Default
  mortgage, 5, 17, 23, 86, 257

Deficit Reductions Act of 1984, 422n11
Deflation, 157–158
Deleveraging, 122–127
Democrats, 36
Department of Housing and Urban Development (HUD), 16–18
  definition, 443
  setting affordable housing goals, 30–31
Department of Veterans Affairs (VA), 39
Deposits, insuring, 179–199
Derivatives
  OTC, 80–81
  technology and, 90–91
  Warren Buffett on, 35–36
Deutsche Bank, 78
DeWitt, Ruth, 15
Discover Financial, 213
Dividend
  limits on, 217–219, 221
Dodd, Christopher J. (Senator), 202
Doha Round, 348–349
Dot-com bubble, 3, 335
Drexel Burnham Lambert, 209
Duff & Phelps, 218

Economic Stabilization Act of 2008, 98, 121
Eichengreen, Barry, 335
Einhorn, David, 105
Eisman, Steve, 75, 84
Emergency Economic Stabilization Act of 2008 (Bailout Act or Bill), 163, 266, 268, 416n7
England, 159, 173
Enron, 105, 270
Escrow account, 13
EU. See European Union
Euro, 330–331
European Union (EU), 173–174, 312, 320, 346, 349
  dollar versus yen and Euro, 330–331
Exceptional assistance, 222–226
Executive compensation, 263–294
  accountable capitalism and, 275–281
  advisory votes and, 289–291
  base salary and bonus, 277–278, 282
  Boards of directors and, 281–285
  bonuses, 269, 281
  broad-based restrictions, 267–275
  CEO salaries, 423n26
  consultants, 273, 423n26
  downside risk and, 277–278
  Federal restrictions, 265–266
  golden parachutes, 265–266, 423n20
  limits, 423n15
  performance measurement, 277
  principles, 282
  quantitative metrics and, 278
  restrictions, 268–275
  say-on-pay, 284, 289–291
  Special Master to approve, 267, 274, 284–285

Executive compensation *(continued)*
   stock options and restricted stock, 278–280, 282
   tax deduction limits, 266
   termination, retirement, and payment deferrals,
      280–281, 282

Fair market value (FMV), 295–318
   adoption of international financial reporting
      standards, 309–314
   changes to, 306–309
   description, 299–302
   historical cost accounting versus, 297–302
   pros and cons, 302–306
   support for, 296–297
Fannie Mae (Federal National Mortgage Association),
    3, 4, 5
   balance sheet liabilities and MBS obligations, 32–34
   charter of, 28
   conservatorship, 98
   definition, 443
   failure of, 107–108
   future of, 38–44
   government charter, 29–30
   history, 28–31
   losses, 396n1
   reorganization of functions, 40
   share of residential mortgage debt, 29
   transfer to coop, 44
FAS157. *See Statement of Financial Accounting Standards
    No. 157*
FASB. *See* Financial Accounting Standards Board
Fat tail distribution, 85–86
FDIC. *See* Federal Deposit Insurance Corporation
Fed. *See* Federal Reserve Board of Governors
Federal deficit, 327–328
Federal Deposit Insurance Corporation (FDIC), 29–30,
    55, 412n9
   for bank deposits, 180–186
   debt guarantee, xvii
   definition, 443
   description, 396–397n3
   guarantee of borrowings of banks and holding
      companies, 169–175
   inflation adjusted increased in insured-deposit limit, 181
Federal funds rate, 154, 156
Federal Home Loan Mortgage Corporation (Freddie
    Mac), 3, 4, 5–6, 27
   definition, 443
Federal Housing Administration (FHA), 28
   General Accounting Office and, 20–21
   mortgage insurance and, 25
   no down payment loans and, 20–21
Federal National Mortgage Association (Fannie Mae),
    3, 4, 5, 27
   definition, 443
Federal Reserve Act, 163
Federal Reserve Bank of Cleveland, 182

Federal Reserve Bank of New York (FRBNY), 163, 334
Federal Reserve Board of Governors (Fed), 93, 333
   bail out of AIG and, 98
   definition, 443
   description, 166
   exposure to financial bail out, 168
   exposure to losses, 166–169
   Federal funds rates, 156
   LIBOR versus Fed funds rate, 154–155
   outline of new lending programs, 161–165,
      161–169
   role in elevating U.S. housing prices, 9
Federal Reserve discount window, 161
Federal Trade Commission (FTC), 17
   definition, 443
FGIC, 76
FHA. *See* Federal Housing Administration
FICO scores, 87
Fidelity Investments, 84, 92, 137, 142–143, 415n59
FIFO. *See* First in, first out
Financial Accounting Standards Board (FASB), 51, 296,
    310, 398n9
   accounting rules, 53–54
   definition, 443
Financial bailouts
   AIG and, 77–79, 98
   Congress and, 140
   decisions made by President and executive branch,
      167
   exposure of Federal Reserve and, 168
   Federal Reserve and, 98
Financial bubble, 92
   psychological and economic causes, 336–339
Financial crisis, xi–xx, 1–6
   accounting rules and, 295–318
   international implications, 321–354
   savings and spending, 324–327
Financial Industry Regulatory Authority (FINRA), 137
   definition, 443
Financial institutions, short-selling and, 106–108
Financial Services Authority (FSA), 314–316
Financial Stability Forum, 340–341, 428n9
FinCredit, xii
FINRA. *See* Financial Industry Regulatory Authority
First in, first out (FIFO), 311, 427n31
First-time home purchasers, 395n33
   tax credits, 20–21
Fishbein, Allen, 31
Fisher, Richard, 159
Fitch, 58
Fitch Reports, 257
Five Investment Banks, 131. *See also* Bear Stearns;
    Goldman Sachs; Lehman Brothers; Merrill
    Lynch; Morgan Stanley
   demise of, 131–138, 139
   gross leverage ratios, 133
   leverage ratio effects, 134

Fixed-rate mortgage
  interest rates, 239, 260
FMV. *See* Fair market value
FOFs. *See* Funds of hedge funds
Forbes, Steve, 296
Foreign currency, 8–9, 328–331
France, 173, 308, 314, 320, 344, 346
Frank, Barney, 114, 342, 433n26
FRBNY. *See* Federal Reserve Bank of New York
Freddie Mac (Federal Home Loan Mortgage
      Corporation), 3, 4, 5–6. *See also* Mortgage-
      backed securities
  balance sheet liabilities and MBS obligations, 32–34
  charter of, 28
  conservatorship, 98
  definition, 443
  failure of, 107–108
  future of, 38–44
  government charter, 29–30
  history, 28–31
  reorganization of functions, 40
  share of residential mortgage debt, 29
  transfer to coop, 44
FSA. *See* Financial Services Authority
FTC. *See* Federal Trade Commission
Fuld, Richard, 107, 123, 264
Functional regulation, 364–366
Funds of hedge funds (FOFs), 113–114, 126
  protection, 116–118

G20. *See* Group of Twenty
GAAP. *See* Generally accepted accounting principles
GAO. *See* General Accounting Office
GDP. *See* Gross domestic product
Geithner, Timothy, 119, 159, 164, 211, 275, 293,
    423n27
General Accounting Office (GAO)
  definition, 443
  Federal Housing Authority and, 20–21
General Electric Capital, 173, 300
Generally accepted accounting principles (GAAP), 297,
    309–314, 317
  by loan classification, 301
  by security classification, 301
General Motors, 214, 346
Genworth, 214
German Marshall Fund, 347
Germany, 173, 320, 331, 346
Gingrich, Newt, 296
Ginnie Mae (Government National Mortgage
    Association), 27–28, 39–41, 45, 48
  definition, 443
  promotion of government-insured mortgages, 41
Glaser, Howard, 20
Glass-Steagall Act, 138–143
  "lite," 140–142
  reinstatement, 138–140, 384–385, 391

repeal, 138
revenue synergies, 142–143
GMAC, 213–214
Golden parachutes, 265–266, 270, 272–273, 275, 292,
    423n20. *See also* Executive compensation;
    Severance
Goldman Sachs, 78, 87, 98, 131, 212–213, 383–385
  leveraging and, 130
  preferred stock terms, 219
Goldschmid, Harvey (SEC Commissioner), 132, 134
Good bank, 249–250, 261, 376–377, 390
Goodwill
  write-offs, 308–309
Gorton, Gary, 88, 90
Government
  American Recovery and Reinvestment Act of 2009
    (Stimulus Plan or Act), 252, 265–266, 270–273,
    292–293, 347–348, 395n33, 431n86
  Bailout Act (or Bill) of 2008 and, 206–210
  guarantee of banks and holding companies
    borrowing, 173–174
  models of federal ownership of banks, 223
  money market funds' assets and net new cash
    flows, 191
  subsidization of mortgages, 39
Government National Mortgage Association (Ginnie
    Mae). *See* Ginnie Mae
Gramlich, Edward (Federal Reserve Governor), 11–12
Gramm Leach Bliley Act of 1999, 434n47
Grayson-Himes Pay for Performance Act of 2009,
    422n10
Great Britain, 344
Great Depression, 28, 103
Greenberg, Evan, 172–173, 215
Greenberger, Michael, 80
Greenspan, Alan (Federal Reserve Governor), 11–12,
    80, 91, 335
Gross domestic product (GDP), 158, 322–323, 327–328
Group of 20 (G20), 343, 344, 348–352
  definition, 443
Group of 30, 150, 193, 414n54

Hammergren, John, 280
Hanson, Mark, 257
Hedge funds, 111–122
  asset concentration, 120
  assets and market positions 1990–2008, 112
  "backfill bias," 404n39
  characteristics, 111–112
  client protection, 114–116
  compensation of hedge fund managers, 121–122
  confidential reports and, 118–121
  fund borrowing, 120
  growth of, 112–114
  illiquid assets, 120
  implicit leverage, 120
  protection of funds of hedge funds, 116–118

Hedge funds *(continued)*
  redemption requests, 120
  risk assessment, 120
  structure of, 113
  trading counterparties, 120
  valuation methods, 120
Hedging, 34–35, 41, 105
Held-For-Investment (HFI), 300–301
Hold-For-Sale (HFS), 300–302, 306–307
Held-To-Maturity (HTM), 300–301
Hele, John, 346
Herz, Robert, 296, 305
HFI. *See* Held-For-Investment
HFS. *See* Held-For-Sale
H4H Program, 252–253
Historical cost accounting, 203, 295, 298–299, 309, 312,
     316, 317, 340–341
Holland, 346
Home equity loan, 23–24
Homeowner's HOPE Hotline, 251
Homestead exemptions, 23
Hope Now Alliance, 251
House Banking Committee, 36
House Financial Services Committee, 37
Housing
  lending standards, 32
  low-income, 31–36
  rise and fall of U.S. housing prices, 7–25
  stock market and, 97–99
  U.S. home ownership rates, 30
Housing and Economic Recovery Act of 2008, 37, 396n2
Housing slump, 1–6
HTM. *See* Held-To-Maturity
HUD. *See* Department of Housing and Urban
     Development
Hummel, Alan, 395n26

IASB. *See* International Accounting Standards Board
IBM, 105
IFRS. *See* International financial reporting standards
Illiquid assets, 120, 248, 300, 317, 341
Illiquid markets, 248, 303–305
IMF. *See* International Monetary Fund
Incentive fee, 112–113, 117, 121–122, 126–127
Independent Bank of Michigan, 217
India, 343, 344, 349
Indonesia, 348
Indy Mac, 98, 206, 251
Inflation, 115, 155, 176, 181, 332
  adjusted home price index versus real S&P 500 stock
     price index, 2
  Fed and, 159–161
  investors and, 158–159
  versus short-term rates, 155–161
Inflation target, 159–160, 332–333, 409n14, 429n43
ING, 346

Institute of Certified Financial Analysts, 308
Insurable interest, 72, 92
Insurance, 75–76, 79, 92–93, 142, 146, 170–172, 215
  for deposits, 179–199
  for money market funds, 179–199
  for mortgages, 25
  regulation, 136, 406n13
Insurance contracts, versus credit default swaps, 72–73
Interest rates, 156–158
  Federal funds rates, 156
  high-yield mortgages and, 9–12
  limitations of cutting rates, 156–158
  tax deductions for mortgage interest, 23–24
Internal Revenue Service (IRS), 220, 273
  nonprofit status revocation and, 20
Internal risk models, 130, 131, 134, 144–145
International accounting principles, 297
International Accounting Standards Board (IASB), 296,
     307, 309–314
  debt and, 426n20
  definition, 443
  regulatory systems, 314–316
International Financial Reporting Standards (IFRS),
     297, 309–310, 312–314
International Monetary Fund (IMF), 332, 343
  definition, 444
  financing, xviii
International Organization of Securities Commissioners
     (IOSCO), 345
Internet stocks, 10, 92. *See also* Financial bubble
Investment Advisers Act of 1940, 114, 116, 126, 137,
     366, 389, 404n34
Investment banks, 3, 98, 139, 150–151
  demise of five large, 129–138
Investment Company Act of 1940, 115, 404n32, 415n59
Investment Company Institute, 196, 199
Investor Protection Act of 2009, 423n26
Investors, foreign, 9, 158, 160, 176, 323, 328, 331–334
IOSCO. *See* International Organization of Securities
     Commissioners
IRS. *See* Internal Revenue Service
Isaac, William, 145
Ivashina, Professor, 237

Japan, 308, 328–330, 344
  dollar versus yen and Euro, 330–331
  housing during the 1990s, 1–3
John Deere, 434n47
John F. Kennedy Profiles in Courage Award, 81
Johnson, Ned, 92
Johnson, Simon, 344
Jones, Tom, 302
J.P. Morgan, 63, 98, 211
  leveraging and, 130
Justice Department, Bailout Act of 2008 and, 207–208,
     383–384, 391

Kanjorski, Paul, 305
King, Mervyn, 165
Korea, 165
Kroszner, Professor, 139, 251

Lamy, Pascal, 348
Lay, Ken, 105
Legacy loans, 244–246, 260
Legacy securities, 244–248, 260
Legislation
    American Recovery and Reinvestment Act of 2009,
        266, 270–273, 395n33, 431n86, 435
    antideficiency laws, 22–23
    Bank Holding Company Act, 141–142
    Commodity Futures Modernization Act, 81
    Deficit Reductions Act of 1984, 422n11
    Emergency Economic Stabilization of 2008 (Bailout
        Act or Bill), 98, 121, 163, 201–204, 266, 268,
        272, 437
    Federal Reserve Act, 163
    Glass-Steagall Act, 138–143, 438
    Gramm Leach Bliley Act of 1999, 434n47
    Grayson-Himes Pay for Performance Act of 2009,
        422n10
    homestead exemptions, 438
    Housing and Economic Recovery Act of 2008,
        37–38, 396n2
    Investment Advisers Act of 1940, 114, 116, 126, 137
    Investment Company Act of 1940, 115, 404n32,
        415n59
    Investor Protection Act of 2009, 423n26
    Mortgage Reform and Anti-Predatory Lending
        Act, 14
    Real Estate Settlement and Procedures Act
        (RESPA), 17
    SAFE Mortgage Licensing Act, 16–18
    Sarbanes-Oxley Act of 2002, 270, 276, 335, 441
    Securities Act of 1933, 81, 115, 116
    Stimulus Act of 2009, 17, 203, 221–222, 252,
        292–293, 347, 348
Lending
    legacy loans and legacy securities program, 245–246
    modifications for salvaging toxic assets, 250–251
    moving toxic assets to banks, 249–250
    securitization and, xvii, 237–242
    short-term, 5, 47–67, 153–177
Leverage ratio, 119, 122–134, 139, 146, 149–152
Leveraging, 122–125
    at brokers and banks, 129–152
    implicit leverage, 120
    leverage ratio effects, 134
Levitt, Arthur (SEC Chair), 80
Lewis, Ken, 224
LIBOR. See London interbank offered rate
Liechtenstein, 344
Lincoln National, 214

Liquidity put, 52–53, 55
Liquidity risk, 87–88, 89, 94, 145
Lo, Andrew, 124–125
Loan loss reserve, 54, 147–149, 152, 340, 408n63
Loan modification programs
    under Bush administration, 251–253
    under Obama administration, 253–258, 421n41
    percentage of loans delinquent, 256
    qualifications, 255
Loan-to-value ratio, 87, 146, 152
Lockhart, James, 252
London interbank offered rate (LIBOR)
    versus Feds funds rate, 154–155, 165, 410n24
Long position, 111
Long-Term Capital Management, 81, 118, 334
Low-income housing, 31–36
    lending standards, 32
Ludwig, Eugene, 249
Lump sum payouts, 280–281

MAC. See Material adverse condition clause
Mack, John, 107
Madoff, Bernie, 136–137, 344
Maheras, Thomas, 88–90
Malaysia, 348
Malkiel, Burton G., 117
Market capitalization, 58, 197, 226, 295–296,
    300, 374
Markopolos, Harry, 136–137
Mark-to-market, 300–303, 308, 312
Mark-to-model, 303–306
Marumoto, Kimberly, 13
Material adverse condition (MAC) clause, 224
MBIA, 76, 77
MBS. See Mortgage-backed securities
MCIs. See Mortgage credit institutions
McKesson Corp., 280
McKinnell, Hank, 263–264
Mega banks, 207, 209, 231. See also Banks
    acquisitions, 207, 383–384
    breakup of, 384
    directors of, 276, 281, 283, 285, 386–388
    ownership of, 226, 374–375
Merkel, Angela, 320, 346
Merrill Lynch, 77, 78, 107, 131, 222–226
    acquisition by Bank of America, 98, 107
    leveraging and, 130
Mexico, 165
MFS Investment Management, 283
Middle East, 328–330
Minneapolis Federal Reserve, 237
Mishkin, Frederic, 159
MMIFF. See Money market investor funding facility
Models, 83–92
    for credit default swaps, 83–92
    for fair market value, 305–306

Monaco, 344
Monetary policy
   of the Fed, 166, 388
Money market funds
   assets and net new cash flows, 191
   examples, 65, 415n64
   inflows versus outflows, 415n59
   instruments, 194
   insuring, 179–199
   shareholders, 414n43
   at zero yields, 192–193
Money market investor funding facility (MMIFF),
   163, 168
Monoline insurers, credit default swaps and, 75–77
Moody's, xii, 58, 88
Moral hazard, 170, 380
Moral obligation, 30, 38
Morgan Stanley, 98, 107, 131, 271
   leveraging and, 130
Mortgage-backed securities (MBS), 3, 27, 49, 138
   capital tiers, 144
   guarantee of, 39, 41
   risks, 73–75
   U.S. nonagency, 48
Mortgage credit institutions (MCIs), 56–57
Mortgage Institute, 56
Mortgage modification, 261–262
Mortgage prepayment
   risks, 34, 46
Mortgage Reform and Anti-Predatory
   Lending Act, 14
Mortgages, 395n33
   antideficiency laws, 22–23
   debt in the United States, 5–6
   delinquency rates, 2000–2008, 12
   Fannie Mae and Freddie Mac residential mortgage
      debt, 29
   federal oversight, 395n31
   first and second, 254, 421n41
   fixed-rate, 438
   insurance for, 25
   lending rules, 12–14
   low interest rates and, 9–12
   originations by loan type, 2001 and 2006, 11
   originators, 16
   raising mortgage capital, 41–43
   risks for residential, 143–144
   securitization, xii–xiv
      in the private sector, 47–67
      process, 3, 50
   stabilization of the market in tumultuous times,
      43–44
   subprime, 60, 84–85
   subsidization through government, 39
   U.S. home ownership rates, 30
Mozilo, Angelo, 32

Mudd, Daniel, 32
Musick, Troy, 15
Mutual funds
   banks managing, 141

National Association of Independent Fee Appraisers,
   395n26
National City Corporation, 220–221
Nationalization, 226–228
Nationwide Insurance Co., 214
NAV. See Net asset value
Negative amortization loan, 14
Negrych, Colin, 154
Net asset value (NAV), 187–189, 189–190, 196–197
New Century Financial, 98
New Century Mortgage, 15
New York Federal Reserve Bank, 118
New York State Insurance Department, 76,
   79–80, 93
New York Stock Exchange, 138
New York Times, 106, 252, 264
New Zealand, 186
Niemeier, Charles, 313
Nigeria, 428n9
NINA (no income/no assets) mortgages, 32
9/11, 64
Nonagency mortgage-backed securities, 48
Nonbank lenders, 4, 15–17
Nonrecourse loan, 165, 239–241, 244
Normal distribution curve, 85–86
Norway, 428n9
Notional amount, 71, 400n3

Obama Administration, 38–39, 122, 158, 171, 203, 210,
   221–222, 235, 251, 253, 258, 264–265, 326, 336,
   340, 343, 347, 349
   loan modification program, 253–258, 421n41
   private-public partnerships, 236–237
OCI. See Other comprehensible income
OECD. See Organization for Economic Co-operation
   and Development
Off-balance sheet financing, 49–58
Office of Federal Housing Enterprise Oversight
   (OFHEO), 33
   definition, 444
   regulation of, 36–38
Office of National Insurance, 406n13
Office of the Comptroller of the Currency (OCC),
   367–368
   definition, 444
Office of the Inspector General (OIG), 132
Office of Thrift Supervision (OTS), 367–368
   definition, 444
OFHEO. See Office of Federal Housing Enterprise
   Oversight
OIG. See Office of the Inspector General

Oil
  price fluctuations, 8
  producers, 428n9
One-way capitalism, xviii, 226–228, 376
Oracle, 173
Organization for Economic Co-operation and
    Development (OECD), 345
Originate, definition, 440
Originate-to-sell, 18
OTC. *See* Over-the-counter derivatives
Other comprehensible income (OCI), 307, 425n7
OTS. *See* Office of Thrift Supervision
Over-the-counter (OTC) derivatives, 80

Panama, 349
Paulson, Henry M. (Treasury Secretary), 37–38, 54, 201,
  202, 203, 215–216, 224, 225, 243, 268
PDCF. *See* Primary dealer credit facility
People's Bank of China, 331–332
Permanent Impairment, 298–299
Pfizer, 263–264
Plosser, Charles, 166
PNC Financial Services Group, 220–221
Policy rate, 151–154
Pollock, Alex, 13–14
Ponzi scheme, 137
PPIP. *See* Public-private investment program
Preferred stock, 216–219, 221–222
President's Working Group on Financial Markets
    (PWG), 118–119
  definition, 444
Preston, Steve (Secretary), 17, 252
Price discovery, 241
Pricewaterhouse Coopers (PWC), 35
Primary dealer credit facility (PDCF), 162
Primary dealers, 161
Prime mortgage, 10
Private equity fund, 116, 230, 366
Private sector, securitization, 47–67
Procyclicality, 147, 150
Project Lifeline, 251
Proxy access, 288–289, 424n47
Proxy statement, 288–289
Prudential Insurance Co., 214
Public Company Accounting Oversight Board, 313
Public-private investment program (PPIP), 244–248
Putin, Vladimir (Prime Minister), 319
Putnam Prime Money Market Fund, 188–189
Put option, 90–91
PWC. *See* Pricewaterhouse Coopers
PWG. *See* President's Working Group on Financial
    Markets

Raines, Franklin, 32
Rajan, Professor, 139
Real Estate Settlement and Procedures Act (RESPA), 17

Recapitalization, 210–233
  of insurers, 210–215
Receivership, definition, 441
Reid, Harry, 36
Repos (repurchase agreements), 123
  overnight, 124
Republicans, 36
Repurchase agreements (repos), 123
  definition, 441
  overnight, 124
Resolution Trust Corporation (RTC), 227, 228, 249
  definition, 444
RESPA. *See* Real Estate Settlement and Procedures Act
Reverse auction, 243–244
Risk-weighted assets, 143–144
RTC. *See* Resolution Trust Corporation
Rubin, Robert, 53, 80
Run on the bank, 183, 215
Russell 3000, 109
Russia, 8, 319, 344, 428n9

SAFE Mortgage Licensing Act, 16–18
Saha, Atanu, 117
Sants, Hector, 315
Sarbanes-Oxley Act of 2002 (SOX), 270, 276, 283, 335
Sarkozy, Nicolas, 308, 320
Saudi Arabia, 8, 428n9
Savings and loan associations (S&Ls), 181, 249
Say-on-pay, 284, 289–291
SBA. *See* Small Business Administration
Schapiro, Mary, 137
Scharfstein, Professor, 217, 237
Schwab, 137
Schwarzman, Stephen, 425n3
SDRs. *See* Special Drawing Rights (SDRs)
SEC. *See* Securities and Exchange Commission
Securities Act of 1933, 81, 115, 116
Securities and Exchange Commission (SEC), 3–4,
    29–30, 56, 399n29
  ban on short selling of financial stocks, 98
  boards of directors and, 288–289
  capital requirements, 130
  consolidated regulation and, 135–136,
    405–406n11
  definition, 444
  description, 396–397n3
  FMV and, 296
  leveraging, 132–134
  money market regulation, 186–187
  mortgage-backed, xiv
  reporting requirements, 108, 403n14
  shareholders and, 288–289
  short selling rules, 108
Securitization, xii–xiv, xvi, 237–242
  in the private sector, 47–67
  process, 3, 50

Self-regulatory organizations (SROs), 137, 403n14
Senate Agriculture Committee, 80
Senate Banking Committee, 38
Senior executive officers (SEOs), 269
SEOs. *See* Senior executive officers
Severance, 267, 280, 422n12. *See also* Golden parachutes
Shareholders
    of money market funds, 414n43
    participation in nomination of boards of directors,
        285–291
    proxies and, 288–289, 424n47
    voting standard, 424n41
Short position, 111
Short selling, 104–110, 125
    description, 104–105
    financial institutions and, 106–108
    positives and negatives, 105
    SEC and, 108
    typical, 104
    uptick rule and, 109–110
Short-term lending, 153–177
    Federal Reserve and, 161–169
    versus long-term rates, 157
    in the private sector, 47–67
    process, 3, 50
Sovereign wealth fund, 230–231
Spain, 338
Special Drawing Rights (SDRs), 332
Special Master, 267, 274, 284–285
Statement of Financial Accounting Standards No. 157
        (FAS157), 303–304
    valuation hierarchy, 304
Stimulus Plan or Act. *See* American Recovery and
        Reinvestment Act of 2009
Stock market
    in 2008, 98
    housing prices and, 97–99
    leveraging, 122–125
Stocks
    executive compensation and, 278–280
    Internet, 92
    options and, 278–279
        re-pricing, 279
    preferred, 217–218
    restricted shares, 279–280
    summary of estimated value conclusions, 216
Stock warrants, 216–219, 374–375
Structured finance, 145
Subordinated debt, 146–147
Subprime mortgage, 10–15
Sullivan, Martin, 90
Sun Trust Bank, 148
Super-directors, 284, 387
Superior Bank of Libya, xiv
Sweden, 159, 173–174, 227, 332, 346
Swensen, David, 117
SWF. *See* Sovereign wealth fund

Systemic risk, 359–364
System Open Market Account (SOMA), 162

Tabarrok, Alex, 139
TAF. *See* Term auction facility
TALF. *See* Term asset backed securities loan facility
Tariffs, 348–350
TARP. *See* Troubled Asset Relief Program
Taxes
    credits for first-time home purchasers, 21–22, 395n33
    deductions for mortgage interest, 23–24
    tax deduction limits, 266
Tax haven, 121, 339, 344–345
Tax, John, 209
Taylor rule, 9, 10
Temporary Liquidity Guarantee Program, 169, 180
Term asset backed securities loan facility (TALF), 163,
        168, 239–241, 245, 423n15
Term auction facility (TAF), 162, 168
Term securities lending facility (TSLF), 162, 168
Thain, John, 107
Thrift, 180
Thrift holding company, 172, 411n42
Toxic assets, 235–262
Tranches, 71–75, 88–89
Troubled Asset Relief Program (TARP), 103, 163, 209,
        211, 218, 264, 269, 291–294, 423n20
    powers of, 274
TSLF. *See* Term securities lending facility
Tying arrangements, 141–142

UBS, 78
Umbrella regulator, 370–371
Underwater mortgage, 256–258
United Arab Emirates, 428n9
United Bankshares, Inc., 212
United Kingdom, 46, 332
United States
    debt, 321–324
    decline in personal savings, 326
    dollar versus yen and Euro, 330–331
    foreign investments and, 353–354
    home ownership rates, 30
    percentage of underwater home owners in, 22
    potential and actual exposure to the financial
        bailout, 337
    rise and fall of housing prices, 7–25
    savings and spending, 325–327
    schematic of financial system, xx
    voting share, 344
Universal banks, 132, 140, 385
Uptick rule, 109–110
    reinstating, 110
U.S. Bureau of Economic Analysis, 326
U.S. Department of Agriculture, 21
U.S. House of Representatives Committee on Oversight
        and Government Reform, 423n26

U.S. Treasury, 27–28, 173, 273–274, 423n26
    dollar fluctuations, 9
    insurance program for money market funds,
        179–180
    investments, xviii
U.S. Treasury bills, 192–193
U.S. Treasury bonds, 325–326

VA. *See* Department of Veterans Affairs
Venezuela, 428n9
Volcker, Paul, 150

Wachovia, 220
Washington Mutual Bank, 179
Wells Fargo, 220, 228

Wen Jiabao (Chinese Premier), 158–159, 319
White, Eugene, 139
Whitman, Professor, 219–220
WorldCom, 270
World Trade Organization (WTO), 342, 347, 350
    definition, 444
WTO. *See* World Trade Organization

XLCA, 77

Yen, 330–331
YRC Worldwide Inc., 208

Zhao, Min, 110
Zhou Xiaochuan, 331–332